D0928066

Praise for *.NET Framework Standard Library Annotated Reference*

"This is a complete, authoritative, and truly useful reference for every .NET developer. It covers every aspect of .NET Framework library by providing concise descriptions with just the right number of examples. I would not start development of any significant .NET project without having this book on my bookshelf."

—*Max Loukianov, Vice President of Research and Development, Netpise Inc.*

"The *.NET Framework Standard Library Annotated Reference* is the one reference you really need when you use the .NET Framework library. The annotations provide clear insight into the design choices that the library development team made when building the library. Those explanations will guide you to the best design choices for your own application code."

—*Bill Wagner, Founder/Consultant, SRT Solutions, and author of* Effective C#

"More than just a reference, this book provides great insight into the massive amount of thought that went into designing the Microsoft .NET Framework. It is both entertaining and educational, combining interesting and sometimes amusing annotations along with the reference material."

—*Jordan Matthiesen, Software Engineer*

"Brad Abrams, Tamara Abrams, and the CLR team take readers on a journey through the backstreets of the .NET Framework, pointing out invaluable design decisions and performance best practices along the way. Not to be missed by any developer who has ever wondered why the Framework is designed the way it is."

—*William D. Bartholomew, Senior Software Architect, Orli-TECH Pty Ltd*

"This volume provides an in-depth review for every class method listed, including a CD with many examples of usage. The most valuable aspect of this book is the annotations provided; the annotators' thoughts about the design of the .NET Framework lets the reader develop a crystal-clear understanding of what can be accomplished with this fantastic technology."

—*Bradley Snobar, Software Engineer*

"The utility of a reference book is often a function of how easily you can find a desired subject and, once there, how clearly is it explained. On both counts, you should find that this book stands well."

—*Dr. Wes Boudville, Inventor*

.NET Framework Standard Library
Annotated Reference
Volume 2

Microsoft .NET Development Series

John Montgomery, *Series Advisor*
Don Box, *Series Advisor*
Martin Heller, *Series Editor*

The **Microsoft .NET Development Series** is supported and developed by the leaders and experts of Microsoft development technologies including Microsoft architects and DevelopMentor instructors. The books in this series provide a core resource of information and understanding every developer needs in order to write effective applications and managed code. Learn from the leaders how to maximize your use of the .NET Framework and its programming languages.

Titles in the Series

Brad Abrams, *.NET Framework Standard Library Annotated Reference Volume 1: Base Class Library and Extended Numerics Library*, 0-321-15489-4

Brad Abrams and Tamara Abrams, *.NET Framework Standard Library Annotated Reference, Volume 2: Networking Library, Reflection Library, and XML Library*, 0-321-19445-4

Keith Ballinger, *.NET Web Services: Architecture and Implementation*, 0-321-11359-4

Bob Beauchemin, Niels Berglund, Dan Sullivan, *A First Look at SQL Server 2005 for Developers*, 0-321-18059-3

Don Box with Chris Sells, *Essential .NET, Volume 1: The Common Language Runtime*, 0-201-73411-7

Keith Brown, *The .NET Developer's Guide to Windows Security*, 0-321-22835-9

Mahesh Chand, *Graphics Programming with GDI+*, 0-321-16077-0

Anders Hejlsberg, Scott Wiltamuth, Peter Golde, *The C# Programming Language*, 0-321-15491-6

Alex Homer, Dave Sussman, Mark Fussell, *ADO.NET and System.Xml v. 2.0—The Beta Version*, 0-321-24712-4

Alex Homer, Dave Sussman, Rob Howard, *ASP.NET v. 2.0—The Beta Version*, 0-321-25727-8

James S. Miller and Susann Ragsdale, *The Common Language Infrastructure Annotated Standard*, 0-321-15493-2

Christian Nagel, *Enterprise Services with the .NET Framework: Developing Distributed Business Solutions with .NET Enterprise Services*, 0-321-24673-X

Fritz Onion, *Essential ASP.NET with Examples in C#*, 0-201-76040-1

Fritz Onion, *Essential ASP.NET with Examples in Visual Basic .NET*, 0-201-76039-8

Ted Pattison and Dr. Joe Hummel, *Building Applications and Components with Visual Basic .NET*, 0-201-73495-8

Dr. Neil Roodyn, *eXtreme .NET: Introducing eXtreme Programming Techniques to .NET Developers*, 0-321-30363-6

Chris Sells, *Windows Forms Programming in C#*, 0-321-11620-8

Chris Sells and Justin Gehtland, *Windows Forms Programming in Visual Basic .NET*, 0-321-12519-3

Paul Vick, *The Visual Basic .NET Programming Language*, 0-321-16951-4

Damien Watkins, Mark Hammond, Brad Abrams, *Programming in the .NET Environment*, 0-201-77018-0

Shawn Wildermuth, *Pragmatic ADO.NET: Data Access for the Internet World*, 0-201-74568-2

Paul Yao and David Durant, *.NET Compact Framework Programming with C#*, 0-321-17403-8

Paul Yao and David Durant, *.NET Compact Framework Programming with Visual Basic .NET*, 0-321-17404-6

For more information go to www.awprofessional.com/msdotnetseries/

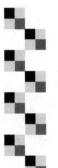

.NET Framework Standard Library Annotated Reference
Volume 2

Networking Library, Reflection Library, and XML Library

- **Brad Abrams**
  Tamara Abrams

✦Addison-Wesley

Upper Saddle River, NJ • Boston • Indianapolis • San Francisco
New York • Toronto • Montreal • London • Munich • Paris • Madrid
Capetown • Sydney • Tokyo • Singapore • Mexico City

The publisher offers excellent discounts on this book when ordered in quantity for bulk purchases or special sales, which may include electronic versions and/or custom covers and content particular to your business, training goals, marketing focus, and branding interests. For more information, please contact:

U.S. Corporate and Government Sales
(800) 382-3419
corpsales@pearsontechgroup.com

For sales outside the U.S., please contact:

International Sales
international@pearsoned.com

Visit us on the Web: www.awprofessional.com

Cataloging-in-Publication data for this book is available from the Library of Congress.

ISBN 0-321-19445-4
Text printed in the United States on recycled paper at Courier in Westford, Massachusetts.
First printing, August 2005

To Our Boys

◼

Contents

Foreword

In 1998 I left the World Wide Web Consortium to work on a small project at Microsoft that was code-named "Lightning," later known as the Common Language Runtime. Our goal was to create the programming platform for the twenty-first century, and Brad Abrams was tasked with designing the classes that are now known as the Microsoft .NET Framework. While Brad worked on the libraries, I worked on the virtual machine.

As time went on, Microsoft decided to standardize much of our work to enable broad adoption of the new programming platform. Brad and I took on this endeavor together, working with Anders Hejlsberg to produce a self-consistent framework that encompassed the most common programming tasks—sort of an updated version of the C Runtime library, but based on a modern object-oriented approach. This framework, along with a description of the architecture, type system, and file format for a virtual machine capable of running the framework, was submitted to ECMA International (formerly known as European Computer Manufacturers Association and refered to simply as ECMA herein), an international standards organization, in October 2000. The original submission included almost 700 classes, divided roughly equally between an abstract operating system API, a common programming library, higher-level programming constructs, low-level virtual machine APIs, and miscellaneous other items.

ECMA accepted the submission and created Task Group 3 of Technical Committee 39 (TC39/TG3) to convert the submission into an ECMA Standard. Brad Abrams was Microsoft's primary representative to the committee for the work on the frameworks, while I was overall editor for the standard. Brad took on the gargantuan task of coordinating changes to the framework proposed by the committee with changes being made by the Microsoft product team, as well as integrating the text of the documentation into the formal XML format being prepared for submission as the eventual standard.

Working under a self-imposed deadline of one year to release the first version of the standard, the committee decided to reduce the scope of the libraries to allow a complete and careful review, whittling the initial submission of 700 classes down to a more manageable 253 classes. They also provided a structure around the framework that allows a variety of implementations based on the size and capabilities of the system on which it will run—the "profiles" and "libraries" of the final standard.

At the end of the year, in October 2001, the standard was approved and ultimately published as ECMA-335, Second Edition, in December 2002. This was then submitted by ECMA to ISO, which adopted a revised version as ISO/IEC 23271:3003(E) about one year later.

Shortly after the adoption of the Standard, Brad and I agreed to provide a more readable version of the standard as part of a series of books being prepared by Addison-Wesley. Little did we know that we'd be producing a trilogy! Susann Ragsdale and I wrote *The Common Language Infrastructure Annotated Standard* (Addison-Wesley, 2004), which deals with the virtual machine. Brad and the .NET Framework Team wrote Volume 1 of the current book, covering roughly two-thirds of the standardized framework. The current book completes this by providing the definitive description of the remaining classes in the framework, including networking, reflection, XML, and infrastructure support.

As with Volume 1, this book goes into considerably more depth than the standard itself. It includes large numbers of examples, as well as information about the intention behind the classes and methods. It provides comments by members of the committee and the Microsoft product team, and discusses differences between the standardized framework and the Microsoft implementation.

In the two years since the adoption of the ECMA Standard, TC39/TG3 has continued to work. At the time of this writing, we anticipate a revised version of the standard to be submitted for consideration within nine months. This version will include a number of additional classes, as well as support for a new underlying technology known as "generics" that allows the framework to provide type-safe abstractions. Look for the new standard, but even more importantly, help me urge Brad to write Volume 3!

James S. Miller
Software Architect
Common Language Runtime
Microsoft Corporation

Preface

This book is intended for anyone building applications using the .NET Framework. It is meant to be a dictionary-style reference to the core types in the Framework.

The .NET Framework is huge. The amount of time that would be required limits our ability to cover the entire .NET Framework in the depth it deserves. As a result, we have focused the scope of this book on the most important, widely used types in the Framework. Luckily, such a subset was already created in the standardization process of the Common Language Runtime and the C# Programming Language. This book covers the second half of that subset (Volume 1 covered the first half). In the printed portion of this volume you will find all the type-level information for these types. Both the type-level information and member-level information are available in electronic form on the CD.

To make the standard more accessible, this book includes the following features:

- Annotations from key folks involved in the design of the .NET Framework
- Namespace overviews
- Type descriptions
- Sample code to illustrate type uses
- A fully searchable CD that includes all source code, descriptions, annotations, and examples

These features not only bring the standard to life, but more importantly, they serve as a convenient, informative reference to the most used types in the .NET Framework.

The Standard

At the Professional Developer's Conference in October 2001, Microsoft, in partnership with HP and Intel, began the ECMA standardization process of three core parts of its new developer platform: the Common Language Infrastructure (CLI), the C# programming language, and a subset of the .NET Framework that is included in the CLI and referenced in the C# specification.

The CLI and the C# programming language are covered in other books in this series. Jim Miller and Susann Ragsdale's *The Common Language Infrastructure Annotated Standard*

(Addison-Wesley, 2004) covers the CLI, which includes the metadata file format, IL Instruction set, and the type system. *The C# Programming Language* (Addison-Wesley, 2004) by Anders Hejlsberg, Scott Wiltamuth, and Peter Golde covers the C# programming language specification.

This book covers the second half of the .NET Framework as standardized in ECMA 335 and ISO 23271. The standards break the .NET Framework into seven different libraries to allow conformant implementations in resource-constrained environments. Those libraries are as follows:

Base Class Library—A simple runtime library for modern programming languages. It serves as the standard for the runtime library for the language C#, as well as one of the CLI standard libraries. It provides types to represent the built-in data types of the CLI, simple file access, custom attributes, security attributes, string manipulation, formatting, streams, collections, and so forth.

Extended Numerics Library—Provides the support for floating-point (System.Single, System.Double) and extended-precision (System.Decimal) data types. Like the Base Class Library, this library is directly referenced by the C# standard.

Network Library—Provides simple networking services, including direct access to network ports and HTTP support.

Reflection Library—Provides the ability to examine the structure of types, create instances of types, and invoke methods on types, all based on a description of the type.

XML Library—Provides a simple "pull-style" parser for XML. It is designed for resource-constrained devices, yet provides a simple user model.

Runtime Infrastructure Library—Provides the services needed by a compiler to target the CLI and the facilities needed to dynamically load types from a stream in the file format specified. For example, it provides System.BadImageFormatException, which is thrown when a stream that does not have the correct format is loaded.

Extended Array Library—Provides support for non-vector arrays, that is, arrays that have more than one dimension and arrays that have non-zero lower bounds.

The first volume of the *.NET Framework Standard Library Reference* covered the Base Class Library, the Extended Numerics Library and the Extended Array Library. This volume will contain the remaining libraries, as well as Microsoft-specific members on those types.

Namespace Overviews

To facilitate reader understanding, for each namespace we cover we provide an overview that describes the functionality and the inheritance hierarchy of types defined in that namespace. At the end of the namespace overview section we include a complete inheritance hierarchy for all the types covered in this volume. In the diagrams we differentiate the various kinds of types that make up the framework as follows:

- For classes, we use a rectangle:

Example of a Class

- For interfaces, we use a rounded rectangle:

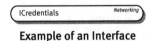

Example of an Interface

- Abstract types are indicated with an "A":

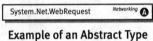

Example of an Abstract Type

- Static types are indicated with a double line:

Example of a Static Type

- Enums are indicated with an "E":

Example of an Enum

- Flag enums are indicated with an "F":

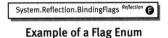

Example of a Flag Enum

- All other value types are indicated with a "V":

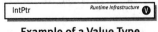

Example of a Value Type

- The library name is indicated in the upper right corner of the box. Items not standardized will be denoted with "Not Standardized" in place of a library name.

Example of a Type in the Xml Library

Note: Some interfaces that exist purely for backwords compatablity with COM have been left off of types for clarity.

Type Chapters
Types are described in their own chapters, which are organized alphabetically by type name.

Header
The header contains the namespace name (1), the type name (2), and the library name from the ECMA/ISO Standard (3).

Type Hierarchy
Under the header we include a diagram representing the full inheritance hierarchy for this type (1), subclasses of this type found in this volume (2), and any interfaces they implement (3). The type being described is shown with a gray background (4).

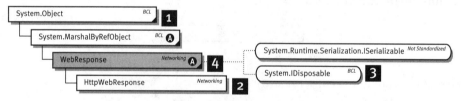

Example of Type Hierarchy for the WebResponse **Class**

Type Summary
This section contains the C# declaration syntax for all members defined on this type. It is meant to provide a quick reference in a very familiar format to what is in the type. In this summary we highlight certain attributes of these members.

CF Indicates the member is not available in the .NET Compact Framework. If not included the member is available.

MS   Indicates that the member is not included in the ECMA/ISO standard.

1.1   Indicates that the member is new in V1.1 of the .NET Framework.

Most of these attributes are shown below.

```
     public class ServicePoint
         {
         // Properties
             public Uri Address { get; }
         MS public X509Certificate Certificate { get; }
     MS CF public X509Certificate ClientCertificate { get; }
             public int ConnectionLimit { get; set; }
             public string ConnectionName { get; }
             public int CurrentConnections { get; }
MS CF 1.1 public bool Expect100Continue { get; set; }
             public DateTime IdleSince { get; }
             public int MaxIdleTime { get; set; }
             public virtual Version ProtocolVersion { get; }
             public bool SupportsPipelining { get; }
MS CF 1.1 public bool UseNagleAlgorithm { get; set; }

         // Methods
         CF public override int GetHashCode();
}
```

Type Description
This section contains a detailed description of how this type is to be used. For the most part this text is taken directly from the standard.

Annotations
Throughout this section we provide annotations from key members of the design team at Microsoft and members of the ECMA standardization committee. The comments in this section vary widely, and include notes on everything from common issues to the history of the class design or standardization process to areas where, in retrospect, the designers feel they could have done better.

Here's an example of an annotation from Brad Abrams on the AppDomain class. Each annotation is attributed to individuals by their initials.

■ **BA** We introduced Application Domains as a lightweight process mechanism. Because managed code can be verifiably type safe (memory safe) we did not need the heavyweight address space barrier that processes provide. This savings works out well most of the time. However, when using interop with unmanaged code it does cause some problems when type safety is violated. One notable example of this is the loader-lock and AppDomain marshaling problem that C++ was succeptible to. We fixed this problem in a service pack of v1.1.

Type Examples

In this section we provide sample code illustrating use of the type. Some samples are from the standard, but we added many more to facilitate a deeper and quicker understanding of the use of the type. All the samples we provide are fully compilable programs (1) and include selected output (2).

1 Example

```
using System;

public class UriSample
{
    public static void Main()
    {
        String baseUrl = "http://microsoft.com";
        Uri baseUri = new Uri(baseUrl);
        String relativePath = "samples/page 1.aspx?q=More#? &> more";
        Uri u = new Uri(baseUri, relativePath, false);
        Console.WriteLine();
        Console.WriteLine("Properties when Don't Escape is False:");
        ShowUriProperties(u);
    }

    private static void ShowUriProperties(Uri u)
    {
        Console.WriteLine("Uri.AbsolutePath = '{0}'", u.AbsolutePath);
        Console.WriteLine("Uri.AbsoluteUri = '{0}'", u.AbsoluteUri);
        Console.WriteLine("Uri.Host = '{0}'", u.Host);
        Console.WriteLine("Uri.HostNameType = '{0}'", u.HostNameType);
        Console.WriteLine("Uri.IsDefaultPort = {0}", u.IsDefaultPort);
        Console.WriteLine("Uri.IsLoopback = '{0}'", u.IsLoopback);
        Console.WriteLine("Uri.LocalPath = '{0}'", u.LocalPath);
        Console.WriteLine("Uri.PathAndQuery = '{0}'", u.PathAndQuery);
        Console.WriteLine("Uri.Port = {0}", u.Port);
        Console.WriteLine("Uri.Query = '{0}'", u.Query);
        Console.WriteLine("Uri.UserEscaped = {0}", u.UserEscaped);
    }
}
```

2   The output is:

```
Properties when Don't Escape is False:
Uri.AbsolutePath = '/samples/page%201.aspx'
Uri.AbsoluteUri = 'http://microsoft.com/samples/page%201.aspx?q=More#?%20&%3E%20
more'
Uri.Host = 'microsoft.com'
Uri.HostNameType = 'Dns'
```

```
Uri.IsDefaultPort = True
Uri.IsLoopback = 'False'
Uri.LocalPath = '/samples/page%201.aspx'
Uri.PathAndQuery = '/samples/page%201.aspx?q=More'
Uri.Port = 80
Uri.Query = '?q=More'
Uri.UserEscaped = False
```

All of these samples have been tested with V1.1 and V2.0 of the .NET Framework and the appropriate ones have been tested on the .NET Compact Framework.

Complete source code for the samples is available on the CD that is included in the back of the book.

Type Members

The detailed descriptions of the members are included in the electronic version of the book on the CD. To facilitate easy look-ups, the member descriptions appear in the same order as the type summary sections. Each member contains some or all of the following fields:

Syntax—C# declaration syntax is provided for familiar reference. ILASM syntax is provided for completeness.

Summary—Short description of the member's purpose.

Parameters—Table of parameters accepted by this member and their meaning.

Description—A complete description of this member.

Return Value—The value and range returned by this method.

Property Value—The value of this property.

Exceptions—Table of the common exceptions thrown by this member.

Permissions—Table of the code access permissions demanded by this method.

Example—An example using this member following the same pattern as the type samples.

Conventions Used in This Book

Courier is used for all source code blocks, including syntax declarations, class names, and member names.

In order to aid readability, the namespace portion of the fully qualified type names were removed when the result was unambigous. The following guidelines were used:

- When referring to a member of the type being addressed, only the member names were used.
- When referring to a type, other than the one being addressed, but in the same namespace, only the type name is used.

Additional Features

In addition to including the content from the ISO CLI standard, this book includes a number of other features:

- For every type covered in the book we include all the members as defined in V1.1 of the .NET Framework. Many members were left out of the ECMA standard to streamline platform work because types in the signature were not in the standard or because of scheduling reasons. As this book is primarily targeted at developers using the .NET Framework, we elected to include all the members of the types we cover, not just those that are standardized.
- Nearly every type contains annotations from key members of the design team at Microsoft and members of the ECMA standards group. These annotations bring rationale, history, and other interesting notes about the types covered.
- We added more than 1,000 samples to the book. Nearly every member has a working sample with output included. All of the samples can be found on the CD.

Acknowledgments

Many people contributed to making this book possible. We would like to thank:

Martin Heller, series editor, for his technical guidance as well as coordinating a myriad of details involved in creating the book.

Joan Murray from Addison-Wesley for her patience and guidance.

David Platt for producing the excellent namespace overviews provided here.

Joel Marcey for providing technical support in working with the Xml doc format used in the ECMA standard and for providing thoughtful and lighthearted annotations.

The contributing members of ECMA TC-39 TG1 and TG2 for formalizing the CLI and C# Standards on which this book is based.

Mike Koenig, my manager here at Microsoft, for allowing me the time to contribute this work.

Alex Homer, Kevin Westhead, and Joel Marcey for sharing their coding expertise through the large set of samples shown in this book.

The many .NET developers who reviewed early versions of the manuscript and provided valuable feedback, including William Bartholomew, Alfred Gary Myers, Jr., Jordan Matthiesen, Kevin Westhead, and Bill Wagner.

Brad Abrams
Lead Program Manager, .NET Framework Team
Microsoft Corporation
June 2005

Annotators' Biographies

In this volume you will find annotations from:

IA—Ihab Abdelhalim is a Lead Software Design Engineer at Microsoft. He led the quality assurance efforts for the .NET Framework globalization functionality (`System.Globalization` and `System.Text`) from 2000 to 2004. Ihab graduated with a B.S. in computer science from The American University in Cairo.

BA—Brad Abrams is a Lead Program Manager on the .NET Framework team at Microsoft, where he has been designing the Framework Class Libraries since 1997. Brad graduated with a B.S. in computer science from North Carolina State University. He is the primary author of the .NET Framework Design Guidelines, the Common Language Specification, and the class libraries for the ECMA/ISO CLI standard and C# language standard. Catch recent musings from Brad at `http://blogs.msdn.com/brada`.

SC—Suzanne Cook is a Software Design Engineer for .NET at Microsoft. She has been part of the Common Language Runtime team since 1998. Suzanne is known for development and design of the "loader" part of the execution engine for the runtime, working with Fusion, compilers, and other partners targeting .NET. Her blog can be viewed at `http://blogs.msdn.com/suzcook`.

KC—Krzysztof Cwalina is a Program Manager on the Common Language Runtime team at Microsoft. He graduated in 1999 with an M.S. in computer science from the University of Iowa, specializing in software engineering. He has participated in the design and implementation of the first release of the .NET Framework. He is also a member of a working group developing the .NET Framework Design Guidelines. For the past two years, he has been helping teams working on the WinFx to design the best ever system API.

MF—Mark Fussell is a Lead Program Manager on XML Technologies team at Microsoft, defining the future direction of XML and data access in the .NET Framework and within

SQL Server. He has worked on the System.Xml design since its inception. He talks regularly at conferences, has recently written a book on the XML programming APIs in .NET and discusses the joys of XML at `http://blogs.msdn.com/mfussell`.

BG—Brian Grunkemeyer has been a Software Design Engineer on the .NET Framework team at Microsoft since 1998. Brian graduated with a B.S. in computer science and a double major in cognitive science from Carnegie Mellon University. He has implemented a large portion of the Framework Class Libraries and contributed to the details of many classes in the ECMA/ISO CLI standard. His previous focuses have included IO, Resources, and Collections. He is currently working on future versions of the .NET Framework, including areas such as managed code reliability and versioning.

RJ—Rex Jaeschke is an independent consultant, author, and developer and leader of seminars, who specializes in programming languages and environments. He is the editor of the C#, CLI, and C++/CLI standards. Rex can be reached at `rex@RexJaeschke.com`.

SK—Sonja Keserovic is a Program Manager on the Common Language Runtime (CLR) team. She worked in COM Interop, Platform Invoke, and cross-AppDomain marshaling areas for almost four years. Recently, she made the transition into JIT area and is spending a lot of time learning about compiler technologies. Sonja joined CLR team in 2000 after working as a software developer for five years. She graduated from the University of Belgrade, Yugoslavia, in computer science and electrical engineering.

HK—Helena Kupkova is a Software Design Engineer on the Webdata team at Microsoft, where she has been working on `System.Xml` library for .NET Framework since 2001. Helena graduated with an M.S. in computer science from Charles University in Prague, Czech Republic.

CL—Chris Lovett is a Software Architect on the XML team at Microsoft where he has worked on XML tools and technologies since joining Microsoft in 1997. Before that Chris worked at IBM in Silicon Valley and joined several startup companies including the Apple/IBM joint venture Taligent, Inc. Chris graduated with a B.S. in science and mathematics, majoring in computer science from NSW University in Sydney, Australia.

JM—Joel Marcey is a Senior Software Engineer at Intel Corporation. He has been with Intel for almost eight years. He graduated in 1997 with a B.S. in computer engineering from North Carolina State University. He is currently doing research in the area of managed runtime environments, specifically around the CLR. He is also a key member and contributor in the CLI standardization process within ECMA. He is the elected chair of ECMA TC39 and the elected convener of the ECMA TC39 TG3 for the 2004/2005 calendar year. He works closely with Microsoft in both his research and standardization efforts.

DM—David Mortenson is the development lead for the core execution engine of the Common Language Runtime. Prior to this, he was one of the main developers responsible for implementing the CLR's support for interoperability between unmanaged and .NET code. He joined the CLR in 1999 after having graduated from Sherbrooke University in Québec, Canada, with a B.S. in computer engineering.

CM—Chad Mumford is a Lead Software Design Engineer for .NET at Microsoft. He has been part of the System.Net team since 2001. Chad graduated with an M.S. in computer science from the University of Washington. In addition to .NET, he has worked on a variety of projects during his time at Microsoft, including NetMeeting, Messenger, and Microsoft Office Developer.

AN—Adam Nathan is a Lead Software Design Engineer on the .NET Framework Quality Assurance team at Microsoft. For more than five years, Adam has driven the quality and usability of COM Interoperability and other Common Language Runtime technologies, and regularly gives talks on these topics. He is the author of *.NET and COM: The Complete Interoperability Guide* (SAMS, 2002), a coauthor of *ASP.NET: Tips, Tutorials, and Code* (SAMS, 2001), and the creator of `www.pinvoke.net`, an online repository of PInvoke signatures. Adam received an honors B.S. in computer science from Cornell University.

LO—Lance Olson was born and raised in Salt Lake City, Utah. He holds a master's degree in business administration from the University of Washington and a bachelor's degree in information systems and technology from Weber State University. Lance works as a Lead Program Manager on the .NET Framework team at Microsoft. He joined Microsoft in 1997 and has been on the .NET Framework since its inception. While working on the .NET Framework, Lance has been actively involved in the developer community. He coauthored *Network Programming for the Microsoft .NET Framework* (Microsoft Press, 2003), presented at numerous developer events including the Microsoft's Professional Developers Conferences (PDC) and Tech Ed, published articles on the Microsoft Developer Network (MSDN), and contributed to various development newsgroups and mailing lists. When he is not working, Lance enjoys fishing, camping, pottery, playing soccer, and spending time with his children and his wife, Julie.

JP—Joel Pobar is a Program Manager in the CLR .NET team working in the Base Class Libraries and the Managed Services teams. Joel shares his time between late-bound dynamic CLR features (reflection, code generation), compiler teams, and the Shared Source CLI (Rotor) program. He graduated with a BIT from the Queensland University of Technology in sunny Brisbane, Australia, where he did research in high-performance computing. You can find his recent CLR-related writings at `http://blogs.msdn.com/joelpob`.

SS—Shawn Steele is a Software Design Engineer for the Windows Global Platforms Technologies and Services team at Microsoft. He implemented many new features in the `System.Text` namespace, with additional work in the `System.Globalization` namespace. In addition to .NET, Shawn does similar globalization work for the Windows APIs.

DT—Danny Thorpe is a Borland Chief Scientist working on software development tools for .NET, Windows, and Linux platforms. Danny graduated with a B.S. in mathematics from Louisiana State University in 1990. He played a small part in the creation of Delphi in 1995, authored "Delphi Component Design" in 1997, and by 2003 was Lead Engineer for the Delphi for .NET project. In 1994, he chipped in with some friends to write a pinball simulation which, later became Microsoft's "Space Cadet Pinball." Danny hosts the Delphi Compiler Core blog at `http://homepages.borland.com/dthorpe/blog/delphi`. In his spare time, he thinks about snowboarding and rewriting "Space Cadet" in .NET managed code.

PART I
Namespace Overviews

The System namespace is the root of all namespaces in the .NET Framework, containing all other namespaces as subordinates. It also contains the types that we felt to be the most fundamental and frequently used. Significant portions of this namespace are covered in Volume 1 of the *.NET Framework Standard Library Annotated Reference*.

Basic Variable Types

The class Object is the root of the inheritance hierarchy in the .NET Framework. Every class in the .NET Framework ultimately derives from this class. If you define a class without specifying any other inheritance, Object is the implied base class. It provides the most basic methods and properties that all objects need to support, such as returning an identifying string, returning a Type object (think of it as a class descriptor) to use for runtime discovery of the object's contents, and providing a location for a garbage collection finalizer.

The .NET Framework provides two kinds of types, value types and reference types. Instances of value types are allocated on the stack or inline inside an object, which incurs a lower overhead than using the managed heap. Value types are most often used for small, lightweight variables accessed primarily for a single data value, while still allowing them to be treated as objects in the inheritance hierarchy (for example, having methods). All value types must derive from the abstract base class ValueType. Table 1 lists the value types in the System namespace covered in this volume of the *.NET Framework Standard Library Annotated Reference*.

TABLE 1

Name	Represents
IntPtr	Platform-specific type that is used to represent a pointer or a handle.
UIntPtr	Platform-specific type that is used to represent a pointer or a handle.
Void	Indicates a method that does not return a value; that is, the method has the void return type.

All objects that are not value types are by definition reference types. Creating an instance of a reference type allocates the new object from the managed heap and returns a reference to it, hence the name. Most objects are reference types.

Attributes

The .NET Framework makes extensive use of attributes, descriptive pieces of read-only information that a programmer can place in an object's metadata. Attributes can be read by any interested piece of code that has the required level of permission. Many attributes are provided and used by the system. Others are defined by programmers and used for their own purposes. All attributes derive from the abstract base class System.Attribute. The attributes in Table 2 were felt to be common enough to occupy the System namespace and are covered in this volume of the *.NET Framework Standard Library Annotated Reference*. Many other subordinate namespaces also define more specialized attributes.

TABLE 2

Attributes	Meaning
ParamArrayAttribute	Indicates that the method will allow a variable number of arguments in its invocation.

Utility Objects

The class AppDomain represents an isolated environment in which applications execute. You generally don't have to worry about creating them and using them; it usually happens behind the scenes. Unmanaged hosts such as the Windows shell and ASP.NET create an application domain and then load and run the user code within that domain.

The Type class (covered in Volume 1) is the basis for all reflection operations. Think of it as a class descriptor. When performing reflection, an internal token is sometimes used to represent a reflected type. A field (object member variable) can be represented by the class RuntimeFieldHandle, a method by the class RuntimeMethodHandle, and a Type object itself by the class RuntimeTypeHandle.

Since the .NET Framework is highly optimized for Internet programming, it contains a number of utility classes to ease the task of handling URIs (uniform resource identifiers). The class Uri is the basic representation of a URI, with methods providing access to individual parts of the URI such as the host name, and utility features such as hex escaping and unescaping. The enumeration UriHostNameType specifies the host name types for the method Uri.CheckHostName, and the enumeration UriPartial specifies the parts of the URI for the method Uri.GetLeftPart. The class UriBuilder provides a custom constructor for Uri objects and provides an easy way to modify an existing Uri.

Delegates

The .NET Framework supports callbacks from one object to another by means of the class Delegate. A Delegate represents a pointer to an individual object method or to a static class method. You generally will not use the Delegate class directly, but instead will use the wrapper provided by your programming language. The .NET Framework event system uses delegates. The object wanting to receive the event provides the sender with a delegate, and the sender calls the function on the delegate to signal the event.

Exceptions

In order to provide a common, rich, easily programmed, and difficult to ignore way of signaling and handling errors, the .NET Framework supports structured exception handling. A caller places an exception handler on the stack at the point at which he wants to catch the error, using the try–catch syntax of his programming language. A called function wanting to signal an error creates an object of class System.Exception (or one derived from it) containing information about the error and throws it. The CLR searches up the call stack until it finds a handler for the type of exception that was thrown, at which time the stack is unwound and control transferred to the catch block, which contains the error handling code.

The class System.Exception is the base class from which all exception objects derive. It contains such basic information as a message provided by the thrower and the stack trace at which the exception took place. The class System.SystemException derives from it, and all system-provided exceptions derive from that. This allows a programmer to differentiate between system-provided and programmer-built exceptions. The system-provided exceptions in Table 3 were felt to be common enough to occupy the base System namespace and are covered in this volume of the *.NET Framework Standard Library Annotated Reference*. Many more specialized exception classes live in subordinate namespaces.

TABLE 3

Exception Class	Meaning
BadImageFormatException	The file image of a DLL or an executable program is invalid.
CannotUnloadAppDomainException	An attempt to unload an application domain fails.
EntryPointNotFoundException	An attempt to load an assembly failed due to the absence of an entry method.
FieldAccessException	An illegal attempt was made to access a field inside a class.

TABLE 3 *(continued)*

Exception Class	Meaning
MemberAccessException	An attempt to access a class member fails.
MethodAccessException	An illegal attempt to access a method inside a class.
MissingFieldException	An attempt to access a field that does not exist.
MissingMemberException	An attempt to access a class member that does not exist.
MissingMethodException	An attempt to access a method that does not exist.
TypeLoadException	Type-loading failure occurred.
TypeUnloadedException	There is an attempt to access an unloaded class.
UriFormatException	An invalid Uniform Resource Identifier (URI) is detected.

Diagram

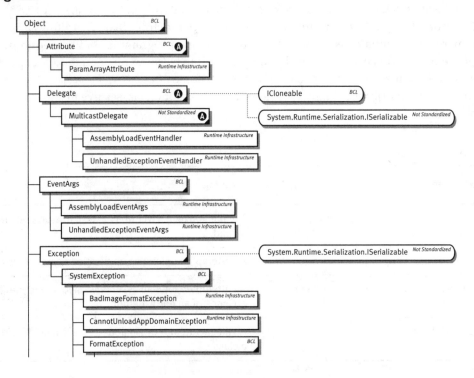

6

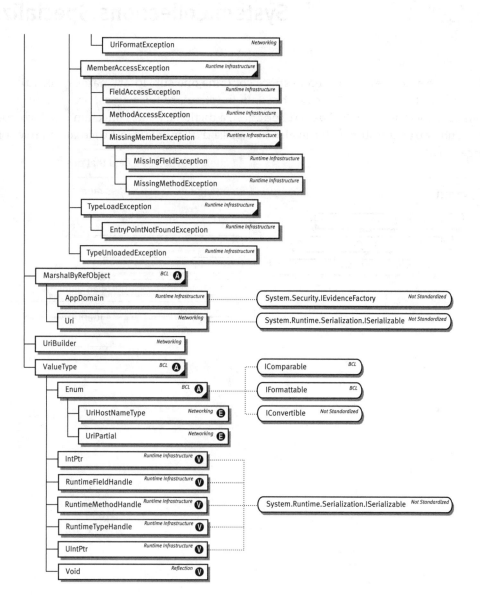

System.Collections.Specialized

The System.Collections namespace contains one subsidiary namespace called System.Collections.Specialized. In the standard this namespace currently contains only the class NameValueCollection, a dictionary-like collection in which both keys and entries are strings. It can also be accessed by numeric index, in the manner of an ArrayList.

Diagram

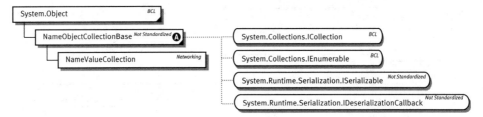

System.Globalization

The global reach of the Internet, which essentially connects every intelligent box in the universe to every other intelligent box in the universe, means that essentially any application can be used by a native speaker of essentially any human language. Presenting numbers and dates in the manner that each user expects and immediately understands is not a matter of cultural sensitivity. It is a critical piece of communication necessary to avoid expensive errors. When you buy your non-refundable airline ticket online, does the departure date of 6–5–02 represent May 6 or June 5? The System.Globalization namespace in the .NET Framework contains classes that provide built-in functionality allowing a programmer to write programs that adjust to the language of its user, particularly in the area of formatting dates and numbers.

Significant portions of this namespace are covered in Volume 1 of the *.NET Framework Standard Library Annotated Reference*.

The class CultureInfo is provided for future standardization.

Diagram

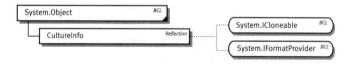

While portions of .NET such as Web Services provide networking functionality at a high level of abstraction, network programmers often need to work at a medium or low level of abstraction, particularly when communicating with non-.NET systems. The System.Net namespace provides objects for performing network operations at these abstraction levels.

Request/Response Objects

A client program generally wants to send a network request to a server and receive some sort of response. The .NET Framework provides a protocol-independent way of doing this through the abstract base classes WebRequest and WebResponse. These protocol-independent classes enforce a common programmatic interface onto their protocol-specific descendant classes, an architecture known as "pluggable protocols." This is analogous to the way the abstract base class System.IO.Stream enforces a common programmatic interface onto all streams regardless of their backing medium.

A client that wants to perform a network request/response operation obtains a WebRequest-derived object by calling the static method WebRequest.Create, passing the URI of the desired target. The system looks up the protocol prefix (e.g., "http:"), finds which WebRequest-derived class is registered as handling that protocol, and returns an instance of it. The creator of the derived instance (often the derived class itself, sometimes a separate factory object) must implement the IWebRequestCreate interface to support this creation mechanism. The protocols are registered with the system at deployment time via the static method WebRequest.Register. The method WebRequest.GetResponse sends the request to the server, optionally uploading data with it, and receives a WebResponse object containing the server's response.

Client applications will often need to set properties of the WebRequest before making the call to GetResponse. For example, servers often require clients to authenticate themselves with some sort of credentials. The WebRequest carries these credentials in a property called Credentials, which contains an object that implements the ICredentials interface. The class NetworkCredential provides a default implementation of this interface which you can use for this purpose. If your application is communicating with several different servers, you might find it easier to use an object of class CredentialCache, which also implements the ICredentials interface. It can hold multiple sets of credentials, each associated with a separate URI. When the server requests authentication credentials, the CredentialCache searches for the URI and returns the right set of credentials for it.

When the client makes a request, a server that requires authentication will send back a challenge to the client, asking for the user's credentials. This challenge is interpreted by an authentication module, which is an object that implements the IAuthenticationModule interface. This interface contains methods that interpret the server's challenge and return an `Authorization` object containing the correct set of user's credentials. The static class `AuthenticationManager` manages one or more authentication modules.

The client may need to supply network headers for its request, and look at the network headers returned by the server. The Headers property of a `WebRequest` or `WebResponse` object contains an object of class `WebHeaderCollection`, which holds the name/value pair headers sent to and received from the server.

Network requests often need to go through proxy servers, for example, to pass through firewalls. Since it is common for all requests in an application to go through the same proxy, the class `GlobalProxySelection` contains static methods to set the proxy server for all `WebRequest`s that don't explicitly override it. You can override the global settings by using the `Proxy` property of the `WebRequest`, supplying an object that implements the `IWebProxy` interface. The class `WebProxy` provides a default implementation of this interface.

The classes `HttpWebRequest` and `HttpWebResponse` provide HTTP-specific implementations of the abstract, protocol-agnostic `WebRequest` and `WebResponse` classes. Internally, they use the object of class `HttpVersion` to specify the version of HTTP that a specific `WebRequest` or `WebResponse` is using. The status of an `HttpWebResponse` is a member of the `HttpStatusCode` enumeration. If you'd like to override the default behavior of a "continue" request in HTTP, you can plug in your own handler using an object of class `HttpContinueDelegate`.

The `WebClient` class provides a simple wrapper through which a client can make a network request and receive a response. It uses the `WebRequest`- and `WebResponse`-derived classes internally without exposing them to the caller. It is simpler to program for the most common cases.

Utility Objects

In addition to `WebRequest` and `WebResponse`, the `System.Net` namespace contains a number of other utility classes useful in network programming. The class `Dns` provides basic access to a domain name service via static methods. The `IPHostEntry` associates a collection of IP addresses with a collection of aliases.

The abstract base class `EndPoint` represents a network resource or service. Descendant classes combine network connection information to form a connection point to a service. The class `IPAddress` holds a dotted quad IP address. The class `IPEndPoint` derives from `EndPoint`, representing a network endpoint as an IP address and a port number. The `ServicePoint` class represents an association between a set of connections and the target host. The `ServicePointManager` manages a collection of instances of `ServicePoint` objects.

Permissions

In my description of the namespaces `System.Security` (in Volume 1 of the *.NET Framework Standard Library Annotated Reference*) and `System.Security.Permissions`, I discussed the nature of permissions and the fact that they could be granted either programmatically or declaratively. The `System.Net` namespace contains three permission objects relating to network programming, each appearing in both programmatic and declarative flavors. The programmatic classes all derive from `System.Security.CodeAccessPermission`, and the declarative classes from `System.Security.CodeAccessSecurityAttribute`. The `NetworkAccess` enumeration is used by the `WebPermission` and `SocketPermission` classes, specifying if the program is allowed to accept incoming connections or make outgoing connections or both. The permissions are listed in Table 4.

TABLE 4

Permission Class	Attribute Class	Controls Access to
WebPermission	WebPermissionAttribute	Using WebRequest class
DnsPermission	DnsPermissionAttribute	Domain name servers
SocketPermission	SocketPermissionAttribute	Socket connections

Exceptions

The `System.Net` namespace contains two exception classes that are listed in Table 5, which are used to signal network-specific error conditions.

TABLE 5

Class	Meaning
ProtocolViolationException	An error is made while using a network protocol.
WebException	An error occurs while accessing the network through a pluggable protocol. Contains status codes from `WebExceptionStatus` enumeration.

Diagram

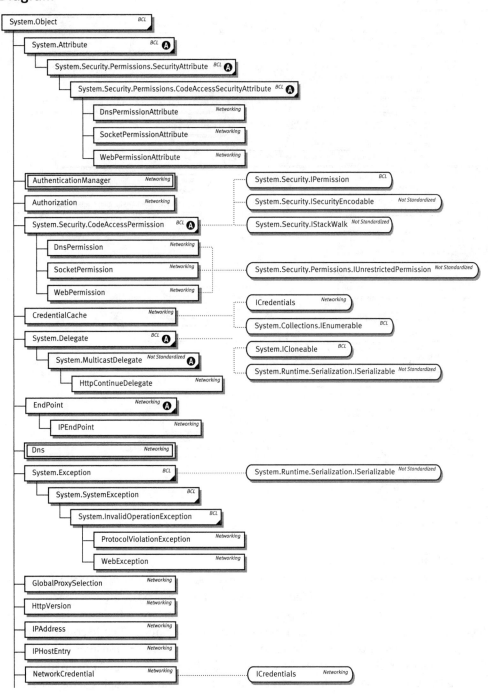

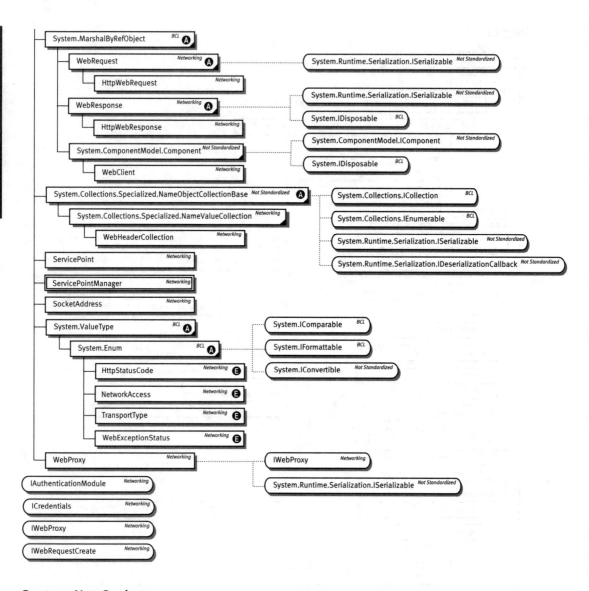

System.Net.Sockets

Sometimes programmers need to work at an even lower level of abstraction than the `WebRequest` and `WebResponse` objects that live in the `System.Net` namespace, particularly when porting legacy code. One popular low-level interface is the Berkeley Sockets interface. The `System.Net.Sockets` interface provides a managed code connection to this subsystem. It uses a number of objects from the `System.Net` namespace.

The base object of the `Socket` subsystem is, naturally, the `Socket`. After creating and configuring the `Socket` to your liking, you read and write data to it using a `Network-`

`Stream` object, which maps the `System.IO.Stream` interface onto the socket's network connection.

The `LingerOption` object contains information about whether the connection should linger after closing the socket, and if so, for how long. The `MulticastOption` object contains the collection of IP addresses to which to send multicast packets.

Table 6 lists a number of enumerations in the socket class for specifying various options.

TABLE 6

Enumeration	Meaning
AddressFamily	Specifies the addressing scheme that an instance of the `Socket` class can use.
ProtocolType	Specifies the protocols that the `Socket` class supports.
SelectMode	Defines the polling modes for the `Socket.Poll` method.
SocketFlags	Provides constant values for socket messages.
SocketOptionLevel	Defines socket option levels for the `Socket.SetSocketOption` and `Socket.GetSocketOption` methods.
SocketOptionName	Defines socket option names for the `Socket` class.
SocketShutdown	Defines constants used by the `Socket.Shutdown` method.
SocketType	Specifies the type of socket an instance of the `Socket` class represents.

The `System.Net.Sockets` namespace contains one new exception class, named `SocketException`.

Diagram

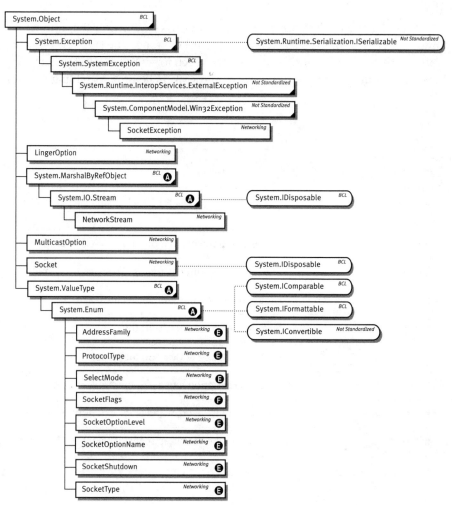

System.Reflection

The System.Reflection namespace contains types that allow programmers to read an object's metadata at runtime to discover and invoke that object's capabilities. You can use reflection to discover an object's members and attributes, for example, in building a browser program. You can also use reflection to access an object's members ("late-bound invocation"), thereby allowing runtime access to objects that you didn't know about at compile time. Invoking an object's members with reflection is slower than performing the same operations with direct compilation; runtime access always is. But the types in the System.Reflection provide a standardized, implementation-independent way of performing these operations across all objects in the system, without requiring the object's implementer to do any work.

The universal base class System.Object contains a method GetType, which returns an object of class System.Type. The Type is the base for all reflection activity. Most of the objects returned by Type's methods belong to the System.Reflection namespace. The property Type.Assembly returns an object of class Assembly, describing the assembly (logical collection of files considered the basic unit of the .NET Framework) within which the type is defined. The property Type.Module returns an object of class Module, describing the module (physical binary file) within which the type is defined.

The Type contains two kinds of methods that return information about the members of individual classes. The methods with plural names, e.g., GetMembers, return an array of all the object's members of that kind. The singular version, e.g., GetMember, searches for the member with a specified name. The base class MemberInfo contains the small amount of information common to all kinds of members, such as the member's name. Each of the derived classes ConstructorInfo, EventInfo, FieldInfo, MethodInfo, and PropertyInfo provides information specific to that kind of member, such as the parameter list of a method. The System.Type methods and the object types they return are listed in Table 7.

TABLE 7

System.Type Methods	Return	Describing
GetConstructor, GetConstructors	ConstructorInfo	Constructors exposed by object
GetEvent, GetEvents	EventInfo	Events fired by object
GetField, GetFields	FieldInfo	Fields (member variables) of object

TABLE 7 *(continued)*

System.Type Methods	Return	Describing
GetMember, GetMembers	MemberInfo	Object's members of all types
GetMethod, GetMethods	MethodInfo	Methods exposed by object
GetProperty, GetProperties	PropertyInfo	Properties exposed by object

Each of the -Info objects listed above contains a property called Attributes, and so does the base class System.Type itself. This property does not return the various System.Attribute-derived classes discussed throughout this book; these live in the CustomAttributes collection. Instead, the Attributes property contains selections from a hardwired enumeration specific to the kind of member that it describes. The enumerations are listed in Table 8.

TABLE 8

Enumeration Name	Information Contained in Enumeration
EventAttributes	Attributes of an event, such as SpecialName
FieldAttributes	Attributes of a field, such as Private, Public, or Literal
MethodAttributes	Attributes of a method or constructor, such as Abstract, Virtual, or Final
ParameterAttributes	Attributes of a method parameter, such as In, Out, Optional, or Retval
PropertyAttributes	Attributes of a property, such as HasDefault
TypeAttributes (from Type.Attributes)	Attributes of a type, such as Class, Interface, or Sealed

When you read the metadata describing a function, you need to know the parameters that the function accepts. The ConstructorInfo and MethodInfo classes derive from the common base class MethodBase. This class contains the method GetParameters, which returns an array of ParameterInfo objects describing the parameters that the method requires.

It is common for a class to specify one member as its default member, the one that gets invoked when the caller omits the method name from a call. For example, the default member of the `Collection` class is `Item`. Writing `SomeCollection[0]` has the same effect as writing `SomeCollection.Item(0)` because Item is the default member of the class. You specify a default member by attaching the attribute `DefaultMemberAttribute` to the member.

As always, objects in the `System.Reflection` namespace throw exceptions when they get annoyed about something. Several exception classes exist to signal the various types of failures that might occur and need to be signaled. Table 9 lists these classes.

TABLE 9

Exception Name	Signals
AmbiguousMatchException	Binding to a method results in more than one method matching the binding criteria.
TargetException	An attempt is made to invoke an invalid target.
TargetInvocationException	A member invoked through reflection threw an exception. *Note:* The exception thrown from the member is available in the `InnerException` property from this exception.
TargetParameterCountException	Number of parameters for an invocation does not match the number expected.

The `BindingFlags` enumeration contains flags that allow a caller to specify the way a reflection function searches the metadata for members and types. Most reflection functions, such as `Type.GetMembers`, contain an overloaded version that allows you to pass a combination of flags from this enumeration. It contains values such as `Public` and `Static`, which limits the search to members of those types, and `IgnoreCase`, which says to pay no attention to the case of a target member's name.

When you call an object method via reflection, you generally pass a parameter list to the method. The reflection system provides an automatic way to coerce the parameter types that you pass into unmanaged types when you are calling a native method, but you might need to override the system behavior and provide your own custom behavior. In this case, you would use an array of `ParameterModifier` objects, saying, "Here's what I want you to make it into." You also need an implementation of the `Binder` class that will read the `ParameterModifier` array and process them. As you can imagine, this technique doesn't get used very often.

Diagram

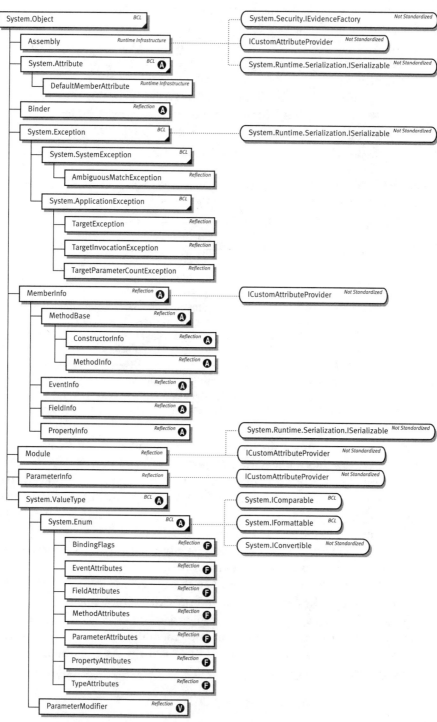

System.Runtime.CompilerServices

The namespace `System.Runtime.CompilerServices` contains objects used by developers of language compilers. Since all source languages have to compile down to the same MSIL, writing a compiler for the .NET Framework requires more intimate and pervasive connection with the target system than a bare Windows compiler.

The class `MethodImplAttribute`, deriving from `System.Attribute`, is a metadata attribute that specifies how a method is implemented. It contains values from the `MethodImplOptions` enumeration. Examples of the options it can specify are `NoInlining`, which specifies that the method must be called by a jump and may not be compiled inline, or `ForwardRef`, which specifies that the method is declared in a particular location but its implementation is elsewhere.

The class `DecimalConstantAttribute`, deriving from `System.Attribute`, stores the value of a `System.Decimal` constant in metadata. The class `IsVolatile`, while not deriving from `System.Attribute`, emits metadata marking a field as volatile.

The `RuntimeHelpers` class is a set of static methods and properties that provide support for certain compiler operations. For example, it contains a method called `GetObjectValue`, which accepts a value type such as an integer and returns it in a `System.Object`, a process known as "boxing," referring to packaging rather than pugilism.

Diagram

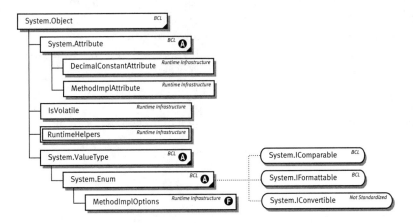

The System.Runtime.InteropServices namespace contains classes for managing the interoperation between .NET Framework managed code and native API functions. Since native APIs will vary greatly from one operating system to the next, this namespace will probably contain additional objects that will vary a great deal from one .NET Framework implementation to another. Consult your particular implementation guide.

The attribute DllImportAttribute is applied to a function declaration to tell the compiler that it represents a call to a method in an unmanaged DLL. This attribute contains a selection from the CallingConvention enumeration, specifying the parameter passing and stack cleanup convention used by the function.

When you pass parameters to an unmanaged method, the CLR converts the managed types (for example, System.String) into corresponding unmanaged types (for example, BSTR). Each type has its own default conversion behavior, but you can use the attribute MarshalAsAttribute if you want to change it. This attribute uses the UnmanagedType enumeration to specify the unmanaged type to which you want the managed parameter converted, and the CharSet enumeration specifies the character set to use in marshaling a string. The attributes InAttribute and OutAttribute denote parameters that are marshaled in only one direction, either in (to the called function) or out (from the called function). The absence of either specifies bidirectional marshaling.

Passing structures between managed and unmanaged code is tricky because the packing and element alignment expectations can vary from one unmanaged application to another. The StructLayoutAttribute specifies the basic rules for packing the unmanaged structure, using the LayoutKind enumeration. The FieldOffsetAttribute specifies the offset of individual fields within the structure.

Marshaling memory blocks between .NET's garbage-collected framework and the non-garbage-collected unmanaged code is also tricky. The GCHandle structure contains methods for obtaining pointers to managed memory objects so that they can be used by unmanaged code. The GCHandleType enumeration contains constants used to control this process, for example, one that specifies that a managed memory block is to be pinned in one location until freed.

Diagram

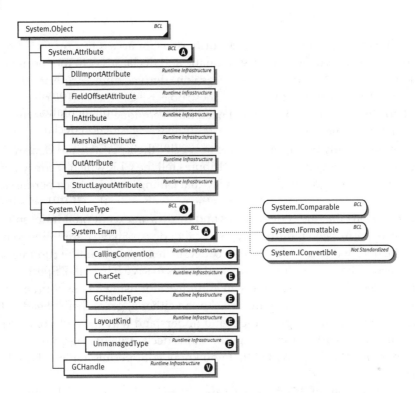

A permission is an object that specifies security rules for access to a protected resource. Permissions come in two flavors, programmatic and declarative. In the former case, the permission class (e.g., `ReflectionPermission`) derives from `CodeAccess-Permission`. You write code that creates these objects, sets their properties, and calls their methods in the usual way. You will need this technique when your security operations can vary dynamically at runtime.

Alternatively, many programmers like to specify their permissions declaratively by marking their code with attributes. The attributes tell the CLR which security permissions the code needs to do its job, in the same way that calling methods on a permission object would do. When a caller attempts to access the marked code, the CLR checks if the caller has the permissions that the code requires and throws an exception if it doesn't. This allows security permission failures (say, your caller doesn't have permission to use the file system) to be detected when code is first loaded instead of later in the runtime session (say, after the user has done a lot of work and needs to save it in a file). Specifying security requirements declaratively also allows an administrator using a viewer program to see which permissions your code requires, so she can either a) grant them ahead of time and avoid the fuss, or b) refuse to grant them and understand why the code, or at least certain portions of it, won't work. Specifying permissions declaratively is usually easier than doing it programmatically provided that you know your permission needs at development time.

Significant portions of this namespace are covered in Volume 1 of the *.NET Framework Standard Library Annotated Reference.*

The permission classes covered in this volume of the the *.NET Framework Standard Library Annotated Reference*, their corresponding attribute classes, and the protected resources to which they control access are listed in Table 10.

TABLE 10

Permission Class	Attribute Class	Controls Access To
`ReflectionPermission`	`ReflectionPermissionAttribute`	Metadata through the `System.Reflection` APIs

A permission object can contain its own fine-grained subdivisions of permissions. Each permission class has its own enumeration specifying the sub-privileges that a piece of code may ask for, as listed in Table 11.

TABLE 11

Enumeration	Meaning
`ReflectionPermissionFlag`	Permitted use of reflection API on members that are not visible, such as invoke or read-only.

Diagram

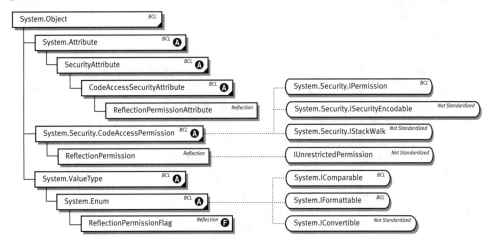

XML is now the universal standard for data interchange between applications systems. XML is not some geeky add-on required in certain obscure cases, but rather a universal requirement of any networked application. Therefore, easy and efficient access to XML by applications is a central requirement of any operating system, and the .NET Framework contains many classes for the easy handling of XML.

The abstract base class XmlReader defines methods for forward-only, read-only access XML documents and streams. The class XmlTextReader derives from Xml-Reader and provides a basic implementation of its logic. It checks a document for being well-formed, but does not validate it against a DTD or schema. It does not read an entire document into memory at a time, as does a DOM parser. Like a SAX parser, it reads a document one node at a time. However, unlike the way a SAX parser pushes data into its client application, the client application must pull data from the XmlTextReader.

The .NET Framework provides conceptually symmetrical classes for writing an XML document or stream. The abstract base class XmlWriter defines methods for fast, non-cached, forward-only writing of XML documents and streams. The class XmlText-Writer derives from XmlWriter and provides a basic implementation of its logic.

The XmlReader and XmlWriter operate on one XML node at a time, advancing through the document in response to calls from the client. They do not return a separate object representing this node, as does a DOM parser. Instead, the properties of the current node (Name, NodeType, Value, etc.) are properties of the XmlReader and XmlWriter themselves.

Despite operating on only one node at a time, an XmlReader-derived object is required to contain a certain amount of per-document data in order to do its job. For example, it can tell you the namespace URI or prefix of the current node, which requires that it remember all of the namespaces and prefixes declared in the document. The .NET Framework contains utility classes to help an implementer provide these capabilities. The class XmlTextReader uses them internally, and so can anyone else.

The class XmlParserContext is a scratchpad object used by a reader. It is intended as a holder, a one-stop shopping location, for all of the per-document information required by the reader. It has properties of its own, such as DocTypeName for the document type declaration and Encoding for the character encoding type used by the document. It also holds utility objects for accessing additional properties.

The XmlParserContext contains an object of class XmlNamespaceManager, a utility class that manages namespaces and their prefixes. This class provides methods that map prefixes onto namespace URIs and vice versa. It also contains a stack for managing the current default namespace scope. Several of the XmlTextReader properties, such as NamespaceURI, map through the XmlParserContext into its XmlNamespace-Manager.

The `XmlParserContext` class also contains a table of names. Since XML element and attribute names are often long and descriptive, so as to have meaning to human designers, storing the string name for every node can consume large amounts of memory. Since the same element and attribute names often repeat many times within an XML document, it makes sense to store each human-meaningful name only once in a table, and use shorter "atomized strings" to refer to each occurrence of it. The abstract base class `Xml-NameTable` defines the methods and properties used for this process, and the derived class `NameTable` provides a default implementation.

The parsing process of an XML document often requires the parser to include other specified documents. For example, the `!DOCTYPE` statement pulls in a DTD, `xsd:include` pulls in a schema, and `xsl:include` pulls in a style sheet. The abstract base class `XmlResolver` contains method definitions for an object that performs this function. The class `XmlUrlResolver` derives from it, providing a default implementation that resolves the inclusion based on a URL.

The class `XmlConvert` is a utility class that contains methods for frequently used data conversions in the XML space. It can convert names that are legal in other applications (for example, names containing spaces) into names that are legal in XML. It also contains methods for converting XML element or attribute values, which are always strings in an XML document, into CLR data types. It is very handy when constructing higher levels of abstraction that automatically convert XML data values into the types specified by a schema before presenting them to a client application.

As with all .NET Framework classes, the ones in this namespace signal errors by throwing exceptions. The class `XmlException` contains the standard exception data, plus additional XML-specific properties such as the line number and column number in the file at which the error occurred.

Diagram

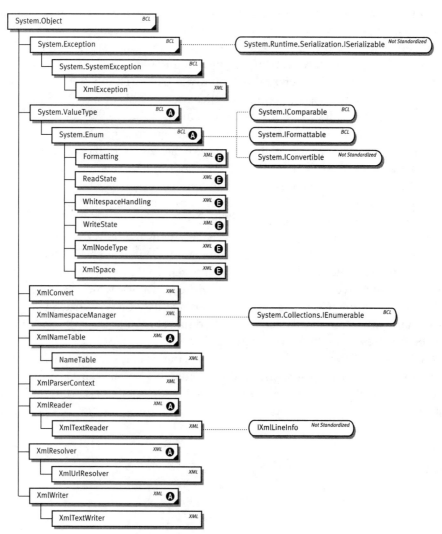

PART II
Class Libraries

System.Net.Sockets
AddressFamily Enum

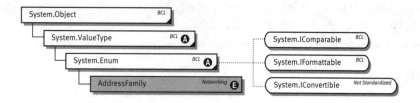

Summary

Specifies the addressing schemes used by the `System.Net.Sockets.Socket` class.

Type Summary

```
public enum AddressFamily
    {
    AppleTalk = 16,
    Atm = 22,
    Banyan = 21,
    Ccitt = 10,
    Chaos = 5,
    Cluster = 24,
    DataKit = 9,
    DataLink = 13,
    DecNet = 12,
    Ecma = 8,
    FireFox = 19,
    HyperChannel = 15,
    Ieee12844 = 25,
    ImpLink = 3,
    InterNetwork = 2,
    InterNetworkV6 = 23,
    Ipx = 6,
    Irda = 26,
    Iso = 7,
    Lat = 14,
MS  Max = 29,
    NetBios = 17,
    NetworkDesigners = 28,
    NS = 6,
    Osi = 7,
    Pup = 4,
    Sna = 11,
    Unix = 1,
    Unknown = -1,
    Unspecified = 0,
    VoiceView = 18,
    }
```

AddressFamily Enum

> ▪ **LO**   This list was derived mainly from the winsock header files. While the socket
> classes included in v1 of the .NET Framework are mostly geared around IP-based
> communication, it is possible to use the EndPoint class to support other protocols
> such as IPX, AppleTalk, Infra Red, and so forth.

Description

An AddressFamily member is specified to the Socket class constructors to identify the
addressing scheme that the socket instance will use to resolve an address. For example,
InterNetwork indicates that an IP version 4 address is expected when a Socket
instance connects to an endpoint.

Example

```csharp
using System;
using System.Net;
using System.Net.Sockets;
using System.Text;

public class AddressFamilySample
{
    public static void Main()
    {
        IPAddress ip = IPAddress.Parse("127.0.0.1");
        Socket skt = new Socket(AddressFamily.InterNetwork,
            SocketType.Dgram, ProtocolType.Udp);
        try
        {
            IPEndPoint ep = new IPEndPoint(ip, 9999);
            skt.Connect(ep);
            Byte[] req = Encoding.ASCII.GetBytes("Test");
            skt.SendTo(req, ep);
            IPEndPoint rep = (IPEndPoint)skt.LocalEndPoint;
            Console.WriteLine("LocalEndPoint details:");
            Console.WriteLine("Address: {0}", rep.Address);
            Console.WriteLine("AddressFamily: {0}", rep.AddressFamily);
            Console.WriteLine("Port: {0}", rep.Port);
        }
        catch (Exception e)
        {
            Console.WriteLine("Error: " + e.Message);
        }
        finally
        {
            skt.Close();
        }
        Console.WriteLine();
        Console.WriteLine();
        Console.WriteLine("Press Enter to continue");
        Console.ReadLine();
    }
}
```

The output is

```
LocalEndPoint details:
Address: 127.0.0.1
AddressFamily: InterNetwork
Port: 4082


Press Enter to continue
```

A
B
C
D
E
F
G
H
I
J
K
L
M
N
O
P
Q
R
S
T
U
V
W
X
Y
Z

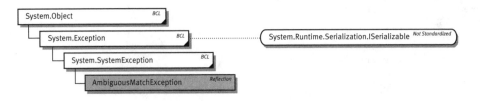

Summary

Represents the error that occurs when binding to a method or retrieving custom attributes results in more than one item matching the specified criteria.

Type Summary

```
public sealed class AmbiguousMatchException : SystemException
    {
    // Constructors
        public AmbiguousMatchException();
        public AmbiguousMatchException(string message);
        public AmbiguousMatchException(string message, Exception inner);
    }
```

■ JP   This exception is commonly thrown when input parameters to various non–plural XXXInfo/Type methods (Type.GetMethod/GetField, etc.) result in multiple matches from the binder. When calling these non–plural methods, it's best to be specific in your BindingFlags and always add type parameters for the methods that can accept them.

I've also seen this exception break deployed code where the code reflects on a library (loaded by name) that is versioned out of band. To illustrate this, a brief example:

```
MyLibrary.dll (Version 1.0)
class Foo
{
    public void MyExtensibilityPoint()
    {}
}

MyLibrary.dll (Version 2.0)
class Foo
{
```

CONTINUED

```
        public void MyExtensibilityPoint()
        {}
        public void MyExtensibilityPoint(int a)
        {}
}
My Deployed Code:
MethodInfo m = typeof(Foo).GetMethod("MyExtensibilityPoint");
```

Version 2 of the MyLibrary dll is deployed with a new overload of `MyExensi-`
`bilityPoint` to type Foo. Rerunning "My Deployed Code" above on Version 2 of
the type results in an ambiguous match exception because we now have two methods
with the same name, and we're not specifying the parameters of the method for binding. To avoid this scenario, always use the GetXXX APIs and supply as many specifics
as possible (in this case, supplying a type array specifying the methods parameters),
and consider including the version part when loading the assembly/library.

A
B
C
D
E
F
G
H
I
J
K
L
M
N
O
P
Q
R
S
T
U
V
W
X
Y
Z

Description

`AmbiguousMatchException` is thrown when a search that is intended to return no
more than one match detects multiple matching items. For example, this exception is
thrown when the `System.Attribute.GetCustomAttribute` methods (which return
a single custom attribute) find multiple occurrences of the attribute.

Example

```csharp
using System;
using System.Reflection;

/// <summary>
/// This sample shows that the AmbiguousMatchException is thrown when we call
/// GetMethod on an overloaded method.  Then it shows how to select the right
/// overload and invoke it.
/// </summary>

public class AmbiguousMatchExceptionSample
{
    public static void Main()
    {
        MethodInfo CompareMethod;
        try
        {
            //Expect GetMethod to throw an exception
            CompareMethod = typeof(String).GetMethod("CompareTo");
        }
        catch (AmbiguousMatchException e)
        {
            Console.WriteLine("'CompareTo' was ambiguous, try again");
            Console.WriteLine("Exception Type: {0}", e.GetType());
```

AmbiguousMatchException Class

```
            }
        CompareMethod = typeof(String).GetMethod("CompareTo",
            new Type[] { typeof(string) });
        string s = "Darb Smarba";
        int value = (int)CompareMethod.Invoke(s, new object[] { "Darb" });
        Console.WriteLine("CompareTo() returned: '{0}'", value);
        Console.WriteLine();
        Console.WriteLine();
        Console.WriteLine("Press Enter to continue");
        Console.ReadLine();
    }
}
```

The output is

```
'CompareTo' was ambiguous, try again
Exception Type: System.Reflection.AmbiguousMatchException
CompareTo() returned: '1'


Press Enter to continue
```

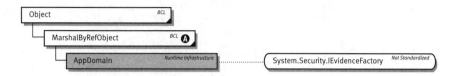

Summary

Represents an application domain, which is an isolated environment where applications execute.

Type Summary

```
    public sealed class AppDomain: MarshalByRefObject, IEvidenceFactory
       {
       // Properties
 MS CF public string BaseDirectory { get; }
 MS CF public static AppDomain CurrentDomain { get; }
 MS CF public string DynamicDirectory { get; }
 MS CF public Evidence Evidence { get; }
       public string FriendlyName { get; }
 MS CF public string RelativeSearchPath { get; }
 MS CF public AppDomainSetup SetupInformation { get; }
 MS CF public bool ShadowCopyFiles { get; }

       // Methods
 MS CF public void AppendPrivatePath(string path);
 MS CF public void ClearPrivatePath();
 MS CF public void ClearShadowCopyPath();
 MS CF public ObjectHandle CreateComInstanceFrom(string assemblyName,
                         string typeName);
 MS CF 1.1 public ObjectHandle CreateComInstanceFrom(string assemblyFile,
                         string typeName, byte[] hashValue,
                         AssemblyHashAlgorithm hashAlgorithm);
    CF public static AppDomain CreateDomain(string friendlyName);
    MS public static AppDomain CreateDomain(string friendlyName,
                         Evidence securityInfo);
 MS CF public static AppDomain CreateDomain(string friendlyName,
                         Evidence securityInfo, AppDomainSetup info);
 MS CF public static AppDomain CreateDomain(string friendlyName,
                         Evidence securityInfo,
                         string appBasePath,
                         string appRelativeSearchPath,
                         bool shadowCopyFiles);
 MS CF public ObjectHandle CreateInstance(string assemblyName,
                         string typeName);
 MS CF public ObjectHandle CreateInstance(string assemblyName,
                         string typeName, bool ignoreCase,
                         BindingFlags bindingAttr, Binder binder,
                         object[] args, CultureInfo culture,
                         object[] activationAttributes,
                         Evidence  securityAttributes);
```

37

```
MS CF public ObjectHandle CreateInstance(string assemblyName,
                        string typeName, object[] activationAttributes);
MS CF public object CreateInstanceAndUnwrap(string assemblyName,
                        string typeName);
MS CF public object CreateInstanceAndUnwrap(string assemblyName,
                        string typeName, bool ignoreCase,
                        BindingFlags bindingAttr, Binder binder,
                        object[] args, CultureInfo culture,
                        object[] activationAttributes,
                        Evidence securityAttributes);
MS CF public object CreateInstanceAndUnwrap(string assemblyName,
                        string typeName, object[] activationAttributes);
MS CF public ObjectHandle CreateInstanceFrom(string assemblyFile,
                        string typeName);
MS CF public ObjectHandle CreateInstanceFrom(string assemblyFile,
                        string typeName, bool ignoreCase,
                        BindingFlags bindingAttr, Binder binder,
                        object[] args, CultureInfo culture,
                        object[] activationAttributes,
                        Evidence securityAttributes);
MS CF public ObjectHandle CreateInstanceFrom(string assemblyFile,
                        string typeName,
                        object[] activationAttributes);
MS CF public object CreateInstanceFromAndUnwrap(string assemblyName,
                        string typeName);
MS CF public object CreateInstanceFromAndUnwrap(string assemblyName,
                        string typeName, bool ignoreCase,
                        BindingFlags bindingAttr, Binder binder, object[] args,
                        CultureInfo culture, object[] activationAttributes,
                        Evidence securityAttributes);
MS CF public object CreateInstanceFromAndUnwrap(string assemblyName,
                        string typeName, object[] activationAttributes);
MS CF public AssemblyBuilder DefineDynamicAssembly(AssemblyName name,
                        AssemblyBuilderAccess access);
MS CF public AssemblyBuilder DefineDynamicAssembly( AssemblyName name,
                        AssemblyBuilderAccess access,
                        Evidence evidence);
MS CF public AssemblyBuilder DefineDynamicAssembly(AssemblyName name,
                        AssemblyBuilderAccess access,
                        Evidence evidence,
                        PermissionSet requiredPermissions,
                        PermissionSet optionalPermissions,
                        PermissionSet refusedPermissions);
MS CF public AssemblyBuilder DefineDynamicAssembly(AssemblyName name,
                        AssemblyBuilderAccess access,
                        PermissionSet requiredPermissions,
                        PermissionSet optionalPermissions,
                        PermissionSet refusedPermissions);
MS CF public AssemblyBuilder DefineDynamicAssembly(AssemblyName name,
                        AssemblyBuilderAccess access, string dir);
MS CF public AssemblyBuilder DefineDynamicAssembly(AssemblyName name,
                        AssemblyBuilderAccess access, string dir,
                        Evidence evidence);
MS CF public AssemblyBuilder DefineDynamicAssembly(AssemblyName name,
                        AssemblyBuilderAccess access, string dir,
                        Evidence evidence,
                        PermissionSet requiredPermissions,
                        PermissionSet optionalPermissions,
                        PermissionSet refusedPermissions);
```

```
     MS CF public AssemblyBuilder DefineDynamicAssembly(AssemblyName name,
                             AssemblyBuilderAccess access, string dir,
                             Evidence evidence,
                             PermissionSet requiredPermissions,
                             PermissionSet optionalPermissions,
                             PermissionSet refusedPermissions,
                             bool isSynchronized);
     MS CF public AssemblyBuilder DefineDynamicAssembly(AssemblyName name,
                             AssemblyBuilderAccess access, string dir,
                             PermissionSet requiredPermissions,
                             PermissionSet optionalPermissions,
                             PermissionSet refusedPermissions);
     MS CF public void DoCallBack(CrossAppDomainDelegate callBackDelegate);
        MS public int ExecuteAssembly(string assemblyFile);
     MS CF public int ExecuteAssembly(string assemblyFile,
                     Evidence assemblySecurity);
        MS public int ExecuteAssembly(string assemblyFile,
                     Evidence assemblySecurity, string[] args);
  MS CF 1.1 public int ExecuteAssembly(string assemblyFile,
                     Evidence assemblySecurity,
                     string[] args, byte[] hashValue,
                     AssemblyHashAlgorithm hashAlgorithm);
     MS CF public Assembly[] GetAssemblies();
     MS CF public static int GetCurrentThreadId();
     MS CF public object GetData(string name);
     MS CF public Type GetType();
     MS CF public override object InitializeLifetimeService();
     MS CF public bool IsFinalizingForUnload();
     MS CF public Assembly Load(AssemblyName assemblyRef);
     MS CF public Assembly Load(AssemblyName assemblyRef,
                     Evidence assemblySecurity);
     MS CF public Assembly Load(byte[] rawAssembly);
     MS CF public Assembly Load(byte[] rawAssembly, byte[] rawSymbolStore);
     MS CF public Assembly Load(byte[] rawAssembly, byte[] rawSymbolStore,
                     Evidence securityEvidence);
     MS CF public Assembly Load(string assemblyString);
     MS CF public Assembly Load(string assemblyString,
                     Evidence assemblySecurity);
     MS CF public void SetAppDomainPolicy(PolicyLevel domainPolicy);
     MS CF public void SetCachePath(string path);
     MS CF public void SetData(string name, object data);
     MS CF public void SetDynamicBase(string path);
     MS CF public void SetPrincipalPolicy(PrincipalPolicy policy);
     MS CF public void SetShadowCopyFiles();
     MS CF public void SetShadowCopyPath(string path);
     MS CF public void SetThreadPrincipal(IPrincipal principal);
        CF public override string ToString();
        CF public static void Unload(AppDomain domain);

     // Events
        CF public event AssemblyLoadEventHandler AssemblyLoad;
     MS CF public event ResolveEventHandler AssemblyResolve;
        CF public event EventHandler DomainUnload;
     MS CF public event EventHandler ProcessExit;
     MS CF public event ResolveEventHandler ResourceResolve;
     MS CF public event ResolveEventHandler TypeResolve;
        CF public event UnhandledExceptionEventHandler UnhandledException;
     }
```

■ BA   We introduced Application Domains as a lightweight process mechanism. Because managed code can be verifiably type safe (memory safe) we did not need the heavyweight address space barrier that processes provide. This savings works out well most of the time. However, when using interop with unmanaged code it does cause some problems when type safety is violated. One notable example of this is the loader-lock and `AppDomain` marshaling problem that C++ was susceptible to. We fixed this problem in a service pack of v1.1.

■ JM   The ECMA standard `AppDomain` only inherits from `MarshalByRefObject`. `IEvidenceFactory` and `_AppDomain` are Microsoft implementation–specific "extensions" to support functionality (e.g., security) added by Microsoft.

■ JM   You can notice quite easily that the ECMA standard `AppDomain` contains minimal functionality as compared with the Microsoft implementation. Basically, the ECMA standard `AppDomain` type only provides mechanisms to create and unload application domains. Reasons for this include the minimum security sets for the ECMA standard, Microsoft-specific functionality, as well as lack of type availability within the standard.

■ JM   Partition I of the ECMA standards describes, in relatively minute detail, the concept of application domains. Only single application domain support is required for a conformant CLI implementation, although the usefulness of application domains really stems from the isolation and remoting capabilities they provide when multiple application domain support is available.

■ BG   Originally, we added `AppDomains` just to support the notion of unloading assemblies. Unloading code is somewhat tricky, especially if you don't want to pay some penalties every time you call a virtual method. `AppDomains` were a rather heavyweight mechanism, but they solved this goal. They also greatly complicated the CLR (Common Language Runtime) internally, especially when we tried to add features like generics in version 2.

However, the concept of an application domain as a unit of state isolation within the process has proved invaluable for our reliability story in version 2. In ASP.NET, the server was very successful with process recycling, i.e., restarting the server's worker processes when they ran out of memory or hit some other potentially critical failure. Here, all state in the process was thrown away when a critical resource failure occurred. We're leveraging the same idea of `AppDomain` recycling to achieve our reliability goals for SQL Server and other similar managed hosts, where you don't

CONTINUED

want to recycle the server process. `AppDomain` recycling is the key to being able to kill errant parts of an application, then throw away potentially corrupt state. In a transacted environment like a database, you can (generally) safely throw away all state within the `AppDomain` if you detect that any shared state within that `AppDomain` has been corrupted. (By shared state, I mean any state accessible from a static variable or some other cross-thread sharing mechanism.)

We have a pretty good heuristic for detecting corruption to shared state. Assuming there are no bugs in the code you're running, the only time you'll see shared state corruption is when an asynchronous exception (such as an `OutOfMemoryException`, `ThreadAbortException`, or `StackOverflowException`) occurs within a method that holds a lock. The idea here is that all synchronous exceptions should be handled by the application and the application generally shouldn't be written to deal with asynchronous exceptions. Then the natural way to edit shared state in a multi-threaded system is to take a lock.

For SQL Server, we have a system for escalating failures based on the above notions. If we get an `OutOfMemoryException` on a thread that isn't editing shared state (i.e., doesn't hold any locks), then we simply abort that thread. If the thread did hold a lock, then we pessimistically assume that at least some amount of shared state within that application domain is corrupt, so we escalate this failure to an `AppDomain` unload. This way we can tear down any threads that may potentially generate incorrect results. In this way, we escalate critical resource failures to `AppDomain` unloads.

There are a lot more subtleties to how we have implemented our escalation policy and the extremely corrupting nature of asynchronous exceptions, which led to the design of new reliability primitives like constrained execution regions, critical finalization, and `SafeHandle`. An example would be critical finalization. If a critical resource failure occurs when running a finalizer during an `AppDomain` unload (such as running out of memory to JIT compile the method), then we've introduced the notion of normal `AppDomain` unloads and rude `AppDomain` unloads. During a rude `AppDomain` unload, we won't run arbitrary user finalizers, but only trusted finalizers that have been eagerly prepared. This is known as critical finalization, and was designed to support `SafeHandle` so that a library developer has a chance to free OS resources even when we're escalating a critical failure.

Anyone who is building a host for running other managed code in-process with strict reliability concerns should research this area in great detail. This same escalation policy is accessible via our unmanaged hosting API for the CLR, and a carefully

CONTINUED

written all-managed application can probably achieve the same level of reliability with careful use of AppDomain's Unload method in conjunction with some other reliability primitives.

■ **AN**   AppDomain is one of the few classes in the .NET Framework that is commonly used via COM Interop (often for CLR hosting scenarios), so we made a point of exposing most of its functionality via an interface called _AppDomain. Exposing a real managed interface to COM consumers is much better than taking advantage of our regrettable "class interface" functionality, since we avoid a host of versioning problems by being in complete control of what gets exposed. The unfortunate thing about _AppDomain (besides the non-standard name, which I know drives folks like Brad crazy) is that the overloaded members are still just as clunky to use from COM. For example, the Load overloads are exposed as Load, Load_2, Load_3, and so on. But because of the versioning benefits, expect more of our COM-visible classes in the .NET Framework to start implementing real interfaces like _AppDomain and stop exposing class interfaces in the future.

Description

Application domains, which are represented by AppDomain objects, provide isolation, unloading, and security boundaries for executing managed code.

Multiple application domains can run in a single process; however, there is not a one-to-one correlation between application domains and threads. Several threads can belong to a single application domain, and while a given thread is not confined to a single application domain, at any given time, a thread executes in a single application domain.

Application domains are created using the CreateDomain method. AppDomain instances are used to load and execute assemblies (System.Reflection.Assembly). When an AppDomain is no longer in use, it can be unloaded.

The AppDomain class implements a set of events to enable applications to respond to the following conditions:

Condition	Event
An assembly was loaded.	System.AppDomain.AssemblyLoad
An application domain will be unloaded.	System.AppDomain.DomainUnload
An unhandled exception was thrown.	System.AppDomain.UnhandledException

Example

```
using System;

public class AppDomainSample
{
    public static void Main()
    {
        AppDomain domain = AppDomain.CreateDomain("MyNewDomain");
        domain.AssemblyLoad +=
            new AssemblyLoadEventHandler(MyLoadHandler);
        Console.WriteLine("FriendlyName is '{0}'", domain.FriendlyName);
        Console.WriteLine("Attempting to execute HelloWorld.exe...");
        domain.ExecuteAssembly("HelloWorld.exe");
        Console.WriteLine("Finished executing HelloWorld.exe.");
        AppDomain.Unload(domain);
        Console.WriteLine("AppDomain unloaded.");
        Console.WriteLine();
        Console.WriteLine();
        Console.WriteLine("Press Enter to continue");
        Console.ReadLine();
    }

    public static void MyLoadHandler(object sender,
        AssemblyLoadEventArgs args)
    {
        Console.WriteLine("Loaded assembly {0}",
            args.LoadedAssembly.FullName);
    }

}
```

The output is

```
FriendlyName is 'MyNewDomain'
Attempting to execute HelloWorld.exe...
Loaded assembly HelloWorld, Version=1.0.1767.19756, Culture=neutral, PublicKeyTo
ken=null
Loaded assembly System.Windows.Forms, Version=1.0.5000.0, Culture=neutral, Publi
cKeyToken=b77a5c561934e089
Loaded assembly System, Version=1.0.5000.0, Culture=neutral, PublicKeyToken=b77a
5c561934e089
Loaded assembly System.Drawing, Version=1.0.5000.0, Culture=neutral, PublicKeyTo
ken=b03f5f7f11d50a3a
Loaded assembly System.Xml, Version=1.0.5000.0, Culture=neutral, PublicKeyToken=
b77a5c561934e089
Finished executing HelloWorld.exe.
AppDomain unloaded.


Press Enter to continue
```

A
B
C
D
E
F
G
H
I
J
K
L
M
N
O
P
Q
R
S
T
U
V
W
X
Y
Z

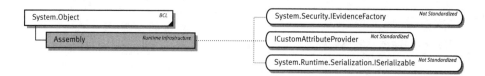

Summary

Defines an Assembly, which is a reusable, versionable, and self-describing building block of an application.

Type Summary

```
      public class Assembly : IEvidenceFactory, ICustomAttributeProvider,
                              ISerializable
         {
         // Properties
   MS CF public virtual string CodeBase { get; }
   MS CF public virtual MethodInfo EntryPoint { get; }
   MS CF public virtual string EscapedCodeBase { get; }
   MS CF public virtual Evidence Evidence { get; }
         public virtual string FullName { get; }
      MS CF public bool GlobalAssemblyCache { get; }
MS CF 1.1 public virtual string ImageRuntimeVersion { get; }
      MS CF public virtual string Location { get; }

         // Methods
         public object CreateInstance(string typeName);
   MS CF public object CreateInstance(string typeName, bool ignoreCase);
   MS CF public object CreateInstance(string typeName, bool ignoreCase,
                        BindingFlags bindingAttr, Binder binder, object[] args,
                        CultureInfo culture, object[] activationAttributes);
   MS CF public static string CreateQualifiedName(string assemblyName,
                              string typeName);
   MS CF public static Assembly GetAssembly(Type type);
      MS public static Assembly GetCallingAssembly();
   MS CF public virtual object[] GetCustomAttributes(bool inherit);
   MS CF public virtual object[] GetCustomAttributes(Type attributeType,
                              bool inherit);
   MS CF public static Assembly GetEntryAssembly();
      MS public static Assembly GetExecutingAssembly();
   MS CF public virtual Type[] GetExportedTypes();
   MS CF public virtual FileStream GetFile(string name);
   MS CF public virtual FileStream[] GetFiles();
   MS CF public virtual FileStream[] GetFiles(bool getResourceModules);
   MS CF public Module[] GetLoadedModules();
   MS CF public Module[] GetLoadedModules(bool getResourceModules);
   MS CF public virtual ManifestResourceInfo GetManifestResourceInfo(
                                       string resourceName);
      MS public virtual string[] GetManifestResourceNames();
      MS public virtual Stream GetManifestResourceStream(string name);
      MS public virtual Stream GetManifestResourceStream(Type type,
                              string name);
```

```
   MS CF public Module GetModule(string name);
      MS public Module[] GetModules();
   MS CF public Module[] GetModules(bool getResourceModules);
      MS public virtual AssemblyName GetName();
      MS public virtual AssemblyName GetName(bool copiedName);
   MS CF public virtual void GetObjectData(SerializationInfo info,
                             StreamingContext context);
   MS CF public AssemblyName[] GetReferencedAssemblies();
      MS public Assembly GetSatelliteAssembly(CultureInfo culture);
      MS public Assembly GetSatelliteAssembly(CultureInfo culture,
                             Version version);
         public virtual Type GetType(string name);
      MS public virtual Type GetType(string name, bool throwOnError);
   MS CF public Type GetType(string name, bool throwOnError, bool ignoreCase);
         public virtual Type[] GetTypes();
   MS CF public virtual bool IsDefined(Type attributeType, bool inherit);
      MS public static Assembly Load(AssemblyName assemblyRef);
   MS CF public static Assembly Load(AssemblyName assemblyRef,
                             Evidence assemblySecurity);
   MS CF public static Assembly Load(byte[] rawAssembly);
   MS CF public static Assembly Load(byte[] rawAssembly,
                             byte[] rawSymbolStore);
   MS CF public static Assembly Load(byte[] rawAssembly, byte[] rawSymbolStore,
                             Evidence securityEvidence);
         public static Assembly Load(string assemblyString);
   MS CF public static Assembly Load(string assemblyString,
                             Evidence assemblySecurity);
MS CF 1.1 public static Assembly LoadFile(string path);
MS CF 1.1 public static Assembly LoadFile(string path,
                             Evidence securityEvidence);
      MS public static Assembly LoadFrom(string assemblyFile);
   MS CF public static Assembly LoadFrom(string assemblyFile,
                             Evidence securityEvidence);
MS CF 1.1 public static Assembly LoadFrom(string assemblyFile,
                             Evidence securityEvidence, byte[] hashValue,
                             AssemblyHashAlgorithm hashAlgorithm);
   MS CF public Module LoadModule(string moduleName, byte[] rawModule);
   MS CF public Module LoadModule(string moduleName, byte[] rawModule,
                             byte[] rawSymbolStore);
   MS CF public static Assembly LoadWithPartialName(string partialName);
   MS CF public static Assembly LoadWithPartialName(string partialName,
                             Evidence securityEvidence);
         public override string ToString();

      // Events
   MS CF public event ModuleResolveEventHandler ModuleResolve;
      }
```

■ SC Calling Load(AssemblyName) is not necessarily the same as calling Load(String). If the AssemblyName.CodeBase is not set, then they do the same thing. So, if you've set the AssemblyName.Name, CultureInfo, public key token/ public key and/or Version properties, it would be the same as if you had specified those properties in a String (as a display name) and passed that to Load(String).

CONTINUED

A
B
C
D
E
F
G
H
I
J
K
L
M
N
O
P
Q
R
S
T
U
V
W
X
Y
Z

However, if the `AssemblyName.CodeBase` is set, but the `AssemblyName.Name` is not, then it's the same as calling `Assembly.LoadFrom()` on that `AssemblyName.CodeBase`. When both the `AssemblyName.CodeBase` and the `AssemblyName.Name` are set, then the bind is tried with all the given binding information, except the `AssemblyName.CodeBase` (so, again, it's just like calling `Load(String)`). If that succeeds, we're done. But, if that fails, then the bind is tried again with just the `AssemblyName.CodeBase` (just like `LoadFrom()`). If it fails again, then of course the whole bind fails. But, if it succeeds, then we verify that the binding properties in the `AssemblyName` match the found assembly. If they don't match, a `FileLoadException` will be thrown for HResult FUSION_E_REF_DEF_MISMATCH.

So, setting both the `AssemblyName.CodeBase` and the `AssemblyName.Name` is useful for when you want to both load an assembly at a given path into the `LoadFrom` context, and verify that it has the public key token, and so forth, that you expect. Of course, as described above (and due to binding context rules), keep in mind that just because you call `Load(AssemblyName)` with a `CodeBase` does not mean that it will be loaded from that path.

Description

An assembly is a reusable, versionable, self-describing deployment unit for types and resources. Assemblies are the fundamental units of deployment, and consist of collections of types and resources that are built to work together and form logical units of functionality.

An assembly consists of the following two logical elements:

* The sets of types and resources that form some logical unit of functionality.
* A manifest, which is the metadata that describes how the types and resources of an assembly relate and what they depend on to work properly.

The following information is captured in an assembly manifest:

* `Identity`—An assembly's identity includes its simple name (also called its weak name), a version number, an optional culture if the assembly contains localized resources, and an optional public key used to guarantee name uniqueness and to "protect" the name from unwanted reuse.
* `Contents`—Assemblies contain types and resources. The manifest lists the names of all the types and resources that are visible outside the assembly, along with information about where they can be found within the assembly.
* `Dependencies`—Each assembly explicitly describes other assemblies that it is dependent upon. Included in this dependency information is the version of each

dependency that was present when the manifest was built and tested. In this way the "known good" configuration is recorded and can be reverted to in case of failures due to version mismatches.

- `Requested Permissions`—As an assembly is being built, the assembly records the set of permissions that the assembly requires to run.

[*Note:* For additional information about assemblies, see Partition II of the CLI Specification.]

Example

```
using System;
using System.Text;
using System.Reflection;

/// <summary>
/// This example shows how to generate ILDASM-like output for an assembly.
/// </summary>

public class AssemblySample
{
    public static void Main()
    {
        Assembly assembly = Assembly.GetExecutingAssembly();
        Console.WriteLine("ILDASM style output for '{0}'",
            assembly.GetName().Name);
        Console.WriteLine("--------------------------------------------------");
        Console.WriteLine("// Metadata version: {0}",
            assembly.ImageRuntimeVersion);

        foreach (AssemblyName refAssemblyName
                    in assembly.GetReferencedAssemblies())
        {
            Console.WriteLine(".assembly extern {0}", refAssemblyName.Name);
            Console.WriteLine("{");
            Console.WriteLine("  .publickeytoken = ({0})",
                ByteArrayToHexString(refAssemblyName.GetPublicKeyToken()));
            Console.WriteLine("  .ver {0}",
                refAssemblyName.Version.ToString().Replace('.', ':'));
            Console.WriteLine("}");
        }
        Console.WriteLine(".assembly {0}",assembly.GetName().Name);
        Console.WriteLine("{");
        foreach (Attribute attrib in assembly.GetCustomAttributes(false))
        {
            Console.WriteLine("  .custom instance {0}", attrib);
        }
        Console.WriteLine("  .hash algorithm {0}",
            assembly.GetName().HashAlgorithm);
        Console.WriteLine("  .ver {0}",
            assembly.GetName().Version.ToString().Replace('.', ':'));
        Console.WriteLine("}");
        foreach (Module currentModule in assembly.GetModules())
```

```
            {
                Console.WriteLine(".module {0}", currentModule.Name);
            }
            Console.WriteLine();
            Console.WriteLine();
            Console.WriteLine("Press Enter to continue");
            Console.ReadLine();
        }//end main

        private static string ByteArrayToHexString(byte[] values)
        {
            StringBuilder hexString = new StringBuilder();
            foreach (byte b in values)
            {
                hexString.AppendFormat("{0:X}", b);
                hexString.Append(' ');
            }
            return hexString.ToString();
        }

    }
```

The output is

```
ILDASM style output for 'Assembly'
---------------------------------------------
// Metadata version: v1.1.4322
.assembly extern mscorlib
{
  .publickeytoken = (B7 7A 5C 56 19 34 E0 89 )
  .ver 1:0:5000:0
}
.assembly Assembly
{
  .custom instance System.Diagnostics.DebuggableAttribute
  .hash algorithm SHA1
  .ver 0:0:0:0
}
.module Assembly.exe


Press Enter to continue
```

Summary

Provides access to the `System.Reflection.Assembly` that was loaded causing an `AppDomain.AssemblyLoad` event.

Type Summary

```
CF public class AssemblyLoadEventArgs : EventArgs
    {
    // Constructors
    CF public AssemblyLoadEventArgs(Assembly loadedAssembly);

    // Properties
    CF public Assembly LoadedAssembly { get; }
    }
```

Description

[*Note:* This class provides the loaded assembly via the `LoadedAssembly` property.]

Example

```
using System;
using System.Reflection;

public class AssemblyLoadEventArgsSample
{
    public static void Main()
    {

        Assembly a = Assembly.GetExecutingAssembly();
        AssemblyLoadEventArgs args = new AssemblyLoadEventArgs(a);
        Console.WriteLine("AssemblyLoad event, "
            + "LoadedAssembly.FullName = {0}",
            args.LoadedAssembly.FullName);
        Console.WriteLine();
        Console.WriteLine();
        Console.WriteLine("Press Enter to continue");
        Console.ReadLine();
    }
}
```

The output is

```
AssemblyLoad event, LoadedAssembly.FullName = AssemblyLoadEventArgs, Version=0.0
.0.0, Culture=neutral, PublicKeyToken=null


Press Enter to continue
```

A
B
C
D
E
F
G
H
I
J
K
L
M
N
O
P
Q
R
S
T
U
V
W
X
Y
Z

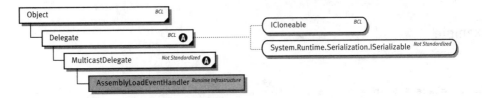

Summary

Defines the shape of methods that are called in response to `AppDomain.AssemblyLoad` events.

Type Summary

```
CF public delegate void AssemblyLoadEventHandler(object sender,
                        AssemblyLoadEventArgs args);
```

> **■ BA**   Looking back on it now, there are way too many types included in the `System` root namespace. This namespace is automatically important in most projects and the proliferation of types causes some degree of developer confusion. In retrospect we should have factored `System` better and put these less commonly used types into a different namespace.

Parameters

Parameter	Description
sender	The `System.AppDomain` that is the source of the event.
args	A `System.AssemblyLoadEventArgs` that contains the event data.

Description

[*Note:* An `AssemblyLoadEventHandler` instance is used to specify the methods that are invoked in response to an `AppDomain.AssemblyLoad` event. To associate an instance of `AssemblyLoadEventHandler` with an event, add the instance to the event. The methods referenced by the `AssemblyLoadEventHandler` instance are invoked whenever an assembly is loaded, until the `AssemblyLoadEventHandler` instance is removed from the event. For additional information about events, see Partitions I and II of the CLI Specification.]

Example

```
using System;

public class AssemblyLoadEventHandlerSample
{
    public static void Main()
    {
        AppDomain domain = AppDomain.CreateDomain("MyNewDomain");
        domain.AssemblyLoad +=
            new AssemblyLoadEventHandler(MyLoadHandler);
        Console.WriteLine("Attempting to execute HelloWorld.exe...");
        domain.ExecuteAssembly("HelloWorld.exe");
        Console.WriteLine("Finished executing HelloWorld.exe.");
        Console.WriteLine();
        Console.WriteLine();
        Console.WriteLine("Press Enter to continue");
        Console.ReadLine();
    }

    public static void MyLoadHandler(object sender,
        AssemblyLoadEventArgs args)
    {
        Console.WriteLine("Loaded assembly {0}",
            args.LoadedAssembly.FullName);
    }

}
```

The output is

```
Attempting to execute HelloWorld.exe...
Loaded assembly HelloWorld, Version=1.0.1767.19756, Culture=neutral, PublicKeyTo
ken=null
Loaded assembly System.Windows.Forms, Version=1.0.5000.0, Culture=neutral, Publi
cKeyToken=b77a5c561934e089
Loaded assembly System, Version=1.0.5000.0, Culture=neutral, PublicKeyToken=b77a
5c561934e089
Loaded assembly System.Drawing, Version=1.0.5000.0, Culture=neutral, PublicKeyTo
ken=b03f5f7f11d50a3a
Loaded assembly System.Xml, Version=1.0.5000.0, Culture=neutral, PublicKeyToken=
b77a5c561934e089
Finished executing HelloWorld.exe.


Press Enter to continue
```

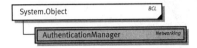

Summary

Manages the authentication modules called during the client authentication process.

Type Summary

```csharp
public class AuthenticationManager
{
    // Properties
    public static IEnumerator RegisteredModules { get; }

    // Methods
    public static Authorization Authenticate(string challenge,
                                  WebRequest request,
                                  ICredentials credentials);
    public static Authorization PreAuthenticate(WebRequest request,
                                  ICredentials credentials);
    public static void Register(IAuthenticationModule
                         authenticationModule);
    public static void Unregister(IAuthenticationModule
                         authenticationModule);
    public static void Unregister(string authenticationScheme);
}
```

Description

The `AuthenticationManager` class manages authentication modules that are responsible for client authentication. [*Note:* The `AuthenticationManager` is called by `Web-Request` instances to provide information that is sent to servers to authenticate the client. The authentication process may consist of requests to an authentication server separate from the resource server, as well as any other activities required to properly authenticate a client.]

The `AuthenticationManager` queries registered authentication modules by calling the `IAuthenticationModule.Authenticate` method for each module. The first authentication module that returns an `Authorization` instance is used to authenticate the request. An authentication module, which can be any object that implements the `IAuthenticationModule` interface, is registered using the `Register` method. Authentication modules are called in the order in which they are registered.

Applications typically do not access this type directly; it provides authentication services for the `WebRequest` type.

Example

```
using System;
using System.Net;
using System.Collections;

public class AuthenticationManagerSample
{
    public class MyModule:IAuthenticationModule
    {
        public MyModule() {}
        public String AuthenticationType
        {
            get
            {
                return "TEST";
            }
        }
        public bool CanPreAuthenticate
        {
            get
            {
                return false;
            }
        }
        public Authorization PreAuthenticate(WebRequest req,
            ICredentials cred)
        {
            return null;
        }
        public Authorization Authenticate(String ch,
            WebRequest req, ICredentials cred)
        {
            return null;
        }
    }

    private static void ShowTestModule()
    {
        IEnumerator rm = AuthenticationManager.RegisteredModules;
        while(rm.MoveNext())
        {
            IAuthenticationModule cm = (IAuthenticationModule) rm.Current;
            if (cm.AuthenticationType == "TEST")
            {
                Console.WriteLine("Module '{0}' is registered:", rm.Current);
                Console.WriteLine(" - AuthenticationType = {0}",
                    cm.AuthenticationType);
                Console.WriteLine(" - CanPreAuthenticate = {0}",
                    cm.CanPreAuthenticate);
                return;
            }
        }
        Console.WriteLine("Could not find module for "
            + "AuthenticationType = TEST");
    }
```

A
B
C
D
E
F
G
H
I
J
K
L
M
N
O
P
Q
R
S
T
U
V
W
X
Y
Z

```
public static void Main()
{
    IAuthenticationModule mod = new MyModule();
    Console.WriteLine();
    Console.WriteLine("Registering module...");
    AuthenticationManager.Register(mod);
    ShowTestModule();
    Console.WriteLine();
    Console.WriteLine("Un-registering module...");
    AuthenticationManager.Unregister("TEST");
    ShowTestModule();
}
}
```

The output is

```
Registering module...
Module 'AuthenticationManagerSample+MyModule' is registered:
 - AuthenticationType = TEST
 - CanPreAuthenticate = False

Un-registering module...
Could not find module for AuthenticationType = TEST
```

A
B
C
D
E
F
G
H
I
J
K
L
M
N
O
P
Q
R
S
T
U
V
W
X
Y
Z

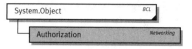

System.Object — BCL
Authorization — Networking

Summary

Supplies authentication messages used to authenticate a client to server.

Type Summary

```
public class Authorization
    {
    // Constructors
    public Authorization(string token);
    public Authorization(string token, bool finished);
CF public Authorization(string token, bool finished,
            string connectionGroupId);

    // Properties
    public bool Complete { get; }
CF public string ConnectionGroupId { get; }
    public string Message { get; }
    public string[] ProtectionRealm { get; set; }
    }
```

■ **DT**   Avoid creating methods with Boolean parameters. Boolean parameters make calls harder to read and harder to write. Quick! What's the difference between Authorization("foo", true) and Authorization("foo", false)? There's no telling what those true/false parameters do on the inside. Adding an enum type AuthorizationCompletion with Pending and Finished members would allow those constructor calls to read Authorization("foo", Authorization-Completion.Pending) and Authorization("foo", Authorization-Completion.Finished). At the same time, it might make sense for the Complete property's type to be the same enum type as the constructor parameters, for consistency.

Description

The Authorization class contains authentication information returned by an IAuthenticationModule module. Authorization instances are used to pass server challenge responses and client preauthentication information.

[*Note:* Applications do not create or access instances of this type directly; instances of this type are created by authentication modules and used by the Authentication-Manager.]

Example

```
using System;
using System.Net;
using System.Text;

public class AuthorizationSample
{
    public static void Main()
    {
        String credentials = "username:password";
        ASCIIEncoding e = new ASCIIEncoding();
        Byte[] bytes = e.GetBytes(credentials);
        String token = "BASIC " + Convert.ToBase64String(bytes);
        Authorization au = new Authorization(token, false, "Group1");
        String realm1 = "c:\\samples\\mytestsamples\\";
        String realm2 = "c:\\data\\mytestdata\\";
        String[] realms = {realm1, realm2};
        au.ProtectionRealm = realms;

        Console.WriteLine("Authorization Complete = {0}",
            au.Complete);
        Console.WriteLine("Authorization ConnectionGroupId = '{0}'",
            au.ConnectionGroupId);
        Console.WriteLine("Authorization.Message = '{0}'",
            au.Message);
        Console.WriteLine();
        Console.WriteLine("Authorization.ProtectionRealm:");
        foreach (String s in au.ProtectionRealm)
        {
            Console.WriteLine(s);
        }
    }
}
```

The output is

```
Authorization Complete = False
Authorization ConnectionGroupId = 'Group1'
Authorization.Message = 'BASIC dXNlcm5hbWU6cGFzc3dvcmQ='

Authorization.ProtectionRealm:
c:\samples\mytestsamples\
c:\data\mytestdata\
```

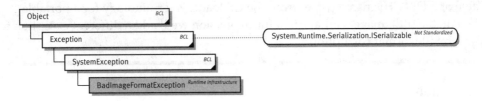

Summary

Represents the error that occurs when an attempt is made to load a `System.Reflection.Assembly` from a file with an invalid file image.

Type Summary

```
CF public class BadImageFormatException : SystemException
    {
    // Constructors
    CF public BadImageFormatException();
 MS CF protected BadImageFormatException(SerializationInfo info,
                StreamingContext context);
    CF public BadImageFormatException(string message);
    CF public BadImageFormatException(string message, Exception inner);
    CF public BadImageFormatException(string message, string fileName);
    CF public BadImageFormatException(string message, string fileName,
            Exception inner);

    // Properties
    CF public string FileName { get; }
 MS CF public string FusionLog { get; }
    CF public override string Message { get; }

    // Methods
 MS CF public override void GetObjectData(SerializationInfo info,
                        StreamingContext context);
    CF public override string ToString();
    }
```

■ **BA**   You have to be careful when you pick a code name for a project as they sometimes leak out into the final product. "Fusion" (as in the `FusionLog` property) is a classic example of that. Fusion is the code name for a set of software lifecycle management infrastructure used in the CLR and some parts of Windows. Now it is immortalized in this property that returns information about the fusion probing history.

CONTINUED

> **BG**   Some people have recently asked what this refers to—does it refer to a corrupt JPEG or bitmap, or a corrupt file of any sort? It was meant to refer to an executable or a DLL. The name comes from the OS loader's terminology for a portable executable (PE) image. Perhaps in a future version we'll add a different exception for general file format corruption.

Description

This exception is thrown when the file image of an executable program is invalid. For example, this exception is thrown when unmanaged code is passed to `System.Reflection.Assembly.Load` for loading.

Example

```
using System;

/// <summary>
/// Attempts to load an executable that is not a valid image
/// Handles the exception and displays the details
/// </summary>
public class BadImageFormatExceptionSample
{
    public static void Main()
    {
        try
        {
            AppDomain domain = AppDomain.CreateDomain("MyNewDomain");
            Console.WriteLine("Attempting to execute BadImage.exe...");
            domain.ExecuteAssembly("BadImage.exe");
        }
        catch (BadImageFormatException bifex)
        {
            Console.WriteLine("BadImageFormatException Thrown ...");
            Console.WriteLine("BadImageFormatException FileName "
                + "= '{0}'", bifex.FileName);
            Console.WriteLine("BadImageFormatException Message "
                + "= '{0}'", bifex.Message);
        }
        Console.WriteLine();
        Console.WriteLine();
        Console.WriteLine("Press Enter to continue");
        Console.ReadLine();
    }
}
```

The output is

```
Attempting to execute BadImage.exe...
BadImageFormatException Thrown ...
BadImageFormatException FileName = 'BadImage.exe'
BadImageFormatException Message = 'The format of the file 'BadImage.exe' is inva
lid.'


Press Enter to continue
```

A
B
C
D
E
F
G
H
I
J
K
L
M
N
O
P
Q
R
S
T
U
V
W
X
Y
Z

System.Reflection
Binder

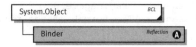

```
System.Object                    BCL

    Binder                    Reflection  A
```

Summary

Performs custom overload resolution and argument coercion to bind a member when reflection is used to invoke a member of a System.Type.

Type Summary

```
public abstract class Binder
    {
    // Constructors
       protected Binder();

    // Methods
       public abstract FieldInfo BindToField(BindingFlags bindingAttr,
                             FieldInfo[] match, object value,
                             CultureInfo culture);
       public abstract MethodBase BindToMethod(BindingFlags bindingAttr,
                             MethodBase[] match, ref object[] args,
                             ParameterModifier[] modifiers,
                             CultureInfo culture,
                             string[] names, out object state);
       public abstract object ChangeType(object value, Type type,
                             CultureInfo culture);
       public abstract void ReorderArgumentArray(ref object[] args,
                             object state);
       public abstract MethodBase SelectMethod(BindingFlags bindingAttr,
                             MethodBase[] match, Type[] types,
                             ParameterModifier[] modifiers);
       public abstract PropertyInfo SelectProperty(BindingFlags bindingAttr,
                             PropertyInfo[] match, Type returnType,
                             Type[] indexes,
                             ParameterModifier[] modifiers);
    }
```

> ■ **BA**   This class is an example of the multilanguage influence on the CLR. We could not assume a standard set of type conversion rules when binding. For example, some languages allow a method that takes an Int32 to be called with a Byte and other languages do not. Introducing the Binder allows each language to customize its own binding rules in late-bound scenarios.

Description

Late binding is controlled by a customized binding interface through reflection. The
Binder class is designed to provide this functionality. Binder objects are used in overload resolution and argument coercion for dynamic invocation of members at runtime.

Access to information obtained from reflection is controlled at two levels: untrusted
code and code with System.Security.Permissions.ReflectionPermission.

Untrusted code is code with no special level of trust (such as code downloaded from
the Internet). Such code is allowed to invoke anything that it would have been able to
invoke in an early bound way.

System.Security.Permissions.ReflectionPermission controls access to
metadata through reflection. If this permission is granted to code, that code has access to
all the types in its application domain, assembly, and module. It can access information
about public, family, and private members of all types it has access to. Two primary capabilities are granted:

- The ability to read the metadata for family and private members of any type.
- The ability to access peer classes in the module and peer modules in the assembly.

[*Note:* The term "reflection" refers to the ability to obtain information about a Sys-
tem.Object during runtime. The primary means through which this information is
accessed is via the System.Type of the object. Reflection allows the programmatic discovery of a type's metadata. The information included in the metadata includes details
about the assembly or module in which the type is defined as well as members of the type.
Reflection uses this information to provide the following primary services: The primary
users of these services are script engines, object viewers, compilers, and object persistence
formatters. Through reflection, methods can be bound and invoked at runtime. If more
than one member exists for a given member name, overload resolution determines which
implementation of that method is invoked by the system. Coercion can occur when a
parameter specified for a method call does not match the type specified for the parameter
in the method signature. When possible, the binder converts the parameter (coerces it) to
the type specified by the method signature. Coercion might not be possible depending on
the types involved. To bind to a method, field, or property, typically a list of probable can-
didates is obtained from the System.Type of a System.Object. That list is then passed
to the appropriate method of a Binder instance. Based on the other parameters passed to
that method, typically (although not necessarily) one of the members of the list is chosen,
and an object that reflects that member is returned. The system supplies a default binder
that provides default binding rules. Because binding rules vary among programming languages, it is recommended that each programming language provide a custom implementation of Binder.]

A
B
C
D
E
F
G
H
I
J
K
L
M
N
O
P
Q
R
S
T
U
V
W
X
Y
Z

Example

```csharp
using System;
using System.Reflection;
using System.Globalization;

/// <summary>
/// This is a simple binder that allows callers to use a string for
/// any method that takes one of the base data types (int, double, short,
/// etc)
/// Notice, we punt if there is an overload issue that needs to be resolved.
/// </summary>

public class BinderSample
{
    public static void Main()
    {
        int sum;

        sum = (int)typeof(BinderSample).InvokeMember("Sum",
            BindingFlags.InvokeMethod | BindingFlags.NonPublic |
            BindingFlags.Static,
            new StringBinder(), null, new object[] { "4", "2" });
        Console.WriteLine("Sum ('4','2') => {0}", sum);

        sum = (int)typeof(BinderSample).InvokeMember("Sum",
            BindingFlags.InvokeMethod | BindingFlags.NonPublic |
            BindingFlags.Static,
            null, null, new object[] { 4, 2 });
        Console.WriteLine("Sum (4,2) => {0}",sum);

        try
        {
            Console.WriteLine("Sum (4.0,2.5) => ");
            sum = (int)typeof(BinderSample).InvokeMember("Sum",
                BindingFlags.InvokeMethod | BindingFlags.NonPublic |
                BindingFlags.Static,
                new StringBinder(), null, new object[] { 4.0, 2.5 });
        }
        catch (ArgumentException e)
        {
            Console.WriteLine("Expected error: could not convert arguments.");
            Console.WriteLine(e);
        }
        Console.WriteLine();
        Console.WriteLine();
        Console.WriteLine("Press Enter to continue");
        Console.ReadLine();
    }

    static private int Sum(int value1, int value2)
    {
        return value1 + value2;
    }
}
```

```csharp
public class StringBinder : Binder
{
    public override FieldInfo BindToField(BindingFlags bindingAttr,
        FieldInfo[] match, object value,
        CultureInfo culture)
    {
        if (match.Length > 1) throw new AmbiguousMatchException();
        return match[0];
    }

    public override MethodBase BindToMethod(BindingFlags bindingAttr,
        MethodBase[] match, ref object[] args,
        ParameterModifier[] modifiers,
        CultureInfo culture,
        string[] names, out object state)
    {
        state = null;
        if (match.Length > 1) throw new AmbiguousMatchException();
        return match[0];
    }
    public override void ReorderArgumentArray(ref object[] args,
        object state)
    {
        //none needed
    }

    public override MethodBase SelectMethod(BindingFlags bindingAttr,
        MethodBase[] match, Type[] types, ParameterModifier[] modifiers)
    {
        if (match.Length > 1) throw new AmbiguousMatchException();
        return match[0];
    }

    public override PropertyInfo SelectProperty(BindingFlags bindingAttr,
        PropertyInfo[] match, Type returnType, Type[] indexes,
        ParameterModifier[] modifiers)
    {
        if (match.Length > 1) throw new AmbiguousMatchException();
        return match[0];
    }


    public override object ChangeType(object value, Type type,
        CultureInfo culture)
    {
        if (value.GetType() == typeof(string))
        {
            Console.WriteLine("Change '{0}' to type {1}", value, type);
            return Convert.ChangeType(value, type);
        }
        return value;
    }
}
```

A
B
C
D
E
F
G
H
I
J
K
L
M
N
O
P
Q
R
S
T
U
V
W
X
Y
Z

The output is

```
Change '4' to type System.Int32
Change '2' to type System.Int32
Sum ('4','2') => 6
Sum (4,2) => 6
Sum (4.0,2.5) =>
Expected error: could not convert arguments.
System.ArgumentException: Cannot widen from target type to primitive type.
    at System.Reflection.RuntimeMethodInfo.InternalInvoke(Object obj, BindingFlag
s invokeAttr, Binder binder, Object[] parameters, CultureInfo culture, Boolean
isBinderDefault, Assembly caller, Boolean verifyAccess)
    at System.Reflection.RuntimeMethodInfo.InternalInvoke(Object obj, BindingFlag
s invokeAttr, Binder binder, Object[] parameters, CultureInfo culture, Boolean
verifyAccess)
    at System.Reflection.RuntimeMethodInfo.Invoke(Object obj, BindingFlags invoke
Attr, Binder binder, Object[] parameters, CultureInfo culture)
    at System.RuntimeType.InvokeMember(String name, BindingFlags invokeAttr, Bind
er binder, Object target, Object[] args, ParameterModifier[] modifiers, CultureI
nfo culture, String[] namedParameters)
    at System.Type.InvokeMember(String name, BindingFlags invokeAttr, Binder bind
er, Object target, Object[] args)
    at BinderSample.Main() in c:\System.Reflection\Binder\Binder.cs:line 34


Press Enter to continue
```

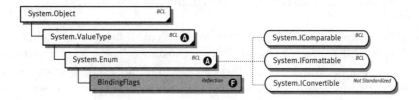

Summary

Specifies flags that control the binding and the invocation processes conducted by reflection.

Type Summary

```
public enum BindingFlags
    {
       CreateInstance = 0x200,
       DeclaredOnly = 0x2,
  MS  Default = 0x0,
       ExactBinding = 0x10000,
  MS  FlattenHierarchy = 0x40,
       GetField = 0x400,
       GetProperty = 0x1000,
       IgnoreCase = 0x1,
  MS  IgnoreReturn = 0x1000000,
       Instance = 0x4,
       InvokeMethod = 0x100,
       NonPublic = 0x20,
       OptionalParamBinding = 0x40000,
       Public = 0x10,
  MS  PutDispProperty = 0x4000,
  MS  PutRefDispProperty = 0x8000,
       SetField = 0x800,
       SetProperty = 0x2000,
       Static = 0x8,
       SuppressChangeType = 0x20000,
    }
```

■ **KC** When we teach API design, we often use this enum as an example of a bad enum design. The problem is that this enum is actually combining several different concepts: visibility selection, member selection, binding algorithm, and so on, yet it claims to be Flags enum, which would imply the values can be used independently or

CONTINUED

together, using the binary OR operator. This is not the case. Just look at the documentation for this enum. It spells out several rules for the usage of the enum. It's probably the most complicated enum documentation in the whole framework.

■ **BG**　This enum has two different axes, and both must be specified when using the enum. The first is the type of method—static or instance. The second is visibility—public or non–public. You must specify one or both of those values when using the BindingFlags enum, and it's remarkably easy to forget to specify one of these. It's a surprisingly common problem for users of Reflection.

■ **JP**　I probably get the most questions about this particular enum, which is a result of bad design choice. So, first off, in all cases where you end up utilizing the BindingFlags overload, you must specify BindingFlags.Instance or BindingFlags.Static and also specify the visibility choice of BindingFlags.Public or BindingFlags.NonPublic to actually get anything to return.

I certainly wish we would have done something a little more explicit here.

■ **JP**　A funny thing about the BindingFlags enum: we originally had a lot more binding flag options (aren't there already enough?!), which we ripped out just before RTM ship. These included things like predefined BindingFlags combinations (BindingFlags.Private, etc.) and more granular binding flags.

■ **JP**　BindingFlags.IgnoreCase has some performance and working set implications associated with it (we double the Reflection string cache and lowercase all strings passed in). If your scenario doesn't need it, try to avoid it.

Description

This enumeration is used by reflection classes such as Binder, Module, and ConstructorInfo. BindingFlags values are used to control binding in methods in classes that find and invoke, create, get, and set members and types.

　　To specify multiple BindingFlags values, use the bitwise "OR" operator.

Example

```
using System;
using System.Reflection;

/// <summary>
/// This example shows the varoius ways of using BindingFlags.
/// First we should al the members of object, then we invoke a
/// method off of System.String.  Then we invoke a property off
```

```
/// string.
/// </summary>

public class BindingFlagsSample
{
    public static void Main()
    {
        Console.WriteLine("Public Members: DeclaredOnly");
        foreach (MemberInfo m in typeof(Int32).GetMembers(
            BindingFlags.Instance | BindingFlags.Static |
            BindingFlags.Public | BindingFlags.DeclaredOnly))
        {
            Console.WriteLine("      {0}",m.Name);
        }

        Console.WriteLine("Public Members: FlattenHierarchy");
        foreach (MemberInfo m in typeof(Int32).GetMembers(
            BindingFlags.Instance | BindingFlags.Static |
            BindingFlags.Public | BindingFlags.FlattenHierarchy))
        {
            Console.WriteLine("      {0}", m.Name);
        }

        Console.WriteLine("Protected and Private Members: FlattenHierarchy");
        foreach (MemberInfo m in typeof(Int32).GetMembers(
            BindingFlags.Instance | BindingFlags.Static |
            BindingFlags.NonPublic | BindingFlags.FlattenHierarchy))
        {
            Console.WriteLine("      {0}", m.Name);
        }

        string s = "Life, The Universe, and Everything ";
        Type type = typeof(String);
        int length;

        //Latebound equivalent to: s = s.Remove(0,6);
        s = (string) type.InvokeMember ("Remove",BindingFlags.InvokeMethod,
            null, s, new Object [] {0,6});
        //Latebound equivalent to: length = s.Length;
        length = (int)type.InvokeMember("Length", BindingFlags.GetProperty,
            null, s, null);

        Console.WriteLine("'{0}'", s);
        Console.WriteLine("Length = {0}", length);
        Console.WriteLine();
        Console.WriteLine();
        Console.WriteLine("Press Enter to continue");
        Console.ReadLine();
    }
}
```

The output is

```
Public Members: DeclaredOnly
      MaxValue
```

```
            MinValue
            ToString
            GetTypeCode
            ToString
            CompareTo
            GetHashCode
            Equals
            ToString
            ToString
            Parse
            Parse
            Parse
            Parse
Public Members: FlattenHierarchy
            MaxValue
            MinValue
            ToString
            GetTypeCode
            ToString
            CompareTo
            GetHashCode
            Equals
            ToString
            ToString
            Parse
            Parse
            Parse
            Parse
            GetType
            Equals
            ReferenceEquals
Protected and Private Members: FlattenHierarchy
            m_value
            System.IConvertible.ToType
            System.IConvertible.ToDateTime
            System.IConvertible.ToDecimal
            System.IConvertible.ToDouble
            System.IConvertible.ToSingle
            System.IConvertible.ToUInt64
            System.IConvertible.ToInt64
            System.IConvertible.ToUInt32
            System.IConvertible.ToInt32
            System.IConvertible.ToUInt16
            System.IConvertible.ToInt16
            System.IConvertible.ToByte
            System.IConvertible.ToSByte
            System.IConvertible.ToChar
            System.IConvertible.ToBoolean
            Finalize
            MemberwiseClone
'The Universe, and Everything '
Length = 29


Press Enter to continue
```

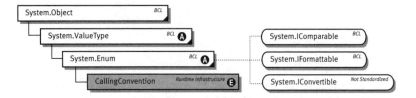

Summary
Indicates the calling convention used by a method located in an unmanaged shared library.

Type Summary
```
public enum CallingConvention
    {
 CF Cdecl = 2,
 CF FastCall = 5,
 CF StdCall = 3,
 CF ThisCall = 4,
 MS Winapi = 1,
    }
```

■ **AN**   Note that the `FastCall` calling convention is not supported by the .NET Framework. At the time this enum was created, we thought it would be supported. But the demand for it was never high enough to actually get it in the product. Per design guidelines for enums, this value should have been removed.

■ **AN**   Starting with version 2.0 of the .NET Framework, you will be able to mark delegates with a `CallingConvention` (using `UnmanagedFunctionPointer-Attribute`) so you are not limited to representing `StdCall` function pointers. There will still be no `FastCall` support, though.

Description
The values of this enumeration are used to specify the calling conventions required to call unmanaged methods implemented in shared libraries.

   [*Note:* Implementers should map the semantics of specified calling conventions onto the calling conventions of the host OS.]

[*Note:* For additional information on shared libraries and an example of the use of the
`CallingConvention` enumeration, see the `DllImportAttribute` class overview.]

Example

```
using System;
using System.Runtime.InteropServices;

/// <summary>
/// Sample demonstrating the use of the CallingConvention enumeration.
/// Use this enumeration to specify the calling convention for methods
/// decorated with DllImportAttribute.
/// </summary>
internal class CallingConventionSample
{

    private static void Main()
    {
        WritePunctuationResultForChar(',');
        WritePunctuationResultForChar('.');
        WritePunctuationResultForChar('!');
        WritePunctuationResultForChar('?');
        WritePunctuationResultForChar('a');
        WritePunctuationResultForChar('2');
        Console.WriteLine();
        Console.WriteLine();
        Console.WriteLine("Press Enter to continue");
        Console.ReadLine();
    }

    private static void WritePunctuationResultForChar(char c)
    {

        // iswpunct returns non-zero if c is a recognized punctuation character.
        if (iswpunct(c) != 0)
        {
            Console.WriteLine("'{0}' is a punctuation character.", c);
        }
        else
        {
            Console.WriteLine("'{0}' is not a punctuation character.", c);
        }

    }

    // C runtime method to determine if a given character represents a
    // punctuation character. This is used purely to demonstrate calling a
    // cdecl method; .NET code should use char.IsPunctuation(char).
    [DllImport(
        "msvcrt.dll",
        CallingConvention=CallingConvention.Cdecl,
        CharSet=CharSet.Unicode)]
    private static extern int iswpunct(char c);

}
```

The output is

```
',' is a punctuation character.
'.' is a punctuation character.
'!' is a punctuation character.
'?' is a punctuation character.
'a' is not a punctuation character.
'2' is not a punctuation character.


Press Enter to continue
```

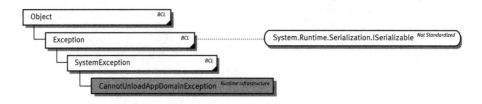

Summary

Represents the error that occurs when an attempt to unload an application domain fails.

Type Summary

```
CF public class CannotUnloadAppDomainException : SystemException
      {
      // Constructors
      CF public CannotUnloadAppDomainException();
   MS CF protected CannotUnloadAppDomainException(SerializationInfo info,
                 StreamingContext context);
      CF public CannotUnloadAppDomainException(string message);
      CF public CannotUnloadAppDomainException(string message,
            Exception innerException);
      }
```

Description

CannotUnloadAppDomainException is thrown when there is an attempt to unload:

- The default application domain, which must remain loaded during the lifetime of the application.
- An application domain with a running thread that cannot immediately stop execution.
- An application domain that has already been unloaded.

Example

```
using System;
using System.Threading;

/// <summary>
/// Shows why a CannotUnloadAppDomainException is thrown
/// and how to handle it
/// </summary>

public class CannotUnloadAppDomainExceptionSample
{
    public static void Main()
    {
        try
        {
            AppDomain ad = Thread.GetDomain();
            AppDomain.Unload(ad);
        }
        catch (CannotUnloadAppDomainException e)
        {
            Console.WriteLine("Caught exception: {0} - '{1}'", e.GetType().Name,
                e.Message);
        }
        Console.WriteLine();
        Console.WriteLine();
        Console.WriteLine("Press Enter to continue");
        Console.ReadLine();
    }
}
```

The output is

```
Caught exception: CannotUnloadAppDomainException - 'The default domain can not b
e unloaded.'


Press Enter to continue
```

A
B
C
D
E
F
G
H
I
J
K
L
M
N
O
P
Q
R
S
T
U
V
W
X
Y
Z

A
B
C
D
E
F
G
H
I
J
K
L
M
N
O
P
Q
R
S
T
U
V
W
X
Y
Z

```
System.Object                    BCL
    System.ValueType             BCL  A
        System.Enum              BCL  A
            CharSet        Runtime Infrastructure  E
```

```
System.IComparable    BCL
System.IFormattable   BCL
System.IConvertible   Not Standardized
```

Summary

Specifies which character set marshaled strings are required to use.

Type Summary

```
public enum CharSet
      {
   CF Ansi = 2,
      Auto = 4,
MS CF None = 1,
      Unicode = 3,
      }
```

AN   The Charset.None value is obsolete and should not be used. It currently has the same behavior as CharSet.Ansi. Like many things, we really wanted to remove it before we shipped v1.0, but with so many dependencies on our APIs it was too risky.

AN   It's somewhat unfortunate that CharSet.Ansi is the default behavior for PInvoke, since managed strings and characters are internally Unicode. Win32 APIs often expose both an ANSI and Unicode export, but by default you end up calling the ANSI one, requiring the Interop marshaler to copy each Unicode string to a new ANSI string! In contrast, by calling the Unicode export, the CLR can just pin the managed strings and expose them directly. You can override the default behavior and explicitly mark each PInvoke signature with CharSet.Auto, although in the future the CLR will provide a module-level DefaultCharSetAttribute that allows you to select your own default for all signatures in your module.

Description

This enumeration is used by the DllImportAttribute to indicate the required modifications to the System.String arguments of an imported function.

[*Note:* See the DllImportAttribute class overview for an example that uses the
CharSet enumeration.]

Example

```
using System;
using System.Runtime.InteropServices;

/// <summary>
/// Sample demonstrating the use of the CharSet enumeration.
/// Use this enumeration to specify how strings should be marshalled to
/// unmanaged code for methods decorated with DllImportAttribute and types
/// decorated with StructLayoutAttribute.
/// </summary>
internal class CharSetSample
{

    private static void Main()
    {
        OSVERSIONINFO ovi = new OSVERSIONINFO();

        // Given that CharSet.Auto was used for OSVERSIONINFO, we can work out
        // how strings are being marshalled by getting the unmanaged size of
        // OSVERSIONINFO.
        ovi.dwOSVersionInfoSize = (uint)Marshal.SizeOf(typeof(OSVERSIONINFO));

        switch (ovi.dwOSVersionInfoSize)
        {

            case 148:
                Console.WriteLine(
                    "OSVERSIONINFO strings will be marshalled as ANSI.");
                break;

            case 276:
                Console.WriteLine(
                    "OSVERSIONINFO strings will be marshalled as Unicode.");
                break;

            default:
                Console.WriteLine(
                    "Unknown marshalling for OSVERSIONINFO strings.");
                break;

        }

        if (GetVersionEx(ref ovi))
        {
        Console.Write(
            "Detected OS version: {0}.{1}.{2}",
            ovi.dwMajorVersion, ovi.dwMinorVersion, ovi.dwBuildNumber);

            if (ovi.szCSDVersion.Length > 0)
            {
                Console.Write(" ({0})", ovi.szCSDVersion);
```

A
B
C
D
E
F
G
H
I
J
K
L
M
N
O
P
Q
R
S
T
U
V
W
X
Y
Z

```
                    }

                    Console.WriteLine();
                }
                else
                {
                    Console.WriteLine("GetVersionEx failed.");
                }

                Console.WriteLine();
                Console.WriteLine();
                Console.WriteLine("Press Enter to continue");
                Console.ReadLine();
            }

        // The OSVERSIONINFO type to use with GetVersionEx. Note that CharSet.Auto
        // is used so the type of string marshalling used is based on the OS.
        [StructLayout(LayoutKind.Sequential, CharSet=CharSet.Auto)]
        private struct OSVERSIONINFO
        {
            public uint dwOSVersionInfoSize;
            public uint dwMajorVersion;
            public uint dwMinorVersion;
            public uint dwBuildNumber;
            public uint dwPlatformId;
            // Note that szCSDVersion is actually limited to SizeConst - 1 chars.
            [MarshalAs(UnmanagedType.ByValTStr, SizeConst=128)]
            public string szCSDVersion;
        }

        // Win32 method to retrieve information about the OS. .NET code would
        // typically use Environment.OSVersion, although it's worth noting that
        // GetVersionEx can retrieve the service pack string as well. Note that
        // CharSet.Auto is used so the type of string marshalling used is based on
        // the OS (Unicode on WinNT family and ANSI on Win9x family).
        [DllImport("kernel32.dll", CharSet=CharSet.Auto, SetLastError=true)]
        private static extern bool GetVersionEx(
            ref OSVERSIONINFO lpVersionInformation);
    }
}
```

The output is

```
OSVERSIONINFO strings will be marshalled as Unicode.
Detected OS version: 5.1.2600 (Service Pack 2)


Press Enter to continue
```

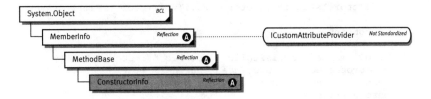

Summary

Provides access to constructor metadata.

Type Summary

```
public abstract class ConstructorInfo : MethodBase
    {
    // Constructors
    protected ConstructorInfo();

    // Fields
    public static readonly string ConstructorName = ".ctor";
    public static readonly string TypeConstructorName = ".cctor";

    // Properties
MS  public override MemberTypes MemberType { get; }

    // Methods
    public abstract object Invoke(BindingFlags invokeAttr, Binder binder,
                        object[] parameters, CultureInfo culture);
    public object Invoke(object[] parameters);
    }
```

Example

```
using System;
using System.Reflection;

/// <summary>
/// This example shows how to print out constructors in C#
/// syntax.
/// </summary>

public class ConstructorInfoSample
{
    public static void Main()
    {
        Type type = typeof(String);

        foreach (ConstructorInfo ctor in type.GetConstructors(
            BindingFlags.NonPublic | BindingFlags.Public |
```

```
                      BindingFlags.Instance ))
          {

              //Skip any constructors that are not publicly accessible
              if (!(ctor.IsPublic || ctor.IsFamily || ctor.IsFamilyOrAssembly))
              {
                  continue;
              }
              Console.Write(ctor.IsPublic ? "public " : ctor.IsFamily ?
                  "protected " : "protected internal ");
              Console.Write(ctor.DeclaringType.Name);
              Console.Write('(');
              ParameterInfo[] parameters = ctor.GetParameters();
              for (int i = 0; i < parameters.Length; i++)
              {
                  Console.Write("{0} {1}", parameters[i].ParameterType,
                      parameters[i].Name);
                  if (i != parameters.Length - 1)
                  {
                      Console.Write(", ");
                  }
              }
              Console.Write(");");
              Console.WriteLine();
          } //end foreach loop

          ConstructorInfo c = typeof(String).GetConstructor(new Type[] {
                                             typeof(char), typeof(int) });
          string s = (string) c.Invoke(new object[] {'.', 7});
          Console.WriteLine ("The result is '{0}'",s);
          Console.WriteLine();
          Console.WriteLine();
          Console.WriteLine("Press Enter to continue");
          Console.ReadLine();
      } //end main
} //end class
```

The output is

```
public String(System.Char* value);
public String(System.Char* value, System.Int32 startIndex, System.Int32 length);
public String(System.SByte* value);
public String(System.SByte* value, System.Int32 startIndex, System.Int32 length);
public String(System.SByte* value, System.Int32 startIndex, System.Int32 length,
System.Text.Encoding enc);
public String(System.Char[] value, System.Int32 startIndex, System.Int32 length);
public String(System.Char[] value);
public String(System.Char c, System.Int32 count);
The result is '.......'

Press Enter to continue
```

Summary

Provides storage for multiple credentials.

Type Summary

```
CF public class CredentialCache :ICredentials, IEnumerable
    {
    // Constructors
    CF public CredentialCache();

    // Properties
    CF public static ICredentials DefaultCredentials { get; }

    // Methods
    CF public void Add(Uri uriPrefix, string authType,
                  NetworkCredential cred);
    CF public NetworkCredential GetCredential(Uri uriPrefix,
                            string authType);
    CF public IEnumerator GetEnumerator();
    CF public void Remove(Uri uriPrefix, string authType);
    }
```

Description

The CredentialCache class stores credentials for multiple Internet resources. Applications that need to access multiple resources can store the credentials for those resources in a CredentialCache instance that then provides the proper set of credentials for a given resource when required. When the GetCredential method is called, it compares the URI and authentication type provided with those stored in the cache, and returns the first set of credentials that match.

Example

```
using System;
using System.Net;
using System.Collections;

/// <summary>
/// Creates two new NetworkCredential instances, adds them to a
/// CredentialCache and then removes one, showing the contents
/// of the CredentialCache cache at each stage
/// </summary>
```

CredentialCache Class

```
public class CredentialCacheSample
{
    private static void ShowContents(CredentialCache cc,
        String caption)
    {
        Console.WriteLine();
        Console.WriteLine(caption + ":");
        foreach (NetworkCredential found in cc)
        {
            Console.WriteLine("User:'{0}'\t Password:'{1}'\t "
                + "Domain:'{2}'", found.UserName,
                found.Password, found.Domain);
        }
    }

    public static void Main()
    {
        Console.WriteLine("DefaultCredentials = '{0}'",
            CredentialCache.DefaultCredentials);
        NetworkCredential nc1 = new
            NetworkCredential("test", "secret");
        NetworkCredential nc2 = new
            NetworkCredential("local", "moresecret", "mydomain");
        Uri path = new Uri("http://mysite.com");
        CredentialCache cc = new CredentialCache();
        cc.Add(path, "BASIC", nc1);
        cc.Add(path, "NTLM", nc2);
        ShowContents(cc, "After adding two credentials");
        cc.Remove(path, "BASIC");
        ShowContents(cc, "After removing BASIC credential");
    }
}
```

The output is

```
DefaultCredentials = 'System.Net.SystemNetworkCredential'

After adding two credentials:
User:'test'      Password:'secret'      Domain:''
User:'local'     Password:'moresecret'  Domain:'mydomain'

After removing BASIC credential:
User:'local'     Password:'moresecret'  Domain:'mydomain'
```

Summary

Represents information about a specific culture including the names of the culture, the writing system, and the calendar used, as well as access to culture-specific objects that provide information for common operations, such as formatting dates and sorting strings.

Type Summary

```
public class CultureInfo : ICloneable, IFormatProvider
    {
        // Constructors
    MS  public CultureInfo(int culture);
    MS  public CultureInfo(int culture, bool useUserOverride);
    MS  public CultureInfo(string name);
    MS  public CultureInfo(string name, bool useUserOverride);

        // Properties
    MS  public virtual Calendar Calendar { get; }
    MS  public virtual CompareInfo CompareInfo { get; }
    MS  public static CultureInfo CurrentCulture { get; }
    MS  public static CultureInfo CurrentUICulture { get; }
    MS  public virtual DateTimeFormatInfo DateTimeFormat { get; set; }
 MS CF  public virtual string DisplayName { get; }
    MS  public virtual string EnglishName { get; }
 MS CF  public static CultureInfo InstalledUICulture { get; }
    MS  public static CultureInfo InvariantCulture { get; }
    MS  public virtual bool IsNeutralCulture { get; }
    MS  public bool IsReadOnly { get; }
    MS  public virtual int LCID { get; }
    MS  public virtual string Name { get; }
    MS  public virtual string NativeName { get; }
    MS  public virtual NumberFormatInfo NumberFormat { get; set; }
    MS  public virtual Calendar[] OptionalCalendars { get; }
    MS  public virtual CultureInfo Parent { get; }
    MS  public virtual TextInfo TextInfo { get; }
    MS  public virtual string ThreeLetterISOLanguageName { get; }
    MS  public virtual string ThreeLetterWindowsLanguageName { get; }
    MS  public virtual string TwoLetterISOLanguageName { get; }
    MS  public bool UseUserOverride { get; }

        // Methods
 MS CF  public void ClearCachedData();
    MS  public virtual object Clone();
    MS  public static CultureInfo CreateSpecificCulture(string name);
    MS  public override bool Equals(object value);
 MS CF  public static CultureInfo[] GetCultures(CultureTypes types);
```

```
MS public virtual object GetFormat(Type formatType);
MS public override int GetHashCode();
MS public static CultureInfo ReadOnly(CultureInfo ci);
MS public override string ToString();
}
```

■ **SS**   For the `CultureInfo` constructor overloads you really want to use names instead of the `int`/LCID. Names allow you to access custom cultures that a user may install for future versions, and will be more extensible in the future. You also really want to use user overrides. User overrides are there because the user did not like the defaults, or because they are inappropriate or ambiguous for the user's environment.

■ **SS**   Always use cultures when appropriate, but be careful where you use them. They are meant to be specific for a user or machine, and they could change. For example, as countries join the EU, their currency symbols or formats change. In other cases, companies or users may prefer a 24-hour clock to a 12-hour default. Culture data is necessary and great when presenting data to the humans who are actually using the computer, but it's an awful way to store data. If you have to read something back later, save it in a binary format, use `CultureInfo.InvariantCulture`, or specify a specific format to the formatting functions. Except for Invariant, don't expect the culture data provided by this class to remain the same, even between instances running as the same user.

■ **BG**   `CultureInfo` is a useful encapsulation of all the culture-specific data that you'll need for your operations. It can be used to control string comparisons, number formatting, date and calendar formatting, and resource lookups. See `Thread`'s `CurrentCulture` and `CurrentUICulture` for ways of setting this culture on your current thread. It is also one of the most interesting types that implement `IFormatProvider`. The `ToString` method on our numeric types and `DateTime` will call `GetFormat(typeof(NumberFormatInfo))` or `GetFormat(typeof (DateTimeFormatInfo))` for formatting and parsing.

■ **BG**   We were never quite sure we got the balance between this type and `RegionInfo` correct. `RegionInfo` is very commonly overlooked, when you'd expect that perhaps some of the features on this class would be on `RegionInfo` instead.

CONTINUED

■. **BG**   In future versions of the Common Language Runtime, look for custom culture support and custom resource fallback support. Custom culture support will allow users to define their own cultures in an easy manner that the entire system will respect.

For the `System.Resources.ResourceManager`, we hope to eventually add in support for fallback along more axes beyond culture, like age (for different scripts like Hiragana or Katakana), gender, and perhaps region or ZIP code (e.g., for different phone numbers).

■. **IA**   One of my biggest regrets is that `CultureInfo.ClearCachedData()` is an instance method rather than a static method. This method actually clears shared (static) caches for system settings like `CurrentCulture`, `CurrentRegion`, and the like. It does nothing to individual instances, so it is very confusing to have this as an instance method. Unfortunately, this was discovered very late in the .NET Framework cycle, and it was considered a breaking change to make it static, so it had to ship this way.

Description

The `System.Globalization.CultureInfo` class holds culture-specific information, such as the associated language, sublanguage, country/region, calendar, and cultural conventions. This class also provides access to culture-specific instances of `System.Globalization.DateTimeFormatInfo`, `System.Globalization.NumberFormatInfo`, `System.Globalization.CompareInfo`, and `System.Globalization.TextInfo`. These objects contain the information required for culture-specific operations, such as casing, formatting dates and numbers, and comparing strings.

The `System.String` class indirectly uses this class to obtain information about the default culture.

The culture names follow the RFC 1766 standard in the format "<languagecode2>-<country/regioncode2>", where <languagecode2> is a lowercase two-letter code derived from ISO 639-1 and <country/regioncode2> is an uppercase two-letter code derived from ISO 3166. For example, U.S. English is "en-US". In cases where a two-letter language code is not available, the three-letter code derived from ISO 639-2 is used; for example, the three-letter code "div" is used for cultures that use the Dhivehi language. Some culture names have suffixes that specify the script; for example, "-Cyrl" specifies the Cyrillic script, "-Latn" specifies the Latin script.

The following predefined `System.Globalization.CultureInfo` names and identifiers are accepted and used by this class and other classes in the `System.Globalization` namespace.

A
B
C
D
E
F
G
H
I
J
K
L
M
N
O
P
Q
R
S
T
U
V
W
X
Y
Z

Culture Name	Culture Identifier	Language-Country/Region
"" (empty string)	0x007F	invariant culture
af	0x0036	Afrikaans
af-ZA	0x0436	Afrikaans - South Africa
sq	0x001C	Albanian
sq-AL	0x041C	Albanian - Albania
ar	0x0001	Arabic
ar-DZ	0x1401	Arabic - Algeria
ar-BH	0x3C01	Arabic - Bahrain
ar-EG	0x0C01	Arabic - Egypt
ar-IQ	0x0801	Arabic - Iraq
ar-JO	0x2C01	Arabic - Jordan
ar-KW	0x3401	Arabic - Kuwait
ar-LB	0x3001	Arabic - Lebanon
ar-LY	0x1001	Arabic - Libya
ar-MA	0x1801	Arabic - Morocco
ar-OM	0x2001	Arabic - Oman
ar-QA	0x4001	Arabic - Qatar
ar-SA	0x0401	Arabic - Saudi Arabia
ar-SY	0x2801	Arabic - Syria
ar-TN	0x1C01	Arabic - Tunisia
ar-AE	0x3801	Arabic - United Arab Emirates
ar-YE	0x2401	Arabic - Yemen
hy	0x002B	Armenian

A
B
C
D
E
F
G
H
I
J
K
L
M
N
O
P
Q
R
S
T
U
V
W
X
Y
Z

Culture Name	Culture Identifier	Language-Country/Region
hy-AM	0x042B	Armenian - Armenia
az	0x002C	Azeri
az-AZ-Cyrl	0x082C	Azeri (Cyrillic) - Azerbaijan
az-AZ-Latn	0x042C	Azeri (Latin) - Azerbaijan
eu	0x002D	Basque
eu-ES	0x042D	Basque - Basque
be	0x0023	Belarusian
be-BY	0x0423	Belarusian - Belarus
bg	0x0002	Bulgarian
bg-BG	0x0402	Bulgarian - Bulgaria
ca	0x0003	Catalan
ca-ES	0x0403	Catalan - Catalan
zh-HK	0x0C04	Chinese - Hong Kong SAR
zh-MO	0x1404	Chinese - Macau SAR
zh-CN	0x0804	Chinese - China
zh-CHS	0x0004	Chinese (Simplified)
zh-SG	0x1004	Chinese - Singapore
zh-TW	0x0404	Chinese - Taiwan
zh-CHT	0x7C04	Chinese (Traditional)
hr	0x001A	Croatian
hr-HR	0x041A	Croatian - Croatia
cs	0x0005	Czech
cs-CZ	0x0405	Czech - Czech Republic

A
B
C
D
E
F
G
H
I
J
K
L
M
N
O
P
Q
R
S
T
U
V
W
X
Y
Z

Culture Name	Culture Identifier	Language-Country/Region
da	0x0006	Danish
da-DK	0x0406	Danish - Denmark
div	0x0065	Dhivehi
div-MV	0x0465	Dhivehi - Maldives
nl	0x0013	Dutch
nl-BE	0x0813	Dutch - Belgium
nl-NL	0x0413	Dutch - The Netherlands
en	0x0009	English
en-AU	0x0C09	English - Australia
en-BZ	0x2809	English - Belize
en-CA	0x1009	English - Canada
en-CB	0x2409	English - Caribbean
en-IE	0x1809	English - Ireland
en-JM	0x2009	English - Jamaica
en-NZ	0x1409	English - New Zealand
en-PH	0x3409	English - Philippines
en-ZA	0x1C09	English - South Africa
en-TT	0x2C09	English - Trinidad and Tobago
en-GB	0x0809	English - United Kingdom
en-US	0x0409	English - United States
en-ZW	0x3009	English - Zimbabwe
et	0x0025	Estonian
et-EE	0x0425	Estonian - Estonia

Culture Name	Culture Identifier	Language-Country/Region
fo	0x0038	Faroese
fo-FO	0x0438	Faroese - Faroe Islands
fa	0x0029	Farsi
fa-IR	0x0429	Farsi - Iran
fi	0x000B	Finnish
fi-FI	0x040B	Finnish - Finland
fr	0x000C	French
fr-BE	0x080C	French - Belgium
fr-CA	0x0C0C	French - Canada
fr-FR	0x040C	French - France
fr-LU	0x140C	French - Luxembourg
fr-MC	0x180C	French - Monaco
fr-CH	0x100C	French - Switzerland
gl	0x0056	Galician
gl-ES	0x0456	Galician - Galician
ka	0x0037	Georgian
ka-GE	0x0437	Georgian - Georgia
de	0x0007	German
de-AT	0x0C07	German - Austria
de-DE	0x0407	German - Germany
de-LI	0x1407	German - Liechtenstein
de-LU	0x1007	German - Luxembourg
de-CH	0x0807	German - Switzerland

A
B
C
D
E
F
G
H
I
J
K
L
M
N
O
P
Q
R
S
T
U
V
W
X
Y
Z

Culture Name	Culture Identifier	Language-Country/Region
el	0x0008	Greek
el-GR	0x0408	Greek - Greece
gu	0x0047	Gujarati
gu-IN	0x0447	Gujarati - India
he	0x000D	Hebrew
he-IL	0x040D	Hebrew - Israel
hi	0x0039	Hindi
hi-IN	0x0439	Hindi - India
hu	0x000E	Hungarian
hu-HU	0x040E	Hungarian - Hungary
is	0x000F	Icelandic
is-IS	0x040F	Icelandic - Iceland
id	0x0021	Indonesian
id-ID	0x0421	Indonesian - Indonesia
it	0x0010	Italian
it-IT	0x0410	Italian - Italy
it-CH	0x0810	Italian - Switzerland
ja	0x0011	Japanese
ja-JP	0x0411	Japanese - Japan
kn	0x004B	Kannada
kn-IN	0x044B	Kannada - India
kk	0x003F	Kazakh
kk-KZ	0x043F	Kazakh - Kazakhstan

A
B
C
D
E
F
G
H
I
J
K
L
M
N
O
P
Q
R
S
T
U
V
W
X
Y
Z

Culture Name	Culture Identifier	Language-Country/Region
kok	0x0057	Konkani
kok-IN	0x0457	Konkani - India
ko	0x0012	Korean
ko-KR	0x0412	Korean - Korea
ky	0x0040	Kyrgyz
ky-KZ	0x0440	Kyrgyz - Kazakhstan
lv	0x0026	Latvian
lv-LV	0x0426	Latvian - Latvia
lt	0x0027	Lithuanian
lt-LT	0x0427	Lithuanian - Lithuania
mk	0x002F	Macedonian
mk-MK	0x042F	Macedonian - FYROM
ms	0x003E	Malay
ms-BN	0x083E	Malay - Brunei
ms-MY	0x043E	Malay - Malaysia
mr	0x004E	Marathi
mr-IN	0x044E	Marathi - India
mn	0x0050	Mongolian
mn-MN	0x0450	Mongolian - Mongolia
no	0x0014	Norwegian
nb-NO	0x0414	Norwegian (BokmÃ¥l) - Norway
nn-NO	0x0814	Norwegian (Nynorsk) - Norway
pl	0x0015	Polish

A
B
C
D
E
F
G
H
I
J
K
L
M
N
O
P
Q
R
S
T
U
V
W
X
Y
Z

CultureInfo Class

Culture Name	Culture Identifier	Language-Country/Region
pl-PL	0x0415	Polish - Poland
pt	0x0016	Portuguese
pt-BR	0x0416	Portuguese - Brazil
pt-PT	0x0816	Portuguese - Portugal
pa	0x0046	Punjabi
pa-IN	0x0446	Punjabi - India
ro	0x0018	Romanian
ro-RO	0x0418	Romanian - Romania
ru	0x0019	Russian
ru-RU	0x0419	Russian - Russia
sa	0x004F	Sanskrit
sa-IN	0x044F	Sanskrit - India
sr-SP-Cyrl	0x0C1A	Serbian (Cyrillic) - Serbia
sr-SP-Latn	0x081A	Serbian (Latin) - Serbia
sk	0x001B	Slovak
sk-SK	0x041B	Slovak - Slovakia
sl	0x0024	Slovenian
sl-SI	0x0424	Slovenian - Slovenia
es	0x000A	Spanish
es-AR	0x2C0A	Spanish - Argentina
es-BO	0x400A	Spanish - Bolivia
es-CL	0x340A	Spanish - Chile
es-CO	0x240A	Spanish - Colombia

A
B
C
D
E
F
G
H
I
J
K
L
M
N
O
P
Q
R
S
T
U
V
W
X
Y
Z

Culture Name	Culture Identifier	Language-Country/Region
es-CR	0x140A	Spanish - Costa Rica
es-DO	0x1C0A	Spanish - Dominican Republic
es-EC	0x300A	Spanish - Ecuador
es-SV	0x440A	Spanish - El Salvador
es-GT	0x100A	Spanish - Guatemala
es-HN	0x480A	Spanish - Honduras
es-MX	0x080A	Spanish - Mexico
es-NI	0x4C0A	Spanish - Nicaragua
es-PA	0x180A	Spanish - Panama
es-PY	0x3C0A	Spanish - Paraguay
es-PE	0x280A	Spanish - Peru
es-PR	0x500A	Spanish - Puerto Rico
es-ES	0x0C0A	Spanish - Spain
es-UY	0x380A	Spanish - Uruguay
es-VE	0x200A	Spanish - Venezuela
sw	0x0041	Swahili
sw-KE	0x0441	Swahili - Kenya
sv	0x001D	Swedish
sv-FI	0x081D	Swedish - Finland
sv-SE	0x041D	Swedish - Sweden
syr	0x005A	Syriac
syr-SY	0x045A	Syriac - Syria
ta	0x0049	Tamil

A
B
C
D
E
F
G
H
I
J
K
L
M
N
O
P
Q
R
S
T
U
V
W
X
Y
Z

Culture Name	Culture Identifier	Language-Country/Region
ta-IN	0x0449	Tamil - India
tt	0x0044	Tatar
tt-RU	0x0444	Tatar - Russia
te	0x004A	Telugu
te-IN	0x044A	Telugu - India
th	0x001E	Thai
th-TH	0x041E	Thai - Thailand
tr	0x001F	Turkish
tr-TR	0x041F	Turkish - Turkey
uk	0x0022	Ukrainian
uk-UA	0x0422	Ukrainian - Ukraine
ur	0x0020	Urdu
ur-PK	0x0420	Urdu - Pakistan
uz	0x0043	Uzbek
uz-UZ-Cyrl	0x0843	Uzbek (Cyrillic) - Uzbekistan
uz-UZ-Latn	0x0443	Uzbek (Latin) - Uzbekistan
vi	0x002A	Vietnamese
vi-VN	0x042A	Vietnamese - Vietnam

The culture identifier "0x0c0a" for "Spanish - Spain" uses the default international sort order; the culture identifier "0x040A", which is also for "Spanish - Spain", uses the traditional sort order. If the System.Globalization.CultureInfo is constructed using the "es-ES" culture name, the new System.Globalization.CultureInfo uses the default international sort order. To construct a System.Globalization.Culture-Info that uses the traditional sort order, use the culture identifier "0x040A" with the constructor.

The cultures are generally grouped into three sets: the invariant culture, the neutral cultures, and the specific cultures.

The invariant culture is culture-insensitive. You can specify the invariant culture by name using an empty string (`""`) or by its culture identifier `0x007F`. `System.Globalization.CultureInfo.InvariantCulture` retrieves an instance of the invariant culture. It is associated with the English language but not with any country/region. It can be used in almost any method in the Globalization namespace that requires a culture. If a security decision depends on a string comparison or a case-change operation, use the `System.Globalization.CultureInfo.InvariantCulture` to ensure that the behavior will be consistent regardless of the culture settings of the system. However, the invariant culture must be used only by processes that require culture-independent results, such as system services; otherwise, it produces results that might be linguistically incorrect or culturally inappropriate.

A neutral culture is a culture that is associated with a language but not with a country/region. A specific culture is a culture that is associated with a language and a country/region. For example, "fr" is a neutral culture and "fr-FR" is a specific culture. Note that "zh-CHS" (Simplified Chinese) and "zh-CHT" (Traditional Chinese) are neutral cultures.

The cultures have a hierarchy, such that the parent of a specific culture is a neutral culture and the parent of a neutral culture is the `System.Globalization.CultureInfo.InvariantCulture`. The `System.Globalization.CultureInfo.Parent` property returns the neutral culture associated with a specific culture.

If the resources for the specific culture are not available in the system, the resources for the neutral culture are used; if the resources for the neutral culture are not available, the resources embedded in the main assembly are used.

The list of cultures in the Windows API is slightly different from the list of cultures in the .NET Framework. For example, the neutral culture zh-CHT "Chinese (Traditional)" with culture identifier 0x7C04 is not available in the Windows API. If interoperability with Windows is required (for example, through the p/invoke mechanism), use a specific culture that is defined in the .NET Framework. This will ensure consistency with the equivalent Windows locale, which is identified with the same `System.Globalization.CultureInfo.LCID`.

A `System.Globalization.DateTimeFormatInfo` or a `System.Globalization.NumberFormatInfo` can be created only for the invariant culture or for specific cultures, not for neutral cultures.

The user might choose to override some of the values associated with the current culture of Windows through Regional and Language Options (or Regional Options or Regional Settings) in Control Panel. For example, the user might choose to display the date in a different format or to use a currency other than the default for the culture.

If `System.Globalization.CultureInfo.UseUserOverride` is `true` and the specified culture matches the current culture of Windows, the `System.Globaliza-`

A
B
C
D
E
F
G
H
I
J
K
L
M
N
O
P
Q
R
S
T
U
V
W
X
Y
Z

tion. `CultureInfo` uses those overrides, including user settings for the properties of the `System.Globalization.DateTimeFormatInfo` instance returned by the `System.Globalization.CultureInfo.DateTimeFormat` property, the properties of the `System.Globalization.NumberFormatInfo` instance returned by the `System.Globalization.CultureInfo.NumberFormat` property, and the properties of the `System.Globalization.CompareInfo` instance returned by the `System.Globalization.CultureInfo.CompareInfo` property. If the user settings are incompatible with the culture associated with the `System.Globalization.CultureInfo` (for example, if the selected calendar is not one of the `System.Globalization.CultureInfo.OptionalCalendars`), the results of the methods and the values of the properties are undefined.

For cultures that use the euro, the .NET Framework and Windows XP set the default currency as euro; however, older versions of Windows do not. Therefore, if the user of an older version of Windows has not changed the currency setting through Regional Options or Regional Settings in Control Panel, the currency might be incorrect. To use the .NET Framework default setting for the currency, use a `System.Globalization.CultureInfo` constructor overload that accepts a *useUserOverride* parameter and set it to `false`.

This class implements the `System.ICloneable` interface to enable duplication of `System.Globalization.CultureInfo` objects. It also implements `System.IFormatProvider` to supply formatting information to applications.

Example

```
using System;
using System.Globalization;

/// <summary>
/// Sample demonstrating the use of the CultureInfo class.
/// Use this class to retrieve information about a specific culture, such as
/// date/time formats and number formats.
/// </summary>
internal class CultureInfoSample
{

    private static void Main()
    {
        Console.WriteLine("Summary for the current thread culture:");
        WriteCultureInfoSummary(CultureInfo.CurrentCulture);
        Console.WriteLine("Summary for the current thread UI culture:");
        WriteCultureInfoSummary(CultureInfo.CurrentUICulture);
        Console.WriteLine("Summary for the operating system UI culture:");
        WriteCultureInfoSummary(CultureInfo.InstalledUICulture);
        Console.WriteLine();
        Console.WriteLine();
        Console.WriteLine("Press Enter to continue");
        Console.ReadLine();
    }
```

```csharp
        // Writes a summary of the specified CultureInfo to the console.
        private static void WriteCultureInfoSummary(CultureInfo info)
        {
            Console.WriteLine(
                "  Culture name:             {0} ({1})",
                info.DisplayName, info.Name);
            WriteDateTimeFormatInfoSummary(info.DateTimeFormat);
            WriteNumberFormatInfoSummary(info.NumberFormat);
            Console.WriteLine();
        }

        // Writes a summary of the specified DateTimeFormatInfo to the console.
        private static void WriteDateTimeFormatInfoSummary(DateTimeFormatInfo info)
        {
            Console.WriteLine(
                "  Long date/time pattern:  {0} {1}",
                info.LongDatePattern, info.LongTimePattern);
            Console.WriteLine(
                "  Short date/time pattern: {0} {1}",
                info.ShortDatePattern, info.ShortTimePattern);
            Console.WriteLine(
                "  AM/PM designators:        {0}/{1}",
                info.AMDesignator, info.PMDesignator);
        }

        // Writes a summary of the specified NumberFormatInfo to the console.
        private static void WriteNumberFormatInfoSummary(NumberFormatInfo info)
        {
            Console.WriteLine(
                "  Currency symbol:          {0}", info.CurrencySymbol);
            Console.WriteLine(
                "  Percent symbol:           {0}", info.PercentSymbol);
            Console.WriteLine(
                "  Negative sign:            {0}", info.NegativeSign);
            Console.WriteLine(
                "  Positive sign:            {0}", info.PositiveSign);
            Console.WriteLine(
                "  Decimal separator:        {0}", info.NumberDecimalSeparator);
            Console.WriteLine(
                "  Thousands separator:      {0}", info.NumberGroupSeparator);
        }
}
```

The output is

```
Summary for the current thread culture:
  Culture name:            English (United States) (en-US)
  Long date/time pattern:  dddd, MMMM dd, yyyy h:mm:ss tt
  Short date/time pattern: M/d/yyyy h:mm tt
  AM/PM designators:        AM/PM
  Currency symbol:          $
  Percent symbol:           %
  Negative sign:            -
  Positive sign:            +
  Decimal separator:        .
  Thousands separator:      ,
```

CultureInfo Class

```
        Summary for the current thread UI culture:
          Culture name:           English (United States) (en-US)
          Long date/time pattern: dddd, MMMM dd, yyyy h:mm:ss tt
          Short date/time pattern: M/d/yyyy h:mm tt
          AM/PM designators:       AM/PM
          Currency symbol:         $
          Percent symbol:          %
          Negative sign:           -
          Positive sign:           +
          Decimal separator:       .
          Thousands separator:     ,

        Summary for the operating system UI culture:
          Culture name:           English (United States) (en-US)
          Long date/time pattern: dddd, MMMM dd, yyyy h:mm:ss tt
          Short date/time pattern: M/d/yyyy h:mm tt
          AM/PM designators:       AM/PM
          Currency symbol:         $
          Percent symbol:          %
          Negative sign:           -
          Positive sign:           +
          Decimal separator:       .
          Thousands separator:     ,


        Press Enter to continue
```

A
B
C
D
E
F
G
H
I
J
K
L
M
N
O
P
Q
R
S
T
U
V
W
X
Y
Z

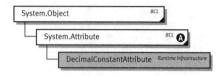

Summary

Stores the value of a `System.Decimal` constant in metadata. This type is not CLS-compliant.

Type Summary

```
public sealed class DecimalConstantAttribute : Attribute
    {
    // Constructors
        public DecimalConstantAttribute(byte scale, byte sign, uint hi,
            uint mid, uint low);

    // Properties
MS public decimal Value { get; }
    }
```

■ JM   Task group work on edition 3 of the ECMA CLI specification consisted of discussion around `Decimal`. Ultimately, the `Decimal` specification was relaxed in order to accommodate a new format coming out of the IEEE 754r specification. While the original format is still supported, a string-based was added to `DecimalConstantAttribute` to accommodate this new format.

■ JM   `DecimalConstantAttribute` is emitted by compilers (e.g., C#) when a field is declared as a `const decimal`.

■ RJ   The metadata does not directly support the representation of constants of type `System.Decimal`. As a result, in the code generated by the C# (and VB) compiler, they are stored as an attribute using the type `DecimalConstantAttribute`. Consider the following C# code:

```
public class Test
{
        private const decimal d = 12.3456m;
}
```

CONTINUED

99

A
B
C
D
E
F
G
H
I
J
K
L
M
N
O
P
Q
R
S
T
U
V
W
X
Y
Z

The relevant MSIL generated is

```
.field private static initonly valuetype [mscorlib]System.Decimal d
.custom instance void
[mscorlib]
System.Runtime.CompilerServices.DecimalConstantAttribute::.ctor(
    uint8, uint8, uint32, uint32, uint32) = ( … hex bytes … )
```

This type is not intended to be used directly by programmers, but rather by compiler writers, based on the programmer's use of some language syntax (such as the keywords const decimal in C#).

Note that it is expected that a future implementation of the CLI will support an alternate representation of the decimal type, which has a much larger range, and a scale that exceeds eight bits. As such, new constructors and methods are likely to be added to this type, as well as to System.Decimal.

■ **DT**   DecimalConstantAttribute provides compilers a place to store decimal constants, since metadata itself can't represent values that big in situ. This attribute is only generated by compilers to indicate the constant value to reflectors and other compilers. The attribute is not used by the runtime or executing code.

■ **DT**   This attribute has been a hot topic in ECMA discussions. A new IEEE 128-bit decimal representation offers more range/precision (in the same number of bits!) than the current CLR implementation. If CLR were to support this new IEEE decimal in the future, this attribute will present a problem because the IEEE decimal's scale is wider than the byte type of the constructor's scale parameter. It is likely that the parameter types of the constructor will be widened and/or additional constructors added in a future release to make an IEEE decimal implementation an option for a future CLR release.

■ **DT**   Some have suggested adding constructors with fewer parameters to make it easier for people to construct DecimalConstantAttributes. The only problem with that is that people don't construct DecimalConstantAttributes—compilers do, so convenience isn't really necessary.

Description

[*Note:* This attribute can be applied to fields and parameters. For more information on storing constants in metadata, see Partition II of the CLI Specification. The types in System.Runtime.CompilerServices are intended primarily for use by compilers, not application programmers. They allow compilers to easily implement certain language features that are not directly visible to programmers.]

Example

```
using System;
using System.Reflection;
using System.Runtime.CompilerServices;

/// <summary>
/// Sample demonstrating the use of the DecimalConstantAttribute class.
/// This attribute is typically used by compiler writers to translate decimal
/// constants in source code into the equivalent IL.
/// </summary>
internal class DecimalConstantAttributeSample
{
    // Compiler adds DecimalConstantAttribute and initializes DecimalConstant1
    // with the specified value. Note that the field will not contain
    // FieldAttributes.Literal even though it looks like a constant.
    public const decimal DecimalConstant1 = 499.9995M;
    // Manually add DecimalConstantAttribute and initialize DecimalConstant2 to
    // a different value.
    [DecimalConstant(4, 0, 0, 0, 4999995)]
    public static readonly decimal DecimalConstant2 = 0;
    // Normal constant.
    public const int IntegerConstant = 500;

    private static void Main()
    {
        FieldInfo[] fields = typeof(DecimalConstantAttributeSample).GetFields();

        foreach (FieldInfo field in fields)
        {
            Console.WriteLine("Field name:       {0}", field.Name);
            Console.WriteLine("Field attributes: {0}", field.Attributes);
            Console.WriteLine("Field value:      {0}", field.GetValue(null));

            foreach (object obj in field.GetCustomAttributes(false))
            {
                DecimalConstantAttribute attr = obj as DecimalConstantAttribute;

                if (attr != null)
                {
                    Console.WriteLine("Constant value:   {0}", attr.Value);
                }
            }

            Console.WriteLine();
        }

        Console.WriteLine();
        Console.WriteLine();
        Console.WriteLine("Press Enter to continue");
        Console.ReadLine();
    }
}
```

A
B
C
D
E
F
G
H
I
J
K
L
M
N
O
P
Q
R
S
T
U
V
W
X
Y
Z

DecimalConstantAttribute Class

The output is

```
Field name:        DecimalConstant1
Field attributes: Public, Static, InitOnly
Field value:       499.9995
Constant value:    499.9995

Field name:        DecimalConstant2
Field attributes: Public, Static, InitOnly
Field value:       0
Constant value:    499.9995

Field name:        IntegerConstant
Field attributes: Public, Static, Literal, HasDefault
Field value:       500


Press Enter to continue
```

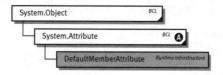

Summary

Defines the member that is invoked when no member name is specified for the type targeted by `DefaultMemberAttribute`.

Type Summary

```
public sealed class DefaultMemberAttribute : Attribute
    {
    // Constructors
        public DefaultMemberAttribute(string memberName);

    // Properties
        public string MemberName { get; }
    }
```

Description

[*Note:* This attribute is used by the `System.Type.InvokeMember` methods. This attribute can be applied to classes, structs, and interfaces.]

Example

```csharp
using System;
using System.Reflection;


/// <summary>
/// This example shows how the DefaultMemberAttribute is used by Reflection.
/// </summary>

public class DefaultMemberAttributeSample
{
    public static void Main()
    {
        foreach (MemberInfo m in typeof(ExampleOne).GetDefaultMembers())
        {
            Console.WriteLine("Default Member == {0}", m);
        }
        foreach (MemberInfo m in typeof(ExampleTwo).GetDefaultMembers())
        {
            Console.WriteLine("Default Member == {0}", m);
```

```
        }
        ExampleTwo exampleTwo = new ExampleTwo();
        int value = (int)typeof(ExampleTwo).InvokeMember(string.Empty,
            BindingFlags.InvokeMethod, null, exampleTwo, null);
        Console.WriteLine("Invoke default member of ExampleTwo: {0} ",
            value);
        Console.WriteLine();
        Console.WriteLine();
        Console.WriteLine("Press Enter to continue");
        Console.ReadLine();
    }
}

    //The C# compiler emits the DefaultMember
    //attribute for types with indexers
public class ExampleOne
{
    //Sample meaningless indexer
    public int this [int index]
    {
        get
        {
            return new Random().Next();
        }
    }
}


    //We customize this example by explicitly telling the runtime
    //what the default member is.
[DefaultMember("GetMeaninglessValue")]
public class ExampleTwo
{
    //Sample meaningless method
    public int GetMeaninglessValue()
    {
        return new Random().Next();
    }
}
```

The output is

```
Default Member == Int32 Item [Int32]
Default Member == Int32 GetMeaninglessValue()
Invoke default member of ExampleTwo: 1342094916


Press Enter to continue
```

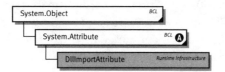

Summary

Indicates that the target method of this attribute is an export from an unmanaged shared library.

Type Summary

```
    public sealed class DllImportAttribute : Attribute
        {
        // Constructors
            public DllImportAttribute(string dllName);

        // Fields
MS CF 1.1 public bool BestFitMapping;
            public CallingConvention CallingConvention;
            public CharSet CharSet;
            public string EntryPoint;
        CF  public bool ExactSpelling;
    MS CF   public bool PreserveSig;
        MS  public bool SetLastError;
MS CF 1.1 public bool ThrowOnUnmappableChar;

        // Properties
            public string Value { get; }
        }
```

> ■ **JM**   Intel's OCL (Open Class Library) made heavy use of the DllImportAttribute in order to reference key functionality in older C/C++ based DLLs. For example, I/O made heavy use of the standard C runtime library in msvcrt.dll and the Windows kernel in kernel32.dll. I would say that in an implementation of the CLI standard, DllImport is one of the most, if not the most, important attribute available.
>
> ■ **AN**   In this attribute, the CharSet value chosen not only affects how Strings, StringBuilders, and Chars are marshaled, but it controls what entry points the CLR will look for (e.g., if it looks for MessageBoxW or MessageBoxA in addition to MessageBox).
>
> *CONTINUED*

A
B
C
D
E
F
G
H
I
J
K
L
M
N
O
P
Q
R
S
T
U
V
W
X
Y
Z

> ■ **AN**   It is kind of strange that `DllImport` has a `Boolean` `PreserveSig` field
> that is completely independent of `PreserveSigAttribute`. The reason for this is
> that we needed a mechanism to "turn off" signature-preserving (which is the
> default behavior for PInvoke), and `PreserveSigAttribute` can only turn it on!
> Had `PreserveSigAttribute` contained any instance data, such as a `Boolean`
> field, then this detail wouldn't have needed to bleed into `DllImportAttribute`.

> ■ **AN**   A little-known fact about `DllImportAttribute`'s `SetLastError` is that
> the CLR pretends that it is always set to true for several Win32 DLLs (`kernel32`,
> `gdi32`, `user32`, etc.) regardless of its real setting. That is because for such DLLs, it is
> almost always the correct behavior and there is very little penalty for having it set on
> APIs that don't make use of the `SetLastError` mechanism. This is similar in spirit
> to the fact that VB.NET Declare statements always set `SetLastError` to true.

Description

This attribute provides the information needed to call a method exported from an unmanaged shared library. This attribute provides the name of the shared library file, the name
of the method within that library, the calling convention, and character set of the unmanaged function.

   [*Note:* A shared library refers to Dynamically Linked Libraries on Windows systems,
and Shared Libraries on UNIX systems.]

   Compilers are required to not preserve this type in metadata as a custom attribute.
Instead, compilers are required to emit it directly in the file format, as described in Partition II of the CLI Specification. Metadata consumers, such as the Reflection API, are
required to retrieve this data from the file format and return it as if it were a custom
attribute.

Example

Example 1
[*Note:* The non-standard `GetLocalTime` API used in this example indicates the current
local system time.]

```
using System;
using System.Runtime.InteropServices;

[ StructLayout( LayoutKind.Sequential )]
public class SystemTime
{
    public ushort year;
    public ushort month;
    public ushort dayOfWeek;
    public ushort day;
```

```
    public ushort hour;
    public ushort minute;
    public ushort second;
    public ushort milliseconds;
}

public class LibWrap
{
    [ DllImportAttribute( "Kernel32", CharSet=CharSet.Auto,
CallingConvention=CallingConvention.StdCall, EntryPoint="GetLocalTime" )]
    public static extern void GetLocalTime( SystemTime st );
}

public class DllImportAttributeTest
{
    public static void Main()
    {

        SystemTime st = new SystemTime();

        LibWrap.GetLocalTime( st );
        Console.Write( "The Date and Time is: " );
        Console.Write( "{0:00}/{1:00}/{2} at ", st.month, st.day, st.year );
        Console.WriteLine( "{0:00}:{1:00}:{2:00}", st.hour, st.minute,
                            st.second );
    }
}
```

When run at the given time on the given date, the output produced was

```
The Date and Time is: 08/21/2004 at 12:59:08
```

Example 2

```
using System;
using System.IO;
using System.Reflection;
using System.Runtime.InteropServices;

/// <summary>
/// Sample demonstrating the use of the DllImportAttribute class.
/// Use this attribute to define unmanaged method signatures that can be called
/// from managed code.
/// </summary>
internal class DllImportAttributeSample
{

    private static void Main()
    {
        bool    fullySigned   = false;
        bool    verified      = false;
        string[] assemblyPaths = new string[2];

        assemblyPaths[0] = Assembly.GetExecutingAssembly().Location;
        assemblyPaths[1] =
            Path.Combine(
                RuntimeEnvironment.GetRuntimeDirectory(),
                "System.Windows.Forms.dll");
```

```csharp
            foreach (string assemblyPath in assemblyPaths)
            {
                // There is no managed API for determining if an assembly's has a
                // valid strong name, although an unmanaged method,
                // StrongNameSignatureVerificationEx, is available and can be
                // called from managed code.
                Console.WriteLine("Verifying {0}...", assemblyPath);
                verified =
                    StrongNameSignatureVerificationEx(
                        assemblyPath, false, ref fullySigned);

                if (verified && fullySigned)
                {
                    Console.WriteLine("  Verified (signed).");
                }
                else if (verified)
                {
                    Console.WriteLine(
                        "  Verified (delay signed, verification skipped).");
                }
                else
                {
                    Console.WriteLine(
                        "  Not verified (not signed or signed and tampered with).");
                }

                Console.WriteLine();
            }

        Console.WriteLine();
        Console.WriteLine();
        Console.WriteLine("Press Enter to continue");
        Console.ReadLine();
    }

    // Unmanaged method for determining if an assembly, identified by a file
    // path, has a valid strong name.
    [DllImport("mscoree.dll", CharSet=CharSet.Unicode)]
    private static extern bool StrongNameSignatureVerificationEx(
        string wszFilePath, bool fForceVerification, ref bool pfWasVerified);

}
```

The output is

```
Verifying
C:\System.Runtime\InteropServices\DllImportAttribute\DllImportAttribute.exe...
  Not verified (not signed or signed and tampered with).

Verifying C:\WINDOWS\Microsoft.NET\Framework\v1.1.4322\System.Windows.Forms.dll...
  Verified (signed).


Press Enter to continue
```

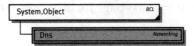

Summary

Obtains domain information from the Domain Name System as defined by IETF RFC 1035 and RFC 1036.

Type Summary

```
public sealed class Dns
{
    // Methods
    public static IAsyncResult BeginGetHostByName(string hostName,
                                AsyncCallback requestCallback,
                                object stateObject);
    public static IAsyncResult BeginResolve(string hostName,
                                AsyncCallback requestCallback,
                                object stateObject);
    public static IPHostEntry EndGetHostByName(IAsyncResult asyncResult);
    public static IPHostEntry EndResolve(IAsyncResult asyncResult);
    public static IPHostEntry GetHostByAddress(IPAddress address);
    public static IPHostEntry GetHostByAddress(string address);
    public static IPHostEntry GetHostByName(string hostName);
    public static string GetHostName();
    public static IPHostEntry Resolve(string hostName);
}
```

> **▪▪ LO**   If you're using sockets in conjunction with this API, remember to construct the socket using the address family from the address in IPHostEntry instead of constructing the socket first. This will ensure that the socket created is compatible in terms of IPv4/IPv6. Also, remember to cycle through the addresses in the list when attempting to connect, rather than just trying the first one and failing if that one doesn't connect.

Description

The Dns class creates and sends queries to obtain information about a host server from the Internet Domain Name System (DNS). In order to access DNS, the machine executing the query is required to be connected to a network. If the query is executed on a machine that does not have access to a domain name server, a System.Net.Sockets.Socket-Exception is thrown.

Information from the DNS query is returned in an instance of the IPHostEntry class. If the specified host has more than one entry in the DNS database, the IPHost-Entry instance contains multiple IP addresses and aliases.

[*Note:* See the IPHostEntry class page for an example that uses the Dns class.]

Example

```
using System;
using System.Net;

public class DnsSample
{
    private static bool bDone = false;

    public static void Main()
    {
        String toFind = "microsoft.com";
        IAsyncResult dummy = Dns.BeginResolve(toFind,
                    new AsyncCallback(DnsCallback), null);
        while(!bDone) {}
    }

    private static void DnsCallback(IAsyncResult ar)
    {
        IPHostEntry host = Dns.EndResolve(ar);
        ShowHostDetails(host);
        bDone = true;
    }

    private static void ShowHostDetails(IPHostEntry host)
    {
        Console.WriteLine("HostName = '{0}'", host.HostName);
        foreach (IPAddress addr in host.AddressList)
        {
            Console.WriteLine("IPAddress = {0}", addr);
        }
        foreach (String alias in host.Aliases)
        {
            Console.WriteLine("Alias = {0}", alias);
        }
    }
}
```

The output is

```
HostName = 'microsoft.com'
IPAddress = 207.46.130.108
IPAddress = 207.46.250.119
```

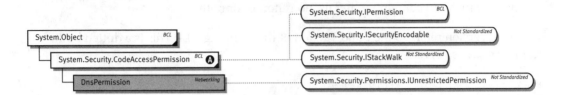

Summary

Controls access to Domain Name System (DNS) servers on the network.

Type Summary

```
CF public sealed class DnsPermission : CodeAccessPermission,
                                       IUnrestrictedPermission
   {
   // Constructors
CF public DnsPermission(PermissionState state);

   // Methods
CF public override IPermission Copy();
CF public override void FromXml(SecurityElement securityElement);
CF public override IPermission Intersect(IPermission target);
CF public override bool IsSubsetOf(IPermission target);
MS CF public bool IsUnrestricted();
CF public override SecurityElement ToXml();
CF public override IPermission Union(IPermission target);
   }
```

Description

The XML encoding of a DnsPermission instance is defined below in EBNF format. The following conventions are used:

- All non-literals in the grammar below are shown in normal type.
- All literals are in bold font.

The following meta-language symbols are used:

- "*" represents a meta-language symbol suffixing an expression that can appear zero or more times.
- "?" represents a meta-language symbol suffixing an expression that can appear zero or one time.
- "+" represents a meta-language symbol suffixing an expression that can appear one or more times.

- "('',')" is used to group literals, non-literals, or a mixture of literals and non-literals.
- " | " denotes an exclusive disjunction between two expressions.
- "::= " denotes a production rule where a left-hand non-literal is replaced by a right-hand expression containing literals, non-literals, or both.

BuildVersion refers to the build version of the shipping CLI. This is a dotted build number such as "2412.0".

```
ECMAPubKeyToken::=b77a5c561934e089
DnsPermissionXML::=
<IPermission
class="
System.Net.DnsPermission,
System,
Version=1.0.BuildVersion,
Culture=neutral,
PublicKeyToken=ECMAPubKeyToken"
version="1"
(
Unrestricted="true"/>
)
|
/>
```

Example

```csharp
using System;
using System.Net;
using System.Security.Permissions;

public class DnsPermissionSample
{
    public static void Main()
    {
        DnsPermission unrestricted1 = new
            DnsPermission(PermissionState.Unrestricted);
        DnsPermission unrestricted2 = new
            DnsPermission(PermissionState.Unrestricted);
        DnsPermission restricted1 = new
            DnsPermission(PermissionState.None);
        DnsPermission restricted2 = new
            DnsPermission(PermissionState.None);

        DnsPermission result =
            (DnsPermission)restricted1.Union(restricted2);
        ShowResult(result, "Union of restricted and "
            + "restricted DnsPermission instances:");
        result = (DnsPermission)unrestricted1.Union(restricted1);
        ShowResult(result, "Union of un-restricted and "
            + "restricted DnsPermission instances:");
        result = (DnsPermission)unrestricted1.Union(unrestricted2);
        ShowResult(result, "Union of un-restricted and "
            + "un-restricted DnsPermission instances:");
```

```
        result = (DnsPermission)unrestricted1.Union(null);
        ShowResult(result, "Union of un-restricted and "
            + "null DnsPermission instances:");
        result = (DnsPermission)unrestricted1.Intersect(restricted1);
        ShowResult(result, "Intersect of un-restricted and "
            + "restricted DnsPermission instances:");
        result = (DnsPermission)unrestricted1.Intersect(unrestricted2);
        ShowResult(result, "Intersect of un-restricted and "
            + "un-restricted DnsPermission instances:");

        Boolean subset = unrestricted1.IsSubsetOf(restricted1);
        Console.WriteLine("\nUn-restricted DnsPermission instance "
            + "IsSubsetOf restricted instance: {0}",
            subset);
        subset = unrestricted1.IsSubsetOf(unrestricted2);
        Console.WriteLine("Un-restricted DnsPermission instance "
            + "IsSubsetOf un-restricted instance: {0}",
            subset);
        subset = restricted1.IsSubsetOf(unrestricted1);
        Console.WriteLine("Restricted DnsPermission instance "
            + "IsSubsetOf un-restricted instance: {0}",
            subset);
        subset = restricted1.IsSubsetOf(restricted2);
        Console.WriteLine("Restricted DnsPermission instance "
            + "IsSubsetOf restricted instance: {0}",
            subset);
        Console.WriteLine();
        Console.WriteLine();
        Console.WriteLine("Press Enter to continue");
        Console.ReadLine();
    }

    private static void ShowResult(DnsPermission result,
        String caption)
    {
        Console.WriteLine();
        Console.WriteLine(caption);
        if (result == null)
        {
            Console.WriteLine("<null>");
        }
        else
        {
            Console.WriteLine("DnsPermission.IsUnrestricted = {0}",
                result.IsUnrestricted());
        }
    }
}
```

The output is

```
Union of restricted and restricted DnsPermission instances:
DnsPermission.IsUnrestricted = False
```

DnsPermission Class

A
B
C
D
E
F
G
H
I
J
K
L
M
N
O
P
Q
R
S
T
U
V
W
X
Y
Z

```
        Union of un-restricted and restricted DnsPermission instances:
        DnsPermission.IsUnrestricted = True

        Union of un-restricted and un-restricted DnsPermission instances:
        DnsPermission.IsUnrestricted = True

        Union of un-restricted and null DnsPermission instances:
        DnsPermission.IsUnrestricted = True

        Intersect of un-restricted and restricted DnsPermission instances:
        <null>

        Intersect of un-restricted and un-restricted DnsPermission instances:
        DnsPermission.IsUnrestricted = True

        Un-restricted DnsPermission instance IsSubsetOf restricted instance: False
        Un-restricted DnsPermission instance IsSubsetOf un-restricted instance: True
        Restricted DnsPermission instance IsSubsetOf un-restricted instance: True
        Restricted DnsPermission instance IsSubsetOf restricted instance: True


        Press Enter to continue
```

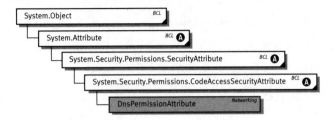

Summary

Used to declaratively specify permission to request information from Domain Name Servers.

Type Summary

```
CF public sealed class DnsPermissionAttribute : CodeAccessSecurityAttribute
    {
    // Constructors
    CF public DnsPermissionAttribute(SecurityAction action);

    // Methods
    CF public override IPermission CreatePermission();
    }
```

Description

[*Note:* The security information declared by a security attribute is stored in the metadata of the attribute target, and is accessed by the system at runtime. Security attributes are used for declarative security only. For imperative security, use the corresponding permission class, DnsPermission. The allowable DnsPermissionAttribute targets are determined by the System.Security.Permissions.SecurityAction passed to the constructor.]

Example

```
using System;
using System.Net;
using System.Security;
using System.Security.Permissions;


[DnsPermission(SecurityAction.Demand, Unrestricted = true)]
public class DnsTest
{
    public static String GetLocalHostName()
```

```
        {
            return Dns.GetHostName();
        }
    }

    public class DnsPermissionAttributeSample
    {
        public static void Main()
        {
            try
            {
                Console.WriteLine("DnsTest.GetLocalHostName returned: '{0}'",
                    DnsTest.GetLocalHostName());
            }
            catch (Exception e)
            {
                Console.WriteLine(e.Message);
            }
            Console.WriteLine();
            Console.WriteLine();
            Console.WriteLine("Press Enter to continue");
            Console.ReadLine();
        }
    }
```

The output is

```
DnsTest.GetLocalHostName returned: 'MachineName'


Press Enter to continue
```

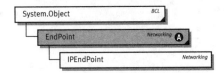

Summary
This is the base class used to derive classes that represent network addresses.

Type Summary

```
public abstract class EndPoint
    {
    // Constructors
        protected EndPoint();

    // Properties
        public virtual AddressFamily AddressFamily { get; }

    // Methods
        public virtual EndPoint Create(SocketAddress socketAddress);
    MS public virtual SocketAddress Serialize();
    }
```

Description
[*Note:* The EndPoint class provides an abstract representation of the address of a network resource or service.]

Example

```
using System;
using System.Net;
using System.Net.Sockets;

public class EndPointSample
{
    public static void Main()
    {
        IPAddress ip = IPAddress.Parse("127.0.0.1");
        IPEndPoint ep = new IPEndPoint(ip, 9999);
        Console.WriteLine("EndPoint.AddressFamily = '{0}'",
            ep.AddressFamily);
        SocketAddress sktaddr = new
            SocketAddress(AddressFamily.InterNetwork);
        EndPoint newep = (EndPoint)ep.Create(sktaddr);
        Console.WriteLine("New EndPoint.AddressFamily = '{0}'",
```

```
                    newep.AddressFamily);
            Console.WriteLine();
            Console.WriteLine();
            Console.WriteLine("Press Enter to continue");
            Console.ReadLine();
        }
    }
```

The output is

```
EndPoint.AddressFamily = 'InterNetwork'
New EndPoint.AddressFamily = 'InterNetwork'


Press Enter to continue
```

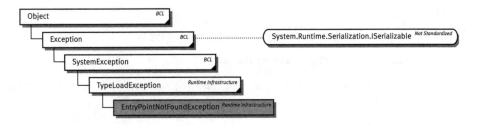

Summary

Represents the error that occurs when an attempt to load a `System.Reflection.Assembly` fails due to the absence of an entry point.

Type Summary

```
public class EntryPointNotFoundException : TypeLoadException
    {
    // Constructors
        public EntryPointNotFoundException();
MS CF protected EntryPointNotFoundException(SerializationInfo info,
                  StreamingContext context);
        public EntryPointNotFoundException(string message);
        public EntryPointNotFoundException(string message, Exception inner);
    }
```

Description

[*Note:* In C#, an entry point is defined through the `Main()` method. For additional information about entry points, see Partition II of the CLI Specification.]

Example

```
using System;
using System.Runtime.InteropServices;

/// <summary>
/// Shows why a EntryPointNotFoundException is thrown
/// and how to handle it
/// </summary>

public class EntryPointNotFoundExceptionSample
{
    // This wrapper causes an exception to be thrown. EntryPoint, CharSet, and
    // ExactSpelling fields are mismatched.
    [DllImport( "User32.dll", EntryPoint="MessageBox",
        CharSet=CharSet.Ansi, ExactSpelling=true )]
    public static extern int MsgBox3( int hWnd, String text,
```

```
        String caption, uint type );

    public static void Main()
    {
        try
        {
            MsgBox3( 0, "No such function", "MsgBox Sample", 0 );
        }
        catch (EntryPointNotFoundException e)
        {
            Console.WriteLine("Caught exception: {0} - '{1}'", e.GetType().Name,
                e.Message);
        }
        Console.WriteLine();
        Console.WriteLine();
        Console.WriteLine("Press Enter to continue");
        Console.ReadLine();
    }
}
```

The output is

```
Caught exception: EntryPointNotFoundException - 'Unable to find an entry point n
amed MessageBox in DLL User32.dll.'


Press Enter to continue
```

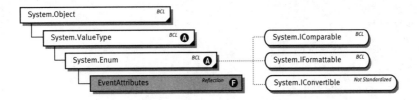

Summary

Specifies the attributes of an event. This enumeration is used by the `EventInfo.Attributes` property.

Type Summary

```
public enum EventAttributes
    {
      None = 0x0,
   MS ReservedMask = 0x400,
   MS RTSpecialName = 0x400,
      SpecialName = 0x200,
    }
```

Example

```csharp
using System;
using System.Reflection;
using System.Runtime.CompilerServices;

/// <summary>
/// This example shows getting the EventInfo from a Type and
/// printing its name and attributes.
/// </summary>

public class EventAttributesSample
{
    public static void Main()
    {
        Type type = typeof(SampleButton);
        EventInfo evnt = type.GetEvent("ClickEvent");
        Console.WriteLine("Event_u39 ?{0}' Attributes: '{1}'",
            evnt.Name, evnt.Attributes);
        Console.WriteLine();
        Console.WriteLine();
        Console.WriteLine("Press Enter to continue");
        Console.ReadLine();
    }
}

public class SampleButton
```

```
    {
        //disabled compiler warning 67: ClickEvent not used.
        public event EventHandler ClickEvent;
    }
```

The output is

```
Event 'ClickEvent' Attributes: 'None'


Press Enter to continue
```

A
B
C
D
E
F
G
H
I
J
K
L
M
N
O
P
Q
R
S
T
U
V
W
X
Y
Z

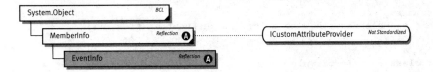

Summary

Provides access to event metadata.

Type Summary

```
public abstract class EventInfo : MemberInfo
   {
   // Constructors
      protected EventInfo();

   // Properties
      public abstract EventAttributes Attributes { get; }
      public Type EventHandlerType { get; }
MS    public bool IsMulticast { get; }
MS    public bool IsSpecialName { get; }
MS    public override MemberTypes MemberType { get; }

   // Methods
      public void AddEventHandler(object target, Delegate handler);
      public MethodInfo GetAddMethod();
      public abstract MethodInfo GetAddMethod(bool nonPublic);
      public MethodInfo GetRaiseMethod();
      public abstract MethodInfo GetRaiseMethod(bool nonPublic);
      public MethodInfo GetRemoveMethod();
      public abstract MethodInfo GetRemoveMethod(bool nonPublic);
      public void RemoveEventHandler(object target, Delegate handler);
   }
```

Description

Events are handled by delegates. An event listener supplies an event-handler delegate
that is invoked whenever the event is raised by an event source. In order to connect to
the event source, the event listener adds this delegate to the invocation list of the source.
When the event is raised, the event-handler delegate invokes the methods in its invocation list. The `GetAddMethod`, `AddEventHandler`, `GetRemoveMethod`, and
`RemoveEventHandler` methods, and the delegate type of the event-handler associated with an event, are required to be marked in the metadata.

[*Note:* For information on delegates, see the `System.Delegate` class overview.]
[*Note:* For information on events, see Partitions I and II of the CLI specification.]

Example

```csharp
using System;
using System.Reflection;

/// <summary>
/// This example shows how to print out an Event in C# syntax
/// </summary>

public class EventInfoSample
{
    public static void Main()
    {
        Type type = typeof(Assembly);

        foreach (EventInfo evnt in type.GetEvents(BindingFlags.NonPublic |
            BindingFlags.Public | BindingFlags.Instance | BindingFlags.Static))
        {
            //All events should at least have an add method, if not, skip it
            if (evnt.GetAddMethod() == null)
            {
                continue;
            }

            //Skip any events that are not publicly accessible.
            //Note: BindingFlags.NonPublic include protected as well
            //private members
            MethodInfo addMethod = evnt.GetAddMethod();
            if (!(addMethod.IsPublic ||
                addMethod.IsFamily ||
                addMethod.IsFamilyOrAssembly))
            {
                return;
            }

            if (addMethod.IsPublic)
            {
                Console.Write("public ");
            }
            else if (addMethod.IsFamily)
            {
                Console.Write("protected ");
            }
            else if (addMethod.IsFamilyOrAssembly)
            {
                Console.Write("protected internal ");
            }

            Console.Write("event ");
            Console.Write(evnt.EventHandlerType.Name);
            Console.Write(" ");
            Console.Write(evnt.Name);
            Console.WriteLine(";");
        }
        Assembly a = Assembly.GetAssembly(typeof(object));
        EventInfo e = type.GetEvent("ModuleResolve");
```

```
        e.AddEventHandler(a, new ModuleResolveEventHandler(ModuleResolver));
        Console.WriteLine();
        Console.WriteLine();
        Console.WriteLine("Press Enter to continue");
        Console.ReadLine();
    }
    static Module ModuleResolver(object sender, ResolveEventArgs e)
    {
        //TODO: insert code to handle event
        return null;
    }

} //end class
```

The output is

```
public event ModuleResolveEventHandler ModuleResolve;


Press Enter to continue
```

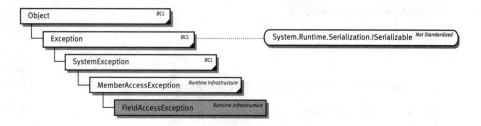

Summary

Represents the error that occurs when there is an attempt to access a field outside the scope in which access is permitted.

Type Summary

```
CF public class FieldAccessException : MemberAccessException
    {
    // Constructors
    CF public FieldAccessException();
MS CF protected FieldAccessException(SerializationInfo info,
                    StreamingContext context);
    CF public FieldAccessException(string message);
    CF public FieldAccessException(string message, Exception inner);
    }
```

Description

[*Note:* This exception is typically thrown when the access level of a field in a class library is changed, and one or more assemblies referencing the library have not been recompiled.]

Example

```
using System;
using System.Reflection;

/// <summary>
/// Shows a FieldAccessException being thrown
/// because we try to SetValue on an enum field, which
/// is read-only.
/// </summary>
///

enum Color
{
    Brown = 0,
    Red = 1,
    Blue = 2,
```

FieldAccessException Class

```
        Green = 3,
    }


class FieldAccessExceptionSample
{
    static void Main()
    {
        try
        {
            typeof(Color).GetField("Red").SetValue(null, (Color)42);
        }
        catch (FieldAccessException fae)
        {
            Console.WriteLine("Caught exception: {0} - '{1}'",
                                fae.GetType().Name, fae.Message);
        }
        Console.WriteLine();
        Console.WriteLine();
        Console.WriteLine("Press Enter to continue");
        Console.ReadLine();

    }
}
```

The output is

```
Caught exception: FieldAccessException - 'Cannot set a final field.'


Press Enter to continue
```

System.Reflection
FieldAttributes Enum

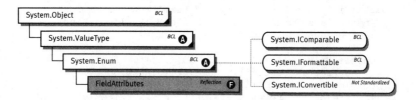

Summary

Specifies flags that describe the attributes of a field.

Type Summary

```
public enum FieldAttributes
    {
        Assembly = 0x3,
        FamANDAssem = 0x2,
        Family = 0x4,
        FamORAssem = 0x5,
        FieldAccessMask = 0x7,
   MS   HasDefault = 0x8000,
   MS   HasFieldMarshal = 0x1000,
   MS   HasFieldRVA = 0x100,
        InitOnly = 0x20,
        Literal = 0x40,
   MS   NotSerialized = 0x80,
        PinvokeImpl = 0x2000,
        Private = 0x1,
        PrivateScope = 0x0,
        Public = 0x6,
   MS   ReservedMask = 0x9500,
   MS   RTSpecialName = 0x400,
        SpecialName = 0x200,
        Static = 0x10,
    }
```

Description

This enumeration is used by the `FieldInfo.Attributes` property.

Example

```
using System;
using System.Reflection;

/// <summary>
/// This example gets all the fields from an example class and
/// shows how to interpret the fields attributes.
/// </summary>
```

```
public class FieldAttributesSample
{
    public static void Main()
    {
        foreach (FieldInfo field in typeof(DemoClass).GetFields(
            BindingFlags.Public | BindingFlags.NonPublic | BindingFlags.Static |
            BindingFlags.Instance))
        {
            Console.Write("{0,-25}    {1,-10}", "'" + field.Name + "'",
                GetPrettyAccessibilityName(field.Attributes));
            Console.Write("   ");
            if ((field.Attributes & FieldAttributes.InitOnly) != 0)
            {
                Console.Write ("readonly ");
            }
            if ((field.Attributes & FieldAttributes.Literal) != 0)
            {
                Console.Write("literal ");
            }
            if ((field.Attributes & FieldAttributes.NotSerialized) != 0)
            {
                Console.Write("[NonSerialized]");
            }
            if ((field.Attributes & FieldAttributes.Static) != 0)
            {
                Console.Write("static ");
            }
            Console.WriteLine();
        }

        Console.WriteLine();
        Console.WriteLine();
        Console.WriteLine("Press Enter to continue");
        Console.ReadLine();
    }
    private static string GetPrettyAccessibilityName(FieldAttributes attributes)
    {
        switch (attributes & FieldAttributes.FieldAccessMask)
        {
            case FieldAttributes.Assembly:
                return "internal";

            case FieldAttributes.Family:
                return "protected";

            case FieldAttributes.Public:
                return "public";

            case FieldAttributes.Private:
                return "private";

            default:
                return (attributes & FieldAttributes.FieldAccessMask).ToString();
        }
    }
}
```

A B C D E F G H I J K L M N O P Q R S T U V W X Y Z

```
[Serializable]
class DemoClass
{
    public readonly int ReadonlyField = 29;
    public const int ConstField= 2;
    [NonSerialized] public int NonSerializableValue = 42;
    public static readonly int StaticReadonlyField = 29;
    protected static int FamilyStaticField = 33;
    private static int PrivateField = 7;

}
```

The output is

```
'ReadonlyField'           public        readonly
'NonSerializableValue'    public        [NonSerialized]
'StaticReadonlyField'     public        readonly static
'FamilyStaticField'       protected     static
'PrivateField'            private       static
'ConstField'              public        literal static


Press Enter to continue
```

A
B
C
D
E
F
G
H
I
J
K
L
M
N
O
P
Q
R
S
T
U
V
W
X
Y
Z

Summary

Provides access to field metadata.

Type Summary

```
public abstract class FieldInfo : MemberInfo
   {
   // Constructors
      protected FieldInfo();

   // Properties
      public abstract FieldAttributes Attributes { get; }
MS    public abstract RuntimeFieldHandle FieldHandle { get; }
      public abstract Type FieldType { get; }
MS    public bool IsAssembly { get; }
MS    public bool IsFamily { get; }
MS    public bool IsFamilyAndAssembly { get; }
MS    public bool IsFamilyOrAssembly { get; }
MS    public bool IsInitOnly { get; }
MS    public bool IsLiteral { get; }
MS    public bool IsNotSerialized { get; }
MS    public bool IsPinvokeImpl { get; }
MS    public bool IsPrivate { get; }
MS    public bool IsPublic { get; }
MS    public bool IsSpecialName { get; }
MS    public bool IsStatic { get; }
MS    public override MemberTypes MemberType { get; }

   // Methods
MS    public static FieldInfo GetFieldFromHandle(RuntimeFieldHandle handle);
      public abstract object GetValue(object obj);
MS CF public virtual object GetValueDirect(TypedReference obj);
      public void SetValue(object obj, object value);
      public abstract void SetValue(object obj, object value,
                          BindingFlags invokeAttr, Binder binder,
                          CultureInfo culture);
MS CF public virtual void SetValueDirect(TypedReference obj, object value);
   }
```

Example

```
using System;
using System.Reflection;

/// <summary>
/// This example prints all the fields of a Type in C# syntax.
/// </summary>

public class FieldInfoSample
{
    public static void Main()
    {
        PrintFields (typeof(Int32));
        PrintFields(typeof(DayOfWeek));
        Console.WriteLine();
        Console.WriteLine();
        Console.WriteLine("Press Enter to continue");
        Console.ReadLine();
    }
    public static void PrintFields (Type type)
    {
        Console.WriteLine("Fields for {0}", type);
        foreach (FieldInfo field in type.GetFields(BindingFlags.NonPublic |
            BindingFlags.Public | BindingFlags.Instance | BindingFlags.Static))
        {
            //skip any fields that are not public or protected
            if (!(field.IsPublic || field.IsFamily || field.IsFamilyOrAssembly))
            {
                continue;
            }
            if (field.DeclaringType.IsEnum)
            {
                if (field.IsStatic)
                {
                    Console.Write(field.Name);
                    Console.Write(" = ");
                    Console.Write(Convert.ChangeType(field.GetValue(null),
                        Enum.GetUnderlyingType(type)));
                    Console.WriteLine(',');
                }
            }
            else
            {
                Console.Write(field.IsPublic ? "public " : field.IsFamily ?
                    "protected " : "protected internal ");

                if (field.IsStatic && field.IsLiteral)
                {
                    Console.Write("const ");
                }
                else
                {
                    if (field.IsStatic)
                    {
                        Console.Write("static ");
```

```
                              }
                              if (field.IsInitOnly)
                              {
                                   Console.Write("readonly ");
                              }
                         }
                         Console.Write(field.FieldType);
                         Console.Write(' ');
                         Console.Write(field.Name);
                         if (field.IsStatic)
                         {
                              Console.Write(" = ");
                              Console.Write(field.GetValue(null));
                         }
                         Console.WriteLine(';');
                    }
               }

          }
     } //end class
```

The output is

```
Fields for System.Int32
public const System.Int32 MaxValue = 2147483647;
public const System.Int32 MinValue = -2147483648;
Fields for System.DayOfWeek
Sunday = 0,
Monday = 1,
Tuesday = 2,
Wednesday = 3,
Thursday = 4,
Friday = 5,
Saturday = 6,


Press Enter to continue
```

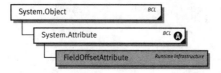

A
B
C
D
E
F
G
H
I
J
K
L
M
N
O
P
Q
R
S
T
U
V
W
X
Y
Z

Summary

Indicates the physical position of a field within the unmanaged representation of a class or structure.

Type Summary

```
CF public sealed class FieldOffsetAttribute : Attribute
    {
    // Constructors
    CF public FieldOffsetAttribute(int offset);

    // Properties
    CF public int Value { get; }
    }
```

> **■ AN**   The most common use of `FieldOffsetAttribute` is to create a union. But whenever you use `FieldOffsetAttribute`, make sure that you avoid burning in platform-specific memory offsets. This isn't easy, since you can't get around specifying the absolute offsets at compile time, but you can create substructures to restrict the number of fields whose offsets need to be specified. This is demonstrated by the following C# definitions for a structure containing a union that follows a pointer-sized field:
>
> ```
> // This definition is bad because it's only correct when
> // the size of a pointer is 32-bits.
> [StructLayout(LayoutKind.Explicit)]
> struct Bad
> {
>     [FieldOffset(0)] public IntPtr pointerSizedField;
>     [FieldOffset(4)] public short unionField1;
>     [FieldOffset(4)] public double unionField2;
> }
> // This definition is good because it leverages sequential
> // layout to handle the structure's varying size, and only
> // uses explicit layout where absolutely necessary.
> ```
>
> *CONTINUED*

```
[StructLayout(LayoutKind.Sequential)]
struct Good
{
    public IntPtr pointerSizedField;
    public GoodUnion union;
}

[StructLayout(LayoutKind.Explicit)]
struct GoodUnion
{
    [FieldOffset(0)] public short unionField1;
    [FieldOffset(0)] public double unionField2;
}
```

Having to create the substructures is a bit of a pain, but in the absence of being able to give sizeof(IntPtr) as a field offset or mixing sequential and explicit layout in the same structure, this is the way to do it.

Description

The target objects for this attribute are non-static fields of classes and structures qualified with the StructLayoutAttribute set to LayoutKind.Explicit. All non-static fields within an object with an explicit layout are required to have this attribute. No static or constant fields within an object with explicit layout are allowed to have this attribute.

The physical layout of the data members of a class or structure is automatically arranged in managed memory. When a managed object is passed as an argument to unmanaged code, the system creates its unmanaged representation. StructLayout-Attribute provides explicit control over this unmanaged representation. FieldOff-setAttribute indicates the offset of a target data member within the unmanaged representation of a class or structure.

If FieldOffsetAttribute instances on target fields of an exported object are set to overlap each other, one field is overwritten by another field. For example, if an integer field has the FieldOffsetAttribute set to 4, and another integer field has the Field-OffsetAttribute set to 6, the last two bytes of the unmanaged representation of the first integer overlap the first two bytes of the second integer. In such a situation writing to one of the fields might corrupt the data in the other.

[*Note:* See the StructLayoutAttribute class overview for an example that uses FieldOffsetAttribute.]

Compilers are required to not preserve this type in metadata as a custom attribute. Instead, compilers are required to emit it directly in the file format, as described in Partition II of the CLI Specification. Metadata consumers, such as the Reflection API, are required to retrieve this data from the file format and return it as if it were a custom attribute.

Example

```csharp
using System;
using System.Runtime.InteropServices;

/// <summary>
/// Sample demonstrating the use of the FieldOffsetAttribute class.
/// Use this attribute to specify the physical position of fields in types
/// decorated with StructLayoutAttribute and LayoutKind.Explicit.
/// </summary>
internal class FieldOffsetAttributeSample
{

    private static void Main()
    {
        TIME_ZONE_INFORMATION tzi = new TIME_ZONE_INFORMATION();

        if (GetTimeZoneInformation(out tzi) != -1)
        {
            Console.WriteLine(
                "The current time-zone standard name is '{0}'",
                tzi.StandardName);
            Console.WriteLine(
                "The current time-zone daylight name is '{0}'",
                tzi.DaylightName);
        }
        else
        {
            Console.WriteLine("GetTimeZoneInformation failed.");
        }

        Console.WriteLine();
        Console.WriteLine();
        Console.WriteLine("Press Enter to continue");
        Console.ReadLine();
    }

    // The SYSTEMTIME type to use with TIME_ZONE_INFORMATION.
    [StructLayout(LayoutKind.Explicit)]
    private struct SYSTEMTIME
    {
        [FieldOffset(0)]
        public ushort wYear;
        [FieldOffset(2)]
        public ushort wMonth;
        [FieldOffset(4)]
        public ushort wDayOfWeek;
        [FieldOffset(6)]
        public ushort wDay;
        [FieldOffset(8)]
        public ushort wHour;
        [FieldOffset(10)]
        public ushort wMinute;
        [FieldOffset(12)]
        public ushort wSecond;
        [FieldOffset(14)]
```

A
B
C
D
E
F
G
H
I
J
K
L
M
N
O
P
Q
R
S
T
U
V
W
X
Y
Z

FieldOffsetAttribute Class

```
        public ushort wMilliseconds;
    }

    // The TIME_ZONE_INFORMATION type to use with GetTimeZoneInformation. Note
    // that strings must be marshalled as Unicode.
    [StructLayout(LayoutKind.Explicit, CharSet=CharSet.Unicode)]
    private struct TIME_ZONE_INFORMATION
    {
        [FieldOffset(0)]
        public int Bias;
        [FieldOffset(4)]
        [MarshalAs(UnmanagedType.ByValTStr, SizeConst=32)]
        public string StandardName;
        [FieldOffset(68)]
        public SYSTEMTIME StandardDate;
        [FieldOffset(84)]
        public int StandardBias;
        [FieldOffset(88)]
        [MarshalAs(UnmanagedType.ByValTStr, SizeConst=32)]
        public string DaylightName;
        [FieldOffset(172)]
        public SYSTEMTIME DaylightDate;
        [FieldOffset(188)]
        public int DaylightBias;
    }

    // Win32 method to retrieve information about the current time-zone.  This
    // is used purely to demonstrate using FieldOffsetAttribute; .NET code
    // would typically use TimeZone.CurrentTimeZone to retrieve the same
    // information.
    [DllImport("kernel32.dll", SetLastError=true)]
    private static extern int GetTimeZoneInformation(
        out TIME_ZONE_INFORMATION lpTimeZoneInformation);

}
```

The output is

```
The current time-zone standard name is 'Pacific Standard Time'
The current time-zone daylight name is 'Pacific Standard Time'


Press Enter to continue
```

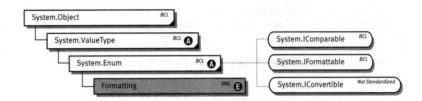

Summary

Specifies formatting options for the `XmlTextWriter` class.

Type Summary

```
public enum Formatting
    {
    Indented = 1,
    None = 0,
    }
```

> ■ **JM**   Back on February 28, 2001, when the first edition of the CLI specification was being standardized, there was a meeting in Redmond, Washington, amongst the co-sponsors of the standardization process (Microsoft, Intel, Hewlett-Packard). During this meeting we were slated to do a pre-review of the XML, Networking, and Reflection classes. Well, for those of you who were in the Seattle area that day, I don't have to remind you of the 6.8 earthquake that occurred at around 10:54 AM (and 32 seconds). We were on a break and everyone except for Brad, myself, and an HP representative had left the meeting room. Luckily for Brad and me, the HP representative was on top of things because, as Brad and I were looking like deer in the headlights, listening to the walls creak, she said we should get under the table (as any basic earthquake drill will tell you). And, hence, we got under the table and came out unscathed. I wish I had a picture of the three of us huddled under there.

Example

```
using System;
using System.Xml;


/// <summary>
/// This sample shows writing a simple Xml document to the console with no
/// formatting and with Indented formatting
/// </summary>
```

```
public class FormattingSample
{
    public static void Main()
    {
        WriteSomeElements(Formatting.None);
        WriteSomeElements(Formatting.Indented);
        Console.WriteLine();
        Console.WriteLine();
        Console.WriteLine("Press Enter to continue");
        Console.ReadLine();
    }

    static void WriteSomeElements(Formatting wformat)
    {
        Console.WriteLine();
        Console.WriteLine();
        Console.WriteLine("With Formatting {0}:", wformat);
        XmlTextWriter w = new XmlTextWriter(Console.Out);
        w.Formatting = wformat;
        w.WriteStartDocument();
        w.WriteStartElement("root");
        w.WriteElementString("subelement", "sample");
        w.WriteEndElement();
        w.WriteEndDocument();
        w.Close();
    }

}
```

The output is

```
With Formatting None:
<?xml version="1.0" encoding="IBM437"?><root><subelement>sample</subelement></ro
ot>

With Formatting Indented:
<?xml version="1.0" encoding="IBM437"?>
<root>
  <subelement>sample</subelement>
</root>

Press Enter to continue
```

A
B
C
D
E
F
G
H
I
J
K
L
M
N
O
P
Q
R
S
T
U
V
W
X
Y
Z

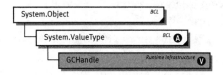

Summary

Provides a means for referencing a managed object from unmanaged memory.

Type Summary

```
public struct GCHandle
    {
    // Properties
        public bool IsAllocated { get; }
        public object Target { get; set; }

    // Methods
        public IntPtr AddrOfPinnedObject();
        public static GCHandle Alloc(object value);
        public static GCHandle Alloc(object value, GCHandleType type);
        public void Free();
        public static explicit operator GCHandle(IntPtr value);
        public static explicit operator IntPtr(GCHandle value);
    }
```

> **■ DM** The behavior of the GCHandle type is controlled by the GCHandleType enumeration optionally passed into the constructor. Here are the different behaviors the GCHandle type supports:
>
> • GCHandleType.Normal: This is the default mode if no GCHandleType is specified. In this mode, the GCHandle represents a new reference to the object that prevents it from being collected. The main reason for using this mode is to keep a reference to the object from native code. The gc_root class in C++ actually works by wrapping a GCHandle.
> • GCHandleType.Pinned: This mode prevents the GC from moving the object the GCHandle represents. It can be useful when doing asynchronous writes directly to the memory the object occupies. However it should be used with extreme caution since it's very easy to cause corruption when writing directly into GC memory space. Using too many pinned GCHandles can also slow down the GC since it
>
> *CONTINUED*

A
B
C
D
E
F
G
H
I
J
K
L
M
N
O
P
Q
R
S
T
U
V
W
X
Y
Z

limits the amount of compaction it can do. Note that some languages, such as C#, have support for pinned local variables. Whenever possible, the language support should be used since it guarantees the object will be unpinned in a timely fashion and is also more performant.

- `GCHandleType.Weak`: In this mode, the `GCHandle` represents a weak reference to an object; that is, it's a reference that allows the object to be accessed, but doesn't cause the GC to keep it alive. This means that if there aren't any other references to this type, it will be eligible for collecting. If the object does indeed get collected, then the `Target` property for this `GCHandle` will return `null`. This can be useful for implementing advanced forms of caching, among other things.

- `GCHandleType.WeakTrackResurrection`: This mode is very similar to the first mode, the only difference being if the object is resurrected then the handle will be reset to point to the object. The way an object can be resurrected is if from its finalizer it causes new references to be created that keep it alive. An example of this is setting a static variable to "this" from inside the finalizer.

Regardless of the type of `GCHandle` used, it's essential to properly free the `GCHandle` once done with it. Failure to do this will cause memory leaks that can be hard to track down.

Description

Use a `GCHandle` when an object reference is required to be accessible from unmanaged memory.

The `GCHandleType` enumeration describes the possible `GCHandle` types.

[*Note:* If the type of the `GCHandle` is `GCHandleType.Normal`, then it is an opaque handle, and the address of the object it references cannot be resolved through it.]

Example

```csharp
using System;
using System.Runtime.InteropServices;
using System.Text;

/// <summary>
/// Sample demonstrating the use of the GCHandle structure.
/// Use this structure to provide unmanaged code with access to managed objects.
/// </summary>
internal class GCHandleSample
{

    private static void Main()
    {
        StringBuilder    sb      = new StringBuilder();
        GCHandle         gch     = GCHandle.Alloc(sb);
```

```
        EnumWindowsProc ewproc = new EnumWindowsProc(EnumWindowsCallBack);

        try
        {

            if (!EnumWindows(ewproc, (IntPtr)gch))
            {
                Console.WriteLine("EnumWindows failed.");
            }

        }
        finally
        {

            if (gch.IsAllocated)
            {
                gch.Free();
            }

        }

        Console.WriteLine("List of current window handles:");
        Console.Write(sb);
        Console.WriteLine();
        Console.WriteLine();
        Console.WriteLine("Press Enter to continue");
        Console.ReadLine();
    }

    // The callback to use with EnumWindows.
    private static bool EnumWindowsCallBack(IntPtr hwnd, IntPtr lParam)
    {
        GCHandle     gch = (GCHandle)lParam;
        StringBuilder sb  = (StringBuilder)gch.Target;

        sb.AppendFormat("  0x{0}", ((int)hwnd).ToString("x8"));
        sb.Append("\n");
        return true;
    }

    // Managed definition for EnumWindowsProc to use with EnumWindows.
    private delegate bool EnumWindowsProc(IntPtr hwnd, IntPtr lParam);

    // Win32 method to enumerate all top-level windows by passing the handle of
    // each window to an application-defined callback.
    [DllImport("user32.dll", SetLastError=true)]
    private static extern bool EnumWindows(
        EnumWindowsProc lpEnumFunc, IntPtr lParam);

}
```

A
B
C
D
E
F
G
H
I
J
K
L
M
N
O
P
Q
R
S
T
U
V
W
X
Y
Z

GCHandle Structure

The output is

```
List of current window handles:
  0x008201ac
  0x0001005e
  0x006b04a4
  0x000105e2
  0x00380604
  0x004a05b2
  0x0047054e
  0x002705ce
  0x0057048c
  0x0001006e
  0x00010062
    [output truncated]
```

A
B
C
D
E
F
G
H
I
J
K
L
M
N
O
P
Q
R
S
T
U
V
W
X
Y
Z

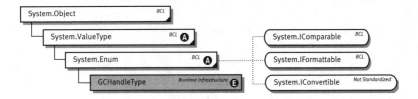

Summary

Represents the types of handles the GCHandle class can allocate.

Type Summary

```
public enum GCHandleType
   {
   Normal = 2,
   Pinned = 3,
MS Weak = 0,
MS WeakTrackResurrection = 1,
   }
```

Example

```csharp
using System;
using System.Runtime.InteropServices;

/// <summary>
/// Sample demonstrating the use of the GCHandleType enumeration.
/// Use this enumeration to specify the type of handle allocated by the
/// GCHandle class.
/// </summary>
internal class GCHandleTypeSample
{

    private static void Main()
    {
        DemoClass demo = new DemoClass();
        GCHandle  gch  =
            GCHandle.Alloc(demo, GCHandleType.WeakTrackResurrection);

        Console.WriteLine(
            "'gch' allocated for 'demo' (GCHandleType.WeakTrackResurrection)");
        // Enable resurrection and run the object's finalizer.
        demo.Resurrectable = true;
        demo = null;
        GC.Collect();
        GC.WaitForPendingFinalizers();
        demo = gch.Target as DemoClass;
```

```
                    if (demo == null)
                    {
                        Console.WriteLine("'gch' target lost after resurrection");
                    }
                    else
                    {
                        Console.WriteLine("'gch' target retained after resurrection");
                    }

                    Console.WriteLine();

                    gch = GCHandle.Alloc(demo, GCHandleType.Weak);

                    Console.WriteLine("'gch' allocated for 'demo' (GCHandleType.Weak)");
                    // Enable resurrection and run the object's finalizer.
                    demo.Resurrectable = true;
                    demo = null;
                    GC.Collect();
                    GC.WaitForPendingFinalizers();
                    demo = gch.Target as DemoClass;

                    if (demo == null)
                    {
                        Console.WriteLine("'gch' target lost after resurrection");
                    }
                    else
                    {
                        Console.WriteLine("'gch' target retained after resurrection");
                    }

                    Console.WriteLine();
                    Console.WriteLine();
                    Console.WriteLine("Press Enter to continue");
                    Console.ReadLine();
            }

    }

    internal class DemoClass
    {
        public bool Resurrectable = false;

        ~DemoClass()
        {
            Console.WriteLine("  Finalizing DemoClass");

            if (Resurrectable)
            {
                // Make sure that resurrection is turned off otherwise the object
                // will never be finalized.
                Resurrectable = false;
                Console.WriteLine("  Resurrecting DemoClass");
                GC.ReRegisterForFinalize(this);
            }

        }

    }
```

The output is

```
'gch' allocated for 'demo' (GCHandleType.WeakTrackResurrection)
  Finalizing DemoClass
  Resurrecting DemoClass
'gch' target retained after resurrection

'gch' allocated for 'demo' (GCHandleType.Weak)
  Finalizing DemoClass
  Resurrecting DemoClass
'gch' target lost after resurrection


Press Enter to continue
  Finalizing DemoClass
```

A
B
C
D
E
F
G
H
I
J
K
L
M
N
O
P
Q
R
S
T
U
V
W
X
Y
Z

A
B
C
D
E
F
G
H
I
J
K
L
M
N
O
P
Q
R
S
T
U
V
W
X
Y
Z

Summary

Contains a global default proxy instance for all HTTP requests.

Type Summary

```
public class GlobalProxySelection
    {
    // Constructors
    public GlobalProxySelection();

    // Properties
    public static IWebProxy Select { get; set; }

    // Methods
    public static IWebProxy GetEmptyWebProxy();
    }
```

> **■ LO**   Ugh, we'd all love to rename this class. You set the default proxy server for
> the application domain using `GlobalProxySelection.Select`.

Description

The `GlobalProxySelection` stores the proxy settings for the default proxy that `System.Net.WebRequest` instances use to contact Internet sites beyond the local network.
The default proxy settings are initialized from a global or application configuration file,
and can be overridden for individual requests, or disabled by setting the `HttpWebRequest.Proxy` property to the object returned by the `GlobalProxySelection.GetEmptyWebProxy` method.

The proxy settings stored in `GlobalProxySelection` are used by an `HttpWebRequest` instance if its `HttpWebRequest.Proxy` property is not set.

Example

```
using System;
using System.Net;


public class GlobalProxySelectionSample
```

```
{
  public static void Main()
  {
      Uri target = new Uri("http://microsoft.com");
      WebProxy wp = (WebProxy)GlobalProxySelection.Select;
    Uri defaultProxy = wp.Address;
    if (defaultProxy == null)
    {
      Console.WriteLine("No default proxy address found");
    }
    else
    {
      Console.WriteLine("Default proxy address is '{0}'",
                        defaultProxy);
    }
  }
}
```

The output is

```
Default proxy address is 'http://itgproxy/'
```

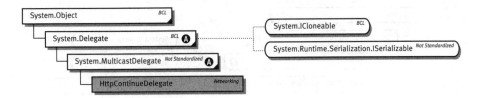

Summary

Defines the shape of methods that are invoked when an `HttpStatusCode.Continue` response is received by a web client.

Type Summary

```
public delegate void HttpContinueDelegate(int StatusCode,
                     WebHeaderCollection httpHeaders);
```

Parameters

Parameter	Description
StatusCode	A System.Int32 containing the numeric value of the HTTP status from the server.
httpHeaders	A System.Net.WebHeaderCollection containing the headers returned with the response.

Description

Use an `HttpContinueDelegate` instance to specify the methods that are automatically invoked whenever HTTP 100 (`HttpStatusCode.Continue`) responses are received from a web server.

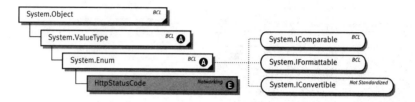

Summary

Contains the values of status codes defined for the Hypertext Transfer Protocol (HTTP).

Type Summary

```
public enum HttpStatusCode
    {
    Accepted = 202,
    Ambiguous = 300,
    BadGateway = 502,
    BadRequest = 400,
    Conflict = 409,
    Continue = 100,
    Created = 201,
    ExpectationFailed = 417,
    Forbidden = 403,
    Found = 302,
    GatewayTimeout = 504,
    Gone = 410,
    HttpVersionNotSupported = 505,
    InternalServerError = 500,
    LengthRequired = 411,
    MethodNotAllowed = 405,
    Moved = 301,
    MovedPermanently = 301,
    MultipleChoices = 300,
    NoContent = 204,
    NonAuthoritativeInformation = 203,
    NotAcceptable = 406,
    NotFound = 404,
    NotImplemented = 501,
    NotModified = 304,
    OK = 200,
    PartialContent = 206,
    PaymentRequired = 402,
    PreconditionFailed = 412,
    ProxyAuthenticationRequired = 407,
    Redirect = 302,
    RedirectKeepVerb = 307,
    RedirectMethod = 303,
    RequestedRangeNotSatisfiable = 416,
    RequestEntityTooLarge = 413,
    RequestTimeout = 408,
```

A
B
C
D
E
F
G
H
I
J
K
L
M
N
O
P
Q
R
S
T
U
V
W
X
Y
Z

```
        RequestUriTooLong = 414,
        ResetContent = 205,
        SeeOther = 303,
        ServiceUnavailable = 503,
        SwitchingProtocols = 101,
        TemporaryRedirect = 307,
        Unauthorized = 401,
        UnsupportedMediaType = 415,
        Unused = 306,
        UseProxy = 305,
    }
```

Description

This enumeration is used by HttpWebResponse.

[*Note:* The HttpStatusCode enumeration contains the values of the status codes defined in IETF RFC 2616 - HTTP/1.1. The status of an HTTP request is contained in the HttpWebResponse.StatusCode property.]

Example

Example 1
The following example compares the status returned by an HttpWebResponse with an HttpStatusCode value to determine the status of the response.

```
using System;
using System.Net;

public class HttpStatusCodeExample
{

    public static void Main()
    {
        string serverName = "http://www.contoso.com";
        HttpWebRequest httpReq = (HttpWebRequest) WebRequest.Create(serverName);
        httpReq.AllowAutoRedirect = false;
        HttpWebResponse httpRes = (HttpWebResponse) httpReq.GetResponse();
        if (httpRes.StatusCode==HttpStatusCode.Found)
        {
            Console.WriteLine("Request for {0} was redirected.", serverName);
        }
    }
}
```

The output is

```
Request for http://www.contoso.com was redirected.
```

A
B
C
D
E
F
G
H
I
J
K
L
M
N
O
P
Q
R
S
T
U
V
W
X
Y
Z

Example 2

```
using System;
using System.Net;


public class HttpStatusCodeSample
{
    public static void Main()
    {
        HttpWebRequest req = (HttpWebRequest)
            WebRequest.Create("http://microsoft.com");
        HttpWebResponse result = (HttpWebResponse)req.GetResponse();
        Console.WriteLine("HttpWebResponse.StatusCode = {0}",
            result.StatusCode);
    }
}
```

The output is

```
HttpWebResponse.StatusCode = OK
```

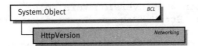

Summary
Defines the HTTP version numbers supported by `HttpWebRequest` and `HttpWeb-Response`.

Type Summary

```
public class HttpVersion
{
// Constructors
    public HttpVersion();

// Fields
    public static readonly Version Version10 = 1.0;
    public static readonly Version Version11 = 1.1;
}
```

> **■ BA** It's pretty odd to have a constructor in this class, isn't it? The truth is we never meant for the class to be created. If you look at the source code in ROTOR you can see that the developer never explicitly put a constructor in this source. The C# compiler added one implicitly. While this language feature may be a good thing for application developers, it is bad for library developers. This is why we have a guideline that all types should explicitly have a constructor, and in this case it should have been a private one. Also note that in C# 2.0, we added "static classes" that avoid this problem.

Description

[*Note:* This class defines the HTTP versions supported by `HttpWebRequest` and `Http-WebResponse`. The HTTP version number is used to control version-specific features of HTTP, such as pipelining and chunking.]

Example

```
using System;
using System.Net;

public class HttpVersionSample
{
    public static void Main()
```

HttpVersion Class

```
        {
            ShowAllVersions();
            HttpWebRequest req = (HttpWebRequest)
                WebRequest.Create("http://www.microsoft.com/");
            req.ProtocolVersion = HttpVersion.Version10;
            Console.WriteLine("HttpWebRequest.ProtocolVersion set "
                + "to HttpVersion.Version10");
            HttpWebResponse result = (HttpWebResponse)req.GetResponse();
            Console.WriteLine("HttpWebResponse.ProtocolVersion is {0}",
                result.ProtocolVersion);
            Console.WriteLine();
            Console.WriteLine();
            Console.WriteLine("Press Enter to continue");
            Console.ReadLine();
        }

        public static void ShowAllVersions()
        {
            Version ver = HttpVersion.Version10;
            Console.WriteLine("HttpVersion.Version10.Major = {0}",
                ver.Major);
            Console.WriteLine("HttpVersion.Version10.Minor = {0}",
                ver.Minor);
            Console.WriteLine("HttpVersion.Version10.Build = {0}",
                ver.Build);
            Console.WriteLine("HttpVersion.Version10.Revision = {0}",
                ver.Revision);
            ver = HttpVersion.Version11;
            Console.WriteLine("HttpVersion.Version11.Major = {0}",
                ver.Major);
            Console.WriteLine("HttpVersion.Version11.Minor = {0}",
                ver.Minor);
            Console.WriteLine("HttpVersion.Version11.Build = {0}",
                ver.Build);
            Console.WriteLine("HttpVersion.Version11.Revision = {0}",
                ver.Revision);
            Console.WriteLine();
        }

    }
```

The output is

```
HttpVersion.Version10.Major = 1
HttpVersion.Version10.Minor = 0
HttpVersion.Version10.Build = -1
HttpVersion.Version10.Revision = -1
HttpVersion.Version11.Major = 1
HttpVersion.Version11.Minor = 1
HttpVersion.Version11.Build = -1
HttpVersion.Version11.Revision = -1

HttpWebRequest.ProtocolVersion set to HttpVersion.Version10
HttpWebResponse.ProtocolVersion is 1.1


Press Enter to continue
```

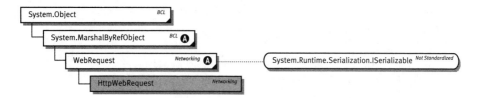

Summary

Provides an HTTP-specific implementation of the WebRequest class.

Type Summary

```
public class HttpWebRequest : WebRequest, ISerializable
   {
   // Constructors
MS CF protected HttpWebRequest(SerializationInfo serializationInfo,
               StreamingContext streamingContext);

   // Properties
      public string Accept { get; set; }
      public Uri Address { get; }
      public bool AllowAutoRedirect { get; set; }
      public bool AllowWriteStreamBuffering { get; set; }
MS CF public X509CertificateCollection ClientCertificates { get; }
      public string Connection { get; set; }
   CF public override string ConnectionGroupName { get; set; }
      public override long ContentLength {get; set; }
      public override string ContentType { get; set; }
      public HttpContinueDelegate ContinueDelegate { get; set; }
MS CF public CookieContainer CookieContainer { get; set; }
      public override ICredentials Credentials { get; set; }
MS CF 1.1 public static int DefaultMaximumResponseHeadersLength { get; set; }
      public string Expect { get; set; }
      public bool HaveResponse { get; }
      public override WebHeaderCollection Headers { get; set; }
      public DateTime IfModifiedSince { get; set; }
      public bool KeepAlive { get; set; }
      public int MaximumAutomaticRedirections { get; set; }
MS CF 1.1 public int MaximumResponseHeadersLength { get; set; }
      public string MediaType { get; set; }
      public override string Method { get; set; }
      public bool Pipelined { get; set; }
      public override bool PreAuthenticate { get; set; }
      public Version ProtocolVersion { get; set; }
      public override IWebProxy Proxy { get; set; }
MS CF 1.1 public int ReadWriteTimeout { get; set; }
      public string Referer { get; set; }
      public override Uri RequestUri { get; }
      public bool SendChunked { get; set; }
      public ServicePoint ServicePoint { get; }
```

HttpWebRequest Class

```
            public override int Timeout { get; set; }
            public string TransferEncoding { get; set; }
MS CF 1.1   public bool UnsafeAuthenticatedConnectionSharing { get; set; }
            public string UserAgent { get; set; }

        // Methods
            public override void Abort();
            public void AddRange(int range);
            public void AddRange(int from, int to);
            public void AddRange(string rangeSpecifier, int range);
            public void AddRange(string rangeSpecifier, int from, int to);
            public override IAsyncResult BeginGetRequestStream(
                                    AsyncCallback callback,
                                    object state);
            public override IAsyncResult BeginGetResponse(AsyncCallback callback,
                                    object state);
            public override Stream EndGetRequestStream(IAsyncResult asyncResult);
            public override WebResponse EndGetResponse(IAsyncResult asyncResult);
 CF         public override int GetHashCode();
            public override Stream GetRequestStream();
            public override WebResponse GetResponse();

        // Explicit Interface Members
MS CF   void ISerializable.GetObjectData(
                SerializationInfo serializationInfo,
                StreamingContext streamingContext);
    }
```

> ▪▪ **LO**   We've gone through years of debate over whether or not `HttpWebRequest` should have a public constructor. The original intention was to make it so that everyone goes through the `WebRequest.Create` mechanism so that `Create` can be used reliably as an interception mechanism. In hindsight, many developers have indicated they'd like to have the option of constructing the class directly. It is likely that we'll put a public constructor in a future version.

> ▪▪ **LO**   Note, in the future there will be an overload for `AddRange` that takes a long. In the meantime, don't request a range that is above 2 GB.

> ▪▪ **LO**   The history on `UnsafeAuthenticationConnectionSharing`: In the beginning of `HttpWebRequest`, it reused connections to the server whenever it could. We then discovered in the betas that because some Web servers cached NTLM connections it was possible—and in fact probable—that a client impersonating different accounts and using NTLM authentication could end up hitting the back end server using a connection that had been authenticated using a different set of credentials from the ones belonging to the currently impersonated client. To mitigate against this, `HttpWebRequest` was changed to close NTLM authenticated connections after use.

> *CONTINUED*

However, clients who weren't doing impersonation or who were aware of this issue and were using `ConnectionGroupName` to mitigate it didn't have a way to reuse the connection and performance suffered. `UnsafeAuthenticatedConnection-Sharing` was introduced as a result. It gives the developer a bit to flip to get back the performance wins of caching NTLM authenticated connections.

Description

This class implements properties and methods defined in `WebRequest` and provides additional properties and methods that enable the user to interact directly with servers using the Hypertext Transfer Protocol (HTTP).

[*Note:* Instances of this class are automatically created by the `WebRequest` class. For example, an instance of `HttpWebRequest` is created when the `WebRequest.Create` method is called and a Uniform Resource Identifier (URI) beginning with `http://` is specified. It is expected that an instance of this class will be constructed for every request made to the server. For example, after a call to `Abort` cancels an asynchronous operation, a call to `GetRequestStream` causes a `WebException` to be thrown. Requests can be sent synchronously or asynchronously. The `GetResponse` method sends a request to a server synchronously and returns an `HttpWebResponse` instance containing the response. An asynchronous request for a resource is sent using the `BeginGetResponse` and `EndGetResponse` methods. Request data is sent using a request stream. The `GetRequestStream`, `BeginGetRequestStream`, and `EndGetRequestStream` methods return a `System.IO.Stream` instance used to send data. When errors occur while accessing an Internet resource, the `HttpWebRequest` class throws a `WebException`, and the `WebException.Status` property that indicates the source of the error. When `WebException.Status` is `WebExceptionStatus.ProtocolError`, the `WebException.Response` property contains the `HttpWebResponse` received from the Internet resource. Certain HTTP headers are protected; the user cannot set them directly in the header collection obtained from the `Headers` property. Instead, these headers are set using the associated properties of an `HttpWebRequest` instance, or are set by the system.

Example

```
using System;
using System.Net;
using System.IO;
using System.Threading;

public class HttpWebRequestSample
{
    public static void Main()
    {
        try
```

```
        {
            String target = "http://www.microsoft.com/";
            HttpWebRequest req = (HttpWebRequest)
                WebRequest.Create(target);
            req.Method = "GET";
            req.UserAgent = "Custom (my own sample code)";
            req.Headers.Add("WINDOW-TARGET", "my-window");
            req.Referer = "http://yoursite.com/yourpage.htm";
            req.Timeout = 2000;
            Console.WriteLine("HttpWebRequest.ContentLength = {0}",
                req.ContentLength);
            IAsyncResult ar = req.BeginGetResponse(
                new AsyncCallback(GetResponseHandler), req);
            while (!bDone)
            {
                Thread.Sleep(500);
            }
        }
        catch (Exception e)
        {
            Console.WriteLine("*ERROR: " + e.Message);
        }
        Console.WriteLine();
        Console.WriteLine();
        Console.WriteLine("Press Enter to continue");
        Console.ReadLine();
    }

    private static Boolean bDone = false;

    private static void GetResponseHandler(IAsyncResult ar)
    {
      try
      {
        HttpWebRequest req = (HttpWebRequest)ar.AsyncState;
        HttpWebResponse result = (HttpWebResponse)
                                    req.EndGetResponse(ar);
        Console.WriteLine("HttpWebResponse.StatusCode = {0}",
                        result.StatusCode.ToString());
        StreamReader reader = new
                    StreamReader(result.GetResponseStream());
        Console.WriteLine("Contents of the returned page:");
        Console.WriteLine(reader.ReadToEnd());
        reader.Close();
        result.Close();
      }
      catch (Exception e)
      {
        Console.WriteLine("*ERROR: " + e.Message);
      }
      finally
      {
        bDone = true;
      }
    }
  }
}
```

The output is

```
HttpWebRequest.ContentLength = -1
HttpWebResponse.StatusCode = OK
Contents of the returned page:
<!DOCTYPE HTML PUBLIC "-//W3C//DTD HTML 4.0 Transitional//EN" ><html><head><META
 http-equiv="Content-Type" content="text/html; charset=utf-8"><!--TOOLBAR_EXEMPT
--><meta http-equiv="PICS-Label" content="(PICS-1.1 &quot;http://www.rsac.org/ra
tingsv01.html&quot; l gen true r (n 0 s 0 v 0 l 0))"><meta name="KEYWORDS" conte
nt="products; headlines; downloads; news; Web site; what's new; solutions; servi
ces; software; contests; corporate news;"><meta name="DESCRIPTION" content="The
entry page to Microsoft's Web site. Find software, solutions, answers, support,
and Microsoft news."><meta name="MS.LOCALE" content="EN-US"><meta name="CATEGORY
" content="home page"><title>Microsoft Corporation</title><style type="text/css"
 media="all">@import "/h/en-us/r/hp.css";</style><script type="text/javascript"
    [output truncated]
```

A
B
C
D
E
F
G
H
I
J
K
L
M
N
O
P
Q
R
S
T
U
V
W
X
Y
Z

Summary

Provides an HTTP-specific implementation of the `WebResponse` class.

Type Summary

```
public class HttpWebResponse : WebResponse, ISerializable, IDisposable
   {

   // Constructors
MS CF protected HttpWebResponse(SerializationInfo serializationInfo,
                StreamingContext streamingContext);

   // Properties
      public string CharacterSet { get; }
      public string ContentEncoding { get; }
      public override long ContentLength { get; }
      public override string ContentType { get; }
MS CF public CookieCollection Cookies { get; set; }
      public override WebHeaderCollection Headers { get; }
      public DateTime LastModified { get; }
      public string Method { get; }
      public Version ProtocolVersion { get; }
      public override Uri ResponseUri { get; }
      public string Server { get; }
      public HttpStatusCode StatusCode { get; }
      public string StatusDescription { get; }

   // Methods
      public override void Close();
 CF protected virtual void Dispose(bool disposing);
 CF public override int GetHashCode();
      public string GetResponseHeader(string headerName);
      public override Stream GetResponseStream();

   // Explicit Interface Members
MS CF void ISerializable.GetObjectData(SerializationInfo serializationInfo,
             StreamingContext streamingContext);
MS CF void IDisposable.Dispose();
   }
```

> **■ JM**   There was a relatively big debate within the ECMA committee regarding strong typing. Notice the Method property. It returns a string. In reality, it does return a well-defined set of HTTP protocols (e.g., GET, POST, etc.). So why didn't it return an enum with these protocols defined? Well, the adage of extensibility and "user-customization" possibilities won out here, even though there was strong support within committee for strong typing—practice won over design again.
>
> **■ CM**   It's very easy to forget to use the Close Method. The Response or ResponseStream must always be closed when you're done with the response. Failure to do this can either cause hangs or slow down your application dramatically.

Description

[*Note:* The HttpWebResponse class contains support for the properties and methods included in WebResponse with additional elements that enable the user to interact directly with the Hypertext Transfer Protocol (HTTP). Expected usage is that instances of this class are not created directly but are obtained by calling HttpWebRequest.Get-Response. To obtain the response from the Internet resource as a System.IO.Stream, call the HttpWebResponse.GetResponseStream method. Certain HTTP headers are protected such that the user cannot set them directly in the header collection. Instead, these headers can be set via the properties of the HttpWebRequest class or are set by the system.

Example

```
using System;
using System.Net;
using System.IO;

public class HttpWebResponseSample
{
    public static void Main()
    {
        try
        {
            String target = "http://www.microsoft.com/";
            HttpWebRequest req = (HttpWebRequest)
                WebRequest.Create(target);
            HttpWebResponse result = (HttpWebResponse)req.GetResponse();
            Console.WriteLine("HttpWebResponse.StatusCode = {0}",
                result.StatusCode);
            Console.WriteLine("HttpWebResponse.StatusDescription = {0}",
                result.StatusDescription);
            Console.WriteLine("HttpWebResponse.ContentEncoding = {0}",
                result.ContentEncoding);
            Console.WriteLine("HttpWebResponse.ContentLength = {0}",
```

A
B
C
D
E
F
G
H
I
J
K
L
M
N
O
P
Q
R
S
T
U
V
W
X
Y
Z

HttpWebResponse Class

```
                    result.ContentLength.ToString());
                Console.WriteLine("HttpWebResponse.ContentType = '{0}'",
                    result.ContentType);
                Console.WriteLine("HttpWebResponse.LastModified = {0}\n",
                    result.LastModified);
                StreamReader reader = new
                    StreamReader(result.GetResponseStream());
                Console.WriteLine("Contents of the returned page:");
                Console.WriteLine(reader.ReadToEnd());
                reader.Close();
                result.Close();
            }
            catch (Exception e)
            {
                Console.WriteLine("*ERROR: " + e.Message);
            }
            Console.WriteLine();
            Console.WriteLine();
            Console.WriteLine("Press Enter to continue");
            Console.ReadLine();
        }
    }
```

The output is

```
HttpWebResponse.StatusCode = OK
HttpWebResponse.StatusDescription = OK
HttpWebResponse.ContentEncoding =
HttpWebResponse.ContentLength = 16843
HttpWebResponse.ContentType = 'text/html'
HttpWebResponse.LastModified = 2/13/2005 8:33:36 AM

Contents of the returned page:
<!DOCTYPE HTML PUBLIC "-//W3C//DTD HTML 4.0 Transitional//EN" ><html><head><META
 http-equiv="Content-Type" content="text/html; charset=utf-8"><!--TOOLBAR_EXEMPT
--><meta http-equiv="PICS-Label" content="(PICS-1.1 &quot;http://www.rsac.org/ra
tingsv01.html&quot; l gen true r (n 0 s 0 v 0 l 0))"><meta name="KEYWORDS" conte
nt="products; headlines; downloads; news; Web site; what's new; solutions; servi
ces; software; contests; corporate news;"><meta name="DESCRIPTION" content="The
entry page to Microsoft's Web site. Find software, solutions, answers, support,
and Microsoft news."><meta name="MS.LOCALE" content="EN-US"><meta name="CATEGORY
" content="home page"><title>Microsoft Corporation</title><style type="text/css"
 media="all">@import "/h/en-us/r/hp.css";</style><script type="text/javascript"
    [output truncated]
```

System.Net
IAuthenticationModule Interface

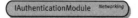

Summary

Implemented by types that perform client authentication.

Type Summary

```
public interface IAuthenticationModule
    {
    // Properties
        string AuthenticationType { get; }
        bool CanPreAuthenticate { get; }

    // Methods
        Authorization Authenticate(string challenge, WebRequest request,
                    ICredentials credentials);
        Authorization PreAuthenticate(WebRequest request,
                    ICredentials credentials);
    }
```

Description

The IAuthenticationModule interface defines the properties and methods that types are required to implement to handle client authentication. Types that implement this interface are called authentication modules. In addition to implementing this interface, an authentication module implements an authentication protocol, such as the Kerberos protocol. The IAuthenticationModule.AuthenticationType property value is a case-insensitive string that typically indicates the protocol implemented by the module. Each authentication module registered with the authentication manager is required to have a unique IAuthenticationModule.AuthenticationType. The following string values are reserved for use by modules implementing the indicated protocols:

AuthenticationType	Protocol
"basic"	Basic as defined by IETF RFC 2617
"digest"	Digest access as defined by IETF RFC 2617
"kerberos"	Kerberos as defined by IETF RFC 1510

A
B
C
D
E
F
G
H
I
J
K
L
M
N
O
P
Q
R
S
T
U
V
W
X
Y
Z

IAuthenticationModule Interface

[*Note:* Authentication modules are registered with the authentication manager (AuthenticationManager) by calling the AuthenticationManager.Register method. When the authentication manager receives an authentication request, registered authentication modules are given the opportunity to handle the authentication in their Authenticate method. Similarly, when a client wishes to avoid waiting for the server to request authentication, it can request preauthentication information to send with a request. If the CanPreAuthenticate property of a registered module returns true, it is among the modules that are given the opportunity to provide the preauthentication information via the PreAuthenticate method. Not all modules receive all authentication and preauthentication requests. The authentication manager searches for an authentication module by invoking the Authenticate or PreAuthenticate method of each registered module in the order in which it was registered. Once a module returns an Authorization instance, indicating that it handles the authentication, the authentication manager terminates the search.]

Example

```
using System;
using System.Net;
using System.Collections;

public class IAuthenticationModuleSample
{
    public static void Main()
    {
        IEnumerator rm = AuthenticationManager.RegisteredModules;
        Console.WriteLine("Authentication.RegisteredModules returned:");
        while(rm.MoveNext())
        {
            Console.WriteLine("Module '{0}'", rm.Current);
            IAuthenticationModule cm = (IAuthenticationModule) rm.Current;

            if (cm.CanPreAuthenticate == true
                && cm.AuthenticationType == "Basic")
            {
                String target = "http://localhost/";
                HttpWebRequest req = (HttpWebRequest)
                    WebRequest.Create(target);
                NetworkCredential nc = new NetworkCredential("username",
                    "password", "domain");
                Authorization preauth = cm.PreAuthenticate(req, nc);
                Console.WriteLine("PreAuthentication result = '{0}'",
                    preauth.Message);
            }

            if (cm.AuthenticationType == "Basic")
            {
                String challenge = "testchallenge";
                String target = "http://localhost/";
                HttpWebRequest req = (HttpWebRequest)
```

```
            WebRequest.Create(target);
        NetworkCredential nc = new NetworkCredential("username",
            "password", "domain");
        Authorization auth = cm.Authenticate(challenge, req, nc);
        if (auth == null)
        {
            Console.WriteLine("Authentication failed");
        }
        else
        {
            Console.WriteLine("Authentication result = '{0}'",
                auth.Message);
        }
        }
    }
    Console.WriteLine();
    Console.WriteLine();
    Console.WriteLine("Press Enter to continue");
    Console.ReadLine();
    }
}
```

The output is

```
Authentication.RegisteredModules returned:
Module 'System.Net.DigestClient'
Module 'System.Net.NegotiateClient'
Module 'System.Net.KerberosClient'
Module 'System.Net.NtlmClient'
Module 'System.Net.BasicClient'
PreAuthentication result = 'Basic ZG9tYWluXHVzZXJuYW1lOnBhc3N3b3Jk'
Authentication failed


Press Enter to continue
```

A
B
C
D
E
F
G
H
I
J
K
L
M
N
O
P
Q
R
S
T
U
V
W
X
Y
Z

A
B
C
D
E
F
G
H
I
J
K
L
M
N
O
P
Q
R
S
T
U
V
W
X
Y
Z

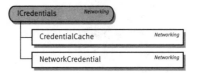

Summary

Implemented by types that supply network credentials used to authenticate clients.

Type Summary

```
public interface ICredentials
    {
    // Methods
        NetworkCredential GetCredential(Uri uri, string authType);
    }
```

Description

The ICredentials interface defines the GetCredential method, which is used to supply network credentials for client authentication.

Example

```
using System;
using System.Net;


public class ICredentialsSample
{
    public static void Main()
    {
        NetworkCredential nc = new NetworkCredential("test", "secret");
        Uri path = new Uri("http://mysite.com");
        CredentialCache cc = new CredentialCache();
        cc.Add(path, "BASIC", nc);
        ICredentials ic = (ICredentials) cc;
        NetworkCredential found =
            ic.GetCredential(path, "BASIC");
        Console.WriteLine("CredentialCache contains:");
        Console.WriteLine("UserName:'{0}' Password:'{1}'",
            found.UserName, found.Password);
        Console.WriteLine();
        Console.WriteLine();
        Console.WriteLine("Press Enter to continue");
        Console.ReadLine();
    }
}
```

The output is

```
CredentialCache contains:
UserName:'test' Password:'secret'


Press Enter to continue
```

A
B
C
D
E
F
G
H
I
J
K
L
M
N
O
P
Q
R
S
T
U
V
W
X
Y
Z

```
System.Object                                    BCL
    System.Attribute                             BCL  A
        InAttribute                    Runtime Infrastructure
```

Summary

Indicates that a parameter will be marshaled from the caller to the callee.

Type Summary

```
public sealed class InAttribute : Attribute
    {
    // Constructors
        public InAttribute();
    }
```

> **■ AN**   What is confusing with both `InAttribute` and `OutAttribute` is that you can only use them to override default behavior for non-blittable types—types whose memory representation isn't identical in the managed and unmanaged worlds. That is because the CLR doesn't copy blittable types back and forth; it just hands out direct pointers as a performance optimization. So, marking a by-ref integer as "in-only" or "out-only" does nothing, but marking a by-ref `DateTime` this way does what you would expect. The bad thing about these performance optimizations for blittable types is that it is not transparent to your code. It muddles the rules for when these attributes have meaning, and it prevents the CLR from making further such optimizations without potentially breaking user code.
>
> **■ BG**   See my comments on `OutAttribute`.

Description

[*Note:* The `InAttribute` and `OutAttribute` are not required. In the absence of explicit settings, the system assumes that all arguments passed by reference are passed in/out and that all non-reference parameters are in. The only exception is the `System.Text.StringBuilder` class, which is always assumed to be in/out. The `InAttribute` and `OutAttribute` are particularly useful when applied to formatted types that cannot be block-copied. Since these types require copying during marshaling, you can use `InAttribute` and `OutAttribute` to eliminate the generation of unnecessary copies.]

Compilers are required to not preserve this type in metadata as a custom attribute. Instead, compilers are required to emit it directly in the file format, as described in Partition II of the CLI Specification. Metadata consumers, such as the Reflection API, are required to retrieve this data from the file format and return it as if it were a custom attribute.

Example

```
using System;
using System.Runtime.InteropServices;

/// <summary>
/// Sample demonstrating the use of the InAttribute class.
/// Use this class to indicate how parameters should be marshalled to unmanaged
/// code.
/// </summary>
internal class InAttributeSample
{

    private static void Main()
    {
        // Get the ProgId for InAttribute.
        Guid inGuid = typeof(InAttribute).GUID;

        Console.WriteLine(
            "InAttribute ProgId: {0}", ProgIDFromCLSID(ref inGuid));
        Console.WriteLine();
        Console.WriteLine();
        Console.WriteLine("Press Enter to continue");
        Console.ReadLine();
    }

    // Win32 method to retrieve the ProgId for a given CLSID. The ref keyword
    // means [in,out], so [In] is used to override the normal marshalling. Note
    // that PreserveSig is used to transform the final [out] parameter into a
    // return value and the HRESULT into an exception if the call fails.
    [DllImport("ole32.dll", CharSet=CharSet.Unicode, PreserveSig=false)]
    private static extern string ProgIDFromCLSID([In]ref Guid clsid);

}
```

The output is

```
InAttribute ProgId: System.Runtime.InteropServices.InAttribute


Press Enter to continue
```

Summary

An implementation-specific type that is used to represent a pointer or a handle.

Type Summary

```
public struct IntPtr : ISerializable
{
    // Constructors
    public IntPtr(int value);
    public IntPtr(long value);
MS  public unsafe IntPtr(void* value);

    // Fields
    public static readonly IntPtr Zero = 0;

    // Properties
    public static int Size { get; }

    // Methods
    public override bool Equals(object obj);
    public override int GetHashCode();
    public int ToInt32();
    public long ToInt64();
    public unsafe void* ToPointer();
    public override string ToString();
    public static bool operator ==(IntPtr value1, IntPtr value2);
    public static bool operator !=(IntPtr value1, IntPtr value2);
MS  public static explicit operator int(IntPtr value);
MS  public static explicit operator IntPtr(int value);
MS  public static explicit operator IntPtr(long value);
MS  public unsafe static explicit operator IntPtr(void* value);
MS  public static explicit operator long(IntPtr value);
MS  public unsafe static explicit operator void*(IntPtr value);

    // Explicit Interface Members
MS CF void ISerializable.GetObjectData(SerializationInfo info,
        StreamingContext context);
}
```

■ **BA**   We spent a fair amount of time arguing about what to name this type. In the end, we decided it was better to follow the pattern we established with Int16, Int32, and Int64, that is Int*Size*. In this case *Size* is the size of a pointer, which is 32 on a 32-bit machine and 64 on a 64-bit machine.

■ **BA**   Even though it has a custom signature like Int32 and Double, it is fair to say that `IntPtr` is not a first class base datatype. Many programming languages such as C# and VB.Net do not support literals of type `IntPtr`, nor do they support arithmetic operations even though such operations are supported in the IL instruction set. In addition, some areas of the runtime don't support `IntPtr`. For example it cannot be used for the underlying type of an enum. I think this is a reasonable design decision, even in light of the transition to 64-bit computing, because it turns out `IntPtr` is not a good replacement for `Int32` in most cases as many programs do need to know the size of the data type they are working with.

■ **BA**   `IntPtr` is a super common type for interop scenarios, but is not used very frequently outside of interop. As such it would have been better to have this type in the `System.Runtime.InteropServices` namespace.

■ **JP**   While common for interop scenarios, `IntPtr` also gets a fair workout in the code generation (`Reflection.Emit` and the new Lightweight Code Generation [LCG] APIs in CLR 2.0) namespaces. We can use it to represent things like method code pointers for IL instructions like "calli". You can call `RuntimeMethodHandle.Get-Function Pointer()` which will hand you back a `System.IntPtr`.

It's also found under the hood of the delegate type implementation.

■ **AN**   When you use `IntPtr` to represent an operating system handle (HWND, HKEY, HDC, etc.), it's far too easy to be vulnerable to leaks, lifetime issues, or handle recycling attacks. The .NET Framework's `System.Runtime.InteropServices.HandleRef` class can be used in place of `IntPtr` to address lifetime issues; it guarantees that the managed object wrapping the handle won't be collected until the call to unmanaged code finishes. But to help you battle all three issues, look for a new type to be added to the .NET Framework in the future called `SafeHandle`. Once this is available, it should be used wherever you used `IntPtr` or `HandleRef` to represent a handle.

CONTINUED

A
B
C
D
E
F
G
H
I
J
K
L
M
N
O
P
Q
R
S
T
U
V
W
X
Y
Z

System

> **■■ BG**   `IntPtr` is of course the bare minimum type you need to represent handles in PInvoke calls because it is the correct size to represent a handle on all platforms, but it isn't what you want for a number of subtle reasons. We came up with two hacky versions of handle wrappers in our first version (`HandleRef` and the not-publicly exposed `HandleProtector` class), but they were horribly incomplete and limited. I've long wanted a formal OS Handle type of some sort, and we finally designed one in our version 2 release called `SafeHandle`.
>
> Another interesting point is a subtle race condition that can occur when you have a type that uses a handle and provides a finalizer. If you have a method that uses the handle in a PInvoke call and never references `this` after the PInvoke call, then the `this` pointer may be considered dead by our GC. If a garbage collection occurs while you are blocked in that PInvoke call (such as a call to `ReadFile` on a socket or a file), the GC could detect the object was dead, then run the finalizer on the finalizer thread. You'll get unexpected results if your handle is closed while you're also trying to use it at the same time, and these races will only get worse if we add multiple finalizer threads. To work around this problem, you can stick calls to `GC.KeepAlive(this);` in your code after your PInvoke call, or you could use `HandleRef` to wrap your handle and the `this` pointer.
>
> Of course, the `SafeHandle` class (added in version 2) solves this problem and five others, most of which can't be fully appreciated without understanding thread aborts and our reliability story. See my comments on the `AppDomain` class for more details.

Description

The `IntPtr` type is designed to be an implementation-sized pointer. An instance of this type is expected to be the size of a `native int` for the current implementation.

For more information on the `native int` type, see Partition II of the CLI Specification.

[*Note:* The `IntPtr` type provides CLS-compliant pointer functionality. `IntPtr` instances can also be used to hold handles. The `IntPtr` type is CLS-compliant while the `UIntPtr` type is not. The `UIntPtr` type is provided mostly to maintain architectural symmetry with the `IntPtr` type.]

Example

```
using System;

public class IntPtrSample
{
```

```
public static void Main()
{
    Int32 i1 = 2000000000;
    Int32 i2 = 2000000000;
    Int32 i3 = 0;
    IntPtr ip1 = new IntPtr(i1);
    IntPtr ip2 = new IntPtr(i2);
    IntPtr ip3 = new IntPtr(i3);
    Console.WriteLine("IntPtr.Size = {0} bytes",
        IntPtr.Size);
    Console.WriteLine("IntPtr(2000000000).Equals(IntPtr(2000000000) ? {0}",
        ip1.Equals(ip2));
    Console.WriteLine("IntPtr(2000000000).Equals(IntPtr(0) ? {0}",
        ip1.Equals(ip3));
    Console.WriteLine("IntPtr(2000000000) == (IntPtr(2000000000) ? {0}",
        (ip1 == ip2));
    Console.WriteLine("IntPtr(2000000000) == (IntPtr(0) ? {0}",
        (ip1 == ip3));
    Console.WriteLine("IntPtr(2000000000) == IntPtr.Zero ? {0}",
        (ip1 == IntPtr.Zero));
    Console.WriteLine("IntPtr(0) == IntPtr.Zero ? {0}",
        (ip3 == IntPtr.Zero));
    Console.WriteLine();
    Console.WriteLine();
    Console.WriteLine("Press Enter to continue");
    Console.ReadLine();
}
}
```

The output is

```
IntPtr.Size = 4 bytes
IntPtr(2000000000).Equals(IntPtr(2000000000) ? True
IntPtr(2000000000).Equals(IntPtr(0) ? False
IntPtr(2000000000) == (IntPtr(2000000000) ? True
IntPtr(2000000000) == (IntPtr(0) ? False
IntPtr(2000000000) == IntPtr.Zero ? False
IntPtr(0) == IntPtr.Zero ? True


Press Enter to continue
```

A
B
C
D
E
F
G
H
I
J
K
L
M
N
O
P
Q
R
S
T
U
V
W
X
Y
Z

A
B
C

Summary

D

Represents an Internet Protocol (IP) address.

E

F

Type Summary

G

```
      public class IPAddress
          {
          // Constructors
MS CF 1.1 public IPAddress(byte[] address);
MS CF 1.1 public IPAddress(byte[] address, long scopeid);
          public IPAddress(long newAddress);

          // Fields
          public static readonly IPAddress Any =
                              new IPAddress(0x0000000000000000);    //0.0.0.0
          public static readonly IPAddress Broadcast =
                              new IPAddress(0x00000000FFFFFFFF);   //255.255.255.255
MS CF 1.1 public static readonly IPAddress IPv6Any = new IPAddress(new
                  byte[]{0,0,0,0,0,0,0,0,0,0,0,0,0,0,0,0 },0); //0:0:0:0:0:0:0:0
MS CF 1.1 public static readonly IPAddress IPv6Loopback = new IPAddress(new
                  byte[]{0,0,0,0,0,0,0,0,0,0,0,0,0,0,0,1 },0);  //0:0:0:0:0:0:0:1
MS CF 1.1 public static readonly IPAddress IPv6None = new IPAddress(new
                  byte[]{0,0,0,0,0,0,0,0,0,0,0,0,0,0,0,0 },0);  //0:0:0:0:0:0:0:0
          public static readonly IPAddress Loopback = new
                                  IPAddress(0x000000000100007F); //127.0.0.1
          public static readonly IPAddress None = Broadcast;  //255.255.255.255

          // Properties
          public long Address { get; set; }
       CF public AddressFamily AddressFamily { get; }
MS CF 1.1 public long ScopeId { get; set; }

          // Methods
          public override bool Equals(object comparand);
MS CF 1.1 public byte[] GetAddressBytes();
          public override int GetHashCode();
          public static int HostToNetworkOrder(int host);
          public static long HostToNetworkOrder(long host);
          public static short HostToNetworkOrder(short host);
          public static bool IsLoopback(IPAddress address);
          public static int NetworkToHostOrder(int network);
          public static long NetworkToHostOrder(long network);
          public static short NetworkToHostOrder(short network);
          public static IPAddress Parse(string ipString);
          public override string ToString();
          }
```

H
I
J
K
L
M
N
O
P
Q
R
S
T
U
V
W
X
Y
Z

> ■ **CM**   Expect to see `IsIPv6Multicast`, `IsIPv6SiteLocal`, and `IsIPv6Link-Local` in v2.0 of the .NET Framework.

Description

An instance of the `IPAddress` class contains the value of an address on an IP network. This address is stored internally as a `System.Int64` in network-byte-order.

[*Note:* Different conventions are in use for ordering bytes within multi-byte data types. All IP address values must be sent over the network in network-byte-order. Network-byte-order puts the most significant byte first (also known as big-endian order). On the host, the ordering of bytes is platform-specific and this ordering is referred to as host-byte-order.]

The IP address can be represented as four numbers in the range 0–255 separated by periods (for example, `"192.168.1.2"`), known as dotted-quad notation.

[*Note:* The address space is fragmented into different types determined by bits 31–28 as shown in the following table.]

Instances of the `IPAddress` class are provided for common IP address values as shown in the following table.

Field	IP Address
Any	0.0.0.0
Broadcast	255.255.255.255
Loopback	127.0.0.1
None	255.255.255.255

Example

```
using System;
using System.Net;


public class IPAddressSample
{
    public static void Main()
    {
        IPAddress addr1 = IPAddress.Parse("10.0.0.1");
        Console.WriteLine("IPAddress = '{0}'",
            addr1);
        Console.WriteLine("IPAddress.AddressFamily = '{0}'",
```

```
                    addr1.AddressFamily);
        Console.WriteLine("IPAddress.IsLoopback(10.0.0.1) = '{0}'",
            IPAddress.IsLoopback(addr1));
        IPAddress addr2 = IPAddress.Loopback;
        Console.WriteLine("IPAddress.IsLoopback(127.0.0.1) = '{0}'",
            IPAddress.IsLoopback(addr2));
        Console.WriteLine("IPAddress.(10.0.0.1) == "
            + "IPAddress(127.0.0.1) ? = {0}",
            addr1.Equals(addr2));
        Console.WriteLine();
        Console.WriteLine();
        Console.WriteLine("Press Enter to continue");
        Console.ReadLine();
    }
}
```

The output is

```
IPAddress = '10.0.0.1'
IPAddress.AddressFamily = 'InterNetwork'
IPAddress.IsLoopback(10.0.0.1) = 'False'
IPAddress.IsLoopback(127.0.0.1) = 'True'
IPAddress.(10.0.0.1) == IPAddress(127.0.0.1) ? = False


Press Enter to continue
```

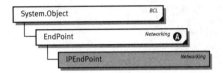

Summary

Represents a network endpoint as an Internet Protocol (IP) address and a port number.

Type Summary

```csharp
public class IPEndPoint : EndPoint
{
// Constructors
    public IPEndPoint(IPAddress address, int port);
    public IPEndPoint(long address, int port);

// Fields
    public const int MaxPort = 65535;
    public const int MinPort = 0;

// Properties
    public IPAddress Address { get; set; }
    public override AddressFamily AddressFamily { get; }
    public int Port { get; set; }

// Methods
    public override EndPoint Create(SocketAddress socketAddress);
    public override bool Equals(object comparand);
    public override int GetHashCode();
MS  public override SocketAddress Serialize();
    public override string ToString();
}
```

Description

The IPEndPoint class contains the IP address of a host system and the number of a port to access on the host. The IPEndPoint class represents a connection point used by the System.Net.Sockets.Socket class.

Example

```csharp
using System;
using System.Net;
using System.Net.Sockets;

public class IPEndPointSample
{
```

```
public static void Main()
{
    IPAddress addr = IPAddress.Parse("10.0.0.1");
    IPEndPoint ep = new IPEndPoint(addr, 80);
    Console.WriteLine("IPEndPoint(10.0.0.1, 80)"
        + ".AddressFamily = '{0}'",
        ep.AddressFamily);
    Console.WriteLine("Address = '{0}'",
        ep.Address);

    SocketAddress sktaddr = new
        SocketAddress(AddressFamily.InterNetwork);
    IPEndPoint newep = (IPEndPoint) ep.Create(sktaddr);
    Console.WriteLine("New IPEndPoint.AddressFamily = '{0}'",
        newep.AddressFamily);
    Console.WriteLine("New IPEndPoint.Address = '{0}'",
        newep.Address);
    Console.WriteLine();
    Console.WriteLine();
    Console.WriteLine("Press Enter to continue");
    Console.ReadLine();
}
}
```

The output is

```
IPEndPoint(10.0.0.1, 80).AddressFamily = 'InterNetwork'
Address = '10.0.0.1'
New IPEndPoint.AddressFamily = 'InterNetwork'
New IPEndPoint.Address = '0.0.0.0'


Press Enter to continue
```

Summary

Provides a container class for Internet host address information.

Type Summary

```csharp
public class IPHostEntry
{
// Constructors
   public IPHostEntry();

// Properties
   public IPAddress[] AddressList { get; set; }
   public string[] Aliases { get; set; }
   public string HostName { get; set; }
}
```

Description

The IPHostEntry class associates a Domain Name System (DNS) host name with an array of aliases and an array of matching IP addresses.

The IPHostEntry class is used as a helper class with the Dns class.

Example

```csharp
using System;
using System.Net;

public class IPHostEntrySample
{
    public static void Main()
    {
        String toFind = "microsoft.com";
        IPHostEntry host = Dns.Resolve(toFind);
        Console.WriteLine("HostName = '{0}'", host.HostName);
        foreach (IPAddress addr in host.AddressList)
        {
            Console.WriteLine("IPAddress = {0}", addr);
        }
        foreach (String alias in host.Aliases)
        {
            Console.WriteLine("Alias = {0}", alias);
        }
        Console.WriteLine();
```

```
            Console.WriteLine();
            Console.WriteLine("Press Enter to continue");
            Console.ReadLine();
        }
    }
```

The output is

```
HostName = 'microsoft.com'
IPAddress = 207.46.250.119
IPAddress = 207.46.130.108


Press Enter to continue
```

A
B
C
D
E
F
G
H
I
J
K
L
M
N
O
P
Q
R
S
T
U
V
W
X
Y
Z

```
System.Object                          BCL
        IsVolatile        Runtime Infrastructure
```

Summary

Marks a field as volatile.

Type Summary

```
CF public sealed class IsVolatile
   {
   }
```

■ RJ   The type `IsVolatile` is a required custom modifier type (`modreq`). Custom modifiers are similar to custom attributes except that modifiers are part of a signature rather than being attached to a declaration. Each modifier associates a type reference with an item in the signature. Two signatures that differ only by the addition of a custom modifier shall not be considered to match.

This custom modifier is used to indicate that a location in the memory store is "volatile." That is, that location is not owned completely by the executing thread; one or more other threads (or the hardware) could be accessing that location at the same time. Any compiler that imports metadata that describes a memory location as "volatile" is required to use the volatile prefixed instructions to access such locations. Examples of such locations are volatile fields, volatile targets of pointers, and volatile elements of arrays.

Consider the following C# code:

```
public class Test
{
        private volatile int count;
        public void ClearCount() { count = 0; }
}
```

The relevant MSIL generated is

```
.field private int32 modreq(
    [mscorlib]System.Runtime.CompilerServices.IsVolatile) count
```

CONTINUED

A
B
C
D
E
F
G
H
I
J
K
L
M
N
O
P
Q
R
S
T
U
V
W
X
Y
Z

```
.method public hidebysig instance void ClearCount() cil managed
{
  .maxstack 8
  ldarg.0
  ldc.i4.0
  volatile.
  stfld int32 modreq([mscorlib]System.Runtime.CompilerServices.IsVolatile)
     Test::count
  ret
}
```

This type is not intended to be used directly by programmers, but rather, by compiler writers, based on the programmer's use of some language syntax (such as the keyword volatile in C# and C++).

C++/CLI provides more interesting uses of this modifier by allowing pointers to volatile objects; for example:

```
public class Test
{
      volatile int* pvi;
      public:
      int* M(int* pvi) { /* … */ }
      volatile int* M(volatile int* pvi) { /* … */ }
}
```

Even though both versions of method M take and return a pointer to int, the overload is permitted as the presence of the required modifier in one signature differentiates it from that without.

Note that the CLS does not allow publicly visible required modifiers.

Description

IsVolatile is a class used only in custom modifiers of method signatures to indicate that the field it marks is "volatile". Any compiler that imports metadata with one or more fields marked as "volatile" is required to use volatile. prefixed instructions to access such fields.

[*Note:* For most languages, it is recommended that the notion of "volatile" be attached to fields using language syntax instead of custom modifiers. The types in System.Runtime.CompilerServices are intended primarily for use by compilers, not application programmers. They allow compilers to easily implement certain language features that are not directly visible to programmers.] For more information on custom modifiers, see Partition II of the CLI Specification.

Summary

Defines the methods and properties required by types that support accessing hosts via proxy servers.

Type Summary

```
public interface IWebProxy
    {
    // Properties
    ICredentials Credentials { get; set; }

    // Methods
    Uri GetProxy(Uri destination);
    bool IsBypassed(Uri host);
    }
```

Description

[*Note:* This interface is implemented by the `WebRequest` type.]

Example

```
using System;
using System.Net;


public class IWebProxySample
{
    public static void Main()
    {
        IWebProxy wp = GlobalProxySelection.GetEmptyWebProxy();
        Uri target = new Uri("http://localhost");
        Uri proxyUri = wp.GetProxy(target);
        Console.WriteLine("IWebProxy.Uri is '{0}'", proxyUri);
        Console.WriteLine("IWebProxy.IsBypassed(\"http://localhost\") = {0}",
            wp.IsBypassed(proxyUri));
        Console.WriteLine();
        Console.WriteLine();
        Console.WriteLine("Press Enter to continue");
        Console.ReadLine();
    }
}
```

IWebProxy Interface

The output is

```
IWebProxy.Uri is 'http://localhost/'
IWebProxy.IsBypassed("http://localhost") = True


Press Enter to continue
```

A
B
C
D
E
F
G
H
I
J
K
L
M
N
O
P
Q
R
S
T
U
V
W
X
Y
Z

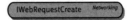

Summary

Provides a mechanism for creating new System.Net.WebRequest instances.

Type Summary

```
public interface IWebRequestCreate
    {
    // Methods
        WebRequest Create(Uri uri);
    }
```

Description

[*Note:* The IWebRequestCreate.Create method is implemented by types that derive from WebRequest. The IWebRequestCreate.Create method is invoked via the WebRequest.Create method. Types that implement the IWebRequestCreate interface are associated with a specific URI scheme and registered with the WebRequest class. When an application requests a WebRequest object for a specific URI, WebRequest calls the IWebRequestCreate.Create method of the type associated with the requested URI.]

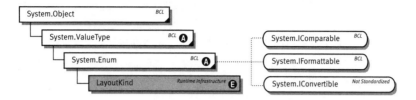

Summary

Indicates the physical memory layout of objects exported to unmanaged code.

Type Summary

```
public enum LayoutKind
    {
    Auto = 3,
    Explicit = 2,
    Sequential = 0,
    }
```

■ AN   Auto is the CLR's default behavior, although compilers such as Visual C# and Visual Basic mark value types with Sequential by default. Auto is naturally preferred for types that aren't exposed to unmanaged code (since the CLR has the option of optimizing the layout), but you must not use Auto for types that are directly passed out to unmanaged code as structures. So why did the compilers choose Sequential as their default? Because many structures tend to be passed to unmanaged code, and Auto layout would cause subtle bugs that would be extremely difficult to diagnose!

■ DT   Avoid explicit layout unless absolutely necessary. Explicit pretty much kills any hope of running the IL code on any other hardware platforms (Compact Framework, 64 bit) and can produce suboptimal performance on the beefier x86 chips as well. Sequential is required for any structure passed to unmanaged code via PInvoke. Auto gives the class loader/JITer the most flexibility to align fields for performance as well as reorder fields to minimize memory bloat owing to padding (C# default for structs is sequential).

Example

```csharp
using System;
using System.Runtime.InteropServices;

/// <summary>
/// Sample demonstrating the use of the LayoutKind enumeration.
/// Use this enumeration to control the binary layout of types passed to
/// unmanaged code.
/// </summary>
internal class LayoutKindSample
{

    private static void Main()
    {
        POINT_EXPLICIT pte = new POINT_EXPLICIT();

        if (GetCursorPos(out pte))
        {
            Console.WriteLine(
                "GetCursorPos (explicit-layout):   {0},{1}", pte.X, pte.Y);
        }
        else
        {
            Console.WriteLine("GetCursorPos (explicit-layout):   failed");
        }

        POINT_SEQUENTIAL pts = new POINT_SEQUENTIAL();

        if (GetCursorPos(out pts))
        {
            Console.WriteLine(
                "GetCursorPos (sequential-layout): {0},{1}", pts.X, pts.Y);
        }
        else
        {
            Console.WriteLine("GetCursorPos (sequential-layout): failed");
        }

        // Note that auto-layout types cannot be passed to unmanaged code.
        POINT_AUTO pta = new POINT_AUTO();

        try
        {
            GetCursorPos(out pta);
        }
        catch (MarshalDirectiveException)
        {
            Console.WriteLine("GetCursorPos (auto-layout):       failed");
        }

        Console.WriteLine();
        Console.WriteLine();
        Console.WriteLine("Press Enter to continue");
        Console.ReadLine();
    }
```

```
// Auto-layout version of the POINT type to use with GetCursorPos.
[StructLayout(LayoutKind.Auto)]
private struct POINT_AUTO
{
    public int X;
    public int Y;
}

// Explicit-layout version of the POINT type to use with GetCursorPos.
[StructLayout(LayoutKind.Explicit)]
private struct POINT_EXPLICIT
{
    [FieldOffset(0)]
    public int X;
    [FieldOffset(4)]
    public int Y;
}

// Sequential-layout version of the POINT type to use with GetCursorPos.
[StructLayout(LayoutKind.Sequential)]
private struct POINT_SEQUENTIAL
{
    public int X;
    public int Y;
}

// Win32 method to retrieve the current cursor position in screen
// co-ordinates. The method is overloaded to demonstrate the different
// definitions of POINT. This is used purely to demonstrate using
// LayoutKind; .NET code should use Cursor.Position to retrieve the same
// information.
[DllImport("user32.dll", SetLastError=true)]
private static extern bool GetCursorPos(out POINT_AUTO lpPoint);
[DllImport("user32.dll", SetLastError=true)]
private static extern bool GetCursorPos(out POINT_EXPLICIT lpPoint);
[DllImport("user32.dll", SetLastError=true)]
private static extern bool GetCursorPos(out POINT_SEQUENTIAL lpPoint);

}
```

The output is

```
GetCursorPos (explicit-layout):   808,545
GetCursorPos (sequential-layout): 808,545
GetCursorPos (auto-layout):       failed


Press Enter to continue
```

A
B
C
D
E
F
G
H
I
J
K
L
M
N
O
P
Q
R
S
T
U
V
W
X
Y
Z

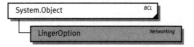

Summary

Maintains information that specifies how a `Socket` instance with pending data behaves when the `Close` method of the socket is called.

Type Summary

```
public class LingerOption
    {
    // Constructors
        public LingerOption(bool enable, int seconds);

    // Properties
        public bool Enabled { get; set; }
        public int LingerTime { get; set; }
    }
```

Description

An instance of this class is passed into the `Socket.SetSocketOption` method and is returned by the `Socket.GetSocketOption` method when the *optionName* parameter is set to `SocketOptionName.Linger`.

When the `Enabled` property is `true`, any queued data continues to be sent until time equal to the setting of the `LingerTime` property has passed or until the input queue is empty. At this time, the connection is closed.

When the `LingerTime` property is zero or the `Enabled` property is `false`, calling `Socket.Close` immediately closes the socket and any pending data is lost.

When setting the `SocketOptionName.Linger` option of an instance of the `Socket` class, a `System.ArgumentException` exception is thrown if the `LingerOption.LingerTime` property is less than zero or greater than `System.UInt16.MaxValue`.

Example

```
using System;
using System.Net;
using System.Net.Sockets;
using System.Text;

public class LingerOptionSample
```

```
{
    public static void Main()
    {
        LingerOption lo = new LingerOption(true, 5);
        TestLinger(lo);
        lo.Enabled = false;
        TestLinger(lo);
        Console.WriteLine();
        Console.WriteLine();
        Console.WriteLine("Press Enter to continue");
        Console.ReadLine();
    }

    private static void TestLinger(LingerOption lo)
    {
        IPAddress ip = IPAddress.Parse("127.0.0.1");
        IPEndPoint ep = new IPEndPoint(ip, 80);
        Socket skt = new Socket(AddressFamily.InterNetwork,
            SocketType.Stream, ProtocolType.Tcp);
        skt.SetSocketOption(SocketOptionLevel.Socket,
            SocketOptionName.Linger, lo);
        Console.Write("LingerOption.Enabled = {0} ... ", lo.Enabled);
        try
        {
            skt.Connect(ep);
            Byte[] req = Encoding.ASCII.GetBytes("Test");
            skt.SendTo(req, ep);
            skt.Shutdown(SocketShutdown.Both);
            Console.WriteLine("Request sent.");
        }
        catch (Exception e)
        {
            Console.WriteLine("Error: " + e.Message);
        }
        finally
        {
            skt.Close();
        }
    }
}
```

The output is

```
LingerOption.Enabled = True ... Request sent.
LingerOption.Enabled = False ... Request sent.

Press Enter to continue
```

A
B
C
D
E
F
G
H
I
J
K
L
M
N
O
P
Q
R
S
T
U
V
W
X
Y
Z

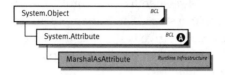

Summary

Specifies how data is to be marshaled between managed and unmanaged code.

Type Summary

```
CF public sealed class MarshalAsAttribute : Attribute
    {
    // Constructors
    CF public MarshalAsAttribute(short unmanagedType);
    CF public MarshalAsAttribute(UnmanagedType unmanagedType);

    // Fields
    CF public UnmanagedType ArraySubType;
    CF public string MarshalCookie;
    CF public string MarshalType;
    CF public Type MarshalTypeRef;
 MS CF public VarEnum SafeArraySubType;
 MS CF public Type SafeArrayUserDefinedSubType;
    CF public int SizeConst;
    CF public short SizeParamIndex;

    // Properties
    CF public UnmanagedType Value { get; }
    }
```

▪ **SK** SizeParamIndex is one of the most confusing MarshalAs fields. People are very surprised when they learn that the SizeParamIndex only applies in one direction. The SizeParamIndex field applies when a managed method is exposed to COM callers where an array parameter is declared as a C-style array. It doesn't work in what is possibly a more common situation, when a managed client calls a COM method with an in/out array parameter. In this situation, there is no way to pass a new array of a particular size since SizeParamIndex can't be applied to by-reference parameters.

▪ **AN** MarshalType and MarshalTypeRef serve the same purpose. With UnmanagedType.CustomMarshaler, you must specify the type of the custom

CONTINUED

A
B
C
D
E
F
G
H
I
J
K
L
M
N
O
P
Q
R
S
T
U
V
W
X
Y
Z

marshaler using one (and only one) of these fields. At first we only had the string field, but once custom attributes gained the ability to use `Type` fields (before we shipped v1.0), the other field seemed like a natural addition since it is much easier to use and less error prone than a string. The only problem was that we couldn't remove the string field, and we couldn't give both fields the same name (at least in C#)! `MarshalTypeRef` was the best name we could come up with, but I wish we could have just gotten rid of the string field instead.

■ AN   The `SafeArrayUserDefinedSubType` field was a late addition that was required to support VT_RECORD SAFEARRAYs, but it also enables you to expose a managed array as a SAFEARRAY using a specific interface type. For example, rather than seeing SAFEARRAY(IDispatch*) in your exported type library, you can use this setting with a VT_DISPATCH SAFEARRAY to instead see SAFEARRAY(IMyInterface*).

Description

This attribute can be applied to parameters, fields, or return values.

Each data type has a default marshaling behavior that is used if this attribute is not present. This attribute is only required when a type can be marshaled as more than one possible type. [*Note:* The `UnmanagedType` enumeration specifies possible data types.]

Compilers are required to not preserve this type in metadata as a custom attribute. Instead, compilers are required to emit it directly in the file format, as described in Partition II of the CLI Specification. Metadata consumers, such as the Reflection API, are required to retrieve this data from the file format and return it as if it were a custom attribute.

Example

```
using System;
using System.Runtime.InteropServices;

/// <summary>
/// Sample demonstrating the use of the MarshalAsAttribute class.
/// Use this attribute to control the marshalling of data between managed and
/// unmanaged code.
/// </summary>
internal class MarshalAsAttributeSample
{

    private static void Main()
    {
        Guid    objectGuid       = typeof(object).GUID;
        string objectGuidString = ProgIDFromCLSID(objectGuid);

        Console.WriteLine("ProgId for object: {0}", objectGuidString);
        Console.WriteLine();
```

```csharp
    const ushort VARIANT_LOCALBOOL = 0x0010;

    object src  = true;
    object dest = null;

    int hr =
        VariantChangeType(
            out dest, ref src, VARIANT_LOCALBOOL, VarEnum.VT_BSTR);

    if (hr == 0)
    {
        Console.WriteLine(
            "src type = {0}, value = {1}", src.GetType(), src);
        Console.WriteLine(
            "dest type = {0}, value = {1}", dest.GetType(), dest);
    }
    else
    {
        Console.WriteLine("VariantChangeType failed.");
    }

    Console.WriteLine();
    Console.WriteLine();
    Console.WriteLine("Press Enter to continue");
    Console.ReadLine();
}

// Win32 method to retrieve the ProgId for a given CLSID. The
// UnmanagedType.LPStruct value allows the Guid to be passed to unmanaged
// code that expects GUID* or REFGUID parameters. Note that PreserveSig is
// used to transform the final [out] parameter into a return value and the
// HRESULT into an exception if the call fails.
[DllImport("ole32.dll", CharSet=CharSet.Unicode, PreserveSig=false)]
private static extern string ProgIDFromCLSID(
    [In, MarshalAs(UnmanagedType.LPStruct)]Guid clsid);

// Win32 method to convert a VARIANT from one type to another. This is used
// purely to demonstrate the use of UnmanagedType.Struct; .NET code would
// typically use Convert.ChangeType.
[DllImport("oleaut32.dll")]
private static extern int VariantChangeType(
    [MarshalAs(UnmanagedType.Struct)]out object pvargDest,
    [In, MarshalAs(UnmanagedType.Struct)]ref object pvargSrc,
    ushort wFlags, VarEnum vt);
}
```

The output is

```
ProgId for object: System.Object

src type = System.Boolean, value = True
dest type = System.String, value = True


Press Enter to continue
```

A
B
C
D
E
F
G
H
I
J
K
L
M
N
O
P
Q
R
S
T
U
V
W
X
Y
Z

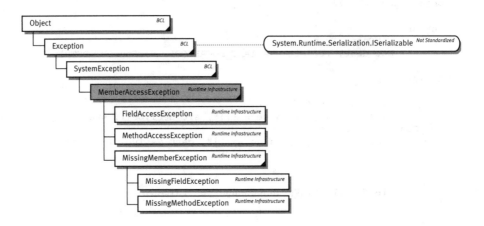

Summary

MemberAccessException is the base class for exceptions that occur when an attempt to locate or access a type member fails.

Type Summary

```
public class MemberAccessException : SystemException
    {
    // Constructors
    public MemberAccessException();
MS CF protected MemberAccessException(SerializationInfo info,
                StreamingContext context);
    public MemberAccessException(string message);
    public MemberAccessException(string message, Exception inner);
    }
```

■ **BA** In retrospect we should have put these Reflection exceptions (MemberAccessException, MethodAccessException, MissingFieldException, MissingMemberException, and MissingMethodException) in the System.Reflection namespace even though they can be thrown from code that doesn't use Reflection and from System.Type, as they are most commonly associated with System.Reflection.

Description

[*Note:* MemberAccessException exceptions are typically thrown by the system when members in a class library have been changed or removed, and an assembly that references the class library has not been recompiled. The Base Class Library includes the following derived types: FieldAccessException, MethodAccessException, MissingFieldException, and MissingMethodException. When appropriate, use these types instead of MemberAccessException.]

Example

```
using System;
using System.Reflection;

/// <summary>
/// Shows a MemberAccessException being thrown
/// because we try to trying to create an instance
///  of an abstract class.
/// </summary>
///

abstract class TestAbstractClass
{
    public TestAbstractClass()
    {
        Console.WriteLine("here");
    }
}



class Program
{
    static void Main()
    {
        try
        {
            Type type = typeof(TestAbstractClass);
            ConstructorInfo ci =  type.GetConstructor(Type.EmptyTypes);
            ci.Invoke(null);
        }
        catch (MemberAccessException mae)
        {
            Console.WriteLine("Caught exception: {0} - '{1}'",
                mae.GetType().Name, mae.Message);
        }
        Console.WriteLine();
        Console.WriteLine();
        Console.WriteLine("Press Enter to continue");
        Console.ReadLine();


    }
}
```

The output is

```
Caught exception: MemberAccessException - 'Cannot create an abstract class.'

Press Enter to continue
```

A
B
C
D
E
F
G
H
I
J
K
L
M
N
O
P
Q
R
S
T
U
V
W
X
Y
Z

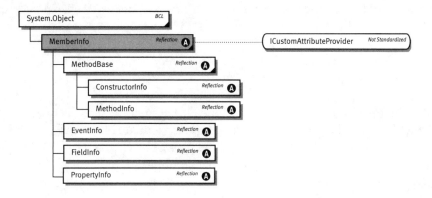

Summary

Provides access to member metadata.

Type Summary

```
public abstract class MemberInfo : ICustomAttributeProvider
{
// Constructors
   protected MemberInfo();

// Properties
   public abstract Type DeclaringType { get; }
MS public abstract MemberTypes MemberType { get; }
   public abstract string Name { get; }
   public abstract Type ReflectedType { get; }

// Methods
MS public abstract object[] GetCustomAttributes(bool inherit);
MS public abstract object[] GetCustomAttributes(
                        Type attributeType, bool inherit);
MS public abstract bool IsDefined(Type attributeType, bool inherit);
}
```

KC   I wish the MemberInfo interface was a bit richer. For example, I think it would be completely reasonable to have a Visibility property on MemberInfo. PropertyInfo would return appropriate visibility if both the get and set accessors had the same visibility and "Mixed" (or something like that) if their visibility was different. In general, I wish I could write most Reflection code using MemberInfo.

CONTINUED

▪ JM If one looks at `System.Type` within the ECMA standard, one will see that it inherits from `Object`. However, looking at the Microsoft implementation of the CLR, one will notice that it inherits from `MemberInfo`. What gives? Well, since `Member-Info` is a part of the Reflection library, `Type` will inherit from `Object` if the Reflection library is not available (i.e., only the kernel profile is implemented). If the Reflection library is available, then `Type` is required to inherit from `MemberInfo` and support all members associated with it.

▪ JP The reasoning behind the XXXInfo APIs being derivable was to allow for the construction of a user-defined, extensible `Type` system. `Reflection.Emit` was a classic example of how the derivation model paid off. JScript.NET is another good example (if you're interested, the JScript.NET compiler source code is distributed with the SSCLI download: http://msdn.microsoft.com/net/sscli/).

The bad news is that it's difficult to call it an extensible type system. In some scenarios it works reasonably well, in others it doesn't. In retrospect, we probably wouldn't have pursued the option of allowing customization via deriving from XXXInfo classes. Some of this extensibility story has introduced performance penalties. For instance, every common use of the real type system (`RuntimeType`) is often penalized by virtual method call invocation all over the place. You could envisage extension in a different way without this penalization but for now, we're stuck with it. Extensible type systems are just hard!

▪ JP Custom Attributes have been a very successful extensibility and augmentation mechanism for the runtime, however Reflecting over these things tends to be performance-heavy. CAs are odd in the sense that they force you into the execution context, which alone adds significant semantic complexities. For a start, Reflection must adhere to the inheritance semantic of CAs, which generally means more work for the APIs to give the user back the correct result.

▪ JP The `Name` property is mostly uninteresting—however, most people rely on `Name` as an identity attribute, mostly because of its ability to be round-tripped through `GetType()`, `GetMember()`, `GetMethod()`, and so forth. In Reflection this is not the case—we identify `MemberInfo` identity via the Metadata token, `Module`, and `ReflectedType`. The implication of this semantic is that entities that are identical or equal to the runtime are not equal in Reflection. This is shown in the following code snippet:

CONTINUED

```
class Foo
{
    public virtual void M()
    {}
}

class Bar : Foo
{
}

class MyClass
{
    public static void Main(string[] args)
    {
        Console.WriteLine(typeof(Foo).GetMethod("M") ==
                                    typeof(Bar).GetMethod("M"));
    }
}
```

This outputs:

```
False
```

Description

[*Note:* MemberInfo is used to represent all members of a type: nested types, fields, events, properties, methods, and constructors. The Base Class Library includes the following derived types:

- FieldInfo
- EventInfo
- PropertyInfo
- Type]

Example

```
using System;
using System.Reflection;

/// <summary>
/// This example shows the number of members for a given Type.
/// </summary>

public class MemberInfoSample
{
    public static void Main()
    {
        Type type = typeof(String);
        int declaredMethods = 0;
        int inheritedMethods = 0;
        int declaredProperties = 0;
```

```csharp
            int inheritedProperties = 0;
            int total = 0;

            foreach (System.Reflection.MemberInfo m in type.GetMembers(
                BindingFlags.Public | BindingFlags.FlattenHierarchy |
                BindingFlags.Instance |BindingFlags.Static))
            {
                total++;
                switch (m.MemberType)
                {
                    case MemberTypes.Method:
                        if (m.DeclaringType == m.ReflectedType)
                        {
                            declaredMethods++;
                        }
                        else
                        {
                            inheritedMethods++;
                        }
                        break;
                    case MemberTypes.Property:
                        if (m.DeclaringType == m.ReflectedType)
                        {
                            declaredProperties++;
                        }
                        else
                        {
                            inheritedProperties++;
                        }
                        break;
                }
            }
            Console.WriteLine("{0} has {1} public members.", type, total);
            Console.WriteLine(" {0} methods ({1} inherited)",
                declaredMethods + inheritedMethods, inheritedMethods);
            Console.WriteLine(" {0} properties ({1} inherited)",
                declaredProperties + inheritedProperties, inheritedProperties);
            Console.WriteLine(" {0} other members", total - (declaredProperties +
                inheritedProperties + declaredMethods + inheritedMethods),
                inheritedProperties);
            Console.WriteLine();
            Console.WriteLine();
            Console.WriteLine("Press Enter to continue");
            Console.ReadLine();
        }

    }
```

The output is

```
System.String has 99 public members.
 88 methods (3 inherited)
 2 properties (0 inherited)
 9 other members


Press Enter to continue
```

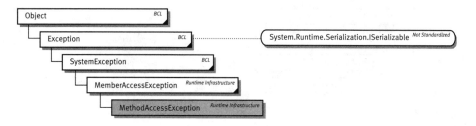

Summary

Represents the error that occurs when there is an attempt to access a method outside the scope in which access is permitted.

Type Summary

```
CF public class MethodAccessException : MemberAccessException
    {
    // Constructors
    CF public MethodAccessException();
 MS CF protected MethodAccessException(SerializationInfo info,
                StreamingContext context);
    CF public MethodAccessException(string message);
    CF public MethodAccessException(string message, Exception inner);
    }
```

Description

[*Note:* This exception is thrown when the access level of a method in a class library is changed, and one or more assemblies referencing the library have not been recompiled. This exception is also thrown when an attempt to invoke a method via reflection fails because the caller does not have the required permissions.]

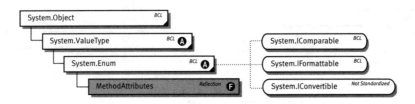

Summary

Specifies flags for method attributes.

Type Summary

```
public enum MethodAttributes
    {
        Abstract = 0x400,
        Assembly = 0x3,
MS CF 1.1 CheckAccessOnOverride = 0x200,
        FamANDAssem = 0x2,
        Family = 0x4,
        FamORAssem = 0x5,
        Final = 0x20,
    MS HasSecurity = 0x4000,
        HideBySig = 0x80,
        MemberAccessMask = 0x7,
        NewSlot = 0x100,
        PinvokeImpl = 0x2000,
        Private = 0x1,
        PrivateScope = 0x0,
        Public = 0x6,
    MS RequireSecObject = 0x8000,
    MS ReservedMask = 0xd000,
        ReuseSlot = 0x0,
    MS RTSpecialName = 0x1000,
        SpecialName = 0x800,
        Static = 0x10,
    MS UnmanagedExport = 0x8,
        Virtual = 0x40,
        VtableLayoutMask = 0x100,
    }
```

Description

This enumeration is used by the `MethodBase.Attributes` property.

Example

```
using System;
using System.Reflection;
```

```
/// <summary>
/// This example shows how to retrieve the attributes of a method.
/// </summary>

public class MethodAttributesSample
{
    public static void Main()
    {
        foreach (MethodInfo method in typeof(DemoClass).GetMethods())
        {
            Console.WriteLine("'{0}' ", method.Name);
            Console.Write("     ");

            if ((method.Attributes & MethodAttributes.MemberAccessMask)
                == MethodAttributes.Public)
            {
                Console.Write("public ");
            }
            if ((method.Attributes & MethodAttributes.Static) != 0)
            {
                Console.Write("static ");
            }
            if ((method.Attributes & MethodAttributes.Final) != 0)
            {
                Console.Write("final ");
            }
            if ((method.Attributes & MethodAttributes.Virtual) != 0)
            {
                Console.Write("virtual ");
            }
            if ((method.Attributes & MethodAttributes.Abstract) != 0)
            {
                Console.Write("abstract ");
            }
            Console.WriteLine();
        }
        Console.WriteLine();
        Console.WriteLine();
        Console.WriteLine("Press Enter to continue");
        Console.ReadLine();
    }
}

public abstract class DemoClass
{
    public static void Method1() { }
    public abstract void Method2();
    public override sealed string ToString() { return "foo"; }

}
```

The output is

```
'Method2'
    public virtual abstract
'GetHashCode'
```

A
B
C
D
E
F
G
H
I
J
K
L
M
N
O
P
Q
R
S
T
U
V
W
X
Y
Z

MethodAttributes Enum

```
        public virtual
'Equals'
        public virtual
'ToString'
        public final virtual
'Method1'
        public static
'GetType'
        public


Press Enter to continue
```

A
B
C
D
E
F
G
H
I
J
K
L
M
N
O
P
Q
R
S
T
U
V
W
X
Y
Z

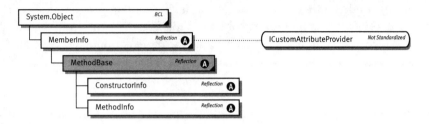

Summary

Provides access to method and constructor metadata.

Type Summary

```
public abstract class MethodBase : MemberInfo
    {
    // Constructors
        protected MethodBase();

    // Properties
        public abstract MethodAttributes Attributes { get; }
MS   public virtual CallingConventions CallingConvention { get; }
MS   public bool IsAbstract { get; }
MS   public bool IsAssembly { get; }
MS   public bool IsConstructor { get; }
MS   public bool IsFamily { get; }
MS   public bool IsFamilyAndAssembly { get; }
MS   public bool IsFamilyOrAssembly { get; }
MS   public bool IsFinal { get; }
MS   public bool IsHideBySig { get; }
MS   public bool IsPrivate { get; }
MS   public bool IsPublic { get; }
MS   public bool IsSpecialName { get; }
MS   public bool IsStatic { get; }
MS   public bool IsVirtual { get; }
MS   public abstract RuntimeMethodHandle MethodHandle { get; }

    // Methods
MS CF public static MethodBase GetCurrentMethod();
       public static MethodBase GetMethodFromHandle(
                            RuntimeMethodHandle handle);
MS CF public abstract MethodImplAttributes GetMethodImplementationFlags();
       public abstract ParameterInfo[] GetParameters();
       public abstract object Invoke(object obj, BindingFlags invokeAttr,
                            Binder binder, object[] parameters,
                            CultureInfo culture);
       public object Invoke(object obj, object[] parameters);
    }
```

A
B
C
D
E
F
G
H
I
J
K
L
M
N
O
P
Q
R
S
T
U
V
W
X
Y
Z

> ■ JP   The IsXXXX family of APIs, while seemingly simple, can be the second most
> confusing APIs in the Reflection namespace after `BindingFlags`. To gain a better
> understanding of the more obscure IsXXXX APIs, it's generally a good idea to refer to
> definitions of the type and member attributes in the ECMA Partition II Metadata spec.
> It would be nice to add more APIs that execute the more common predicates.

Description

[*Note:* `MethodBase` is used to represent method types. The Base Class Library includes
the following derived types:

- MethodInfo
- ConstructorInfo]

Example

```
using System;
using System.Reflection;


/// <summary>
/// This example prints the MethodBase for the currently executing
/// method and the target site of an exception.
/// </summary>

public class MethodBaseSample
{
    public static void Main()
    {
        MethodBaseSample p = new MethodBaseSample();
        int i = p.Value;
        Console.WriteLine();
        Console.WriteLine();
        Console.WriteLine("Press Enter to continue");
        Console.ReadLine();
    }

    public static void PrintMethodBase(MethodBase method)
    {
        switch (method.Attributes & MethodAttributes.MemberAccessMask)
        {
            case MethodAttributes.Public:
                Console.Write("public ");
                break;
            case MethodAttributes.Private:
                Console.Write("private ");
                break;
            case MethodAttributes.Family:
                Console.Write("protectedx");
                break;
```

```csharp
            case MethodAttributes.FamANDAssem:
                Console.Write("protected internal");
                break;
            case MethodAttributes.Assembly:
                Console.Write("internal ");
                break;
            default:
                Console.Write("Unknown "0u59 ?
                break;
        }
        if (method.IsStatic)
        {
            Console.Write("static ");
        }
        if (method.MemberType == MemberTypes.Constructor)
        {
            Console.Write("{0} (", method.DeclaringType.Name);
        }
        else
        {
            Console.Write("{0} (", method.Name);
        }
        ParameterInfo[] parameters = method.GetParameters();
        for (int i = 0; i < parameters.Length; i++)
        {
            Console.Write("{0} {1}", parameters[i].ParameterType.Name,
                parameters[i].Name);
            if (i != parameters.Length - 1)
            {
                Console.Write(", ");
            }
        }
        Console.WriteLine(")");
    }

    protected int Value
    {
        get
        {
            PrintMethodBase(MethodBase.GetCurrentMethod());
            return 42;
        }
    }

    static MethodBaseSample()
    {
        PrintMethodBase(MethodBase.GetCurrentMethod());
    }

    internal MethodBaseSample ()
    {
        PrintMethodBase(MethodBase.GetCurrentMethod());
        try
        {
            //causes an exception to be raised
            string temp = new String('c', -1);
```

A
B
C
D
E
F
G
H
I
J
K
L
M
N
O
P
Q
R
S
T
U
V
W
X
Y
Z

```
            }
            catch (ArgumentException e)
            {
                PrintMethodBase(e.TargetSite);
            }
    } //end ctor

} //end class
```

The output is

```
private static MethodBaseSample ()
internal MethodBaseSample ()
public String (Char c, Int32 count)
protected get_Value ()


Press Enter to continue
```

A
B
C
D
E
F
G
H
I
J
K
L
M
N
O
P
Q
R
S
T
U
V
W
X
Y
Z

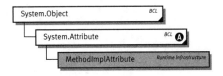

Summary

Specifies the details of how a method is implemented.

Type Summary

```
public sealed class MethodImplAttribute : Attribute
    {
    // Constructors
       public MethodImplAttribute();
       public MethodImplAttribute(MethodImplOptions methodImplOptions);
       public MethodImplAttribute(short value);

    // Fields
 MS public MethodCodeType MethodCodeType;

    // Properties
       public MethodImplOptions Value { get; }
    }
```

Description

Compilers are required to not preserve this type in metadata as a custom attribute.
Instead, compilers are required to emit it directly in the file format, as described in Partition II of the CLI Specification. Metadata consumers, such as the Reflection API, are
required to retrieve this data from the file format and return it as if it were a custom
attribute.

[*Note:* This class uses the `MethodImplOptions` enumeration to describe the implementation details of methods. For most languages, it is recommended that the notions of
"forward" and "synchronized" be attached to methods using language syntax instead of
custom attributes.]

Example

```
using System;
using System.Runtime.CompilerServices;
using System.Threading;

/// <summary>
/// Sample demonstrating the use of the MethodImplAttribute class.
```

MethodImplAttribute Class

```
/// Use this attribute to provide information about a method implementation.
/// </summary>
internal class MethodImplAttributeSample
{

    private static void Main()
    {
        DemoClass demo = new DemoClass();

        // Use a couple of threads from the thread pool to call the
        // synchronized an unsynchronized methods on DemoClass.
        ThreadPool.QueueUserWorkItem(new WaitCallback(ThreadProc1), demo);
        ThreadPool.QueueUserWorkItem(new WaitCallback(ThreadProc2), demo);
        Thread.Sleep(8000);

        Console.WriteLine();
        Console.WriteLine();
        Console.WriteLine("Press Enter to continue");
        Console.ReadLine();
    }

    // ThreadProc1 will call GetStatus first but, because of a shorter delay,
    // ThreadProc2 will call GetStatusSynchronized first. The result is that
    // ThreadProc1 will be blocked from calling GetStatusSynchronized until
    // the call finishes on ThreadProc2.
    private static void ThreadProc1(object stateInfo)
    {
        DemoClass demo = (DemoClass)stateInfo;

        demo.GetStatus(1, 1500);
        demo.GetStatusSynchronized(1, 2000);
    }

    private static void ThreadProc2(object stateInfo)
    {
        DemoClass demo = (DemoClass)stateInfo;

        demo.GetStatus(2, 1000);
        demo.GetStatusSynchronized(2, 3000);
    }

    private class DemoClass
    {
        static int syncCount = 0;
        static int count    = 0;

        [MethodImpl(MethodImplOptions.Synchronized)]
        public void GetStatusSynchronized(int threadIndex, int delay)
        {
            Console.WriteLine(
                "Thread {0} entering GetStatusSynchronized", threadIndex);
            syncCount++;
            Console.WriteLine("  {0} thread(s) in critical section", syncCount);
            Thread.Sleep(delay);
            syncCount--;
            Console.WriteLine(
```

```
                    "Thread {0} leaving GetStatusSynchronized", threadIndex);
        }

        public void GetStatus(int threadIndex, int delay)
        {
            Console.WriteLine("Thread {0} entering GetStatus", threadIndex);
            count++;
            Console.WriteLine("  {0} thread(s) in critical section", count);
            Thread.Sleep(delay);
            count--;
            Console.WriteLine("Thread {0} leaving GetStatus", threadIndex);
        }

    }

}
```

The output is

```
Thread 1 entering GetStatus
  1 thread(s) in critical section
Thread 2 entering GetStatus
  2 thread(s) in critical section
Thread 2 leaving GetStatus
Thread 2 entering GetStatusSynchronized
  1 thread(s) in critical section
Thread 1 leaving GetStatus
Thread 2 leaving GetStatusSynchronized
Thread 1 entering GetStatusSynchronized
  1 thread(s) in critical section
Thread 1 leaving GetStatusSynchronized


Press Enter to continue
```

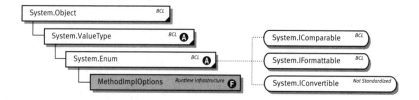

Summary

Defines the details of how a method is implemented.

Type Summary

```
public enum MethodImplOptions
    {
        ForwardRef = 0x10,
        InternalCall = 0x1000,
        NoInlining = 0x8,
    MS  PreserveSig = 0x80,
        Synchronized = 0x20,
        Unmanaged = 0x4,
    }
```

▪ **AN**   The `PreserveSig` bit corresponds to the `System.Runtime.InteropServices.PreserveSigAttribute` pseudo-custom attribute. This controls whether a managed signature's return value should be treated as the unmanaged signature's last parameter ([retval] in IDL-speak) or as a true return value. As part of this, it controls whether the CLR transforms an unhandled exception into an HRESULT and vice versa. We debated a long time over the name of this bit and what the default behavior should be, considering suggestions like `IgnoreHResult`, `HideHResult`, and `TransformSig`, but I'm pleased with where we ended up. Now if only there was an easy way to automatically set this bit on imported COM signatures!

▪ **BA**   Unlike the Java language, C#, VB, and other languages opted to not expose a keyword to mark a method as synchronized, meaning a lock is taken on method enter and removed on method exit. The rationale is that while this looks like an attractive feature at first, better scalability is available if you use coarser grain locks such as on a whole set of methods from different classes. Taking locks at this fine level of granularity creates lock contention and often does not meet the real need for synchronization.

CONTINUED

216

> That said, because some languages do support fine-grained locks, the CLR supports
> them. Since they are supported by the runtime, you are able to access them from C#,
> even though method level locking is not supported by C#. The following code shows
> how:
>
> ```
> [MethodImpl(MethodImplOptions.Synchronized)]
> public void Withdraw(int amount){
>
>     if(amount < this.amount)
>        this.amount - amount;
>
> }
> ```

Description

This enumeration is used by `MethodImplAttribute`.

Example

```csharp
using System;
using System.Reflection;
using System.Runtime.CompilerServices;

/// <summary>
/// Sample demonstrating the use of the MethodImplOptions enumeration.
/// Use this enumeration to provide information about the implementation of
/// methods decorated with MethodImplAttribute.
/// </summary>
internal class MethodImplOptionsSample
{

    private static void Main()
    {
        AppDomain domain = AppDomain.CreateDomain("Test domain 1");

        domain.DomainUnload += new EventHandler(Handler1);
        AppDomain.Unload(domain);

        domain = AppDomain.CreateDomain("Test domain 2");
        domain.DomainUnload += new EventHandler(Handler2);
        AppDomain.Unload(domain);

        Console.WriteLine();
        Console.WriteLine();
        Console.WriteLine("Press Enter to continue");
        Console.ReadLine();
    }

    // Must be public for serialization support.
    public static void Handler1(object sender, EventArgs e)
    {
```

```
              Console.WriteLine("The caller of GetCallingAssemblyName1() is:");
              Console.WriteLine(GetCallingAssemblyName1());
              Console.WriteLine();
          }

          // Returns the name of the calling assembly. The use of
          // MethodImplOptions.NoInlining prevents the jitter from inlining the
          // method.
          [MethodImpl(MethodImplOptions.NoInlining)]
          private static string GetCallingAssemblyName1()
          {
              return Assembly.GetCallingAssembly().FullName;
          }

          // Must be public for serialization support.
          public static void Handler2(object sender, EventArgs e)
          {
              Console.WriteLine("The caller of GetCallingAssemblyName2() is:");
              Console.WriteLine(GetCallingAssemblyName2());
              Console.WriteLine();
          }

          // Returns the name of the calling assembly. The jitter is free to inline
          // this method. Note that inlining will only occur in release builds with
          // no debugger attached, e.g. CTRL+F5.
          private static string GetCallingAssemblyName2()
          {
              return Assembly.GetCallingAssembly().FullName;
          }
      }
```

The output is

```
The caller of GetCallingAssemblyName1() is:
MethodImplOptions, Version=0.0.0.0, Culture=neutral, PublicKeyToken=null

The caller of GetCallingAssemblyName2() is:
MethodImplOptions, Version=0.0.0.0, Culture=neutral, PublicKeyToken=null


Press Enter to continue
```

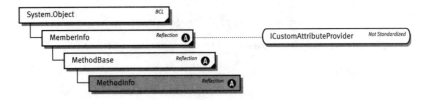

Summary

Provides access to method metadata.

Type Summary

```
public abstract class MethodInfo : MethodBase
    {
    // Constructors
        protected MethodInfo();

    // Properties
MS  public override MemberTypes MemberType { get; }
        public abstract Type ReturnType { get; }
MS  public abstract ICustomAttributeProvider ReturnTypeCustomAttributes
                                            { get; }

    // Methods
        public abstract MethodInfo GetBaseDefinition();
    }
```

Example

```
using System;
using System.Reflection;

/// <summary>
/// Shows how to print a method in C# syntax
/// </summary>

public class MethodInfoSample
{
    public static void Main()
    {
        Type type = typeof(MethodInfoSample);

        foreach (MethodInfo method in
            type.GetMethods(BindingFlags.NonPublic | BindingFlags.Public |
            BindingFlags.Instance | BindingFlags.Static))
        {
            //Skip any methods that are not publicly accessible
            if (!(method.IsPublic || method.IsFamily ||
```

```
                            method.IsFamilyOrAssembly))
                    {
                        continue;
                    }

                    //Skip any method with special names (such as constructors or
                    //property\event methods)
                    if (method.IsSpecialName)
                    {
                        continue;
                    }

                    Console.Write(method.IsPublic ? "public " : "protected ");
                    if (method.IsStatic)
                    {
                        Console.Write("static ");
                    }
                    PrintMethodModifiers(method);
                    Console.WriteLine("{0} (...)", method.Name);
                }

            MethodInfo m = type.GetMethod("ToString",
                BindingFlags.Public | BindingFlags.Instance);
            string ret = (string)m.Invoke(new MethodInfoSample(), null);
            Console.WriteLine("The result is '{0}'", ret);
            Console.WriteLine();
            Console.WriteLine();
            Console.WriteLine("Press Enter to continue");
            Console.ReadLine();
        }

        public override string ToString()
        {
            return "In MethodInfoSample ToString()";
        }

        static void PrintMethodModifiers(MethodInfo method)
        {
            if (method.DeclaringType.IsInterface)
            {
                return;
            }
            MethodAttributes attrs = method.Attributes;
            if ((attrs & MethodAttributes.Final) != 0)
            {
                Console.Write("sealed ");
            }
            if ((attrs & MethodAttributes.Virtual) != 0)
            {
                //consider only the NewSlot and Abstract bits...
                switch (attrs &
                    (MethodAttributes.NewSlot | Method_ttributes.Abstract))
                {
                    case 0: //if none are set, it must be an override
                        Console.Write("override ");
                        break;
```

```
            case MethodAttributes.NewSlot:
                Console.Write("virtual ");
                break;
            case MethodAttributes.Abstract:
                Console.Write("abstract override ");
                break;
            case MethodAttributes.NewSlot | MethodAttributes.Abstract:
                Console.Write("abstract ");
                break;
        } //end switch
    }
} //end method
} //end class
```

The output is

```
protected override Finalize (...)
public virtual GetHashCode (...)
public virtual Equals (...)
public override ToString (...)
public static Main (...)
public GetType (...)
protected MemberwiseClone (...)
The result is 'In MethodInfoSample ToString()'


Press Enter to continue
```

A
B
C
D
E
F
G
H
I
J
K
L
M
N
O
P
Q
R
S
T
U
V
W
X
Y
Z

Summary

Represents the error that occurs when there is an attempt to dynamically access a field that does not exist.

Type Summary

```
public class MissingFieldException : MissingMemberException, ISerializable
   {
   // Constructors
      public MissingFieldException();
MS CF protected MissingFieldException(SerializationInfo info,
               StreamingContext context);
      public MissingFieldException(string message);
      public MissingFieldException(string message, Exception inner);
      public MissingFieldException(string className, string fieldName);

   // Properties
MS CF public override string Message { get; }
   }
```

Description

Normally a compilation error is generated if code attempts to access a nonexistent member of a class. MissingFieldException is designed to handle cases where an attempt is made to dynamically access a renamed or deleted field of an assembly that is not referenced by its strong name. The MissingFieldException is thrown when code in a dependent assembly attempts to access a missing field in an assembly that was modified.

Example

```
using System;
using System.Reflection;

/// <summary>
/// Shows why a MissingFieldException is thrown
/// and how to handle it
/// </summary>

public class MissingFieldExceptionSample
{
    public static void Main()
    {
        try
        {
            Type type = typeof(string);
            type.InvokeMember("NonExistFld", BindingFlags.GetField, null,
                null, null);

        }
        catch (MissingFieldException e)
        {
            Console.WriteLine("Caught exception: {0} - '{1}'", e.GetType().Name,
                e.Message);
        }
        Console.WriteLine();
        Console.WriteLine();
        Console.WriteLine("Press Enter to continue");
        Console.ReadLine();
    }
}
```

The output is

```
Caught exception: MissingFieldException - 'Field System.String.NonExistFld not f
ound.'


Press Enter to continue
```

A
B
C
D
E
F
G
H
I
J
K
L
M
N
O
P
Q
R
S
T
U
V
W
X
Y
Z

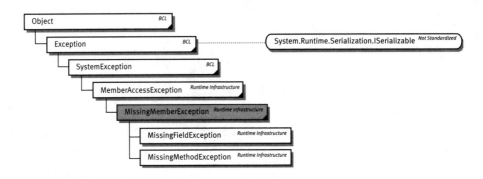

Summary

Represents the error that occurs when there is an attempt to dynamically access a class member that does not exist.

Type Summary

```
public class MissingMemberException : MemberAccessException, ISerializable
      {
      // Constructors
         public MissingMemberException();
MS CF  protected MissingMemberException(SerializationInfo info,
                    StreamingContext context);
         public MissingMemberException(string message);
         public MissingMemberException(string message, Exception inner);
MS CF  public MissingMemberException(string className, string memberName);

      // Fields
MS    protected string ClassName;
MS    protected string MemberName;
MS CF protected byte[] Signature;

      // Properties
MS CF public override string Message { get; }

      // Methods
MS CF public override void GetObjectData(SerializationInfo info,
                         StreamingContext context);
      }
```

Description

Normally a compilation error is generated if code attempts to access a nonexistent member of a class. MissingMemberException is designed to handle cases where an attempt is made to dynamically access a renamed or deleted member of an assembly that is not referenced by its strong name. The `MissingMemberException` is thrown when code in a dependent assembly attempts to access a missing member in an assembly that was modified.

   [*Note:* The Base Class Library includes the following derived types: `MissingField-Exception`, `MissingMethodException`. When appropriate, use these types instead of `MissingMemberException`.]

Example

```
using System;
using System.Reflection;

/// <summary>
/// Shows why a MissingMemberException is thrown
/// and how to handle it
/// </summary>

public class MissingMemberExceptionSample
{
    public static void Main()
    {
        try
        {
            Type type = typeof(string);
            type.InvokeMember("Splitt", BindingFlags.InvokeMethod, null,
                null, null);
        }
        catch (MissingMemberException e)
            //traps MissingMemberException, but reports MissingMethodException
            //because the subclass is more specific:
            //MissingMethodException IS-A MissingMemberException
        {
            Console.WriteLine("Caught MissingMemberException\n"+
                "e.GetType reports exception: {0} - '{1}'",
                e.GetType().Name, e.Message);
        }
        Console.WriteLine();
        Console.WriteLine();
        Console.WriteLine("Press Enter to continue");
        Console.ReadLine();
    }
}
```

   The output is

```
Caught MissingMemberException
e.GetType reports exception: MissingMethodException - 'Method System.String.Spli
tt not found.'


Press Enter to continue
```

225

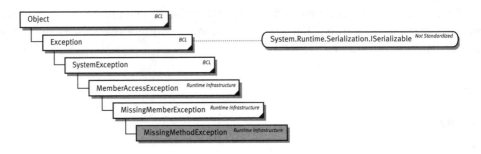

Summary

Represents the error that occurs when there is an attempt to dynamically access a method that does not exist.

Type Summary

```
public class MissingMethodException : MissingMemberException,
                                      ISerializable
   {
   // Constructors
      public MissingMethodException();
MS CF protected MissingMethodException(SerializationInfo info,
             StreamingContext context);
      public MissingMethodException(string message);
      public MissingMethodException(string message, Exception inner);
MS CF public MissingMethodException(string className, string methodName);

   // Properties
MS CF public override string Message { get; }
   }
```

> **■_ SC**   Say you've just installed some assemblies from a third party, and now, during the run of an application using those assemblies, you're seeing a MissingMethod-Exception. The following are the common causes:
>
> **Loading failures**
>
> First, check for assembly binding failures by getting the Fusion log. Look for the assembly containing the missing method, or assemblies containing types referenced by that method. If an assembly failed to load, use the instructions at the same link to help resolve that issue.
>
> *CONTINUED*

Unexpected assembly version loaded

But, if that's not the problem, turn on the Fusion log for everything—not just failures—and check to see if the wrong version of those assemblies is being loaded. Look at the display names requested. Are any requesting outdated versions, even after policy has been applied (see farther down in the log for the post-policy display name)? If so, you may want to recompile part of your app so that it has current references.

Loaded from unexpected path

If that doesn't help, run filever.exe on the file at the path it was loaded from. You can get that from the loaded modules list in a debugger. It's also the last path listed in the Fusion log, for a successful log (if it's in the GAC, no path is listed). Make sure the path is the same as you would expect.

Method not in this version of the assembly

Next, run ildasm.exe on the file at the path it was loaded from at runtime, and make sure the method is there. Maybe the file has changed, adding or removing methods, but the assembly version and location have stayed the same.

Invalid IL

Now, try running peverify.exe on the file containing the method, using the path it was loaded from at runtime. If it gives an error, check back to see if there was a warning at compile time for this file.

Description

Normally a compilation error is generated if code attempts to access a nonexistent method of a class. `MissingMethodException` is designed to handle cases where an attempt is made to dynamically access a renamed or deleted method of an assembly that is not referenced by its strong name. The `MissingMethodException` is thrown when code in a dependent assembly attempts to access a missing method in an assembly that was modified.

[*Note:* The following IL instructions throw `MissingMethodException`:

- `callvirt`
- `newobj`]

Example

```
using System;
using System.Reflection;
```

MissingMethodException Class

```csharp
/// <summary>
/// Shows why a MissingMethodException is thrown
/// and how to handle it
/// </summary>

public class MissingMethodExceptionSample
{
    public static void Main()
    {
        try
        {
            Type type = typeof(string);
            type.InvokeMember("Splitt", BindingFlags.InvokeMethod, null,
                null, null);
        }
        catch (MissingMethodException e)
        {
            Console.WriteLine("Caught exception: {0} - '{1}'", e.GetType().Name,
                e.Message);
        }
        Console.WriteLine();
        Console.WriteLine();
        Console.WriteLine("Press Enter to continue");
        Console.ReadLine();
    }
}
```

The output is

```
Caught exception: MissingMethodException - 'Method System.String.Splitt not foun
d.'


Press Enter to continue
```

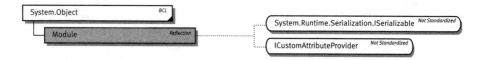

Summary

Provides access to module metadata.

Type Summary

```
public class Module : ISerializable, ICustomAttributeProvider
    {
    // Fields
MS CF public static readonly TypeFilter FilterTypeName =
                                        System.Reflection.TypeFilter;
MS CF public static readonly TypeFilter FilterTypeNameIgnoreCase =
                                        System.Reflection.TypeFilter;

    // Properties
       public Assembly Assembly { get; }
       public virtual string FullyQualifiedName { get; }
       public string Name { get; }
MS CF public string ScopeName { get; }

    // Methods
MS CF public virtual Type[] FindTypes(TypeFilter filter,
                           object filterCriteria);
MS CF public virtual object[] GetCustomAttributes(bool inherit);
MS CF public virtual object[] GetCustomAttributes(Type attributeType,
                              bool inherit);
   CF public FieldInfo GetField(string name);
   CF public FieldInfo GetField(string name, BindingFlags bindingAttr);
   CF public FieldInfo[] GetFields();
      public FieldInfo[] GetFields(BindingFlags bindingAttr);
   CF public MethodInfo GetMethod(string name);
MS CF public MethodInfo GetMethod(string name, BindingFlags bindingAttr,
                        Binder binder, CallingConventions callConvention,
                        Type[] types, ParameterModifier[] modifiers);
   CF public MethodInfo GetMethod(string name, Type[] types);
MS CF protected virtual MethodInfo GetMethodImpl(string name,
                                   BindingFlags bindingAttr, Binder binder,
                                   CallingConventions callConvention,
                                   Type[] types,
                                   ParameterModifier[] modifiers);
   CF public MethodInfo[] GetMethods();
      public MethodInfo[] GetMethods(BindingFlags bindingAttr);
MS CF public virtual void GetObjectData(SerializationInfo info,
                          StreamingContext context);
MS CF public X509Certificate GetSignerCertificate();
   MS public virtual Type GetType(string className);
MS CF public virtual Type GetType(string className, bool ignoreCase);
```

```
MS CF public virtual Type GetType(string className, bool throwOnError,
                            bool ignoreCase);
   MS public virtual Type[] GetTypes();
MS CF public virtual bool IsDefined(Type attributeType, bool inherit);
MS CF public bool IsResource();
       public override string ToString();
   }
```

■ JM   It was noticed at some point during the standardization process that while C# does not allow overloading on return types, the CLI does allow it (as well as other languages). The GetMethod methods in class Module do not allow the retrieval of a singular MethodInfo based on this one distinction.

■ BA   The GetType() overloads have two design problems. First, the methods are not overloaded in a consistent order; it should have been

```
public virtual Type GetType(string className);
public virtual Type GetType(string className, bool ignoreCase);
public virtual Type GetType(string className, bool ignoreCase, bool
throwOnError);
```

Second, as Danny Thorpe commented on WebProxy, using enums would have been more self-documenting.

Description

A module is a single portable executable (PE) file. [*Note:* One or more modules deployed as a unit composes an assembly. For more information on modules, see Partition II of the CLI Specification.]

Example

```
using System;
using System.Reflection;

/// <summary>
/// This example prints our information about a module.
/// </summary>

[module: TestAttribute("Darb")]

public class ModuleSample
{
    public static void Main()
    {
        foreach (Module module in Assembly.GetExecutingAssembly().GetModules())
        {
```

```
            Console.WriteLine(module.Name);
            foreach (Attribute attr in module.GetCustomAttributes(false))
            {
                Console.WriteLine(attr.ToString());
                TestAttribute testAttr = attr as TestAttribute;
                if (testAttr != null)
                {
                    Console.WriteLine("TestAttr.Name == '{0}'", testAttr.Name);
                }
            }
        }
        Console.WriteLine();
        Console.WriteLine();
        Console.WriteLine("Press Enter to continue");
        Console.ReadLine();
    }
} //end class

[AttributeUsage(AttributeTargets.Module, AllowMultiple = false,
Inherited = false)]
public sealed class TestAttribute : Attribute
{
    private string name;
    public TestAttribute(string name)
    {
        this.name = name;
    }
    public string Name
    {
        get
        {
            return name;
        }
    }
}
```

The output is

```
Module.exe
TestAttribute
TestAttr.Name == 'Darb'


Press Enter to continue
```

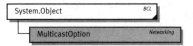

Summary

Contains Internet Protocol (IP) addresses used when joining or leaving an IP multicast group.

Type Summary

```
public class MulticastOption
{
    // Constructors
    public MulticastOption(IPAddress group);
    public MulticastOption(IPAddress group, IPAddress mcint);

    // Properties
    public IPAddress Group { get; set; }
    public IPAddress LocalAddress { get; set; }
}
```

Description

Collectively, the hosts listening to a specific IP multicast address (the group address) are called a multicast group. Each member of the group receives any IP messages sent to the group address.

An instance of this class is passed into the `Socket.SetSocketOption` method and returned by the `Socket.GetSocketOption` method when the *optionName* parameter is set to `SocketOptionName.AddMembership` or `SocketOptionName.DropMembership`.

because if you are dealing with completely open-ended input, then someone can spam you with degenerate XML that causes your NameTable to explode; for example, if I return the following XML to you every time you call me:

```
XmlWriter w = new XmlTextWriter("output.xml");
 Random r = new Random(Environment.TickCount);
 w.WriteStartElement("RandomName"+r.Next());
 w.WriteEndElement();
```

and if you never recycle your NameTable, then you will have a memory bloat.

Description

Only a single instance of any given string is stored even if the string is added multiple times to the table.

Using this class provides an efficient means for an XML parser to use the same String object for all repeated element and attribute names in an XML document. If the same object is used for all repeated names, the efficiency of name comparisons is increased by allowing the names to be compared using object comparisons rather than string comparisons.

[*Note:* This class implements a single-threaded XmlNameTable. This class is used internally by the XmlNamespaceManager, XmlParserContext, and XmlTextReader classes to store element and attribute names.]

Example

Example 1
The following example demonstrates the difference between equal string values and equal String objects using the NameTable class.

```
using System;
using System.Text;
using System.Xml;

class Ntable
{

    public static void Main()
    {

        NameTable nameTable = new NameTable();

        string str1 = "sunny";
        StringBuilder strBuilder = new StringBuilder();
        string str2 =
```

NameTable Class

```
                strBuilder.Append("sun").Append("ny").ToString();
            Console.WriteLine( "{0}: {1}",
                str1, str2 );
            Console.WriteLine( "{0}: {1}",
                str1 == str2,
                (Object)str1==(Object)str2 );

            string str3 = nameTable.Add(str1);
            string str4 = nameTable.Add(str2);
            Console.WriteLine( "{0}: {1}",
                str3, str4 );
            Console.WriteLine( "{0}: {1}",
                str3 == str4,
                (Object)str3==(Object)str4 );
        }
    }
```

The output is

```
sunny: sunny
True: False
sunny: sunny
True: True
```

Example 2

```
using System;
using System.Xml;

/// <summary>
/// Reads a sample xml document into an XmlReader, gets the NameTable out
/// of the XmlReader, adds another value to the NameTable then shows how
/// to get values out of the NameTable.
/// </summary>

public class NameTableSample
{
    public static void Main()
    {
        XmlTextReader r = new XmlTextReader("sample.xml");
        while (r.Read());
        NameTable n = (NameTable) r.NameTable;
        n.Add("another");
        Console.WriteLine("String 'test:first' is in NameTable: {0}",
            n.Get("test:first") == "test:first");
        Console.WriteLine("String 'one' is in NameTable: {0}",
            n.Get("one") == "one");
        Console.WriteLine("String 'child' is in NameTable: {0}",
            n.Get("child") == "child");
        Console.WriteLine("String 'not-there' is in NameTable: {0}",
            n.Get("not-there") == "not-there");
        Console.WriteLine("String 'another' is in NameTable: {0}",
            n.Get("another") == "another");
        Console.WriteLine();
        Console.WriteLine();
```

```
        Console.WriteLine("Press Enter to continue");
        Console.ReadLine();
    }
}
```

The output is

```
String 'test:first' is in NameTable: True
String 'one' is in NameTable: False
String 'child' is in NameTable: False
String 'not-there' is in NameTable: False
String 'another' is in NameTable: True


Press Enter to continue
```

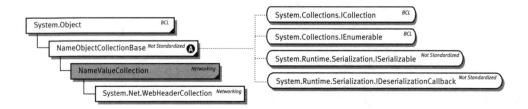

Summary

Represents a collection of associated `String` keys and `String` values.

Type Summary

```
public class NameValueCollection : NameObjectCollectionBase
    {
    // Constructors
        public NameValueCollection();
        public NameValueCollection(IHashCodeProvider hashProvider,
            IComparer comparer);
        public NameValueCollection(int capacity);
        public NameValueCollection(int capacity,
            IHashCodeProvider hashProvider,
            IComparer comparer);
        public NameValueCollection(int capacity, NameValueCollection col);
        public NameValueCollection(NameValueCollection col);
    MS CF protected NameValueCollection(SerializationInfo info,
                 StreamingContext context);

    // Properties
        public virtual string[] AllKeys { get; }
        public string this[int index] { get; }
        public string this[string name] { get; set; }

    // Methods
        public void Add(NameValueCollection c);
        public virtual void Add(string name, string value);
        public void Clear();
    CF public void CopyTo(Array dest, int index);
        public virtual string Get(int index);
        public virtual string Get(string name);
        public virtual string GetKey(int index);
        public virtual string[] GetValues(int index);
        public virtual string[] GetValues(string name);
        public bool HasKeys();
        protected void InvalidateCachedArrays();
        public virtual void Remove(string name);
        public virtual void Set(string name, string value);
    }
```

> ▪ **JM**   You might be wondering about this one specialized collection class
> that made it into the ECMA standard. I was too, at the time. Why this weird
> `NameValueCollection` class and no Stack or Queue, for example? Well, it turns out
> the networking types make use of this class (see `WebHeaderCollection`). Rather
> than try to redesign the networking classes to make use of another type or remove the
> culprit members altogether, the committee just decided to standardize Microsoft
> existing practice in this case.

Description

This class can be used for headers, query strings, and form data. Each key in the collection
is associated with one or more values. Multiple values for a particular key are contained in
a single `String`.

The capacity is the number of key-and-value pairs that the `NameValueCollection`
can contain. The default initial capacity is zero. The capacity is automatically increased as
required.

The hash code provider dispenses hash codes for keys in the `NameValueCollection`.
The comparer determines whether two keys are equal.

Example

```
using System;
using System.Collections.Specialized;

public class NameValueCollectionSample
{
    public static void Main()
    {
        NameValueCollection nv1 = new NameValueCollection();
        nv1.Add("name1", "value1");
        nv1.Add("name2", "value2a");
        nv1.Add("name2", "value2b");
        ShowContents("Contents of NameValueCollection1:", nv1);
        NameValueCollection nv2 = new NameValueCollection();
        nv2.Add("name3", "value3");
        nv2.Add("name4", "value4a");
        nv2.Add("name4", "value4b");
        ShowContents("Contents of NameValueCollection2:", nv2);
        string[] a = new string[4];
        nv1.CopyTo(a, 0);
        ShowArrayValues("Array contents after NameValueCollection1"
            + ".CopyTo(array, 0):", a);
        nv2.CopyTo(a, 2);
        ShowArrayValues("Array contents after NameValueCollection2"
            + ".CopyTo(array, 2):", a);
        Console.WriteLine();
        Console.WriteLine();
```

A
B
C
D
E
F
G
H
I
J
K
L
M
N
O
P
Q
R
S
T
U
V
W
X
Y
Z

```
            Console.WriteLine("Press Enter to continue");
            Console.ReadLine();
        }

        private static void ShowContents(string t,
            NameValueCollection nv)
        {
            Console.WriteLine();
            Console.WriteLine(t);
            foreach (string k in nv.AllKeys)
            {
                Console.WriteLine("Key: '{0}', Value: '{1}'",
                    k, nv[k]);
            }
        }
        private static void ShowArrayValues(string t, string[] a)
        {
            Console.WriteLine("\n" + t);
            for (int i = 0; i < a.Length; i++)
            {
                Console.WriteLine("Index: {0}, Value: '{1}'",
                    i, a[i]);
            }
        }
    }
}
```

The output is

```
Contents of NameValueCollection1:
Key: 'name1', Value: 'value1'
Key: 'name2', Value: 'value2a,value2b'

Contents of NameValueCollection2:
Key: 'name3', Value: 'value3'
Key: 'name4', Value: 'value4a,value4b'

Array contents after NameValueCollection1.CopyTo(array, 0):
Index: 0, Value: 'value1'
Index: 1, Value: 'value2a,value2b'
Index: 2, Value: ''
Index: 3, Value: ''

Array contents after NameValueCollection2.CopyTo(array, 2):
Index: 0, Value: 'value1'
Index: 1, Value: 'value2a,value2b'
Index: 2, Value: 'value3'
Index: 3, Value: 'value4a,value4b'


Press Enter to continue
```

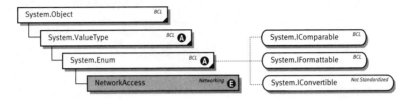

Summary

Specifies network access permission types.

Type Summary

```
CF public enum NetworkAccess
    {
    CF Accept = 128,
    CF Connect = 64,
    }
```

Description

This enumeration is used to indicate whether a permission object secures connect (client-side) or accept (server-side) operations.

[*Note:* The `NetworkAccess` enumeration is used with the `WebPermission` and `SocketPermission` classes.]

Example

```
using System;
using System.Net;
using System.Collections;

public class NetworkAccessSample
{
    public static void Main()
    {
        String target = "http://localhost/";
        WebPermission wp = new
            WebPermission(NetworkAccess.Connect, target);
        IEnumerator list = wp.ConnectList;
        while (list.MoveNext())
        {
            Console.WriteLine("NetworkAccess.Connect specified for {0}",
                list.Current);
        }
        Console.WriteLine();
        Console.WriteLine();
```

```
            Console.WriteLine("Press Enter to continue");
            Console.ReadLine();
        }
    }
```

The output is

NetworkAccess.Connect specified for http://localhost/

Press Enter to continue

Summary

Provides credentials for password-based authentication.

Type Summary

```
public class NetworkCredential : ICredentials
{
    // Constructors
        public NetworkCredential();
        public NetworkCredential(string userName, string password);
        public NetworkCredential(string userName, string password,
                string domain);

    // Properties
        public string Domain { get; set; }
        public string Password { get; set; }
        public string UserName { get; set; }

    // Methods
        public NetworkCredential GetCredential(Uri uri, string authType);
}
```

Description

The `NetworkCredential` class supplies client credentials used in password-based authentication schemes such as Kerberos.

[*Note:* Classes that implement the `ICredentials` interface, such as the `CredentialCache` class, return `NetworkCredential` instances. This class does not support public key-based authentication methods such as SSL client authentication.]

Example

```
using System;
using System.Net;

public class NetworkCredentialSample
{
    public static void Main()
    {
        NetworkCredential nc = new NetworkCredential("test", "secret");
        Uri path = new Uri("http://mysite.com");
        HttpWebRequest req = (HttpWebRequest) WebRequest.Create(path);
```

```
        req.Credentials = nc.GetCredential(path, "BASIC");
        NetworkCredential found =
            req.Credentials.GetCredential(path, "BASIC");
        Console.WriteLine("HttpWebRequest.Credentials contains:");
        Console.WriteLine("UserName:'{0}' Password:'{1}' Domain:'{2}'",
            found.UserName, found.Password, found.Domain);
        Console.WriteLine();
        Console.WriteLine();
        Console.WriteLine("Press Enter to continue");
        Console.ReadLine();
    }
}
```

The output is

```
HttpWebRequest.Credentials contains:
UserName:'test' Password:'secret' Domain:''


Press Enter to continue
```

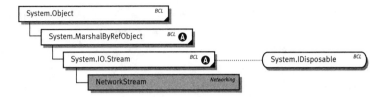

Summary
Implements the standard stream mechanism to read and write network data through an instance of the Socket class.

Type Summary

```
public class NetworkStream : Stream, IDisposable
    {
    // Constructors
        public NetworkStream(Socket socket);
        public NetworkStream(Socket socket, bool ownsSocket);
        public NetworkStream(Socket socket, FileAccess access);
        public NetworkStream(Socket socket, FileAccess access,
                bool ownsSocket);

    // Properties
        public override bool CanRead { get; }
        public override bool CanSeek { get; }
        public override bool CanWrite { get; }
        public virtual bool DataAvailable { get; }
        public override long Length { get; }
        public override long Position { get; set; }
MS CF protected bool Readable { get; set; }
MS CF protected Socket Socket { get; }
MS CF protected bool Writeable { get; set; }

    // Methods
        public override IAsyncResult BeginRead(byte[] buffer, int offset,
                                    int size, AsyncCallback callback,
                                    object state);
        public override IAsyncResult BeginWrite(byte[] buffer, int offset,
                                    int size, AsyncCallback callback,
                                    object state);
        public override void Close();
        protected virtual void Dispose(bool disposing);
        public override int EndRead(IAsyncResult asyncResult);
        public override void EndWrite(IAsyncResult asyncResult);
        ~NetworkStream();
        public override void Flush();
        public override int Read(byte[] buffer, int offset, int size);
        public override long Seek(long offset, SeekOrigin origin);
        public override void SetLength(long value);
        public override void Write(byte[] buffer, int offset, int size);
```

```
                // Explicit Interface Members
        MS void IDisposable.Dispose();
        }
```

> **■ LO**   Many network sources provide data in a way that makes it impossible to seek
> directly against the network stream. Classes that require streams to be seekable can be
> problematic in these cases and should be avoided whenever possible. In cases where the
> stream must be seekable, you may be forced to buffer the data into a `MemoryStream`
> and pass that in to the class once the data has all been read from the network.

Description

The `NetworkStream` class allows network data to be read and written in the same manner as the `System.IO.Stream` class.

This class supports simultaneous synchronous and asynchronous access to the network data. Random access is not supported and thus the `CanSeek` property always
returns `false`.

The following properties and methods inherited from the `System.IO.Stream` class
are not supported and throw a `System.NotSupportedException` exception when
accessed:

- `Length`
- `Position`
- `Seek`
- `SetLength`

The `Flush` method is reserved for future use but does not throw an exception.

Example

```
using System;
using System.Net;
using System.Net.Sockets;
using System.Text;

public class NetworkStreamSample
{
    private static bool bDone = false;
    private static Socket skt = null;
    private static NetworkStream ns = null;
    private static Byte[] res = new Byte[1024];

    public static void Main()
    {
        try
        {
```

```csharp
        skt = GetConnectedSocket();
        ns = new NetworkStream(skt, true);
        string targ = "/default.htm";
        byte[] req = Encoding.ASCII.GetBytes("GET " + targ + "\n");
        ns.Write(req, 0, req.Length);
        ns.BeginRead(res, 0 ,res.Length,
            new AsyncCallback(ReadHandler), null);
        Console.WriteLine("BeginRead completed...");
        while(!bDone) {}
    }
    catch (Exception e)
    {
        Console.WriteLine("Error: " + e.Message);
    }
    finally
    {
        ns.Close();
        skt.Close();
    }
    Console.WriteLine();
    Console.WriteLine();
    Console.WriteLine("Press Enter to continue");
    Console.ReadLine();
}

private static Socket GetConnectedSocket()
{
    IPAddress ip = IPAddress.Parse("127.0.0.1");
    Socket skt = new Socket(AddressFamily.InterNetwork,
        SocketType.Stream, ProtocolType.Tcp);
    try
    {
        IPEndPoint ep = new IPEndPoint(ip, 80);
        skt.Connect(ep);
        if (skt.Connected)
        {
            return skt;
        }
        else
        {
            throw new Exception("Cannot connect to host " + ip);
        }
    }
    catch (Exception e)
    {
        throw e;
    }
}


private static void ReadHandler(IAsyncResult ar)
{
    try
    {
        Console.WriteLine("ReadHandler executing...");
        int rec = ns.EndRead(ar);
```

A
B
C
D
E
F
G
H
I
J
K
L
M
N
O
P
Q
R
S
T
U
V
W
X
Y
Z

```
            Console.WriteLine("Received {0} bytes", rec);
            Console.WriteLine(Encoding.ASCII.GetString(res, 0, rec));
        }
        catch (Exception e)
        {
            Console.WriteLine("Error: " + e.Message);
        }
        finally
        {
            ns.Close();
            bDone = true;
        }
    }
}
```

The output is

```
BeginRead completed...
ReadHandler executing...
Received 60 bytes
<html>
<body>
This is the default page
</body>
</html>


Press Enter to continue
```

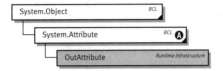

Summary

Indicates that a parameter will be marshaled from the callee back to the caller.

Type Summary

```
public sealed class OutAttribute : Attribute
    {
    // Constructors
        public OutAttribute();
    }
```

∎ SK There is sometimes confusion between this attribute and the `out` keyword in C#. `OutAttribute` (and `InAttribute` as well) are just hints to the interop marshaler so they don't have any effect unless used on interop calls. Typically, this attribute is used on reference types like classes passed *by value*. Without it, the marshaler will not copy back changes made on native side, even though this is inconsistent with the behavior of non-interop calls. Rumor has it that this is done for performance reasons and similarity with COM.

∎ AN The other case where `OutAttribute` is often needed is passing a by-value array of non-blittable types in a PInvoke signature, if you expect to see changes in the contents of the array after the call. The need for an explicit `OutAttribute` often catches people by surprise, because in managed code you expect the array to exhibit "in-out" behavior. But in this case, too, we ended up choosing the higher-performing default that also happened to match MIDL's default.

∎ BG The `InAttribute` and `OutAttribute` classes have some interesting effects in PInvoke calls and Remoting calls. `Stream`'s `Read` is an interesting example. Since `Stream` is a marshal-by-reference object and it writes data into one of its parameters, you must use the `OutAttribute` on the byte[]. As a performance optimization, Remoting assumes all parameters are passed as input parameters. Unfortunately, `InAttribute` and `OutAttribute` aren't part of a method's signature, even though for remoting purposes they are part of the signature.

CONTINUED

249

> Here's an example of using this on the `Stream` class:
>
> ```
> public abstract int Read([In, Out] byte[] buffer, int offset, int count);
> ```

Description

[*Note:* The `InAttribute` and `OutAttribute` are not required. In the absence of explicit settings, the system assumes that all arguments passed by reference are passed in/out and that all non-reference parameters are in. The only exception is the `System.Text.StringBuilder` class, which is always assumed to be in/out. The `InAttribute` and `OutAttribute` are particularly useful when applied to formatted types that cannot be block-copied. Since these types require copying during marshaling, you can use `InAttribute` and `OutAttribute` to eliminate the generation of unnecessary copies.]

Compilers are required to not preserve this type in metadata as a custom attribute. Instead, compilers are required to emit it directly in the file format, as described in Partition II of the CLI Specification. Metadata consumers, such as the Reflection API, are required to retrieve this data from the file format and return it as if it were a custom attribute.

Example

```
using System;
using System.Runtime.InteropServices;
using System.Text;

/// <summary>
/// Sample demonstrating the use of the OutAttribute class.
/// Use this class to indicate how parameters should be marshalled to unmanaged
/// code.
/// </summary>
internal class OutAttributeSample
{

    private static void Main()
    {
        StringBuilder guidString = new StringBuilder(39).Append('\0', 39);
        Guid          newGuid    = Guid.NewGuid();

        if (StringFromGUID2(ref newGuid, guidString, guidString.Length) != 0)
        {
            Console.WriteLine("Generated GUID: {0}", guidString);
        }
        else
        {
            Console.WriteLine("StringFromGUID2 failed.");
        }
```

```
        Console.WriteLine();
        Console.WriteLine();
        Console.WriteLine("Press Enter to continue");
        Console.ReadLine();
    }

    // Win32 method to convert a given GUID to a string. Note that the default
    // marshalling for StringBuilder is [in,out], so [Out] is used to override
    // the normal marshalling. This is used purely to demonstrate using the
    // OutAttribute; .NET code should use Guid.ToString() to perform the same
    // conversion.
    [DllImport("ole32.dll", CharSet=CharSet.Unicode)]
    private static extern int StringFromGUID2(
        [In]ref Guid rguid, [Out]StringBuilder lpsz, int cchMax);

}
```

The output is

```
Generated GUID: {36ED812C-BB9E-4154-B6F6-D8903F81738F}


Press Enter to continue
```

A
B
C
D
E
F
G
H
I
J
K
L
M
N
O
P
Q
R
S
T
U
V
W
X
Y
Z

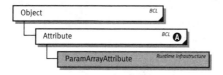

Summary

Indicates that a method allows a variable number of arguments in its invocation.

Type Summary

```
public sealed class ParamArrayAttribute : Attribute
    {
    // Constructors
       public ParamArrayAttribute();
    }
```

BG   A number of people on the CLR team have looked down on param arrays in C#, saying they're not really similar to variable arguments from C\C++ land. The primary criticism is that they allocate an array in the GC heap to pass in data from one spot on the stack to the next. The CLR implemented the `ArgIterator` type to do varargs in a style similar to C++'s `va_list`. But as far as I know, only the C++ compiler from Microsoft supports varargs using the `ArgIterator` class. The C# compiler has limited support for CLR-style varargs methods (you may see `__argList` in the BCL source), but that only exists so we can write the base class libraries in C#, and isn't supported as a general part of the C# language. Param arrays are a hack, but they're usable for multiple languages. I have no idea whether they perform better than our `ArgIterator`. This is yet another example in the history of computing where simplicity and elegance may have won out over complexity and performance; judging by real-world usage, I think param arrays won out over `ArgIterator`.

BA   In retrospect, we should have put this type in the `System.Runtime.CompilerServices` namespaces with all the other types that are only used by the compiler.

CONTINUED

> **▪ BA**   To give you an idea of how this attribute is used, consider how the following C# code translates into IL. Notice how the ILASM code shows the usage of the ParamArrayAttribute. This tells any compiler targeting this method to allow special calling syntax. Examples follow.
>
> C# code:
>
> ```
> public static void PrintArgs (params string[] args) {
> ```
>
> Corresponding ILASM code:
>
> ```
> .method public hidebysig static void PrintArgs(string[] args) cil managed
> {
>   .param [1]
>   .custom instance void [mscorlib]System.ParamArrayAttribute::.ctor() =
>                                                      ( 01 00 00 00 )
> ```
>
> C# calling code examples; notice the final two examples produce identical IL code:
>
> ```
> PrintArgs ("One");
> PrintArgs ("One", "Two");
> PrintArgs ("One","Two","Three");
> PrintArgs (new string[] {"One","Two","Three"});
> ```

Description

This attribute can be applied to parameters. A parameter array allows the specification of an unknown number of arguments. The array is required to be a single-dimensional array that is the last parameter in a formal parameter list. It permits arguments to a method to be specified in two ways:

- A single expression of a type that is implicitly convertible to the parameter array type. The array functions as a value parameter.
- Zero or more arguments where each argument is an expression of a type that is implicitly convertible to the type of the parameter-array element.

Example

```
using System;
using System.Reflection;

/// <summary>
/// This sample shows calling a method defined with a params method
/// and how to access that data via reflection.
/// </summary>
public class ParamArrayAttributeSample
{
    public static void Main()
    {
        Console.WriteLine("Sum(1, 1, 2, 3, 5, 8) == {0}", Sum(1, 1, 2, 3, 5, 8));
```

```
        Console.WriteLine("Sum(2, 3, 5) == {0}", Sum(2, 3, 5));

        MethodInfo[] methods = typeof(ParamArrayAttributeSample).GetMethods(
            BindingFlags.Static | BindingFlags.Public);
        foreach (MethodInfo method in methods)
        {
            Console.Write("public static {0} (", method.Name);
            foreach (ParameterInfo param in method.GetParameters())
            {
                foreach (Attribute attr in param.GetCustomAttributes(true))
                {
                    if (attr is ParamArrayAttribute)
                    {
                        Console.Write("params ");
                    }
                }
                Console.Write("{0} {1}", param.ParameterType, param.Name);
            }
            Console.WriteLine(");");
        }
        Console.WriteLine();
        Console.WriteLine();
        Console.WriteLine("Press Enter to continue");
        Console.ReadLine();
    }

    public static int Sum(params int[] numbers)
    {
        int sum = 0;
        foreach (int value in numbers)
        {
            sum += value;
        }
        return sum;

    }
}
```

The output is

```
Sum(1, 1, 2, 3, 5, 8) == 20
Sum(2, 3, 5) == 10
public static Main ();
public static Sum (params System.Int32[] numbers) ;


Press Enter to continue
```

A
B
C
D
E
F
G
H
I
J
K
L
M
N
O
P
Q
R
S
T
U
V
W
X
Y
Z

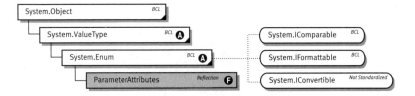

Summary

Defines the attributes for a parameter. This enumeration is used by the `Parameter-Info.Attributes` property.

Type Summary

```
public enum ParameterAttributes
    {
    HasDefault = 0x1000,
    HasFieldMarshal = 0x2000,
MS  In = 0x1,
MS  Lcid = 0x4,
MS  None = 0x0,
MS  Optional = 0x10,
MS  Out = 0x2,
MS  Reserved3 = 0x4000,
MS  Reserved4 = 0x8000,
MS  ReservedMask = 0xf000,
MS  Retval = 0x8,
    }
```

> ■ JP Some developers are curious about the `Reserved3` and `Reserved4` fields. We reserved the bits in metadata in 1.0 and 1.1 and as a result, exposed them in managed code. Funnily enough, the reasons why we reserved them are lost to history. We have since removed the metadata bits in v2.0 of the .NET Framework, but have kept around their managed counterparts for backwards compatibility reasons.

Example

```
using System;
using System.Reflection;
using System.Runtime.InteropServices;
```

```csharp
/// <summary>
/// This example shows how to set and retrieve the attributes of
/// a paramater.
/// </summary>

public class ParameterAttributesSample
{
    public static void Main()
    {
        foreach (MethodInfo method in typeof(DemoClass).GetMethods())
        {
            //ignore anything not declared here...
            if (method.DeclaringType != method.ReflectedType)
            {
                continue;
            }
            Console.WriteLine("'{0}' ", method.Name);
            Console.Write("     ");

            foreach (ParameterInfo pi in method.GetParameters())
            {

                Console.Write(pi.Name);
                Console.Write("( ");
                if ((pi.Attributes & ParameterAttributes.In) != 0)
                {
                    Console.Write("In ");
                }
                if ((pi.Attributes & ParameterAttributes.Out) != 0)
                {
                    Console.Write("Out ");
                }
                if (pi.Attributes == ParameterAttributes.None)
                {
                    Console.Write("None ");
                }
                Console.Write(") ");


            }
            Console.WriteLine();
        }
        Console.WriteLine();
        Console.WriteLine();
        Console.WriteLine("Press Enter to continue");
        Console.ReadLine();
    }
}
public abstract class DemoClass
{
    public static void Method1([In] int value, [Out]int value2) { }
    public static void Method2([In][Out] int value) { }
    public static void Method3(int value) { }
}
```

The output is

```
'Method1'
    value( In ) value2( Out )
'Method2'
    value( In Out )
'Method3'
    value( None )


Press Enter to continue
```

A
B
C
D
E
F
G
H
I
J
K
L
M
N
O
P
Q
R
S
T
U
V
W
X
Y
Z

Summary

Provides access to parameter metadata.

Type Summary

```
public class ParameterInfo : ICustomAttributeProvider
   {
   // Constructors
      protected ParameterInfo();

   // Fields
MS protected ParameterAttributes AttrsImpl;
MS protected Type ClassImpl;
MS protected object DefaultValueImpl;
MS protected MemberInfo MemberImpl;
MS protected string NameImpl;
MS protected int PositionImpl;

   // Properties
      public virtual ParameterAttributes Attributes { get; }
MS    public virtual object DefaultValue { get; }
MS CF public bool IsIn { get; }
MS CF public bool IsLcid { get; }
MS CF public bool IsOptional { get; }
MS CF public bool IsOut { get; }
MS CF public bool IsRetval { get; }
MS    public virtual MemberInfo Member { get; }
      public virtual string Name { get; }
      public virtual Type ParameterType { get; }
MS    public virtual int Position { get; }

   // Methods
MS public virtual object[] GetCustomAttributes(bool inherit);
MS public virtual object[] GetCustomAttributes(Type attributeType,
                        bool inherit);
MS public virtual bool IsDefined(Type attributeType, bool inherit);
   }
```

Example

```
using System;
using System.Reflection;

/// <summary>
/// This example shows how to print out the parameters to a method
```

```
/// in C# syntax.
/// </summary>

public class ParameterInfoSample
{
    public static void Main()
    {
        Type type = typeof(string);

        foreach (MethodInfo method in type.GetMethods(BindingFlags.NonPublic |
            BindingFlags.Public | BindingFlags.Instance | BindingFlags.Static))
        {
            //Skip any methods that are not publicly accessible
            if (!(method.IsPublic || method.IsFamily ||
                method.IsFamilyOrAssembly))
            {
                continue;
            }

            //Skip any methods with special names such as
            //constructors and property\event methods.
            if (method.IsSpecialName)
            {
                continue;
            }

            Console.Write(method.IsPublic ? "public " : "protected ");
            if (method.IsStatic)
            {
                Console.Write("static ");
            }
            Console.Write("{0} (", method.Name);
            PrintParamList(method.GetParameters());
            Console.WriteLine(")");
        }
        Console.WriteLine();
        Console.WriteLine();
        Console.WriteLine("Press Enter to continue");
        Console.ReadLine();
    }
    static void PrintParamList(ParameterInfo[] parameters)
    {
        for (int i = 0; i < parameters.Length; i++)
        {
            ParameterInfo param = parameters[i];
            if (i != 0)
            {
                Console.Write(", ");
            }
            Type type = param.ParameterType;
            if (type.IsArray && Attribute.IsDefined(param,
                typeof(ParamArrayAttribute), true))
            {
                Console.Write("params ");
            }
            Console.Write(type.Name);
```

```
            Console.Write(' ');
            Console.Write(param.Name);
        }
    }
} //end class
```

The output is

```
public ToString (IFormatProvider provider)
public GetTypeCode ()
public Clone ()
public CompareTo (Object value)
protected Finalize ()
public GetHashCode ()
public Equals (Object obj)
public ToString ()
public static Join (String separator, String[] value)
public static Join (String separator, String[] value, Int32 startIndex, Int32
count)
public Equals (String value)
public static Equals (String a, String b)
public CopyTo (Int32 sourceIndex, Char[] destination, Int32 destinationIndex,
Int32 count)
```

    [output truncated]

A
B
C
D
E
F
G
H
I
J
K
L
M
N
O
P
Q
R
S
T
U
V
W
X
Y
Z

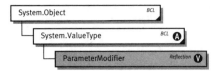

A

B

C

D

Summary

E
Reserved for future use.

F

G
Type Summary

```
public struct ParameterModifier
    {
    // Constructors
MS  public ParameterModifier(int parameterCount);

    // Properties
MS  public bool this[int index] { get; set; }
    }
```

H

I

J

K

L

M
> ■ **DM**   Currently, this type's sole purpose in life is to indicate which arguments passed to `Type.InvokeMember` are meant to be `byref` when invoking on a COM component. The way this is specified is by setting the default property to true for all arguments that are to be passed out `byref` using the index of the argument in the objects array. However, who knows if we will find other interesting uses for this type in the future.

N

O

P

Q

R

S
Description

T
[Note: This class is provided in order to implement the abstract methods that require it in the reflection library. When invoking a method with a parameter that is an array of `ParameterModifier` objects, specify `null`.*]*

U

V

W

X

Y

Z

System.Reflection
PropertyAttributes Enum

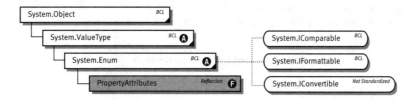

Summary

Defines the attributes that may be associated with a property.

Type Summary

```
public enum PropertyAttributes
    {
    HasDefault = 0x1000,
    None = 0x0,
MS  Reserved2 = 0x2000,
MS  Reserved3 = 0x4000,
MS  Reserved4 = 0x8000,
MS  ReservedMask = 0xf400,
MS  RTSpecialName = 0x400,
    SpecialName = 0x200,
    }
```

> ■ JP   Reflection has always considered its job as rationalizing the type system and exposing metadata bits. `PropertyAttributes` is a basic enum that exposes the metadata flags for Properties. Compilers are the typical consumers and producers of this enum.

Description

This enumeration is used by the `PropertyInfo.Attributes` property.

Example

```
using System;
using System.Reflection;

/// <summary>
/// This example prints out the attributes of a property.
/// </summary>
```

PropertyAttributes Enum

```
public class PropertyAttributesSample
{
    public static void Main()
    {
        Type type = typeof(string);
        foreach (PropertyInfo property in type.GetProperties())
        {
            Console.WriteLine("Property '{0}' Attributes: '{1}'",
                property.Name, property.Attributes);
        }
        Console.WriteLine();
        Console.WriteLine();
        Console.WriteLine("Press Enter to continue");
        Console.ReadLine();
    }
}
```

The output is

```
Property 'Chars' Attributes: 'None'
Property 'Length' Attributes: 'None'


Press Enter to continue
```

Summary
Provides access to property metadata.

Type Summary

```
public abstract class PropertyInfo : MemberInfo
    {
    // Constructors
    protected PropertyInfo();

    // Properties
    public abstract PropertyAttributes Attributes { get; }
    public abstract bool CanRead { get; }
    public abstract bool CanWrite { get; }
MS  public bool IsSpecialName { get; }
MS  public override MemberTypes MemberType { get; }
    public abstract Type PropertyType { get; }

    // Methods
    public MethodInfo[] GetAccessors();
    public abstract MethodInfo[] GetAccessors(bool nonPublic);
    public MethodInfo GetGetMethod();
    public abstract MethodInfo GetGetMethod(bool nonPublic);
    public abstract ParameterInfo[] GetIndexParameters();
    public MethodInfo GetSetMethod();
    public abstract MethodInfo GetSetMethod(bool nonPublic);
    public abstract object GetValue(object obj, BindingFlags invokeAttr,
                        Binder binder, object[] index,
                        CultureInfo culture);
    public virtual object GetValue(object obj, object[] index);
    public abstract void SetValue(object obj, object value,
                        BindingFlags invokeAttr, Binder binder,
                        object[] index, CultureInfo culture);
    public virtual void SetValue(object obj, object value, object[] index);
    }
```

■ JP   There is a friction between the CLI and the type system as a whole. The CLI
has restrictions that are exposed via the languages and compilers that enforce them.
The XXXInfo APIs represent adherence to only the runtime type system rules and do
not follow the CLI rule specifications. Users sometimes find it confusing when
XXXInfo APIs don't match their language expectations.

CONTINUED

A good example of this is the lack of `IsPublic` property on the `PropertyInfo` API. A C# property matches the CLI specification and does not allow for differences in getter and setter accessibility—they must both match the property accessibility. (This has changed for C# 2.0.) You could expect in this case that an `IsPublic` property would make sense. However, property getter and setter methods from the CLR prospective can have difference accessibility associated with them. For this reason alone, we cannot have an `IsPublic` property API on `PropertyInfo`, because the `get` and `set` accessibility could be different.

■ **JP**   Properties are very much a second-class citizen in the runtime, and hence the performance of obtaining `PropertyInfos` tends to be slower than its counterpart XXXInfo APIs. The runtime actually stashes properties in an inconvenient place (property metadata table), with no real direct relational data to its relevant methods (I purposely don't say "get/set" methods here, because the runtime allows for any number of methods, with any name to be tagged against a property) in the method table (`MethodImpl` metadata table). This means Reflection needs to do more work to map property names to their respective methods—it's pretty ugly.

A nice bird's-eye view of the property to method mapping can be found in Partition II (21.31) of the ECMA spec.

Description

A property is a named aspect of an object's state whose value is typically accessible through `get` and `set` accessors. [*Note:* Properties can be read-only, in which case the `set` accessor is not available.]

Several methods in this class assume that the `Get` and `Set` accessors of a property have certain formats. The signatures of the accessors are required to match the following conventions:

The return type of the `Get` accessor and the last argument of the `Set` accessor are required to be identical to the type of the property reflected by the current instance.

The `Get` and `Set` accessors are required to have the same number, type, and order of indices.

If this format is not followed, the behavior of the `GetValue` and `SetValue` methods is undefined.

Example

```
using System;
using System.Reflection;
```

```
/// <summary>
/// This example prints out the properties of a type in C# syntax.
/// </summary>

public class PropertyInfoSample
{
    public static void Main()
    {
        Type type = typeof(String);

        foreach (PropertyInfo property in type.GetProperties(
            BindingFlags.NonPublic | BindingFlags.Public |
            BindingFlags.Instance | BindingFlags.Static))
        {
            //set accessor to the GetMethod if it is there, if not use the
            // set method.  If neither are present this is a badly formed
            // property, skip it.
            MethodInfo accessor = property.GetGetMethod();
            if (accessor == null)
            {
                accessor = property.GetSetMethod();
            }
            if (accessor == null)
            {
                continue;
            }

            //Properties don't themselves have accessibility,
            //only their accessors.
            //Skip this property if the accessor is not publicly accessible.
            if (!(accessor.IsPublic || accessor.IsFamily ||
                accessor.IsFamilyOrAssembly))
            {
                continue;
            }

            Console.Write(accessor.IsPublic ? "public " : "protected ");
            if (accessor.IsStatic)
            {
                Console.Write("static ");
            }

            Console.Write(property.PropertyType.Name + " ");
            ParameterInfo[] parameters = property.GetIndexParameters();
            if (parameters.Length == 0)
            {
                Console.Write(property.Name);
            }
            else
            {
                Console.Write("this[");
                foreach (ParameterInfo p in parameters)
                {
                    Console.Write("{0} {1}", p.ParameterType, p.Name);
                }
```

A
B
C
D
E
F
G
H
I
J
K
L
M
N
O
P
Q
R
S
T
U
V
W
X
Y
Z

267

```
                    Console.Write("]");
                }
                Console.Write(" { ");
                if (property.CanRead)
                {
                    Console.Write("get; ");
                }
                if (property.CanWrite)
                {
                    Console.Write("set; ");
                }
                Console.WriteLine("}");
            }

            PropertyInfo pi = type.GetProperty("Length");
            int ret = (int)pi.GetValue("test input", null);
            Console.WriteLine("The result is '{0}'", ret);
            Console.WriteLine();
            Console.WriteLine();
            Console.WriteLine("Press Enter to continue");
            Console.ReadLine();
        }

    } //end class
```

The output is

```
public Char this[System.Int32 index] { get; }
public Int32 Length { get; }
The result is '10'


Press Enter to continue
```

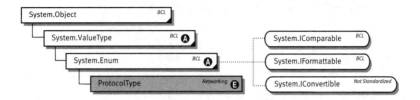

Summary
Specifies the protocols used by the Socket class.

Type Summary
```
public enum ProtocolType
    {
        Ggp = 3,
        Icmp = 1,
        Idp = 22,
        Igmp = 2,
        IP = 0,
MS CF 1.1 IPv6 = 41,
        Ipx = 1000,
        ND = 77,
        Pup = 12,
        Raw = 255,
        Spx = 1256,
        SpxII = 1257,
        Tcp = 6,
        Udp = 17,
        Unknown = -1,
        Unspecified = 0,
    }
```

Description
The ProtocolType enumeration is used with the Socket class. This enumeration specifies the protocols that a socket instance can use to transport data.

Example
```
using System;
using System.Net;
using System.Net.Sockets;
using System.Text;

public class ProtocolTypeSample
{
    public static void Main()
```

A
B
C
D
E
F
G
H
I
J
K
L
M
N
O
P
Q
R
S
T
U
V
W
X
Y
Z

```csharp
        {
            IPAddress ip = IPAddress.Parse("127.0.0.1");
            string targ = "/default.htm";
            Socket skt = new Socket(AddressFamily.InterNetwork,
                SocketType.Stream, ProtocolType.Tcp);
            try
            {
                IPEndPoint ep = new IPEndPoint(ip, 80);
                skt.Connect(ep);
                if (skt.Connected)
                {
                    Byte[] req = Encoding.ASCII.GetBytes("GET " + targ + "\n");
                    skt.Send(req);
                    Byte[] res = new Byte[1024];
                    int rec = skt.Receive(res);
                    skt.Shutdown(SocketShutdown.Both);
                    Console.WriteLine("Received {0} bytes for {1}:",
                        rec, targ);
                    Console.WriteLine(Encoding.ASCII.GetString(res, 0, rec));
                }
                else
                {
                    Console.WriteLine("Cannot connect to host {0}", ip);
                }
            }
            catch (Exception e)
            {
                Console.WriteLine("Error: " + e.Message);
            }
            finally
            {
                skt.Close();
            }
            Console.WriteLine();
            Console.WriteLine();
            Console.WriteLine("Press Enter to continue");
            Console.ReadLine();
        }
    }
```

The output is

```
Received 60 bytes for /default.htm:
<html>
<body>
This is the default page
</body>
</html>


Press Enter to continue
```

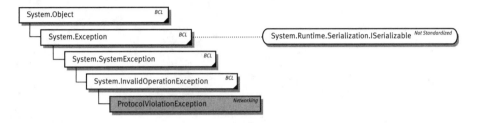

Summary

Represents errors that occur due to violating the rules of a network protocol.

Type Summary

```
public class ProtocolViolationException : InvalidOperationException,
                                          ISerializable
   {
   // Constructors
   public ProtocolViolationException();
MS CF protected ProtocolViolationException(
               SerializationInfo serializationInfo,
               StreamingContext streamingContext);
   public ProtocolViolationException(string message);

   // Explicit Interface Members
MS CF void ISerializable.GetObjectData(SerializationInfo serializationInfo,
         StreamingContext streamingContext);
   }
```

Description

A `ProtocolViolationException` is thrown by types derived from `WebRequest` and `WebResponse` to indicate that an error has occurred as defined by the rules of the underlying protocol. For example, the `HttpWebRequest` type throws a `ProtocolViolationException` when an application attempts to send content without specifying the content length.

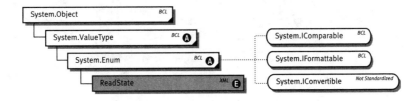

Summary

Specifies the read state of an instance of a class derived from the XmlReader class.

Type Summary

```
public enum ReadState
    {
    Closed = 4,
    EndOfFile = 3,
    Error = 2,
    Initial = 0,
    Interactive = 1,
    }
```

Description

When a reader is instantiated, the read state is set to Initial. When the Xml-Reader.Read method is called, the read state is changed to Interactive. If an error occurs during a read operation, the read state is changed to Error. When the end of the XML data is reached, the read state is set to EndOfFile. When the XmlReader.Close method is called, the read state is set to Closed.

Example

```
using System;
using System.Xml;

/// <summary>
/// Writes the ReadState at each point in the reading of an .xml input file
/// </summary>

public class ReadStateSample
{
    public static void Main()
    {
        string s = "sample.xml";
        Console.WriteLine("Reading file '{0}'", s);
        XmlTextReader r = new XmlTextReader(s);
        Console.WriteLine("Before first Read, ReadState is {0}", r.ReadState);
```

```
                    while(r.Read())
                    {
                        ShowReadState(r);
                    }
                    r.Close();
                    Console.WriteLine("After Close, ReadState is {0}", r.ReadState);
                    Console.WriteLine();
                    Console.WriteLine();
                    Console.WriteLine("Press Enter to continue");
                    Console.ReadLine();
                }

                static void ShowReadState(XmlTextReader r)
                {
                    Console.WriteLine("Node {0} {1}, ReadState is {2}", r.NodeType, r.Name,
                                        r.ReadState);
                }

            }
```

The output is

```
Reading file 'sample.xml'
Before first Read, ReadState is Initial
Node XmlDeclaration xml, ReadState is Interactive
Node Element root, ReadState is Interactive
Node Text , ReadState is Interactive
Node EndElement root, ReadState is Interactive
Node Whitespace , ReadState is Interactive
After Close, ReadState is Closed


Press Enter to continue
```

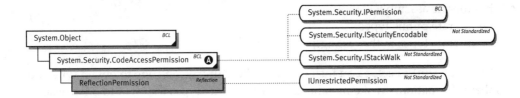

Summary

Secures access to the metadata of non-public types and members through reflection.

Type Summary

```
CF public sealed class ReflectionPermission : CodeAccessPermission,
                                              IUnrestrictedPermission
      {
      // Constructors
MS CF public ReflectionPermission(PermissionState state);
   CF public ReflectionPermission(ReflectionPermissionFlag flag);

      // Properties
MS CF public ReflectionPermissionFlag Flags { get; set; }

      // Methods
   CF public override IPermission Copy();
   CF public override void FromXml(SecurityElement esd);
   CF public override IPermission Intersect(IPermission target);
   CF public override bool IsSubsetOf(IPermission target);
MS CF public bool IsUnrestricted();
   CF public override SecurityElement ToXml();
   CF public override IPermission Union(IPermission other);

      // Explicit Interface Members
MS CF int IBuiltInPermission.GetTokenIndex();
      }
```

Description

Code with the appropriate ReflectionPermission has access to non-public members of a type. Without ReflectionPermission, code can access only the public members of assemblies.

[*Note:* Without ReflectionPermission, untrusted code can perform the following operations on members of loaded assemblies:

- Obtain type information from metadata for public types and members.
- Invoke public members.
- Invoke members defined with family access in the calling code's base classes.

- Invoke members defined with assembly access in the calling code's assembly.
- Invoke members defined with FamilyAndAssembly or FamilyOrAssembly access in the calling code's base classes and/or assembly.
- Enumerate assemblies.
- Enumerate public types.
- Enumerate types in the calling.]

`ReflectionPermission` instances can allow untrusted code to obtain type and member information, invoke members, and enumerate types that would otherwise be inaccessible. [*Note:* Because `ReflectionPermission` can provide access to members and information that were not intended for public access, it is recommended that `ReflectionPermission` be granted only to trusted code.]

The XML encoding of a `ReflectionPermission` instance is defined below in EBNF format. The following conventions are used:

- All non-literals in the grammar below are shown in normal type.
- All literals are in bold font.

The following meta-language symbols are used:

- "*" represents a meta-language symbol suffixing an expression that can appear zero or more times.
- "?" represents a meta-language symbol suffixing an expression that can appear zero or one time.
- "+" represents a meta-language symbol suffixing an expression that can appear one or more times.
- "(',')" is used to group literals, non-literals, or a mixture of literals and non-literals.
- " | " denotes an exclusive disjunction between two expressions.
- "::= " denotes a production rule where a left-hand non-literal is replaced by a right-hand expression containing literals, non-literals, or both.

BuildVersion refers to the build version of the shipping CLI. This is specified as a dotted build number such as"2412.0".
ECMAPubKeyToken::= `b77a5c561934e089`
ReflectionPermissionFlag = `MemberAccess` | `TypeInformation`
Each ReflectionPermissionFlag can appear in the XML no more than once. For example, Flags=MemberAccess,MemberAccess is illegal.
The XML encoding of a `ReflectionPermission` instance is as follows:

ReflectionPermissionXML::=

```
<IPermission
class="
System.Security.Permissions.ReflectionPermission, mscorlib,
```

```
Version=1.0.BuildVersion,
Culture=neutral,
PublicKeyToken=ECMAPubKeyToken"
version="1"
(
Unrestricted="true"
)
|
(
Flags="NoFlags | (ReflectionPermissionFlag
(,ReflectionPermissionFlag)*"
)
/>
```

Example

```
using System;
using System.Reflection;
using System.Security;
using System.Security.Permissions;

/// <summary>
/// Sample demonstrating the use of the ReflectionPermission class.
/// Use this class to imperatively control access to type information with
/// reflection.
/// </summary>
internal class ReflectionPermissionSample
{

    private static void Main()
    {
        // Deny ReflectionPermission to all callees.
        ReflectionPermission perm =
            new ReflectionPermission(ReflectionPermissionFlag.AllFlags);

        perm.Deny();

        try
        {
            // Get the assembly name by calling GetName() directly. Note that
            // ReflectionPermission has no effect.
            Console.WriteLine("Retrieving current assembly name...");
            Console.WriteLine(GetCurrentAssemblyName().FullName);
            Console.WriteLine();
            // Get the assembly name by calling GetName() with reflection. Note
            // that ReflectionPermission is enforced.
            Console.WriteLine(
                "Retrieving current assembly name with reflection...");
            Console.WriteLine(GetCurrentAssemblyNameWithReflection().FullName);
        }
        catch (SecurityException ex)
        {
            Console.WriteLine(ex.Message);
        }
```

```
            Console.WriteLine();
            Console.WriteLine();
            Console.WriteLine("Press Enter to continue");
            Console.ReadLine();
        }

        private static AssemblyName GetCurrentAssemblyName()
        {
            return Assembly.GetExecutingAssembly().GetName();
        }

        private static AssemblyName GetCurrentAssemblyNameWithReflection()
        {
            return (AssemblyName)typeof(Assembly).InvokeMember(
                "GetName", BindingFlags.InvokeMethod, null,
                Assembly.GetExecutingAssembly(), null);
        }

    }
}
```

The output is

```
Retrieving current assembly name...
ReflectionPermission, Version=0.0.0.0, Culture=neutral, PublicKeyToken=null

Retrieving current assembly name with reflection...
Request for the permission of type System.Security.Permissions.ReflectionPermiss
ion, mscorlib, Version=1.0.5000.0, Culture=neutral, PublicKeyToken=b77a5c561934e
089 failed.


Press Enter to continue
```

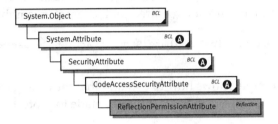

Summary

Used to declaratively specify security actions to control access to non-public types using reflection.

Type Summary

```
CF public sealed class ReflectionPermissionAttribute :
                                      CodeAccessSecurityAttribute
    {
    // Constructors
    CF public ReflectionPermissionAttribute(SecurityAction action);

    // Properties
    CF public ReflectionPermissionFlag Flags { get; set; }
MS CF public bool MemberAccess { get; set; }
MS CF public bool ReflectionEmit { get; set; }
MS CF public bool TypeInformation { get; set; }

    // Methods
    CF public override IPermission CreatePermission();
    }
```

Description

[*Note:* The level of access to non-public types and members is specified using the ReflectionPermissionAttribute.Flags property and the ReflectionPermis-sionFlag enumeration. The security information declared by a security attribute is stored in the metadata of the attribute target, and is accessed by the system at runtime. Security attributes are used for declarative security only. For imperative security, use the corresponding permission class, ReflectionPermission. The allowable Reflec-tionPermissionAttribute targets are determined by the SecurityAction passed to the constructor.]

ReflectionPermissionAttribute Class

Example

The following example shows a declarative request for access to non-public members of loaded assemblies. The `SecurityAction.RequestMinimum` security action indicates that this is the minimum permission required for the target assembly to be able to execute.

```
[assembly:ReflectionPermissionAttribute(SecurityAction.RequestMinimum,
MemberAccess=true)]
```

The following example shows how to demand that the calling code has unrestricted access to non-public types. Demands are typically made to protect methods or classes from malicious code.

```
[ReflectionPermissionAttribute(SecurityAction.Demand, Unrestricted=true)]
```

The following example demonstrates the use of the `ReflectionPermission-Attribute` class.

```
using System;
using System.Reflection;
using System.Security;
using System.Security.Permissions;

/// <summary>
/// Sample demonstrating the use of the ReflectionPermissionAttribute class.
/// Use this class to declaratively control access to type information with
/// reflection.
/// </summary>
internal class ReflectionPermissionAttributeSample
{

    private static void Main()
    {

        try
        {
            // Get the assembly name by calling GetName() directly. Note that
            // ReflectionPermissionAttribute has no effect.
            Console.WriteLine("Retrieving current assembly name...");
            Console.WriteLine(GetCurrentAssemblyName().FullName);
            Console.WriteLine();
            // Get the assembly name by calling GetName() with reflection. Note
            // that ReflectionPermissionAttribute is enforced.
            Console.WriteLine(
                "Retrieving current assembly name with reflection...");
            Console.WriteLine(GetCurrentAssemblyNameWithReflection().FullName);
        }
        catch (SecurityException ex)
        {
            Console.WriteLine(ex.Message);
        }

        Console.WriteLine();
```

```
        Console.WriteLine();
        Console.WriteLine("Press Enter to continue");
        Console.ReadLine();
    }

    // Deny ReflectionPermission to this method and all of its callees.
    [ReflectionPermission(
        SecurityAction.Deny, Flags=ReflectionPermissionFlag.AllFlags)]
    private static AssemblyName GetCurrentAssemblyName()
    {
        return Assembly.GetExecutingAssembly().GetName();
    }

    // Deny ReflectionPermission to this method and all of its callees.
    [ReflectionPermission(
        SecurityAction.Deny, Flags=ReflectionPermissionFlag.AllFlags)]
    private static AssemblyName GetCurrentAssemblyNameWithReflection()
    {
        return (AssemblyName)typeof(Assembly).InvokeMember(
            "GetName", BindingFlags.InvokeMethod, null,
            Assembly.GetExecutingAssembly(), null);
    }

}
```

The output is

```
Retrieving current assembly name...
ReflectionPermissionAttribute, Version=0.0.0.0, Culture=neutral,
PublicKeyToken=null

Retrieving current assembly name with reflection...
Request for the permission of type System.Security.Permissions.ReflectionPermiss
ion, mscorlib, Version=1.0.5000.0, Culture=neutral, PublicKeyToken=b77a5c561934e
089 failed.


Press Enter to continue
```

A
B
C
D
E
F
G
H
I
J
K
L
M
N
O
P
Q
R
S
T
U
V
W
X
Y
Z

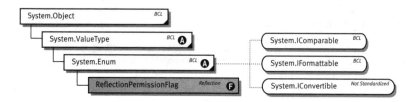

Summary

Represents levels of access to the metadata for non-public types and members accessed using reflection.

Type Summary

```
CF public enum ReflectionPermissionFlag
        {
  MS CF  AllFlags = 0x7,
     CF  MemberAccess = 0x2,
     CF  NoFlags = 0x0,
  MS CF  ReflectionEmit = 0x4,
     CF  TypeInformation = 0x1,
        }
```

Description

[*Note:* This enumeration is used by ReflectionPermission.]

Example

```csharp
using System;
using System.Reflection;
using System.Security;
using System.Security.Permissions;

/// <summary>
/// Sample demonstrating the use of the ReflectionPermissionFlag enumeration.
/// Use this enumeration with ReflectionPermission or
/// ReflectionPermissionAttribute to to control access to type information with
/// reflection.
/// </summary>
internal class ReflectionPermissionFlagSample
{

    private static void Main()
    {
        // Deny access to non-public type information to all callees.
        ReflectionPermission perm =
            new ReflectionPermission(ReflectionPermissionFlag.TypeInformation);
```

```
        perm.Deny();
        WriteNonPublicInstanceMethodsForType(typeof(Assembly));
        // Restore access to non-public type information to its previous
        // setting.
        CodeAccessPermission.RevertDeny();
        WriteNonPublicInstanceMethodsForType(typeof(Assembly));
        Console.WriteLine();
        Console.WriteLine();
        Console.WriteLine("Press Enter to continue");
        Console.ReadLine();
    }

    // Writes a list of the non-public methods for the specified Type.
    private static void WriteNonPublicInstanceMethodsForType(Type t)
    {
        Console.WriteLine("Non-public instance methods for '{0}'", t);

        MethodInfo[] methods =
            t.GetMethods(BindingFlags.Instance | BindingFlags.NonPublic);

        foreach (MethodInfo method in methods)
        {
            Console.WriteLine("  {0}", method.Name);
        }

        Console.WriteLine("Total number of methods: {0}", methods.Length);
        Console.WriteLine();
    }

}
```

The output is

```
Non-public instance methods for 'System.Reflection.Assembly'
Total number of methods: 0

Non-public instance methods for 'System.Reflection.Assembly'
  GetManifestResourceStream
  GetManifestResourceStream
  Finalize
  nGetManifestResourceNames
  GetTypeInternal
  nLoadModule
  nGlobalAssemblyCache
  nGetImageRuntimeVersion
  nPrepareForSavingManifestToDisk
  nSaveToFileList
  nSetHashValue
  nSaveExportedType
  nSavePermissionRequests
  nSaveManifestToDisk
  nAddFileToInMemoryFileList
  nGetOnDiskAssemblyModule
  nGetInMemoryAssemblyModule
  nGetExportedTypeLibGuid
  DecodeSerializedEvidence
```

A
B
C
D
E
F
G
H
I
J
K
L
M
N
O
P
Q
R
S
T
U
V
W
X
Y
Z

ReflectionPermissionFlag Enum

```
        AddX509Certificate
        AddStrongName
        CreateSecurityIdentity
        GetVersion
        GetLocale
        nGetLocale
        nGetVersion
        nGetManifestResourceInfo
        VerifyCodeBaseDiscovery
        GetLocation
        nGetPublicKey
        nGetSimpleName
        nGetCodeBase
        nGetHashAlgorithm
        nGetFlags
        nForceResolve
        nGetEvidence
        nGetGrantSet
        GetFullName
        nGetEntryPoint
        GetResource
        OnModuleResolveEvent
        InternalGetSatelliteAssembly
        get_Cache
        OnCacheClear
        nAddStandAloneResource
        nGetModules
        MemberwiseClone
  Total number of methods: 47



  Press Enter to continue
```

A
B
C
D
E
F
G
H
I
J
K
L
M
N
O
P
Q
R
S
T
U
V
W
X
Y
Z

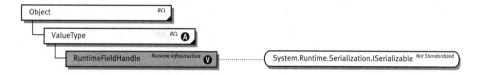

Summary

Serves as a metadata token for a field.

Type Summary

```
public struct RuntimeFieldHandle : ISerializable
    {
    // Properties
       public IntPtr Value { get; }

    // Methods
 MS CF public void GetObjectData(SerializationInfo info,
                 StreamingContext context);
    }
```

Description

RuntimeFieldHandle objects are created only through the use of IL instruction
ldtoken.

> [*Note:* For more information on ldtoken, see Partition III of the CLI Specification.]

Example

```
using System;
using System.Reflection;

/// <summary>
/// Sample demonstrating the use of the RuntimeFieldHandle structure.
/// Use this structure when retrieving the internal handle for a field.
/// </summary>
internal class RuntimeFieldHandleSample
{
    public const int SampleInt32 = int.MaxValue;
    public static readonly Guid SampleGuid = Guid.NewGuid();
    public DateTime SampleDateTime = DateTime.Now;

    private static void Main()
    {
        FieldInfo[] fields = typeof(RuntimeFieldHandleSample).GetFields();

        foreach (FieldInfo field in fields)
```

```
        {
            RuntimeFieldHandle fieldHandle = field.FieldHandle;

            Console.WriteLine("Summary for '{0}'", field.Name);
            Console.WriteLine(
                "   fieldHandle.Value = 0x{0}",
                ((int)fieldHandle.Value).ToString("x8"));
            Console.WriteLine();
        }

        Console.WriteLine();
        Console.WriteLine();
        Console.WriteLine("Press Enter to continue");
        Console.ReadLine();
    }

}
```

The output is

```
Summary for 'SampleDateTime'
   fieldHandle.Value = 0x00975064

Summary for 'SampleGuid'
   fieldHandle.Value = 0x00975070

Summary for 'SampleInt32'
   fieldHandle.Value = 0x02c63be0



Press Enter to continue
```

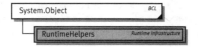

A

B

Summary

Implements static methods and properties that provide special support for compilers.

C

D

E

Type Summary

F

```
      public sealed class RuntimeHelpers
      {
      // Properties
CF    public static int OffsetToStringData { get; }

      // Methods
MS CF 1.1 public static bool Equals(object o1, object o2);
MS CF 1.1 public static int GetHashCode(object o);
      MS public static object GetObjectValue(object obj);
      public static void InitializeArray(Array array,
                            RuntimeFieldHandle fldHandle);
CF    public static void RunClassConstructor(RuntimeTypeHandle type);
      }
```

G

H

I

J

K

L

M

N

▪ DT   I was certainly delighted to discover `RunClassConstructor()`. We rely on it in Delphi codegen to implement some of the Delphi language's order of initialization semantics (more explicit ordering/earlier execution than `BeforeFieldInit`). It is a shame that it doesn't exist in the .NET Compact Framework.

O

P

Q

R

Description

S

[*Note:* The types in `System.Runtime.CompilerServices` are intended primarily for use by compilers, not application programmers. They allow compilers to easily implement certain language features that are not directly visible to programmers.]

T

U

V

Example

W

```
using System;
using System.Runtime.CompilerServices;

/// <summary>
/// Sample demonstrating the use of the RuntimeHelpers class.
/// This class is typically only used by compiler writers.
/// </summary>
internal class RuntimeHelpersSample
```

X

Y

Z

RuntimeHelpers Class

```csharp
{
    private static void Main()
    {
        // Explicitly call the class constructor on DemoClass1.
        RuntimeTypeHandle demo1Handle = typeof(DemoClass1).TypeHandle;

        Console.WriteLine("Explicity run demo1's type constructor");
        RuntimeHelpers.RunClassConstructor(demo1Handle);
        Console.WriteLine();

        // Initialize instances of DemoClass2 and DemoClass1. Note that the
        // class constructor for DemoClass1 has already run.
        Console.WriteLine("Create an instance of demo2");
        DemoClass2 demo2 = new DemoClass2();
        Console.WriteLine();

        Console.WriteLine("Create an instance of demo1");
        DemoClass1 demo1 = new DemoClass1();

        Console.WriteLine();
        Console.WriteLine();
        Console.WriteLine("Press Enter to continue");
        Console.ReadLine();
    }
}

internal class DemoClass1
{

    static DemoClass1()
    {
        Console.WriteLine("Running DemoClass1.cctor()");
    }

    public DemoClass1()
    {
        Console.WriteLine("Running DemoClass1.ctor()");
    }

}

internal class DemoClass2
{

    static DemoClass2()
    {
        Console.WriteLine("Running DemoClass2.cctor()");
    }

    public DemoClass2()
    {
        Console.WriteLine("Running DemoClass2.ctor()");
    }

}
```

The output is

```
Explicity run demo1's type constructor
Running DemoClass1.cctor()

Create an instance of demo2
Running DemoClass2.cctor()
Running DemoClass2.ctor()

Create an instance of demo1
Running DemoClass1.ctor()


Press Enter to continue
```

A
B
C
D
E
F
G
H
I
J
K
L
M
N
O
P
Q
R
S
T
U
V
W
X
Y
Z

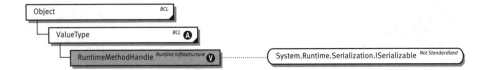

Summary

The RuntimeMethodHandle is a handle to the internal metadata representation of a method.

Type Summary

```
public struct RuntimeMethodHandle : ISerializable
    {
    // Properties
       public IntPtr Value { get; }

    // Methods
MS CF public IntPtr GetFunctionPointer();
MS CF public void GetObjectData(SerializationInfo info,
                  StreamingContext context);
    }
```

Example

```
using System;
using System.Reflection;

/// <summary>
/// Sample demonstrating the use of the RuntimeMethodHandle structure.
/// Use this structure when retrieving the internal handle for a method.
/// </summary>
internal class RuntimeMethodHandleSample
{

    private static void Main()
    {
        MethodInfo[] methods = typeof(RuntimeMethodHandleSample).GetMethods();

        foreach (MethodInfo method in methods)
        {
            RuntimeMethodHandle methodHandle = method.MethodHandle;

            Console.WriteLine("Summary for '{0}'", method.Name);
            Console.WriteLine(
                "  methodHandle.Value                  = 0x{0}",
                ((int)methodHandle.Value).ToString("x8"));
            Console.WriteLine(
                "  methodHandle.GetFunctionPointer() = 0x{0}",
```

```
                ((int)methodHandle.GetFunctionPointer()).ToString("x8"));
            Console.WriteLine();
        }

        Console.WriteLine();
        Console.WriteLine();
        Console.WriteLine("Press Enter to continue");
        Console.ReadLine();
    }

    public static void Method1() {}
    public void Method2() {}

}
```

The output is

```
Summary for 'GetHashCode'
  methodHandle.Value                  = 0x79b90f60
  methodHandle.GetFunctionPointer() = 0x79b90f5b

Summary for 'Equals'
  methodHandle.Value                  = 0x79b90f48
  methodHandle.GetFunctionPointer() = 0x79b90f43

Summary for 'ToString'
  methodHandle.Value                  = 0x79b90fc0
  methodHandle.GetFunctionPointer() = 0x79b90fbb

Summary for 'Method1'
  methodHandle.Value                  = 0x00975090
  methodHandle.GetFunctionPointer() = 0x0097508b

Summary for 'Method2'
  methodHandle.Value                  = 0x009750a0
  methodHandle.GetFunctionPointer() = 0x0097509b

Summary for 'GetType'
  methodHandle.Value                  = 0x79b90ff0
  methodHandle.GetFunctionPointer() = 0x79b90feb


Press Enter to continue
```

A
B
C
D
E
F
G
H
I
J
K
L
M
N
O
P
Q
R
S
T
U
V
W
X
Y
Z

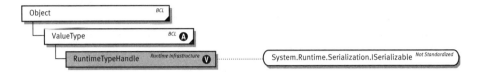

Summary

Provides a handle to the internal metadata representation of a type.

Type Summary

```
public struct RuntimeTypeHandle : ISerializable
    {
    // Properties
       public IntPtr Value { get; }

    // Methods
 MS CF public void GetObjectData(SerializationInfo info,
                 StreamingContext context);
    }
```

▪▪ JP   RuntimeTypeHandles are an abstraction for strong type identity. If you do a typeof(MyClass) in C#, you're essentially getting back a RuntimeTypeHandle that identifies the "MyClass" type. The other alternative we could have gone with is simply using System.Type for this abstraction, however, a small, lean struct has both performance and working set benefits over a GC handled class.

▪▪ JP   Most type identity code sequences are performance-optimized. An example of this is the code sequence typeof(Foo) == foo.GetType(). The IL disassembly of this code looks like the following:

```
newobj     instance void Foo::.ctor()
stloc.0
ldtoken    Foo
call       class [mscorlib]System.Type
                  [mscorlib]System.Type::GetTypeFromHandle(
                  valuetype [mscorlib]System.RuntimeTypeHandle)
ldloc.0
callvirt   instance class [mscorlib]System.Type
                  [mscorlib]System.Object::GetType()
ceq
```

CONTINUED

While the IL suggests we're comparing two System.Types, the JIT ends up comparing two RuntimeTypeHandles instead. Comparing two small, stack-based structs is much faster than comparing two heap-based System.Type objects.

■ JP We've worked on improving the handle story for the v2.0 release. We've introduced metadata token/runtime handle/XXXInfo resolution APIs (we call the feature Token Handle resolution), to quickly jump around the triangle. This API introduces a new set of cool performance and working set tricks—you can now cache a token or handle, instead of holding on to the overweight XXXInfo/Type objects.

Example

```
using System;
using System.Reflection;

/// <summary>
/// Sample demonstrating the use of the RuntimeTypeHandle structure.
/// Use this structure when retrieving the internal handle for a type.
/// </summary>
internal class RuntimeTypeHandleSample
{

    private static void Main()
    {
        // Get the RuntimeTypeHandle from an instance.
        RuntimeTypeHandleSample sample         = new RuntimeTypeHandleSample();
        RuntimeTypeHandle       instanceHandle = Type.GetTypeHandle(sample);

        Console.WriteLine("Summary for instanceHandle:");
        Console.WriteLine(
            "  instanceHandle.Value                 = 0x{0}",
            ((int)instanceHandle.Value).ToString("x8"));
        Console.WriteLine(
            "  instanceHandle.GetType()             = {0}",
            instanceHandle.GetType());
        Console.WriteLine(
            "  Type.GetTypeFromHandle(instanceHandle) = {0}",
            Type.GetTypeFromHandle(instanceHandle));
        Console.WriteLine();

        // Get the RuntimeTypeHandle from the type.
        RuntimeTypeHandle typeHandle =
            typeof(RuntimeTypeHandleSample).TypeHandle;

        Console.WriteLine("Summary for typeHandle:");
        Console.WriteLine(
            "  typeHandle.Value                 = 0x{0}",
            ((int)typeHandle.Value).ToString("x8"));
        Console.WriteLine(
            "  typeHandle.GetType()             = {0}",
            typeHandle.GetType());
```

RuntimeTypeHandle Structure

```
            Console.WriteLine(
                "  Type.GetTypeFromHandle(typeHandle) = {0}",
                Type.GetTypeFromHandle(typeHandle));

            Console.WriteLine();
            Console.WriteLine();
            Console.WriteLine("Press Enter to continue");
            Console.ReadLine();
        }

    }
```

The output is

```
Summary for instanceHandle:
  instanceHandle.Value                   = 0x00975098
  instanceHandle.GetType()               = System.RuntimeTypeHandle
  Type.GetTypeFromHandle(instanceHandle) = RuntimeTypeHandleSample

Summary for typeHandle:
  typeHandle.Value                   = 0x00975098
  typeHandle.GetType()               = System.RuntimeTypeHandle
  Type.GetTypeFromHandle(typeHandle) = RuntimeTypeHandleSample


Press Enter to continue
```

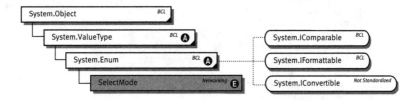

Summary

Specifies the mode used by the `Poll` method of the `Socket` class.

Type Summary

```
public enum SelectMode
    {
    SelectError = 2,
    SelectRead = 0,
    SelectWrite = 1,
    }
```

Description

A `SelectMode` member specifies the status information (read, write, or error) to retrieve from the current `Socket` instance.

Example

```
using System;
using System.Net;
using System.Net.Sockets;
using System.Text;

public class SelectModeSample
{
    private static void ShowSelectMode(Socket skt)
    {
        if (skt.Poll(1000, SelectMode.SelectRead) == true)
            Console.WriteLine(" - You can read from this Socket");
        if(skt.Poll(1000, SelectMode.SelectWrite) == true)
            Console.WriteLine(" - You can write to this Socket");
        if (skt.Poll(1000, SelectMode.SelectError))
            Console.WriteLine(" - There was an error connecting");
    }
    public static void Main()
    {
        IPAddress ip = IPAddress.Parse("127.0.0.1");
        Socket skt = new Socket(AddressFamily.InterNetwork,
            SocketType.Stream, ProtocolType.Tcp);
```

A
B
C
D
E
F
G
H
I
J
K
L
M
N
O
P
Q
R
S
T
U
V
W
X
Y
Z

```
        try
        {
            IPEndPoint ep = new IPEndPoint(ip, 80);
            Console.WriteLine("Opening connection...");
            skt.Connect(ep);
            ShowSelectMode(skt);
            Console.WriteLine("Sending request...");
            string targ = "/default.htm";
            Byte[] req = Encoding.ASCII.GetBytes("GET " + targ + "\n");
            skt.Send(req);
            Console.WriteLine("Awaiting response...");
            Byte[] res = new Byte[512];
            int rec = skt.Receive(res);
            ShowSelectMode(skt);
            Console.WriteLine("Received {0} bytes for {1}:",
                rec, targ);
            Console.WriteLine(Encoding.ASCII.GetString(res, 0, rec));
            skt.Shutdown(SocketShutdown.Both);
        }
        catch (Exception e)
        {
            Console.WriteLine("Error: " + e.Message);
        }
        finally
        {
            skt.Close();
        }
        Console.WriteLine();
        Console.WriteLine();
        Console.WriteLine("Press Enter to continue");
        Console.ReadLine();
    }
}
```

The output is

```
Opening connection...
 - You can write to this Socket
Sending request...
Awaiting response...
 - You can read from this Socket
 - You can write to this Socket
Received 60 bytes for /default.htm:
<html>
<body>
This is the default page
</body>
</html>


Press Enter to continue
```

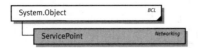

Summary

Represents connections to Internet hosts.

Type Summary

```
public class ServicePoint
    {
    // Properties
        public Uri Address { get; }
    MS  public X509Certificate Certificate { get; }
  MS CF public X509Certificate ClientCertificate { get; }
        public int ConnectionLimit { get; set; }
        public string ConnectionName { get; }
        public int CurrentConnections { get; }
MS CF 1.1 public bool Expect100Continue { get; set; }
        public DateTime IdleSince { get; }
        public int MaxIdleTime { get; set; }
        public virtual Version ProtocolVersion { get; }
        public bool SupportsPipelining { get; }
MS CF 1.1 public bool UseNagleAlgorithm { get; set; }

    // Methods
    CF  public override int GetHashCode();
    }
```

Description

The `ServicePoint` class handles connections to a resource based on the host information passed in the Uniform Resource Identifier (URI) of the resource. The initial connection to the host determines the information the `ServicePoint` maintains, which is then
shared by all subsequent requests for resources residing on the host.

[*Note:* `ServicePoint` instances are created and managed by the `ServicePoint-
Manager` class. The maximum number of `ServicePoint` instances is set by the
`ServicePointManager.MaxServicePoints` property. A `System.Net.Service-
Point` instance that is not connected to any host is idle. An idle `ServicePoint` is man-
aged by the `ServicePointManager` only until it has been idle longer than the time
specified in its `ServicePoint.MaxIdleTime` property. After a . `ServicePoint`
instance exceeds the `ServicePoint.MaxIdleTime`, it is released by the service point
manager and subsequently freed. The default value of `ServicePoint.MaxIdleTime` is
set by the `ServicePointManager.MaxServicePointIdleTime` property.]

A
B
C
D
E
F
G
H
I
J
K
L
M
N
O
P
Q
R
S
T
U
V
W
X
Y
Z

Example

```
using System;
using System.Net;

public class ServicePointSample
{
    public static void Main()
    {
        try
        {
            String target = "http://www.microsoft.com/";
            HttpWebRequest req = (HttpWebRequest)
                WebRequest.Create(target);
            HttpWebResponse result = (HttpWebResponse)req.GetResponse();
            result.Close();
            ServicePoint sp = req.ServicePoint;
            Console.WriteLine("ServicePoint.Address = {0}",
                sp.Address);
            Console.WriteLine("ServicePoint.ConnectionName = {0}",
                sp.ConnectionName);
            Console.WriteLine("ServicePoint.ConnectionLimit = {0}",
                sp.ConnectionLimit);
            Console.WriteLine("ServicePoint.ProtocolVersion = {0}",
                sp.ProtocolVersion);
            Console.WriteLine("ServicePoint.CurrentConnections = {0}",
                sp.CurrentConnections);
            Console.WriteLine("ServicePoint.SupportsPipelining = {0}",
                sp.SupportsPipelining);
            Console.WriteLine("ServicePoint.MaxIdleTime = {0}",
                sp.MaxIdleTime);
            Console.WriteLine("ServicePoint.IdleSince = {0}",
                sp.IdleSince);
        }
        catch (Exception e)
        {
            Console.WriteLine("*ERROR: " + e.Message);
        }
        Console.WriteLine();
        Console.WriteLine();
        Console.WriteLine("Press Enter to continue");
        Console.ReadLine();
    }
}
```

The output is

```
ServicePoint.Address = http://www.microsoft.com/
ServicePoint.ConnectionName = http
ServicePoint.ConnectionLimit = 2
ServicePoint.ProtocolVersion = 1.1
ServicePoint.CurrentConnections = 0
ServicePoint.SupportsPipelining = True
ServicePoint.MaxIdleTime = 900000
ServicePoint.IdleSince = 2/13/2005 10:52:34 AM


Press Enter to continue
```

Summary

Manages `ServicePoint` instances.

Type Summary

```
public class ServicePointManager
{
    // Fields
 CF public const int DefaultNonPersistentConnectionLimit = 4;
    public const int DefaultPersistentConnectionLimit = 2;

    // Properties
       MS public static ICertificatePolicy CertificatePolicy { get; set; }
MS CF 1.1 public static bool CheckCertificateRevocationList { get; set; }
          public static int DefaultConnectionLimit { get; set; }
MS CF 1.1 public static bool Expect100Continue { get; set; }
          public static int MaxServicePointIdleTime { get; set; }
       CF public static int MaxServicePoints { get; set; }
MS CF 1.1 public static SecurityProtocolType SecurityProtocol { get; set; }
MS CF 1.1 public static bool UseNagleAlgorithm { get; set; }

    // Methods
    public static ServicePoint FindServicePoint(string uriString,
                                    IWebProxy proxy);
    public static ServicePoint FindServicePoint(Uri address);
    public static ServicePoint FindServicePoint(Uri address,
                                    IWebProxy proxy);
}
```

■ **CM**   If you are seeing a lot of mysterious 350-ms delays when sniffing your network traffic, you may want to set the `Expect100Continue` property to `false`. IIS6 does a great job supporting 100-continue, but there are other servers that don't. Internally, we wait up to 350 ms for the server to tell us that it's ready for the content. If we don't see it, we will turn this expectation off for the `ServicePoint`, however if you don't set it to `false`, we may re-enable it if we see the 100-continue header later.

■ **CM**   Be cautious when using `FindServicePoint`. Frequently folks will use this API with the URI of the request. The problem is that if a proxy is being used, then you

CONTINUED

are probably modifying the wrong `ServicePoint`. The URI should be that of the proxy and not the server. A better option is to get the `WebRequest`.

■ **LO**   The `DefaultConnectionLimit` property defaults to two connections as per the HTTP RFC. This is usually the right value for clients going over the Internet directly or through a proxy server. However, applications communicating with an origin server on the LAN can bump this up to much higher levels and see significant performance improvements. Middle-tier clients running on machines with multiple processors should also consider bumping up the limit.

■ **LO**   Note also that requests sent to the local machine "localhost" will bypass this limit.

Description

`ServicePointManager` creates, maintains, and deletes `ServicePoint` instances.

When an application requests a connection to an Internet resource through the `ServicePointManager`, the `ServicePointManager` returns a `ServicePoint` instance containing connection information for the host identified by the Uniform Resource Identifier (URI) of the resource. If there is an existing `ServicePoint` for that host, the `ServicePointManager` returns the existing `ServicePoint`, otherwise the `ServicePointManager` creates a new `ServicePoint` instance.

Example

```
using System;
using System.Net;

public class ServicePointManagerSample
{
    public static void Main()
    {
        ServicePointManager.MaxServicePointIdleTime = 30000;
        ServicePointManager.DefaultConnectionLimit = 10;
        ServicePointManager.MaxServicePoints = 10;

        Console.WriteLine("ServicePointManager."
            + "DefaultNonPersistentConnectionLimit = {0}",
            ServicePointManager.DefaultNonPersistentConnectionLimit);
        Console.WriteLine("ServicePointManager."
            + "DefaultPersistentConnectionLimit = {0}",
            ServicePointManager.DefaultPersistentConnectionLimit);
        Console.WriteLine("ServicePointManager."
            + "MaxServicePointIdleTime = {0}",
            ServicePointManager.MaxServicePointIdleTime);
        Console.WriteLine("ServicePointManager."
```

```
            + "DefaultConnectionLimit = {0}",
            ServicePointManager.DefaultConnectionLimit);
        Console.WriteLine("ServicePointManager."
            + "MaxServicePoints = {0}",
            ServicePointManager.MaxServicePoints);

        Uri target = new Uri("http://www.microsoft.com");
        ServicePoint sp = ServicePointManager.FindServicePoint(target,
            new WebProxy("10.0.0.1"));
        Console.WriteLine("ServicePoint.Address = '{0}'",
            sp.Address);
        Console.WriteLine();
        Console.WriteLine();
        Console.WriteLine("Press Enter to continue");
        Console.ReadLine();
    }
}
```

The output is

```
ServicePointManager.DefaultNonPersistentConnectionLimit = 4
ServicePointManager.DefaultPersistentConnectionLimit = 2
ServicePointManager.MaxServicePointIdleTime = 30000
ServicePointManager.DefaultConnectionLimit = 10
ServicePointManager.MaxServicePoints = 10
ServicePoint.Address = 'http://10.0.0.1/'


Press Enter to continue
```

Summary

Creates a communication endpoint through which an application sends or receives data across a network.

Type Summary

```
public class Socket : IDisposable
{
    // Constructors
    public Socket(AddressFamily addressFamily, SocketType socketType,
            ProtocolType protocolType);

    // Properties
    public AddressFamily AddressFamily { get; }
    public int Available { get; }
    public bool Blocking { get; set; }
    public bool Connected { get; }
    public IntPtr Handle { get; }
    public EndPoint LocalEndPoint { get; }
    public ProtocolType ProtocolType { get; }
    public EndPoint RemoteEndPoint { get; }
    public SocketType SocketType { get; }
MS CF 1.1 public static bool SupportsIPv4 { get; }
MS CF 1.1 public static bool SupportsIPv6 { get; }

    // Methods
    public Socket Accept();
    public IAsyncResult BeginAccept(AsyncCallback callback, object state);
    public IAsyncResult BeginConnect(EndPoint remoteEP,
            AsyncCallback callback, object state);
    public IAsyncResult BeginReceive(byte[] buffer, int offset, int size,
            SocketFlags socketFlags, AsyncCallback callback,
            object state);
    public IAsyncResult BeginReceiveFrom(byte[] buffer, int offset,
            int size, SocketFlags socketFlags,
            ref EndPoint remoteEP, AsyncCallback callback,
            object state);
    public IAsyncResult BeginSend(byte[] buffer, int offset, int size,
            SocketFlags socketFlags, AsyncCallback callback,
            object state);
    public IAsyncResult BeginSendTo(byte[] buffer, int offset, int size,
            SocketFlags socketFlags, EndPoint remoteEP,
            AsyncCallback callback, object state);
    public void Bind(EndPoint localEP);
    public void Close();
    public void Connect(EndPoint remoteEP);
```

```
      protected virtual void Dispose(bool disposing);
      public Socket EndAccept(IAsyncResult asyncResult);
      public void EndConnect(IAsyncResult asyncResult);
      public int EndReceive(IAsyncResult asyncResult);
      public int EndReceiveFrom(IAsyncResult asyncResult,
             ref EndPoint endPoint);
      public int EndSend(IAsyncResult asyncResult);
      public int EndSendTo(IAsyncResult asyncResult);
      ~Socket();
   CF public override int GetHashCode();
      public object GetSocketOption(SocketOptionLevel optionLevel,
                 SocketOptionName optionName);
      public void GetSocketOption(SocketOptionLevel optionLevel,
                 SocketOptionName optionName, byte[] optionValue);
      public byte[] GetSocketOption(SocketOptionLevel optionLevel,
                 SocketOptionName optionName, int optionLength);
      public int IOControl(int ioControlCode, byte[] optionInValue,
                 byte[] optionOutValue);
      public void Listen(int backlog);
      public bool Poll(int microSeconds, SelectMode mode);
      public int Receive(byte[] buffer);
      public int Receive(byte[] buffer, int offset, int size,
                 SocketFlags socketFlags);
      public int Receive(byte[] buffer, int size, SocketFlags socketFlags);
      public int Receive(byte[] buffer, SocketFlags socketFlags);
      public int ReceiveFrom(byte[] buffer, ref EndPoint remoteEP);
      public int ReceiveFrom(byte[] buffer, int offset, int size,
                 SocketFlags socketFlags, ref EndPoint remoteEP);
      public int ReceiveFrom(byte[] buffer, int size,
                 SocketFlags socketFlags, ref EndPoint remoteEP);
      public int ReceiveFrom(byte[] buffer, SocketFlags socketFlags,
                 ref EndPoint remoteEP);
      public static void Select(IList checkRead, IList checkWrite,
                       IList checkError, int microSeconds);
      public int Send(byte[] buffer);
      public int Send(byte[] buffer, int offset, int size,
                 SocketFlags socketFlags);
      public int Send(byte[] buffer, int size, SocketFlags socketFlags);
      public int Send(byte[] buffer, SocketFlags socketFlags);
      public int SendTo(byte[] buffer, EndPoint remoteEP);
      public int SendTo(byte[] buffer, int offset, int size,
                 SocketFlags socketFlags, EndPoint remoteEP);
      public int SendTo(byte[] buffer, int size, SocketFlags socketFlags,
                 EndPoint remoteEP);
      public int SendTo(byte[] buffer, SocketFlags socketFlags,
                 EndPoint remoteEP);
      public void SetSocketOption(SocketOptionLevel optionLevel,
                 SocketOptionName optionName, byte[] optionValue);
      public void SetSocketOption(SocketOptionLevel optionLevel,
                 SocketOptionName optionName, int optionValue);
      public void SetSocketOption(SocketOptionLevel optionLevel,
                 SocketOptionName optionName, object optionValue);
      public void Shutdown(SocketShutdown how);

   // Explicit Interface Members
      void IDisposable.Dispose();
   }
```

A
B
C
D
E
F
G
H
I
J
K
L
M
N
O
P
Q
R
S
T
U
V
W
X
Y
Z

> **■ CM**   Wouldn't it be nice if we let you connect using just the host name and port?
> In v2.0 we will add this, along with a bunch of new features that will make life much
> easier. Of course, if you don't need asynchronous connects, you can always use
> `TcpClient`.

Description

This class enables a `Socket` instance to communicate with another socket across a network. The communication can be through connection-oriented and connectionless protocols using either data streams or datagrams (discrete message packets).

Message-oriented protocols preserve message boundaries and require that for each
`Send` method call there is one corresponding `Receive` method call. For stream-oriented
protocols, data is transmitted without regards to message boundaries. In this case, for
example, multiple `Receive` method calls may be necessary to retrieve all the data from
one `Send` method call. The protocol is set in the `Socket` class constructor.

A `Socket` instance has a local and a remote endpoint associated with it. The local
endpoint contains the connection information for the current socket instance. The remote
endpoint contains the connection information for the socket that the current instance com-
municates with. The endpoints are required to be an instance of a type derived from the
`System.Net.EndPoint` class. For the Transmission Control Protocol (TCP) and User
Datagram Protocol (UDP) protocols, an endpoint includes the address family, an Internet
Protocol (IP) address, and a port number. For connection-oriented protocols (for example,
TCP), the remote endpoint does not have to be specified when transferring data. For connectionless protocols (for example, UDP), the remote endpoint is required to be specified.

Methods are provided for both synchronous and asynchronous operations. A synchronous method can operate in blocking mode, in which it waits (blocks) until the operation is complete before returning, or in non-blocking mode, where it returns immediately,
possibly before the operation has completed. The blocking mode is set through the
`Blocking` property.

An asynchronous method returns immediately and, by convention, relies on a delegate to complete the operation. Asynchronous methods have names which correspond
to their synchronous counterparts prefixed with either "Begin" or "End". For example,
the synchronous `Accept` method has asynchronous counterpart methods named
`BeginAccept` and `EndAccept`. The example for the `BeginAccept` method shows the
basic steps for using an asynchronous operation. A complete working example follows
this discussion.

Connection-oriented protocols commonly use the client/server model. In this model,
one of the sockets is set up as a server, and one or more sockets are set up as clients. A general procedure demonstrating the synchronous communication process for this model is
as follows.

On the server-side:

1. Create a socket to listen for incoming connection requests.
2. Set the local endpoint using the Bind method.
3. Put the socket in the listening state using the Listen method.
4. At this point incoming connection requests from a client are placed in a queue.
5. Use the Accept method to create a server socket for a connection request issued by a client-side socket. This sets the remote endpoint.
6. Use the Send and Receive methods to communicate with the client socket.
7. When communication is finished, terminate the connection using the Shutdown method.
8. Release the resources allocated by the server socket using the Close method.
9. Release the resources allocated by the listener socket using the Close method.

On the client-side:

1. Create the client socket.
2. Connect to the server socket using the Connect method. This sets both the local and remote endpoints for the client socket.
3. Use the Send and Receive methods to communicate with the server socket.
4. When communication is finished, terminate the connection using the Shutdown method.
5. Release the resources allocated by the client socket using the Close method.

The shutdown step in the previous procedure is not necessary but ensures that any pending data is not lost. If the Shutdown method is not called, the Close method shuts down the connection either gracefully or by force. A graceful closure attempts to transfer all pending data before the connection is terminated. Use the SocketOptionName.Linger socket option to specify a graceful closure for a socket.

[*Note:* This implementation is based on the UNIX sockets implementation in the Berkeley Software Distribution (BSD, release 4.3) from the University of California at Berkeley.]

Example

Example 1
The following examples provide a client/server application that demonstrates the use of asynchronous communication between sockets. Run the client and server on different consoles.

The following code is for the server application. Start this application before the client application.

```
using System;
using System.Threading;
using System.Text;
using System.Net;
using System.Net.Sockets;

public class Server
{
    // used to pass state information to delegate
    internal class StateObject
    {
        internal byte[] sBuffer;
        internal Socket sSocket;
        internal StateObject(int size, Socket sock)
        {
            sBuffer = new byte[size];
            sSocket = sock;
        }
    }
    static void Main()
    {
        IPAddress ipAddress =
            Dns.Resolve( Dns.GetHostName() ).AddressList[0];

        IPEndPoint ipEndpoint =
            new IPEndPoint(ipAddress, 1800);

        Socket listenSocket =
            new Socket(AddressFamily.InterNetwork,
            SocketType.Stream,
            ProtocolType.Tcp);

        listenSocket.Bind(ipEndpoint);
        listenSocket.Listen(1);
        IAsyncResult asyncAccept = listenSocket.BeginAccept(
            new AsyncCallback(Server.acceptCallback),
            listenSocket );

        // could call listenSocket.EndAccept(asyncAccept) here
        // instead of in the callback method, but since
        // EndAccept blocks, the behavior would be similar to
        // calling the synchronous Accept method

        Console.Write("Connection in progress.");
        if( writeDot(asyncAccept) == true )
        {
            // allow time for callbacks to
            // finish before the program ends
            Thread.Sleep(3000);
        }
    }

    public static void
        acceptCallback(IAsyncResult asyncAccept)
    {
        Socket listenSocket = (Socket)asyncAccept.AsyncState;
```

```
    Socket serverSocket =
        listenSocket.EndAccept(asyncAccept);

    // arriving here means the operation completed
    // (asyncAccept.IsCompleted = true) but not
    // necessarily successfully
    if( serverSocket.Connected == false )
    {
        Console.WriteLine( ".server is not connected." );
        return;
    }
    else Console.WriteLine( ".server is connected." );

    listenSocket.Close();

    StateObject stateObject =
        new StateObject(16, serverSocket);

    // this call passes the StateObject because it
    // needs to pass the buffer as well as the socket
    IAsyncResult asyncReceive =
        serverSocket.BeginReceive(
        stateObject.sBuffer,
        0,
        stateObject.sBuffer.Length,
        SocketFlags.None,
        new AsyncCallback(receiveCallback),
        stateObject);

    Console.Write("Receiving data.");
    writeDot(asyncReceive);
}

public static void
    receiveCallback(IAsyncResult asyncReceive)
{
    StateObject stateObject =
        (StateObject)asyncReceive.AsyncState;
    int bytesReceived =
        stateObject.sSocket.EndReceive(asyncReceive);

    Console.WriteLine(
        ".{0} bytes received: {1}",
        bytesReceived.ToString(),
        Encoding.ASCII.GetString(stateObject.sBuffer) );

    byte[] sendBuffer =
        Encoding.ASCII.GetBytes("Goodbye");
    IAsyncResult asyncSend =
        stateObject.sSocket.BeginSend(
        sendBuffer,
        0,
        sendBuffer.Length,
        SocketFlags.None,
        new AsyncCallback(sendCallback),
        stateObject.sSocket);
```

A
B
C
D
E
F
G
H
I
J
K
L
M
N
O
P
Q
R
S
T
U
V
W
X
Y
Z

```
            Console.Write("Sending response.");
            writeDot(asyncSend);
        }

        public static void sendCallback(IAsyncResult asyncSend)
        {
            Socket serverSocket = (Socket)asyncSend.AsyncState;
            int bytesSent = serverSocket.EndSend(asyncSend);
            Console.WriteLine(
                ".{0} bytes sent.{1}{1}Shutting down.",
                bytesSent.ToString(),
                Environment.NewLine );

            serverSocket.Shutdown(SocketShutdown.Both);
            serverSocket.Close();
        }

        // times out after 20 seconds but operation continues
        internal static bool writeDot(IAsyncResult ar)
        {
            int i = 0;
            while( ar.IsCompleted == false )
            {
                if( i++ > 40 )
                {
                    Console.WriteLine("Timed out.");
                    return false;
                }
                Console.Write(".");
                Thread.Sleep(500);
            }
            return true;
        }
    }
```

The following code is for the client application. When starting the application, supply the hostname of the console running the server application as an input parameter (for example, ProgramName *hostname*).

```
using System;
using System.Threading;
using System.Text;
using System.Net;
using System.Net.Sockets;

public class Client
{

    // used to pass state information to delegate
    class StateObject
    {
        internal byte[] sBuffer;
        internal Socket sSocket;
        internal StateObject(int size, Socket sock)
```

```
    {
        sBuffer = new byte[size];
        sSocket = sock;
    }
}

static void Main(string[] argHostName)
{
    IPAddress ipAddress =
        Dns.Resolve( argHostName[0] ).AddressList[0];

    IPEndPoint ipEndpoint =
        new IPEndPoint(ipAddress, 1800);

    Socket clientSocket = new Socket(
        AddressFamily.InterNetwork,
        SocketType.Stream,
        ProtocolType.Tcp);

    IAsyncResult asyncConnect = clientSocket.BeginConnect(
        ipEndpoint,
        new AsyncCallback(connectCallback),
        clientSocket );

    Console.Write("Connection in progress.");
    if( writeDot(asyncConnect) == true )
    {
        // allow time for callbacks to
        // finish before the program ends
        Thread.Sleep(3000);
    }
}

public static void
    connectCallback(IAsyncResult asyncConnect)
{
    Socket clientSocket =
        (Socket)asyncConnect.AsyncState;
    clientSocket.EndConnect(asyncConnect);
    // arriving here means the operation completed
    // (asyncConnect.IsCompleted = true) but not
    // necessarily successfully
    if( clientSocket.Connected == false )
    {
        Console.WriteLine( ".client is not connected." );
        return;
    }
    else Console.WriteLine( ".client is connected." );

    byte[] sendBuffer = Encoding.ASCII.GetBytes("Hello");
    IAsyncResult asyncSend = clientSocket.BeginSend(
        sendBuffer,
        0,
        sendBuffer.Length,
        SocketFlags.None,
        new AsyncCallback(sendCallback),
```

A
B
C
D
E
F
G
H
I
J
K
L
M
N
O
P
Q
R
S
T
U
V
W
X
Y
Z

```
                    clientSocket);

                Console.Write("Sending data.");
                writeDot(asyncSend);
        }

        public static void sendCallback(IAsyncResult asyncSend)
        {
                Socket clientSocket = (Socket)asyncSend.AsyncState;
                int bytesSent = clientSocket.EndSend(asyncSend);
                Console.WriteLine(
                    ".{0} bytes sent.",
                    bytesSent.ToString() );

                StateObject stateObject =
                    new StateObject(16, clientSocket);

                // this call passes the StateObject because it
                // needs to pass the buffer as well as the socket
                IAsyncResult asyncReceive =
                    clientSocket.BeginReceive(
                    stateObject.sBuffer,
                    0,
                    stateObject.sBuffer.Length,
                    SocketFlags.None,
                    new AsyncCallback(receiveCallback),
                    stateObject);

                Console.Write("Receiving response.");
                writeDot(asyncReceive);
        }

        public static void
            receiveCallback(IAsyncResult asyncReceive)
        {
                StateObject stateObject =
                    (StateObject)asyncReceive.AsyncState;

                int bytesReceived =
                    stateObject.sSocket.EndReceive(asyncReceive);

                Console.WriteLine(
                    ".{0} bytes received: {1}{2}{2}Shutting down.",
                    bytesReceived.ToString(),
                    Encoding.ASCII.GetString(stateObject.sBuffer),
                    Environment.NewLine );

                stateObject.sSocket.Shutdown(SocketShutdown.Both);
                stateObject.sSocket.Close();
        }

        // times out after 2 seconds but operation continues
        internal static bool writeDot(IAsyncResult ar)
        {
                int i = 0;
                while( ar.IsCompleted == false )
```

```
        {
            if( i++ > 20 )
            {
                Console.WriteLine("Timed out.");
                return false;
            }
            Console.Write(".");
            Thread.Sleep(100);
        }
        return true;
    }
}
```

The output of the server application is

```
Connection in progress..........server is connected.


Receiving data......5 bytes received: Hello


Sending response....7 bytes sent.


Shutting down.


-----------------------------------------
```

The output of the client application is

```
Connection in progress......client is connected.


Sending data......5 bytes sent.


Receiving response......7 bytes received: Goodbye


Shutting down.
```

Example 2

```
using System;
using System.Net;
using System.Net.Sockets;
using System.Text;

public class SocketSample
{
    private static Socket skt = null;
    private static String targ = "/default.htm";
    private static bool bDone = false;

    public static void Main()
```

Socket   System.Net.Sockets

Socket Class

```
    {
        IPAddress ip = IPAddress.Parse("127.0.0.1");
        skt = new Socket(AddressFamily.InterNetwork,
            SocketType.Stream, ProtocolType.Tcp);
        IPEndPoint ep = new IPEndPoint(ip, 80);
        try
        {
            skt.Connect(ep);
            if (skt.Connected)
            {
                Byte[] req = Encoding.ASCII.GetBytes("GET " + targ + "\n");
                skt.BeginSend(req, 0, req.Length, SocketFlags.None,
                    new AsyncCallback(SendHandler), null);
                Console.WriteLine("BeginSend method completed.");
            }
            else
            {
                Console.WriteLine("Cannot connect to host");
            }
        }
        catch (Exception e)
        {
            Console.WriteLine("Error: " + e.Message);
            skt.Close();
        }
        while(!bDone) {}
        Console.WriteLine();
        Console.WriteLine();
        Console.WriteLine("Press Enter to continue");
        Console.ReadLine();
    }

    private static void SendHandler(IAsyncResult ar)
    {
        try
        {
            int bs = skt.EndSend(ar);
            Console.WriteLine("SendHandler sent {0} bytes", bs);
            Byte[] res = new Byte[1024];
            int rec = skt.Receive(res);
            skt.Shutdown(SocketShutdown.Both);
            Console.WriteLine("Received {0} bytes for {1}:",
                rec, targ);
            Console.WriteLine(Encoding.ASCII.GetString(res, 0, rec));
        }
        catch (Exception e)
        {
            Console.WriteLine("Error: " + e.Message);
        }
        finally
        {
            skt.Close();
            bDone = true;
        }
    }
}
```

The output is

```
BeginSend method completed.
SendHandler sent 17 bytes
Received 60 bytes for /default.htm:
<html>
<body>
This is the default page
</body>
</html>


Press Enter to continue
```

A
B
C
D
E
F
G
H
I
J
K
L
M
N
O
P
Q
R
S
T
U
V
W
X
Y
Z

Summary

Provides a socket address stored in a `System.Byte` array.

Type Summary

```
public class SocketAddress
    {
    // Constructors
        public SocketAddress(AddressFamily family);
        public SocketAddress(AddressFamily family, int size);

    // Properties
        public AddressFamily Family { get; }
        public int Size { get; }
        public byte this[int offset] { get; set; }

    // Methods
        public override bool Equals(object comparand);
        public override int GetHashCode();
        public override string ToString();
    }
```

Description

At a minimum, a socket address consists of a member of the `System.Net.Sock-ets.AddressFamily` enumeration stored in the first two bytes of the array.

Example

```
using System;
using System.Net;
using System.Net.Sockets;


public class SocketAddressSample
{
    public static void Main()
    {
        SocketAddress sktaddr1 = new
            SocketAddress(AddressFamily.InterNetwork);
        SocketAddress sktaddr2 = new
            SocketAddress(AddressFamily.InterNetwork, 255);
        Console.WriteLine("SocketAddress.Family = '{0}'",
            sktaddr1.Family);
```

```
        Console.WriteLine("SocketAddress.Size = {0}",
            sktaddr1.Size);
        Console.WriteLine("SocketAddress = '{0}'",
            sktaddr1);
        Console.WriteLine("SocketAddress(AddressFamily.InterNetwork) "
            + "== SocketAddress(AddressFamily.InterNetwork, 255) ? = {0}",
            sktaddr1.Equals(sktaddr2));
        Console.WriteLine();
        Console.WriteLine();
        Console.WriteLine("Press Enter to continue");
        Console.ReadLine();
    }
}
```

The output is

```
SocketAddress.Family = 'InterNetwork'
SocketAddress.Size = 32
SocketAddress = 'InterNetwork:32:{0,0,0,0,0,0,0,0,0,0,0,0,0,0,0,0,0,0,0,0,0,0,0,
0,0,0,0,0,0,0}'
SocketAddress(AddressFamily.InterNetwork) == SocketAddress(AddressFamily.InterNe
twork, 255) ? = False


Press Enter to continue
```

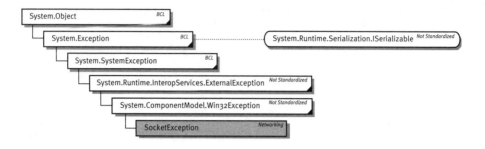

Summary

Represents the error that occurs when a socket error occurs.

Type Summary

```
public class SocketException : Win32Exception
   {
   // Constructors
      public SocketException();
MS public SocketException(int errorCode);
MS CF protected SocketException(SerializationInfo serializationInfo,
                StreamingContext streamingContext);

   // Properties
MS public override int ErrorCode { get; }
   }
```

Description

A `SocketException` is thrown by the `Socket` and `System.Net.Dns` classes when a network error occurs.

Example

```
using System;
using System.Net;
using System.Net.Sockets;
using System.Text;

public class SocketExceptionSample
{
    public static void Main()
    {
        try
        {
            FetchPage();
        }
        catch (SocketException se)
```

```
        {
            Console.WriteLine("Socket Error - code:" + se.ErrorCode);
        }
        catch (Exception e)
        {
            Console.WriteLine("Error: " + e.Message);
        }
        Console.WriteLine();
        Console.WriteLine();
        Console.WriteLine("Press Enter to continue");
        Console.ReadLine();
    }

    private static void FetchPage()
    {
        IPAddress ip = IPAddress.Parse("127.0.0.1");
        string targ = "/default.htm";
        Socket skt = new Socket(AddressFamily.InterNetwork,
            SocketType.Stream, ProtocolType.Tcp);
        try
        {
            IPEndPoint ep = new IPEndPoint(ip, 9999);
            skt.Connect(ep);
            if (skt.Connected)
            {
                Byte[] req = Encoding.ASCII.GetBytes("GET " + targ + "\n");
                skt.Send(req);
                Byte[] res = new Byte[1024];
                int rec = skt.Receive(res);
                skt.Shutdown(SocketShutdown.Both);
                Console.WriteLine("Received {0} bytes for {1}:",
                    rec, targ);
                Console.WriteLine(Encoding.ASCII.GetString(res, 0, rec));
            }
            else
            {
                throw new Exception("Cannot connect to Host");
            }
        }
        catch (Exception e)
        {
            throw new SocketException();
        }
        finally
        {
            skt.Close();
        }
    }
}
```

The output is

```
Socket Error - code:10061


Press Enter to continue
```

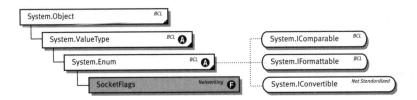

Summary

Controls the transfer behavior when sending and receiving data on a Socket instance.

Type Summary

```
public enum SocketFlags
    {
    DontRoute = 0x4,
MS  MaxIOVectorLength = 0x10,
    None = 0x0,
    OutOfBand = 0x1,
    Partial = 0x8000,
    Peek = 0x2,
    }
```

Description

The following methods use this enumeration:

- Socket.BeginReceive
- Socket.BeginReceiveFrom
- Socket.BeginSend
- Socket.BeginSendTo
- Socket.Receive
- Socket.ReceiveFrom
- Socket.Send
- Socket.SendTo

Example

```
using System;
using System.Net;
using System.Net.Sockets;
using System.Text;

public class SocketFlagsSample
{
```

```csharp
public static void Main()
{
    IPAddress ip = IPAddress.Parse("127.0.0.1");
    string targ = "/default.htm";
    Socket skt = new Socket(AddressFamily.InterNetwork,
        SocketType.Stream, ProtocolType.Tcp);
    try
    {
        IPEndPoint ep = new IPEndPoint(ip, 80);
        skt.Connect(ep);
        if (skt.Connected)
        {
            Byte[] req = Encoding.ASCII.GetBytes("GET " + targ + "\n");
            skt.Send(req, SocketFlags.Partial & SocketFlags.DontRoute);
            Byte[] res = new Byte[1024];
            int rec = skt.Receive(res);
            skt.Shutdown(SocketShutdown.Both);
            Console.WriteLine("Received {0} bytes for {1}:",
                rec, targ);
            Console.WriteLine(Encoding.ASCII.GetString(res, 0, rec));
        }
        else
        {
            Console.WriteLine("Cannot connect to host {0}", ip);
        }
    }
    catch (Exception e)
    {
        Console.WriteLine("Error: " + e.Message);
    }
    finally
    {
        skt.Close();
    }
    Console.WriteLine();
    Console.WriteLine();
    Console.WriteLine("Press Enter to continue");
    Console.ReadLine();
}
}
```

The output is

```
Received 60 bytes for /default.htm:
<html>
<body>
This is the default page
</body>
</html>


Press Enter to continue
```

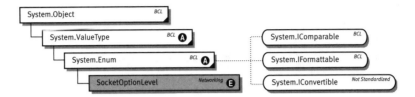

Summary

Specifies the option level associated with the `SocketOptionName` used in the `Socket.SetSocketOption` and `Socket.GetSocketOption` methods of the `Socket` class.

Type Summary

```
public enum SocketOptionLevel
      {
            IP = 0,
MS CF 1.1  IPv6 = 41,
            Socket = 65535,
            Tcp = 6,
            Udp = 17,
      }
```

Description

Some socket options apply only to specific protocols while others apply to all types. Members of this enumeration specify which protocol applies to a specific socket option.

Example

```
using System;
using System.Net;
using System.Net.Sockets;
using System.Text;

public class SocketOptionLevelSample
{
    public static void Main()
    {
        IPAddress ip = IPAddress.Parse("127.0.0.1");
        IPEndPoint ep = new IPEndPoint(ip, 9999);
        Socket skt = new Socket(AddressFamily.InterNetwork,
            SocketType.Dgram, ProtocolType.Udp);
        skt.SetSocketOption(SocketOptionLevel.Socket,
            SocketOptionName.SendTimeout, 5000);
        try
```

```
        {
            Byte[] req = Encoding.ASCII.GetBytes("Test");
            skt.SendTo(req, ep);
        }
        catch (Exception e)
        {
            Console.WriteLine("Error: " + e.Message);
        }
        finally
        {
            skt.Close();
        }
    }
}
```

A
B
C
D
E
F
G
H
I
J
K
L
M
N
O
P
Q
R
S
T
U
V
W
X
Y
Z

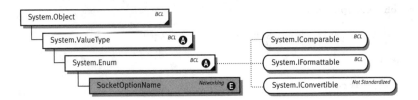

Summary

Specifies option names for use in the `Socket.SetSocketOption` and `Socket.Get-SocketOption` methods of the `Socket` class.

Type Summary

```
public enum SocketOptionName
    {
    AcceptConnection = 2,
    AddMembership = 12,
    AddSourceMembership = 15,
    BlockSource = 17,
    Broadcast = 32,
    BsdUrgent = 2,
    ChecksumCoverage = 20,
    Debug = 1,
    DontFragment = 14,
    DontLinger = -129,
    DontRoute = 16,
    DropMembership = 13,
    DropSourceMembership = 16,
    Error = 4103,
    ExclusiveAddressUse = -5,
    Expedited = 2,
    HeaderIncluded = 2,
    IPOptions = 1,
    IpTimeToLive = 4,
    KeepAlive = 8,
    Linger = 128,
    MaxConnections = 2147483647,
    MulticastInterface = 9,
    MulticastLoopback = 11,
    MulticastTimeToLive = 10,
    NoChecksum = 1,
    NoDelay = 1,
    OutOfBandInline = 256,
    PacketInformation = 19,
    ReceiveBuffer = 4098,
    ReceiveLowWater = 4100,
    ReceiveTimeout = 4102,
    ReuseAddress = 4,
    SendBuffer = 4097,
```

```
            SendLowWater = 4099,
            SendTimeout = 4101,
            Type = 4104,
            TypeOfService = 3,
            UnblockSource = 18,
            UseLoopback = 64,
            }
```

Description

Socket options determine the behavior of an instance of the `Socket` class. Some socket options apply only to specific protocols while others apply to all types. Members of the `SocketOptionLevel` enumeration specify which protocol applies to a specific socket option.

Example

```
using System;
using System.Net;
using System.Net.Sockets;
using System.Text;


public class SocketOptionNameSample
{
    public static void Main()
    {
        IPAddress ip = IPAddress.Parse("127.0.0.1");
        IPEndPoint ep = new IPEndPoint(ip, 9999);
        Socket skt = new Socket(AddressFamily.InterNetwork,
            SocketType.Dgram, ProtocolType.Udp);
        skt.SetSocketOption(SocketOptionLevel.Socket,
            SocketOptionName.SendTimeout, 5000);
        try
        {
            Byte[] req = Encoding.ASCII.GetBytes("Test");
            skt.SendTo(req, ep);
        }
        catch (Exception e)
        {
            Console.WriteLine("Error: " + e.Message);
        }
        finally
        {
            skt.Close();
        }
    }
}
```

A
B
C
D
E
F
G
H
I
J
K
L
M
N
O
P
Q
R
S
T
U
V
W
X
Y
Z

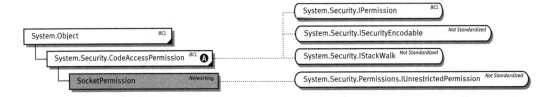

Summary

Secures socket connections.

Type Summary

```
CF public sealed class SocketPermission : CodeAccessPermission,
                                          IUnrestrictedPermission
    {
    // Constructors
CF public SocketPermission(NetworkAccess access, TransportType transport,
            string hostName, int portNumber);
CF public SocketPermission(PermissionState state);

    // Fields
CF public const int AllPorts = -1;

    // Properties
MS CF public IEnumerator AcceptList { get; }
MS CF public IEnumerator ConnectList { get; }

    // Methods
MS CF public void AddPermission(NetworkAccess access,
                    TransportType transport, string hostName, int portNumber);
CF public override IPermission Copy();
CF public override void FromXml(SecurityElement securityElement);
CF public override IPermission Intersect(IPermission target);
CF public override bool IsSubsetOf(IPermission target);
MS CF public bool IsUnrestricted();
CF public override SecurityElement ToXml();
CF public override IPermission Union(IPermission target);
    }
```

Description

`SocketPermission` instances control permission to accept connections or initiate socket
connections. A socket permission can secure access based on host name or IP address, a
port number, and a transport protocol.

The XML encoding of a SocketPermission instance is defined below in EBNF format, in particular the following conventions are used:

- All non-literals in the grammar below are shown in normal type.
- All literals are in bold font.

The following meta-language symbols are used:

- "*" represents a meta-language symbol suffixing an expression that can appear zero or more times.
- "?" represents a meta-language symbol suffixing an expression that can appear zero or one time.
- "+" represents a meta-language symbol suffixing an expression that can appear one or more times.
- "(',')" is used to group literals, non-literals, or a mixture of literals and non-literals.
- "|" denotes an exclusive disjunction between two expressions.
- "::= " denotes a production rule where a left-hand non-literal is replaced by a right-hand expression containing literals, non-literals, or both.

BuildVersion refers to the build version of the shipping CLI. This is a dotted build number such as "2412.0".

ECMAPubKeyToken::= b77a5c561934e089

HostName refers to a host name such as www.contoso.com.

Portnumber denotes a System.Int32 value indicating a port.

```
TransportProtocol::= 1 | 2 | 3 /*1= UDP, 2 = TCP, 3 = both */

SocketPermissionXML::=
<IPermission class="
System.Net.SocketPermission,
System,
Version=1.0.BuildVersion,
Culture=neutral,
PublicKeyToken=ECMAPubKeyToken"
version="1"
(
Unrestricted="true"
)
|
>
(<ConnectAccess>
(
<ENDPOINT>HostName#PortNumber#TransportProtocol</ENDPOINT>
) +
</ConnectAccess>
)
|
>
```

SocketPermission Class

```
(<AcceptAccess>
(
<ENDPOINT>HostName#PortNumber#TransportProtocol</ENDPOINT>
)+
</AcceptAccess>
</IPermission>
)
|
/>
```

Example

```
using System;
using System.Net;
using System.Security;
using System.Security.Permissions;

public class SocketPermissionSample
{
    public static void Main()
    {
        SocketPermission perm = new SocketPermission(
            NetworkAccess.Connect,
            TransportType.Tcp,
            "microsoft.com", 80);
        Console.WriteLine("XML encoding of SocketPermission:");
        SecurityElement sec = perm.ToXml();
        Console.WriteLine(sec);
        SocketPermission permCopy = (SocketPermission)perm.Copy();
        Console.WriteLine("XML encoding of copy of SocketPermission:");
        sec = permCopy.ToXml();
        Console.WriteLine(sec);
        Console.WriteLine();
        Console.WriteLine();
        Console.WriteLine("Press Enter to continue");
        Console.ReadLine();
    }
}
```

The output is

```
XML encoding of SocketPermission:
<IPermission class="System.Net.SocketPermission, System, Version=1.0.5000.0,
Culture=neutral, PublicKeyToken=b77a5c561934e089"
              version="1">
   <ConnectAccess>
      <ENDPOINT host="microsoft.com"
                transport="Tcp"
                port="80"/>
   </ConnectAccess>
</IPermission>

XML encoding of copy of SocketPermission:
<IPermission class="System.Net.SocketPermission, System, Version=1.0.5000.0,
Culture=neutral, PublicKeyToken=b77a5c561934e089"
```

```
            version="1">
  <ConnectAccess>
    <ENDPOINT host="microsoft.com"
              transport="Tcp"
              port="80"/>
  </ConnectAccess>
</IPermission>


Press Enter to continue
```

A
B
C
D
E
F
G
H
I
J
K
L
M
N
O
P
Q
R
S
T
U
V
W
X
Y
Z

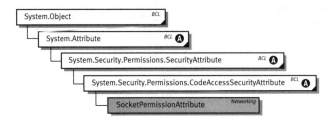

Summary

Used to declaratively specify security actions to control socket connections.

Type Summary

```
CF public sealed class SocketPermissionAttribute : CodeAccessSecurityAttribute
        {
        // Constructors
        CF public SocketPermissionAttribute(SecurityAction action);

        // Properties
        CF public string Access { get; set; }
        CF public string Host { get; set; }
        CF public string Port { get; set; }
        CF public string Transport { get; set; }

        // Methods
        CF public override IPermission CreatePermission();
        }
```

Description

The properties of a `SocketPermissionAttribute` are required to have non-null values. Once set, the values of the properties cannot be changed.

[*Note:* The details of a socket connection are specified using the properties of the current instance. For example, to secure a socket connection to port 80, set the `Port` property equal to "80". The security information declared by a security attribute is stored in the metadata of the attribute target, and is accessed by the system at runtime. Security attributes are used for declarative security only. For imperative security, use the corresponding permission class, `SocketPermission`. The allowable `SocketPermissionAttribute` targets are determined by the `System.Security.Permissions.SecurityAction` passed to the constructor.]

System.Net.Sockets
SocketShutdown Enum

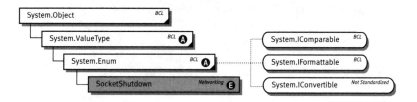

Summary

Specifies whether the ability to send or receive data is terminated when the `Socket.Shutdown` method is called on a connected `Socket` instance.

Type Summary

```
public enum SocketShutdown
    {
    Both = 2,
    Receive = 0,
    Send = 1,
    }
```

Example

```
using System;
using System.Net;
using System.Net.Sockets;
using System.Text;

public class SocketShutdownSample
{
    public static void Main()
    {
        IPAddress ip = IPAddress.Parse("127.0.0.1");
        string targ = "/default.htm";
        Socket skt = new Socket(AddressFamily.InterNetwork,
            SocketType.Stream, ProtocolType.Tcp);
        try
        {
            IPEndPoint ep = new IPEndPoint(ip, 80);
            skt.Connect(ep);
            if (skt.Connected)
            {
                Byte[] req = Encoding.ASCII.GetBytes("GET " + targ + "\n");
                skt.Send(req);
                Byte[] res = new Byte[1024];
                int rec = skt.Receive(res);
                skt.Shutdown(SocketShutdown.Both);
                Console.WriteLine("Received {0} bytes for {1}:",
                    rec, targ);
```

A
B
C
D
E
F
G
H
I
J
K
L
M
N
O
P
Q
R
S
T
U
V
W
X
Y
Z

```
                    Console.WriteLine(Encoding.ASCII.GetString(res, 0, rec));
                }
                else
                {
                    Console.WriteLine("Cannot connect to host {0}", ip);
                }
            }
            catch (Exception e)
            {
                Console.WriteLine("Error: " + e.Message);
            }
            finally
            {
                skt.Close();
            }
            Console.WriteLine();
            Console.WriteLine();
            Console.WriteLine("Press Enter to continue");
            Console.ReadLine();
        }
    }
```

The output is

```
Received 60 bytes for /default.htm:
<html>
<body>
This is the default page
</body>
</html>


Press Enter to continue
```

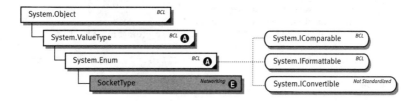

Summary

Specifies the type of socket an instance of the Socket class represents.

Type Summary

```
public enum SocketType
    {
    Dgram = 2,
    Raw = 3,
    Rdm = 4,
    Seqpacket = 5,
    Stream = 1,
    Unknown = -1,
    }
```

Description

A SocketType member is required when constructing instances of the Socket class and specifies the functionality the instance supports.

Example

```
using System;
using System.Net;
using System.Net.Sockets;
using System.Text;

public class SocketTypeSample
{
    public static void Main()
    {
        IPAddress ip = IPAddress.Parse("127.0.0.1");
        string targ = "/default.htm";
        Socket skt = new Socket(AddressFamily.InterNetwork,
            SocketType.Stream, ProtocolType.Tcp);
        try
        {
            IPEndPoint ep = new IPEndPoint(ip, 80);
            skt.Connect(ep);
            if (skt.Connected)
```

A
B
C
D
E
F
G
H
I
J
K
L
M
N
O
P
Q
R
S
T
U
V
W
X
Y
Z

A
B
C
D
E
F
G
H
I
J
K
L
M
N
O
P
Q
R
S
T
U
V
W
X
Y
Z

```
                    {
                        Byte[] req = Encoding.ASCII.GetBytes("GET " + targ + "\n");
                        skt.Send(req);
                        Byte[] res = new Byte[1024];
                        int rec = skt.Receive(res);
                        skt.Shutdown(SocketShutdown.Both);
                        Console.WriteLine("Received {0} bytes for {1}:",
                            rec, targ);
                        Console.WriteLine(Encoding.ASCII.GetString(res, 0, rec));
                    }
                    else
                    {
                        Console.WriteLine("Cannot connect to host {0}", ip);
                    }
                }
                catch (Exception e)
                {
                    Console.WriteLine("Error: " + e.Message);
                }
                finally
                {
                    skt.Close();
                }
                Console.WriteLine();
                Console.WriteLine();
                Console.WriteLine("Press Enter to continue");
                Console.ReadLine();
            }
        }
```

The output is

```
Received 60 bytes for /default.htm:
<html>
<body>
This is the default page
</body>
</html>


Press Enter to continue
```

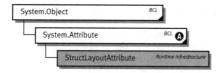

Summary

The `StructLayoutAttribute` allows the user to control the physical layout of the data members of a class or structure.

Type Summary

```
public sealed class StructLayoutAttribute : Attribute
    {
    // Constructors
        public StructLayoutAttribute(LayoutKind layoutKind);
    CF  public StructLayoutAttribute(short layoutKind);

    // Fields
    CF  public CharSet CharSet;
    CF  public int Pack;
        public int Size;

    // Properties
    CF  public LayoutKind Value { get; }
    }
```

■ **JM**   You will notice that this attribute has two constructors. One takes a `LayoutKind` and the other takes a `short`. You can see a possible design problem here, right? The one that takes the `enum` restricts (from a developer's point of view) the layout to the fields defined in `LayoutKind`. A `short` can be any short value inside or outside the range of `LayoutKind`. This can be error-prone. The designers said it was created to make it easier for type library importers to emit Interop assemblies, but even the designers said they dislike the overload.

■ **AN**   A few people have wondered why several of the custom attributes in `System.Runtime.InteropServices` have two constructors—one that takes an enumeration and one that takes a `short`. This is not a recommended design practice; it was done for legacy reasons to make it easier for the type library importer to emit these attributes.

CONTINUED

StructLayoutAttribute Class

> ■ **BG** I found out something a little arcane about declaring PInvoke methods that might save users some amount of time.
>
> If you have a method that takes a native `struct`, you have two options for declaring that `struct`. You can make it a value class ("struct" in C#), or a normal class. This choice doesn't seem very interesting, but your function prototype must use different syntax depending on your choice. For example, if your native method is prototyped as such:
>
> ```
> bool GetVersionEx(OSVERSIONINFO & lposvi);
> ```
>
> you must use one of the two following sets of syntax:
>
> ```
> [StructLayout(LayoutKind.Sequential, CharSet=CharSet.Auto)]
> internal struct OSVERSIONINFO {  ...  }
>
> [DllImport("KERNEL32", CharSet=CharSet.Auto)]
> internal static extern bool GetVersionEx(ref OSVERSIONINFO lposvi);
> ```
>
> or:
>
> ```
> [StructLayout(LayoutKind.Sequential, CharSet=CharSet.Auto)]
> internal class OSVERSIONINFO {  ...  }
>
> [DllImport("KERNEL32", CharSet=CharSet.Auto)]
> internal static extern bool GetVersionEx([In, Out] OSVERSIONINFO lposvi);
> ```
>
> Note that classes require being marked as [In, Out] while value classes must be passed as `ref` parameters.

Description

The target objects for this attribute are classes and structures. By default, the physical layout of the data members of a target object is automatically arranged. When managed objects are passed as arguments to unmanaged code, the system creates their unmanaged representations. These unmanaged representations can be controlled with the `Struct-LayoutAttribute`. Such control is necessary if the unmanaged code expects a specific layout, packing size, or character set.

[*Note:* See the `LayoutKind` enumeration for a description of the possible layout schemes, and the `FieldOffsetAttribute` for further information on the layout of exported objects.]

Compilers are required to not preserve this type in metadata as a custom attribute. Instead, compilers are required to emit it directly in the file format, as described in Partition II of the CLI Specification. Metadata consumers, such as the Reflection API, are required to retrieve this data from the file format and return it as if it were a custom attribute.

Example

Example 1

The following example demonstrates the use of the `StructLayoutAttribute`, and the `FieldOffsetAttribute`.

[*Note:* The non-standard `PtInRect` function used in this example indicates whether the specified point is located inside the specified rectangle. In this example, the layout setting on the `Rect` structure can be set to `LayoutKind.Sequential` with no bearing on the end result.]

```
using System;
using System.Runtime.InteropServices;

[StructLayout(LayoutKind.Sequential)]
public struct Point
{
    public int x;
    public int y;
}

[StructLayout(LayoutKind.Explicit)]
public struct Rect
{
    [FieldOffset(0)]  public int left;
    [FieldOffset(4)]  public int top;
    [FieldOffset(8)]  public int right;
    [FieldOffset(12)] public int bottom;
}


class NativeCodeAPI
{
    [DllImport("User32.dll")]
    public static extern bool PtInRect(ref Rect r, Point p);
}

public class StructLayoutTest
{
    public static void Main()
    {
        Rect r;
        Point p1, p2;

        r.left = 0;
        r.right = 100;
        r.top = 0;
        r.bottom = 100;

        p1.x = 20;
        p1.y = 30;

        p2.x = 110;
        p2.y = 5;
```

StructLayoutAttribute Class

```
        bool isInside1 = NativeCodeAPI.PtInRect(ref r, p1);
        bool isInside2 = NativeCodeAPI.PtInRect(ref r, p2);

        if(isInside1)
            Console.WriteLine("The first point is inside the rectangle.");
        else
            Console.WriteLine("The first point is outside the rectangle.");

        if(isInside2)
            Console.WriteLine("The second point is inside the rectangle.");
        else
            Console.WriteLine("The second point is outside the rectangle.");

    }
}
```

The output is

```
The first point is inside the rectangle.
The second point is outside the rectangle.
```

Example 2

```
using System;
using System.Runtime.InteropServices;

/// <summary>
/// Sample demonstrating the use of the StructLayoutAttribute class.
/// Use this attribute to control the binary layout of types passed to
/// unmanaged code.
/// </summary>
internal class StructLayoutAttributeSample
{

    private static void Main()
    {
        GUITHREADINFO info = new GUITHREADINFO();

        info.cbSize = (uint)Marshal.SizeOf(typeof(GUITHREADINFO));

        // Get information about windows in the active thread, which will
        // typically be the console. Setting a breakpoint on this line will
        // mean the IDE contains the active thread.
        if (GetGUIThreadInfo(0, ref info))
        {
            Console.WriteLine("Window information for the foreground thread:");
            Console.WriteLine(
                "   Active window                      = 0x{0}",
                ((int)info.hwndActive).ToString("x8"));
            Console.WriteLine(
                "   Window that has keyboard focus     = 0x{0}",
                ((int)info.hwndFocus).ToString("x8"));
            Console.WriteLine(
                "   Window that has captured the mouse = 0x{0}",
                ((int)info.hwndCapture).ToString("x8"));
            Console.WriteLine(
```

```
                "   Window displaying the caret           = 0x{0}",
                ((int)info.hwndCaret).ToString("x8"));
            Console.WriteLine(
                "   Caret dimensions (client coordinates)   = {0},{1} {2}x{3}",
                info.rcCaret.Left, info.rcCaret.Top,
                info.rcCaret.Right - info.rcCaret.Left,
                info.rcCaret.Bottom - info.rcCaret.Top);
        }
        else
        {
            Console.WriteLine("GetGUIThreadInfo failed.");
        }

        Console.WriteLine();
        Console.WriteLine();
        Console.WriteLine("Press Enter to continue");
        Console.ReadLine();
    }

    // The RECT type to use with GUITHREADINFO.
    [StructLayout(LayoutKind.Sequential)]
    private struct RECT
    {
        public int Left;
        public int Top;
        public int Right;
        public int Bottom;
    }

    // The GUITHREADINFO to use with GetGUIThreadInfo. Note that this type
    // contains an embedded RECT type.
    [StructLayout(LayoutKind.Sequential)]
    private struct GUITHREADINFO
    {
        public uint cbSize;
        public uint flags;
        public IntPtr hwndActive;
        public IntPtr hwndFocus;
        public IntPtr hwndCapture;
        public IntPtr hwndMenuOwner;
        public IntPtr hwndMoveSize;
        public IntPtr hwndCaret;
        public RECT rcCaret;
    }

    // Win32 method to retrieve information about windows in the specified
    // thread.
    [DllImport("user32.dll", SetLastError=true)]
    private static extern bool GetGUIThreadInfo(
        uint idThread, ref GUITHREADINFO lpgui);

}
```

A
B
C
D
E
F
G
H
I
J
K
L
M
N
O
P
Q
R
S
T
U
V
W
X
Y
Z

StructLayoutAttribute Class

The output is

```
Window information for the foreground thread:
  Active window                          = 0x001d07fe
  Window that has keyboard focus         = 0x001d07fe
  Window that has captured the mouse     = 0x00000000
  Window displaying the caret            = 0x00000000
  Caret dimensions (client coordinates)  = 0,0 0x0


Press Enter to continue
```

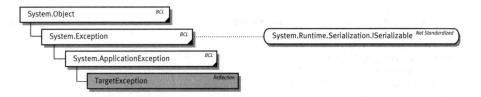

Summary

Represents the error that occurs when an attempt is made to invoke a member on an invalid target.

Type Summary

```
CF public class TargetException : ApplicationException
      {
      // Constructors
      CF public TargetException();
   MS CF protected TargetException(SerializationInfo info,
                    StreamingContext context);
      CF public TargetException(string message);
      CF public TargetException(string message, Exception inner);
      }
```

Description

[*Note:* A TargetException is thrown when an attempt is made to invoke a non-static method using a null object. This exception can also be thrown if the target does not implement the member.]

Example

```
using System;
using System.Reflection;

/// <summary>
/// This example causes a TargetException to be thrown by passing
/// invalid arguments to the String.Split() method.
/// </summary>

public class TargetExceptionSample
{
    public static void Main()
    {
        try
        {
            Type type = typeof(string);
```

```
                   type.InvokeMember("Split", BindingFlags.InvokeMethod, null,
                       null, null);
               }
               catch (TargetException e)
               {
                   Console.WriteLine("Caught exception: {0} - '{1}'", e.GetType().Name,
                       e.Message);
               }
               Console.WriteLine();
               Console.WriteLine();
               Console.WriteLine("Press Enter to continue");
               Console.ReadLine();
           }
       }
```

The output is

```
Caught exception: TargetException - 'Non-static method requires a target.'


Press Enter to continue
```

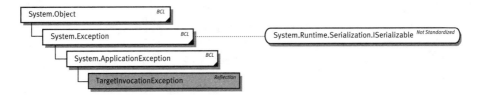

Summary

Represents the error that occurs when a method invoked via reflection throws an exception.

Type Summary

```
public sealed class TargetInvocationException : ApplicationException
    {
    // Constructors
        public TargetInvocationException(Exception inner);
        public TargetInvocationException(string message, Exception inner);
    }
```

> ■ **DM**   This exception is used to wrap any exceptions that occur in user code called via Reflection. This has two unfortunate side effects:
>
> 1. Since the inner exception is caught in order to wrap it, the context where this exception occurred is lost. This makes debugging this type of situation more difficult.
> 2. It makes catching only specific types of exception from code that calls into Reflection more difficult. Instead of simply catching the specific exception type, the TargetInvocationException needs to be caught and the inner exception then needs to be examined to determine whether this is the sought-after exception.

Description

The TargetInvocationException constructors are passed a reference to the exception thrown by the invoked method. [*Note:* The InnerException property inherited from System.Exception holds the exception.]

Example

```
using System;
using System.Reflection;

/// <summary>
/// Shows why a TargetInvocationException is raised
/// and how to handle it
/// </summary>

public class TargetInvocationExceptionSample
{
    public static void Main()
    {
        try
        {
            Type type = typeof(string);
            string str = "do unto others..";
            string result = (string)type.InvokeMember("Remove",
                BindingFlags.InvokeMethod, null, str, new object[] { 7, 60 });
            Console.WriteLine(result);
        }
        catch (TargetInvocationException e)
        {
            Console.WriteLine("Caught exception: {0} ", e.GetType().Name);
            Console.WriteLine("      {0} - '{1}'",
                e.InnerException.GetType().Name, e.InnerException.Message);
        }
        Console.WriteLine();
        Console.WriteLine();
        Console.WriteLine("Press Enter to continue");
        Console.ReadLine();
    }
}
```

The output is

```
Caught exception: TargetInvocationException
    ArgumentOutOfRangeException - 'Index and count must refer to a location
within the string.
Parameter name: count'


Press Enter to continue
```

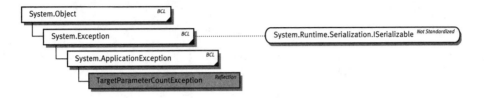

Summary

Represents the error that occurs when the number of parameters passed in the invocation of a member does not match the number of parameters required by the contract of that member.

Type Summary

```
public sealed class TargetParameterCountException : ApplicationException
{
// Constructors
    public TargetParameterCountException();
    public TargetParameterCountException(string message);
    public TargetParameterCountException(string message, Exception inner);
}
```

Description

This exception is thrown by types in the Reflection Library when attempting to dynamically invoke members.

Example

```
using System;
using System.Reflection;

/// <summary>
/// Shows why a TargetParameterCountException is raised
/// and how to handle it
/// </summary>

public class TargetParameterCountExceptionSample
{
    public static void Main()
    {
        try
        {
            Type type = typeof(string);
            string str = "do unto others..";
            MethodInfo RemoveMethod = type.GetMethod("Remove",
```

TargetParameterCountException Class

```
                BindingFlags.Public | BindingFlags.Instance, null,
                new Type[] { typeof(int), typeof(int) }, null);
            string result = (string)RemoveMethod.Invoke(str,
                new object[] { 7, 6, 5 });
            Console.WriteLine(result);
        }
        catch (TargetParameterCountException e)
        {
            Console.WriteLine("Caught exception: {0} - '{1}'",
                e.GetType().Name, e.Message);
        }
        Console.WriteLine();
        Console.WriteLine();
        Console.WriteLine("Press Enter to continue");
        Console.ReadLine();
    }
}
```

The output is

```
Caught exception: TargetParameterCountException - 'Parameter count mismatch.'


Press Enter to continue
```

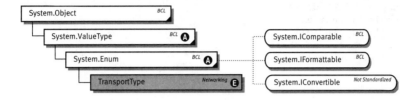

Summary

Specifies transport types.

Type Summary

```
CF public enum TransportType
      {
   CF All = 3,
   CF Connectionless = 1,
   CF ConnectionOriented = 2,
   CF Tcp = 2,
   CF Udp = 1,
      }
```

Description

[*Note:* The TransportType enumeration defines transport types for the SocketPermission and System.Net.Sockets.Socket classes.]

Example

```
using System;
using System.Net;
using System.Security;
using System.Security.Permissions;
using System.Collections;

public class TransportTypeSample
{
    public static void Main()
    {
        SocketPermission perm = new SocketPermission(
            NetworkAccess.Connect,
            TransportType.Tcp,
            "microsoft.com", 80);
        IEnumerator list = perm.ConnectList;
        while(list.MoveNext())
        {
            Console.Write("ConnectList: '{0}' ",list.Current);
            EndpointPermission epp = (EndpointPermission) list.Current;
```

TransportType Enum

```
                    Console.WriteLine("TransportType='{0}'", epp.Transport);
                }
                Console.WriteLine("XML encoding of SocketPermission:");
                SecurityElement sec = perm.ToXml();
                Console.WriteLine(sec);
                Console.WriteLine();
                Console.WriteLine();
                Console.WriteLine("Press Enter to continue");
                Console.ReadLine();
            }
        }
```

The output is

```
ConnectList: 'microsoft.com#80#2' TransportType='Tcp'
XML encoding of SocketPermission:
<IPermission class="System.Net.SocketPermission, System, Version-1.0.5000.0,
Culture=neutral, PublicKeyToken=b77a5c561934e089"
                version="1">
    <ConnectAccess>
        <ENDPOINT host="microsoft.com"
                  transport="Tcp"
                  port="80"/>
    </ConnectAccess>
</IPermission>



Press Enter to continue
```

System.Reflection
TypeAttributes Enum

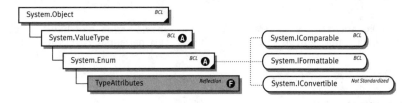

Summary

Specifies attributes of a type. This enumeration is used by the System.Type class.

Type Summary

```
public enum TypeAttributes
     {
     Abstract = 0x80,
     AnsiClass = 0x0,
     AutoClass = 0x20000,
     AutoLayout = 0x0,
     BeforeFieldInit = 0x100000,
     Class = 0x0,
     ClassSemanticsMask = 0x20,
     ExplicitLayout = 0x10,
MS   HasSecurity = 0x40000,
MS   Import = 0x1000,
     Interface = 0x20,
     LayoutMask = 0x18,
     NestedAssembly = 0x5,
     NestedFamANDAssem = 0x6,
     NestedFamily = 0x4,
     NestedFamORAssem = 0x7,
     NestedPrivate = 0x3,
     NestedPublic = 0x2,
     NotPublic = 0x0,
     Public = 0x1,
MS   ReservedMask = 0x40800,
MS   RTSpecialName = 0x800,
     Sealed = 0x100,
     SequentialLayout = 0x8,
MS   Serializable = 0x2000,
     SpecialName = 0x400,
     StringFormatMask = 0x30000,
     UnicodeClass = 0x10000,
     VisibilityMask = 0x7,
     }
```

A
B
C
D
E
F
G
H
I
J
K
L
M
N
O
P
Q
R
S
T
U
V
W
X
Y
Z

Example

```csharp
using System;
using System.Reflection;

/// <summary>
/// Shows how to access the various type attributes a type can have.  Prints
/// all the types (and nested types) in the System namespace of mscorlib.dll
/// </summary>

public class TypeAttributesSample
{
    public static void Main()
    {
        foreach (Type type in typeof(object).Assembly.GetTypes())
        {
            if (type.Namespace != "System")
            {
                continue;
            }
            Console.WriteLine("===>{0}<===",type.Name);
            if ((type.Attributes & TypeAttributes.VisibilityMask)
                == TypeAttributes.NotPublic)
            {
                Console.WriteLine("Not Public");
            }
            if ((type.Attributes & TypeAttributes.VisibilityMask)
                == TypeAttributes.Public)
            {
                Console.WriteLine("Public");
            }
            if ((type.Attributes & TypeAttributes.VisibilityMask)
                == TypeAttributes.NestedPublic)
            {
                Console.WriteLine("Nested Public");
            }

            if ((type.Attributes & TypeAttributes.LayoutMask)
                == TypeAttributes.SequentialLayout)
            {
                Console.WriteLine("Sequential Layout");
            }
            if ((type.Attributes & TypeAttributes.LayoutMask)
                == TypeAttributes.ExplicitLayout)
            {
                Console.WriteLine("Explicit Layout");
            }

            if ((type.Attributes & TypeAttributes.ClassSemanticsMask)
                == TypeAttributes.Class && !type.IsSubclassOf(typeof(ValueType)))
            {
                Console.WriteLine("Class");
            }

            if ((type.Attributes & TypeAttributes.ClassSemanticsMask)
                == TypeAttributes.Interface)
```

```
            {
                Console.WriteLine("interface");
            }
            if ((type.Attributes & TypeAttributes.Abstract) != 0)
            {
                Console.WriteLine("Abstract");
            }
            if ((type.Attributes & TypeAttributes.Sealed) != 0)
            {
                Console.WriteLine("Sealed");
            }

            if ((type.Attributes & TypeAttributes.SpecialName) != 0)
            {
                Console.WriteLine("Special Name");
            }
        }
        Console.WriteLine();
        Console.WriteLine();
        Console.WriteLine("Press Enter to continue");
        Console.ReadLine();
    }
}
```

The output is

```
===>Object<===
Public
Class
===>ICloneable<===
Public
interface
Abstract
===>Array<===
Public
Class
Abstract
===>SorterObjectArray<===
Class
===>SorterGenericArray<===
Class
===>SZArrayEnumerator<===
Class
===>ArrayEnumerator<===
Class
===>IComparable<===
Public
interface
Abstract
===>IConvertible<===
Public
interface
Abstract
===>String<===
Public
Class
```

A
B
C
D
E
F
G
H
I
J
K
L
M
N
O
P
Q
R
S
T
U
V
W
X
Y
Z

TypeAttributes Enum

```
Sealed
===>Exception<===
Public
Class
===>ValueType<===
Public
Class
Abstract

    [output truncated]
```

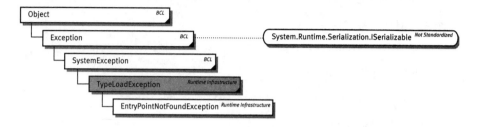

Summary

Represents the error that occurs when the system cannot load a Type.

Type Summary

```csharp
public class TypeLoadException : SystemException, ISerializable
    {
    // Constructors
        public TypeLoadException();
  MS CF protected TypeLoadException(SerializationInfo info,
                    StreamingContext context);
        public TypeLoadException(string message);
        public TypeLoadException(string message, Exception inner);

    // Properties
     CF public override string Message { get; }
     CF public string TypeName { get; }

    // Methods
  MS CF public override void GetObjectData(SerializationInfo info,
                            StreamingContext context);
    }
```

Description

TypeLoadException is thrown when the system cannot load a Type, or cannot locate
the assembly that contains the Type.

Example

```csharp
using System;


public class TypeLoadExceptionSample
{
    public static void Main()
    {
        try
```

```
        {
            String aname = "mscorlib, Version=1.0.5000.0, "+
                "Culture=neutral, PublicKeyToken=b77a5c561934e089";
            AppDomain.CurrentDomain.CreateInstance(aname, "InvalidType");
        }
        catch (TypeLoadException tlex)
        {
            Console.WriteLine("TypeLoadException: {0}", tlex.Message);
        }
        catch (Exception ex)
        {
            Console.WriteLine("Exception: {0}", ex.Message);
        }
        Console.WriteLine();
        Console.WriteLine();
        Console.WriteLine("Press Enter to continue");
        Console.ReadLine();
    }
}
```

The output is

```
TypeLoadException: Could not load type InvalidType from assembly mscorlib, Versi
on=1.0.5000.0, Culture=neutral, PublicKeyToken=b77a5c561934e089.


Press Enter to continue
```

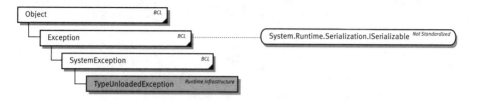

Summary

Represents the error that occurs when there is an attempt to access a Type that has been unloaded.

Type Summary

```
CF public class TypeUnloadedException : SystemException
      {
      // Constructors
      CF public TypeUnloadedException();
 MS CF protected TypeUnloadedException(SerializationInfo info,
                 StreamingContext context);
      CF public TypeUnloadedException(string message);
      CF public TypeUnloadedException(string message, Exception innerException);
      }
```

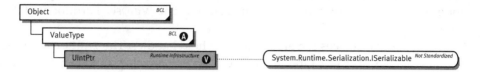

Summary

An implementation-specific type that is used to represent a pointer or a handle. This type is not CLS-compliant.

Type Summary

```
public struct UIntPtr : ISerializable
    {
    // Constructors
       public UIntPtr(uint value);
       public UIntPtr(ulong value);
    MS public unsafe UIntPtr(void* value);

    // Fields
       public static readonly UIntPtr Zero = 0;

    // Properties
       public static int Size { get; }

    // Methods
       public override bool Equals(object obj);
       public override int GetHashCode();
       public unsafe void* ToPointer();
       public override string ToString();
       public uint ToUInt32();
       public ulong ToUInt64();
       public static bool operator ==(UIntPtr value1, UIntPtr value2);
       public static bool operator !=(UIntPtr value1, UIntPtr value2);
    MS public static explicit operator uint(UIntPtr value);
    MS public static explicit operator UIntPtr(uint value);
    MS public static explicit operator UIntPtr(ulong value);
    MS public unsafe static explicit operator UIntPtr(void* value);
    MS public static explicit operator ulong(UIntPtr value);
    MS public unsafe static explicit operator void*(UIntPtr value);

    // Explicit Interface Members
    MS CF void ISerializable.GetObjectData(SerializationInfo info,
             StreamingContext context);
    }
```

A
B
C
D
E
F
G
H
I
J
K
L
M
N
O
P
Q
R
S
T
U
V
W
X
Y
Z

UIntPtr Structure

Description

The UIntPtr type is designed to be an implementation-sized pointer. An instance of this type is expected to be the size of a native unsigned int for the current implementation.

For more information on the native unsigned int type, see Partition II of the CLI Specification.

[*Note:* UIntPtr instances can also be used to hold handles. The IntPtr type is CLS-compliant while the UIntPtr type is not. The UIntPtr type is provided mostly to maintain architectural symmetry with the IntPtr type.]

Example

```
using System;

public class UIntPtrSample
{
    public static void Main()
    {
        Console.WriteLine("UIntPtr.Size = {0} bytes", UIntPtr.Size);

        UInt32 ui1 = 4000000000;
        UInt32 ui2 = 0;
        UIntPtr uip1 = new UIntPtr(ui1);
        UIntPtr uip2 = new UIntPtr(ui2);
        Console.WriteLine("UIntPtr(4000000000) == UIntPtr.Zero ? {0}",
            uip1 == UIntPtr.Zero);
        Console.WriteLine("UIntPtr(0) == UIntPtr.Zero ? {0}",
            uip2 == UIntPtr.Zero);
        Console.WriteLine("UIntPtr(4000000000) = {0}",
            uip1);
        Console.WriteLine();
        Console.WriteLine();
        Console.WriteLine("Press Enter to continue");
        Console.ReadLine();
    }
}
```

The output is

```
UIntPtr.Size = 4 bytes
UIntPtr(4000000000) == UIntPtr.Zero ? False
UIntPtr(0) == UIntPtr.Zero ? True
UIntPtr(4000000000) = 4000000000


Press Enter to continue
```

356

Summary

Provides data for the event that is raised when an exception is not caught by the program code executing in an application domain.

Type Summary

```
CF public class UnhandledExceptionEventArgs : EventArgs
    {
    // Constructors
    CF public UnhandledExceptionEventArgs(object exception,
            bool isTerminating);

    // Properties
    CF public object ExceptionObject { get; }
    CF public bool IsTerminating { get; }
    }
```

> **KC** I really regret that CLR allows exceptions that don't derive from System.Exception. Even though such exceptions are extremely rare, all APIs (not to mention user code) that deal with exceptions (like the ExceptionObject property) have to be typed as System.Object. The main reason CLR supports such exceptions is to be able to interop and support C++, but I think we could have solved the issue with some smart wrapping/unwrapping on the CLR–C++ boundary.

Description

UnhandledExceptionEventArgs provides access to the uncaught Exception and a property indicating whether the system will terminate the current process.

Example

```
using System;

public class UnhandledExceptionEventArgsSample
{
    public static void Main()
    {
        AppDomain domain = AppDomain.CurrentDomain;
        domain.UnhandledException +=
            new UnhandledExceptionEventHandler(MyExceptionHandler);
        Console.WriteLine("Attempting to execute NotThere.exe...");
        domain.ExecuteAssembly("NotThere.exe");
        Console.WriteLine("Finished executing NotThere.exe.");
    }

    public static void MyExceptionHandler(Object sender,
        UnhandledExceptionEventArgs args)
    {
        Exception e = (Exception) args.ExceptionObject;
        Console.WriteLine("UnhandledException event, Message is '{0}'",
            e.Message);
        Console.WriteLine();
        Console.WriteLine();
        Console.WriteLine("Press Enter to continue");
        Console.ReadLine();
    }

}
```

The output is

```
Attempting to execute NotThere.exe...
UnhandledException event, Message is 'File or assembly name NotThere.exe, or one
 of its dependencies, was not found.'


Press Enter to continue
```

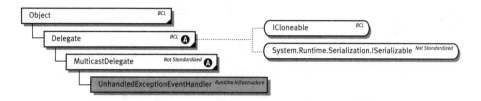

Summary

Defines the shape of methods that handle the event that is raised by the system for uncaught exceptions.

Type Summary

```
CF public delegate void UnhandledExceptionEventHandler(object sender,
                        UnhandledExceptionEventArgs e);
```

Parameters

Parameter	Description
sender	The application domain that handled the `System.AppDomain.UnhandledException` event.
e	A `System.UnhandledExceptionEventArgs` that contains the event data.

Description

An `UnhandledExceptionEventHandler` instance can only be specified for the default application domain that is created by the system to execute an application. Specifying an `UnhandledExceptionEventHandler` for an `AppDomain` created by an application has no effect.

[*Note:* An `UnhandledExceptionEventHandler` instance is used to specify methods that are invoked in response to exceptions that are not caught. To associate an instance of `UnhandledExceptionEventHandler` with an application domain, add the `UnhandledExceptionEventHandler` to the `AppDomain.UnhandledException` event. The methods referenced by the `UnhandledExceptionEventHandler` instance are invoked whenever an object, typically an `Exception`, is thrown and is not caught.]

A
B
C
D
E
F
G
H
I
J
K
L
M
N
O
P
Q
R
S
T
U
V
W
X
Y
Z

[*Note:* For additional information about events, see Partitions I and II of the CLI Specification.]

Example

```
using System;

public class UnhandledExceptionEventHandlerSample
{
    public static void Main()
    {
        AppDomain domain = AppDomain.CurrentDomain;
        domain.UnhandledException +=
            new UnhandledExceptionEventHandler(MyExceptionHandler);
        Console.WriteLine("Attempting to execute NotThere.exe...");
        domain.ExecuteAssembly("NotThere.exe");
        Console.WriteLine("Finished executing NotThere.exe.");
    }

    public static void MyExceptionHandler(object sender,
        UnhandledExceptionEventArgs args)
    {
        Exception e = (Exception) args.ExceptionObject;
        Console.WriteLine("UnhandledException event, Message is '{0}'",
            e.Message);
        Console.WriteLine("IsTerminating property = {0}",
            args.IsTerminating);
        Console.WriteLine();
        Console.WriteLine();
        Console.WriteLine("Press Enter to continue");
        Console.ReadLine();
    }

}
```

The output is

```
Attempting to execute NotThere.exe...
UnhandledException event, Message is 'File or assembly name NotThere.exe, or one
 of its dependencies, was not found.'
IsTerminating property = True


Press Enter to continue
```

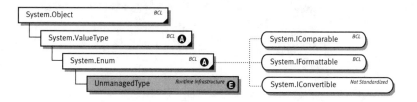

Summary

Identifies how parameters or fields are to be marshaled to unmanaged code.

Type Summary

```
public enum UnmanagedType
      {
   MS AnsiBStr = 35,
   MS AsAny = 40,
      Bool = 2,
   MS BStr = 19,
      ByValArray = 30,
   MS ByValTStr = 23,
MS CF Currency = 15,
      CustomMarshaler = 44,
   MS Error = 45,
      FunctionPtr = 38,
      I1 = 3,
      I2 = 5,
      I4 = 7,
      I8 = 9,
   MS IDispatch = 26,
   MS Interface = 28,
   MS IUnknown = 25,
      LPArray = 42,
      LPStr = 20,
   MS LPStruct = 43,
      LPTStr = 22,
      LPWStr = 21,
      R4 = 11,
      R8 = 12,
   MS SafeArray = 29,
      Struct = 27,
      SysInt = 31,
      SysUInt = 32,
      TBStr = 36,
      U1 = 4,
      U2 = 6,
      U4 = 8,
      U8 = 10,
   MS VariantBool = 37,
   MS VBByRefStr = 34,
      }
```

■■ **SK**   Regarding the `FunctionPtr` member, we had the ability to marshal delegates as native function pointers since v1.0, but reverse functionality was missing.
There was no way to take a native function pointer, wrap it into a delegate, and call it
from managed code. This was one of the most frequently asked-for features ever since
we shipped v1.0. Finally, in v2.0 we added this as a new method on the `Marshal` class
called `GetDelegateForFunctionPointer`.

■■ **SK**   The `Struct` member is one of the very funny ones. Just from the name there
is no chance you can guess what it's doing. Marshal objects as VARIANTs! Or something like that, I always forget. So don't worry, your structures will be marshaled as
structures, no special attributes needed for that case.

■■ **KC**   This enum always reminds me of one of the most pleasant things about the
framework: the fact that we only have one type representing a string! We cherish this
"feature" so much that, when we recently were trying to decide whether to constrain
`Nullable<T>` to value types or leave it unconstrained, one of the strongest arguments for constraining was that otherwise `Nullable<String>` would become an
alternative representation of a `string`.

■■ **AN**   Overwhelmed by the staggering number of choices in the `UnmanagedType`
enumeration to use with `MarshalAsAttribute`? Note that 10 of these values never
need to be used: `I2`, `I4`, `I8`, `R4`, `R8`, `U2`, `U4`, `U8`, `SysInt`, and `SysUInt`. That is
because no data type's marshaling behavior can be overridden in these ways. (In case
you were wondering about `I1` and `U1`, those *can* be used to make a `Boolean` marshal
as a single-byte C-style `bool`.)

■■ **AN**   Next to `UnmanagedType.Struct` that Sonja mentions, the next most confusing value is `UnmanagedType.LPStruct`. It's only supported for one specific
case: marshaling a `System.Guid` with an extra level of indirection (GUID* instead of
just GUID). It can be handy for some cases (e.g., enabling you to define a PInvoke signature for `CoCreateInstanceEx` with a by-value GUID first parameter rather than
a by-reference GUID), but it is probably best to just pretend this setting doesn't exist.
When `LPStruct` was originally created, there was a much grander vision for what it
would enable, but that never happened because of more pressing features that were
needed.

■■ **DT**   If you are doing PInvokes to unmanaged code, `UnmanagedType` is your best
friend.

Example

```csharp
using System;
using System.Runtime.InteropServices;

/// <summary>
/// Sample demonstrating the use of the UnmanagedType enumeration.
/// Use this enumeration to specify how data should be marshalled to unmanaged
/// code for fields and parameters decorated with MarshalAsAttribute.
/// </summary>
internal class UnmanagedTypeSample
{

    private static void Main()
    {
        OSVERSIONINFO ovi = new OSVERSIONINFO();

        ovi.dwOSVersionInfoSize = (uint)Marshal.SizeOf(typeof(OSVERSIONINFO));

        if (GetVersionEx(ref ovi))
        {
            Console.Write(
                "Detected OS version: {0}.{1}.{2}",
                ovi.dwMajorVersion, ovi.dwMinorVersion, ovi.dwBuildNumber);

            if (ovi.szCSDVersion.Length > 0)
            {
                Console.Write(
                    " ({0})",
                    NullTerminatedCharArrayToString(ovi.szCSDVersion));
            }

            Console.WriteLine();
        }
        else
        {
            Console.WriteLine("GetVersionEx failed.");
        }

        Console.WriteLine();
        Console.WriteLine();
        Console.WriteLine("Press Enter to continue");
        Console.ReadLine();
    }

    // Returns a string that contains all of the chars in the specified array,
    // upto the first null character.
    private static string NullTerminatedCharArrayToString(char[] chars)
    {
        int length = Array.IndexOf(chars, '\0');

        if (length == -1)
        {
            length = chars.Length;
        }
```

A
B
C
D
E
F
G
H
I
J
K
L
M
N
O
P
Q
R
S
T
U
V
W
X
Y
Z

```
        return new string(chars, 0, length);
    }

    // The OSVERSIONINFO1 type to use with GetVersionEx1. Note that the use of
    // UnmanagedType.ByValArray means that szCSDVersion is capable of receiving
    // SizeConst chars, although the convenience of a string is lost.
    // UnmanagedType.ByValTStr means that szCSDVersion is actually limited to
    // SizeConst - 1 chars, although it is often more convenient to deal with a
    // string field instead of a char[] field.
    [StructLayout(LayoutKind.Sequential, CharSet=CharSet.Auto)]
    private struct OSVERSIONINFO
    {
        public uint dwOSVersionInfoSize;
        public uint dwMajorVersion;
        public uint dwMinorVersion;
        public uint dwBuildNumber;
        public uint dwPlatformId;
        [MarshalAs(UnmanagedType.ByValArray, SizeConst=128)]
        public char[] szCSDVersion;
    }

    // Win32 method to retrieve information about the OS. .NET code would
    // typically use Environment.OSVersion, although it's worth noting that
    // GetVersionEx can retrieve the service pack string as well.
    [DllImport("kernel32.dll", CharSet=CharSet.Auto, SetLastError=true)]
    private static extern bool GetVersionEx(
        ref OSVERSIONINFO lpVersionInformation);

}
```

The output is

```
Detected OS version: 5.1.2600 (Service Pack 2)


Press Enter to continue
```

A
B
C
D
E
F
G
H
I
J
K
L
M
N
O
P
Q
R
S
T
U
V
W
X
Y
Z

Summary

Provides an object representation of a uniform resource identifier (URI) as defined by IETF RFC 2396.

Type Summary

```
public class Uri : MarshalByRefObject, ISerializable
{
  // Constructors
MS CF protected Uri(SerializationInfo serializationInfo,
               StreamingContext streamingContext);
     public Uri(string uriString);
     public Uri(string uriString, bool dontEscape);
     public Uri(Uri baseUri, string relativeUri);
     public Uri(Uri baseUri, string relativeUri, bool dontEscape);

  // Fields
     public static readonly string SchemeDelimiter = "://";
     public static readonly string UriSchemeFile = "file";
     public static readonly string UriSchemeFtp = "ftp";
     public static readonly string UriSchemeGopher = "gopher";
     public static readonly string UriSchemeHttp = "http";
     public static readonly string UriSchemeHttps = "https";
     public static readonly string UriSchemeMailto = "mailto";
     public static readonly string UriSchemeNews = "news";
     public static readonly string UriSchemeNntp = "nntp";

  // Properties
     public string AbsolutePath { get; }
     public string AbsoluteUri { get; }
     public string Authority { get; }
     public string Fragment { get; }
     public string Host { get; }
     public UriHostNameType HostNameType { get; }
     public bool IsDefaultPort { get; }
     public bool IsFile { get; }
     public bool IsLoopback { get; }
MS   public bool IsUnc { get; }
     public string LocalPath { get; }
     public string PathAndQuery { get; }
     public int Port { get; }
     public string Query { get; }
     public string Scheme { get; }
MS   public string[] Segments { get; }
     public bool UserEscaped { get; }
     public string UserInfo { get; }
```

```
// Methods
    protected virtual void Canonicalize();
    public static UriHostNameType CheckHostName(string name);
    public static bool CheckSchemeName(string schemeName);
    protected virtual void CheckSecurity();
    public override bool Equals(object comparand);
    protected virtual void Escape();
    protected static string EscapeString(string str);
    public static int FromHex(char digit);
    public override int GetHashCode();
    public string GetLeftPart(UriPartial part);
    public static string HexEscape(char character);
    public static char HexUnescape(string pattern, ref int index);
    protected virtual bool IsBadFileSystemCharacter(char character);
    protected static bool IsExcludedCharacter(char character);
    public static bool IsHexDigit(char character);
    public static bool IsHexEncoding(string pattern, int index);
    protected virtual bool IsReservedCharacter(char character);
    public string MakeRelative(Uri toUri);
    protected virtual void Parse();
    public override string ToString();
    protected virtual string Unescape(string path);

// Explicit Interface Members
MS CF void ISerializable.GetObjectData(SerializationInfo serializationInfo,
        StreamingContext streamingContext);
}
```

> **■ JM**   You might wonder why `System.Uri` is in the `System` namespace as
> opposed to the `System.Net` namespace. I wondered that too when we were doing
> the initial review of this type back in 2001 for the ECMA standard. The response I got
> was that there were plans (by Microsoft) to use `Uri` in an expanded role beyond the
> obvious networking cases. Some of these "plans" are noticeable in the `System.Xml`
> namespace and maybe others will come out in a future release of the Microsoft prod-
> uct and/or ECMA standard.
>
> **■ LO**   Given the breadth of a URI, I believe `System.Uri` is the correct location as
> compared with `System.Net.Uri`, which would incorrectly indicate some binding
> between the network and URIs. URIs are much broader than the network. A URI is a
> superset of URL and URN. The key difference between a URL and a URN is that a
> URL can be resolved. URNs can and do exist in all types of places independent of the
> network; for example, as a namespace identifier in the XML stack. URLs, while most
> commonly resolved over a network, can also be resolved without accessing the net-
> work at all; for example, file:URL.
>
> *CONTINUED*

■ LO   This class never should have been `MarshalByRef`. It was a mistake that didn't get caught until it was too late for version 1. It doesn't make sense because `Uri` is immutable and is much more suitable as an object you'd pass by value.

■ LO   One of the biggest challenges we had with `Uri` was how to deal with unknown schemes. If you know the scheme perfectly (as with "http:") then you can guarantee that the parsing is correct. However if the scheme is "foo:" then you don't have any guaranteed knowledge of the scheme-specific part that follows. We could have simply thrown on every scheme we didn't recognize, but that would leave people in a situation where they are using some valid scheme and have to introduce their own URI parsing class because `Uri` doesn't know about their scheme. In the end we decided to test unknown schemes to see if they look like hierarchical URIs similar to http: or some other non-hierarchical URI scheme similar to mailto:. If the unrecognized scheme is determined to be hierarchical then it is parsed in a way similar to http:. If it is non-hierarchical then the parsing is limited. I don't regret this decision, but it isn't perfect, the main flaw being that it is possible for `Uri` to think an unknown scheme fits into one bucket and make assumptions that actually aren't true for that scheme and therefore result in parsing that isn't intuitive.

■ BA   Notice that the only way to find out if a given string is a valid URI given this API is to try to create the URI and catch the exception.

```
try
{
    new Uri(s);
    return true;
}
    catch (UriFormatException)
{
return false;
}
```

Not only is the code ugly to write and read, the performance in the false case is very bad as the entire exception handling infrastructure has to be spun up. In v2.0 we added some other methods to `Uri` to avoid this problem similar to the `TryParse()` pattern on `Double` today.

■ BA   In v1.0 and v1.1, `System.Uri` is `MarshalByRef`. This strikes some people as odd since `MarshalByRef` is designed to be used only for types that encapsulate external resources that need to be shared across `AppDomains`.

CONTINUED

A
B
C
D
E
F
G
H
I
J
K
L
M
N
O
P
Q
R
S
T
U
V
W
X
Y
Z

Well, this has been changed in v2.0. Although technically a breaking change, we don't believe this will actually break any applications as it would have been hard to take advantage of the `MarshalByRef` properties of `System.Uri`. We made this change for a couple of reasons:

1. Security—`Uri` is immutable and yet if you could pass it by ref then there is the potential for it to be changed by the caller without the callee knowing.
2. Performance—MBRObj implied a significant performance hit (~100%) to `System.Uri` with no functional benefit.

■ **BA**   When designing an API, sometimes it is not clear whether to expose it with a `System.Uri` or a `System.String`. Here is some information from the design guidelines that should help.

Use `System.Uri` to represent URI/URL data. This applies to parameter types, property types, and return value types. `System.Uri` is a much safer and richer way of representing URIs. Extensive manipulation of URI-related data using plain strings has been shown to cause many security and correctness problems. An excellent whitepaper describing the issues in more detail is on its way.

Consider providing string-based overloads for most commonly used members with `System.Uri` parameters, but do not automatically overload all `Uri`-based members with a version that accepts a string. In cases where the usage pattern of taking a string from a user will be common enough, you should consider adding a convenience overload accepting a string. The string-based overload should be implemented in terms of the `Uri`-based overload.

Description

[*Note:* A Uniform Resource Identifier (URI) is a compact string of characters used to identify a resource located on a computer. A resource can be anything that has identity. Examples of resources that may be accessed using a URI include an electronic document, an image, a web service, and a collection of other resources. A URI is represented as a sequence of characters. While the exact format of a URI is determined by the protocol used to access the resource, many URIs consist of four major components: *<scheme>://* *<authority><path>?<query>*.

- *Scheme* indicates a protocol used to access the resource.
- *Authority* indicates the naming authority (server or registry) that governs the namespace defined by the remainder of the URI. The authority component is composed of *userinfo*, *host*, and *port* subcomponents in the form *<userinfo>@<host>:<port>*.

— *Userinfo* (a subcomponent of *Authority*) consists of a user name and, optionally, scheme-specific authorization information used to access *Host*. The *userinfo*, if present, is separated from the *Host* component by the "@" character. Note that for some URI schemes, the format of the *userinfo* subcomponent is "username:password". Passing authorization information in this manner is strongly discouraged due to security issues. The *userinfo* information is stored in the `UserInfo` property.

— *Host* (subcomponent of *Authority*) is the Domain Name System (DNS) name or IP4 address of a machine that provides access to the resource. This information is stored in the `Host` property. Only the *host* subcomponent is required to be present in the *Authority* component. Authority information is stored in the `Authority` property.

— *Port* (subcomponent of *Authority*) is the network port number used to connect to the host. If no port number is specified in the URI, most schemes designate protocols that have a default port number. This information is stored in the `Port` property.

- *Path* identifies the resource within the scope of the scheme and, if present, the authority. This information is stored in the `AbsolutePath`, `PathAndQuery`, and `LocalPath` properties.
- *Query* is parameter information that is passed to the executable script identified by the URI. The query, if present, is the last element in a URI and begins with a "?". This information is stored in the `Query` property.
- The *fragment* is not part of the URI, but is used in conjunction with the URI and is included here for completeness. This component contains resource-specific information that is used after a resource is retrieved. The *fragment*, if present, is separated from the URI by the "#" character. This information is stored in the `Fragment` property. URIs include components consisting of or delimited by certain special (reserved) characters that have a special meaning in a URI component. If the reserved meaning is not intended, then the character is required to be escaped in the URI. An escaped character is encoded as a character triplet consisting of the percent character "%" followed by the US-ASCII character code specified as two hexadecimal digits. For example, "%20" is the escaped encoding for the US-ASCII space character. The URI represented by a `Uri` instance is always in "escaped" form. The following characters are reserved:

A
B
C
D
E
F
G
H
I
J
K
L
M
N
O
P
Q
R
S
T
U
V
W
X
Y
Z

Character Name	Example
Semi-colon	;
Forward slash	/
Question mark	?
Colon	:
At-sign	@
Ampersand	&amp;
Equal sign	=
Plus sign	+
US Dollar sign	$
Comma	,

To transform the URI contained in a `Uri` instance from an escape encoded URI to a human-readable URI, use the `ToString` method.]

URIs are stored as canonical URIs in escaped encoding, with all characters with ASCII values greater than 127 replaced with their hexadecimal equivalents. The `Uri` constructors do not escape URI strings if the string is a well-formed URI, including a scheme identifier, that contains escape sequences. To put the URI in canonical form, the `Uri` constructors perform the following steps.

- Converts the URI scheme to lower case.
- Converts the host name to lower case.
- Removes default and empty port numbers.
- Simplifies the URI by removing superfluous segments such as "/" and "/test" segments.

The `Uri` class stores only absolute URIs (for example, "http://www.contoso.com/index.htm"). Relative URIs (for example, "/new/index.htm") are expanded to absolute form using a specified base URI. The `MakeRelative` method converts absolute URIs to relative URIs.

The `Uri` class properties are read-only; to modify a `Uri` instance use the `UriBuilder` class.

Example

```
using System;

public class UriSample
{
    public static void Main()
    {
        String baseUrl = "http://microsoft.com";
        Uri baseUri = new Uri(baseUrl);
        String relativePath = "samples/page 1.aspx?q=More#? &> more";
        Uri u = new Uri(baseUri, relativePath, false);
        Console.WriteLine();
        Console.WriteLine("Properties when Don't Escape is False:");
        ShowUriProperties(u);
        Console.WriteLine();
        Console.WriteLine();
        Console.WriteLine("Press Enter to continue");
        Console.ReadLine();
    }

    private static void ShowUriProperties(Uri u)
    {
        Console.WriteLine("Uri.AbsolutePath = '{0}'", u.AbsolutePath);
        Console.WriteLine("Uri.AbsoluteUri = '{0}'", u.AbsoluteUri);
        Console.WriteLine("Uri.Host = '{0}'", u.Host);
        Console.WriteLine("Uri.HostNameType = '{0}'", u.HostNameType);
        Console.WriteLine("Uri.IsDefaultPort = {0}", u.IsDefaultPort);
        Console.WriteLine("Uri.IsLoopback = '{0}'", u.IsLoopback);
        Console.WriteLine("Uri.LocalPath = '{0}'", u.LocalPath);
        Console.WriteLine("Uri.PathAndQuery = '{0}'", u.PathAndQuery);
        Console.WriteLine("Uri.Port = {0}", u.Port);
        Console.WriteLine("Uri.Query = '{0}'", u.Query);
        Console.WriteLine("Uri.UserEscaped = {0}", u.UserEscaped);
    }
}
```

The output is

```
Properties when Don't Escape is False:
Uri.AbsolutePath = '/samples/page%201.aspx'
Uri.AbsoluteUri = 'http://microsoft.com/samples/page%201.aspx?q=More#?%20&%3E%20
more'
Uri.Host = 'microsoft.com'
Uri.HostNameType = 'Dns'
Uri.IsDefaultPort = True
Uri.IsLoopback = 'False'
Uri.LocalPath = '/samples/page%201.aspx'
Uri.PathAndQuery = '/samples/page%201.aspx?q=More'
Uri.Port = 80
Uri.Query = '?q=More'
Uri.UserEscaped = False


Press Enter to continue
```

A
B
C
D
E
F
G
H
I
J
K
L
M
N
O
P
Q
R
S
T
U
V
W
X
Y
Z

Summary

Provides a mutable version of the Uri class.

Type Summary

```
CF public class UriBuilder
    {
    // Constructors
    CF public UriBuilder();
    CF public UriBuilder(string uri);
    CF public UriBuilder(string schemeName, string hostName);
    CF public UriBuilder(string scheme, string host, int portNumber);
    CF public UriBuilder(string scheme, string host, int port,
            string pathValue);
    CF public UriBuilder(string scheme, string host, int port, string path,
            string extraValue);
    CF public UriBuilder(Uri uri);

    // Properties
    CF public string Fragment { get; set; }
    CF public string Host { get; set; }
    CF public string Password { get; set; }
    CF public string Path { get; set; }
    CF public int Port { get; set; }
    CF public string Query { get; set; }
    CF public string Scheme { get; set; }
    CF public Uri Uri { get; }
    CF public string UserName { get; set; }

    // Methods
    CF public override bool Equals(object rparam);
    CF public override int GetHashCode();
    CF public override string ToString();
    }
```

> **▪ JM**   You might notice a similarity between Uri/UriBuilder and String/
> StringBuilder. That's because they are similar in concept. A Uri/String is
> immutable (read-only, if you will). A UriBuilder/StringBuilder provides a
> mechanism to modify the contents of a Uri/String without having to destroy and
> recreate a Uri/String each time (which, if done often enough, could hurt perfor-
> mance).

Description

The `Uri` and `UriBuilder` classes both represent a Uniform Resource Identifier (URI).
Instances of the `Uri` type are immutable: once the underlying URI is specified, neither it
nor its components, or constituent parts, can be changed. The `UriBuilder` type permits
modifications to the components of the URI it represents. The `Uri` property provides the
current contents of a `UriBuilder` as a `Uri` instance.

> [*Note:* For more information on URI, see IETF RFC 2396.]

Example

```
using System;

public class UriBuilderSample
{
    public static void Main()
    {
        String scheme = "http";
        String target = "microsoft.com";
        int port = 8080;
        String path = "samples/page 1.aspx";
        String query = "?q=my value";
        UriBuilder u = new UriBuilder(scheme, target, port,
            path, query);
        Console.WriteLine("Properties for UriBuilder(''{0}'"
            + ", '{1}', {2}, {3}, {4})",
            scheme, target, port, path, query);
        ShowUriProperties(u);
        Console.WriteLine();
        Console.WriteLine();
        Console.WriteLine("Press Enter to continue");
        Console.ReadLine();
    }

    private static void ShowUriProperties(UriBuilder u)
    {
        Console.WriteLine("UriBuilder.Fragment = '{0}'", u.Fragment);
        Console.WriteLine("UriBuilder.Host = '{0}'", u.Host);
        Console.WriteLine("UriBuilder.Password = '{0}'", u.Password);
        Console.WriteLine("UriBuilder.Path = '{0}'", u.Path);
        Console.WriteLine("UriBuilder.Port = {0}", u.Port);
        Console.WriteLine("UriBuilder.Query = '{0}'", u.Query);
        Console.WriteLine("UriBuilder.Scheme = '{0}'", u.Scheme);
        Console.WriteLine("UriBuilder.Uri = {0}", u.Uri);
        Console.WriteLine("UriBuilder.UserName = '{0}'", u.UserName);
    }

}
```

A
B
C
D
E
F
G
H
I
J
K
L
M
N
O
P
Q
R
S
T
U
V
W
X
Y
Z

The output is

```
Properties for UriBuilder('http', 'microsoft.com', 8080, samples/page 1.aspx, ?q
=my value)
UriBuilder.Fragment = ''
UriBuilder.Host = 'microsoft.com'
UriBuilder.Password = ''
UriBuilder.Path = 'samples/page%201.aspx'
UriBuilder.Port = 8080
UriBuilder.Query = '?q=my value'
UriBuilder.Scheme = 'http'
UriBuilder.Uri = http://microsoft.com:8080/samples/page 1.aspx?q=my value
UriBuilder.UserName = ''


Press Enter to continue
```

A
B
C
D
E
F
G
H
I
J
K
L
M
N
O
P
Q
R
S
T
U
V
W
X
Y
Z

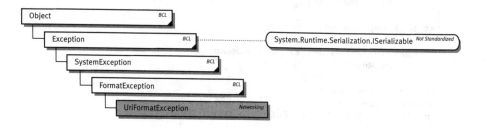

Summary

Represents the error that occurs when a Uniform Resource Identifier (URI) is not correctly formatted.

Type Summary

```
public class UriFormatException : FormatException, ISerializable
    {
    // Constructors
        public UriFormatException();
MS CF protected UriFormatException(SerializationInfo serializationInfo,
                StreamingContext streamingContext);
        public UriFormatException(string textString);

    // Explicit Interface Members
MS CF void ISerializable.GetObjectData(SerializationInfo serializationInfo,
            StreamingContext streamingContext);
    }
```

Description

[*Note:* The format for a valid URI is defined in IETF RFC 2396.]

Example

```
using System;
using System.Net;
using System.IO;

public class UriFormatExceptionSample
{
    public static void Main()
    {
        try
        {
            ThrowException();
        }
```

```
            catch (UriFormatException ufex)
            {
                Console.WriteLine("UriFormatException.Message = '{0}'",
                    ufex.Message);
            }
            catch (Exception ex)
            {
                Console.WriteLine("Exception.Message = '{0}'",
                    ex.Message);
            }
            Console.WriteLine();
            Console.WriteLine();
            Console.WriteLine("Press Enter to continue");
            Console.ReadLine();
        }

        private static void ThrowException()
        {
            try
            {
                Uri u = new Uri("invalid:///some where.com");
            }
            catch (Exception ex)
            {
                throw (ex);
            }
        }
    }
```

The output is

```
UriFormatException.Message = 'Invalid URI: The format of the URI could not be de
termined.'


Press Enter to continue
```

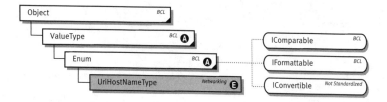

Summary

Specifies the format of host names.

Type Summary

```
public enum UriHostNameType
    {
 MS Basic = 1,
    Dns = 2,
    IPv4 = 3,
    IPv6 = 4,
    Unknown = 0,
    }
```

Description

[*Note:* The UriHostNameType enumeration defines the values returned by the
Uri.CheckHostName method.]

Example

```
using System;

public class UriHostNameTypeSample
{
    public static void Main()
    {
        string target = "microsoft.com";
        Console.WriteLine("Uri.CheckHostName('{0}') = '{1}'",
            target, Uri.CheckHostName(target));
        Console.WriteLine();
        Console.WriteLine();
        Console.WriteLine("Press Enter to continue");
        Console.ReadLine();
    }
}
```

UriHostNameType Enum

The output is

```
Uri.CheckHostName('microsoft.com') = 'Dns'
```

```
Press Enter to continue
```

A
B
C
D
E
F
G
H
I
J
K
L
M
N
O
P
Q
R
S
T
U
V
W
X
Y
Z

System
UriPartial Enum

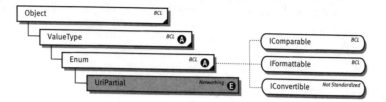

Summary

Specifies URI components.

Type Summary

```
public enum UriPartial
    {
    Authority = 1,
    Path = 2,
    Scheme = 0,
    }
```

Description

[*Note:* The UriPartial enumeration defines the values that are passed to the
Uri.GetLeftPart method.]

Example

```
using System;

public class UriPartialSample
{
    public static void Main()
    {
        Uri u = new Uri("http://microsoft.com/page1.aspx#paragraph1");
        ShowLeftParts(u);
        u = new Uri("ftp://microsoft.com/files/myfile.zip");
        ShowLeftParts(u);
        u = new Uri("file://c:\\temp\\myfile.zip");
        ShowLeftParts(u);
        u = new Uri("mailto:dummy@microsoft.com?subject=test");
        ShowLeftParts(u);
        Console.WriteLine();
        Console.WriteLine();
        Console.WriteLine("Press Enter to continue");
        Console.ReadLine();
    }
```

```
        private static void ShowLeftParts(Uri u)
        {
            Console.WriteLine("Uri('{0}').GetLeftPart(UriPartial"
                + ".Scheme) = {1}", u.ToString(),
                u.GetLeftPart(UriPartial.Scheme));
        }

    }
```

The output is

```
Uri('http://microsoft.com/page1.aspx#paragraph1').GetLeftPart(UriPartial.Scheme)
 = http://
Uri('ftp://microsoft.com/files/myfile.zip').GetLeftPart(UriPartial.Scheme) = ftp
://
Uri('file:///c:/temp/myfile.zip').GetLeftPart(UriPartial.Scheme) = file:///
Uri('mailto:dummy@microsoft.com?subject=test').GetLeftPart(UriPartial.Scheme) =
mailto:


Press Enter to continue
```

A
B
C
D
E
F
G
H
I
J
K
L
M
N
O
P
Q
R
S
T
U
V
W
X
Y
Z

System
Void Structure

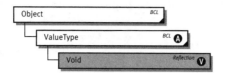

Summary

Indicates a method that does not return a value; that is, the method has a return type of void.

Type Summary

```
CF public struct Void
    {
    }
```

> **BA**   The Void class is a pretty special type. Compilers are supposed to emit it using a special signature encoding for void. The idea behind having the class was to have a way in Reflection to describe the "return type" of a method that returns void.

Description

This class is used by types in the Reflection Library.

System.Net
WebClient

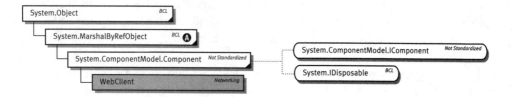

Summary

Provides common methods for sending data to and receiving data from a resource identified by a URI.

Type Summary

```
CF public sealed class WebClient : Component
    {
    // Constructors
    CF public WebClient();

    // Properties
    CF public string BaseAddress { get; set; }
    CF public ICredentials Credentials { get; set; }
    CF public WebHeaderCollection Headers { get; set; }
    CF public NameValueCollection QueryString { get; set; }
    CF public WebHeaderCollection ResponseHeaders { get; }

    // Methods
    CF public byte[] DownloadData(string address);
    CF public void DownloadFile(string address, string fileName);
    CF public Stream OpenRead(string address);
    CF public Stream OpenWrite(string address);
    CF public Stream OpenWrite(string address, string method);
    CF public byte[] UploadData(string address, byte[] data);
    CF public byte[] UploadData(string address, string method, byte[] data);
    CF public byte[] UploadFile(string address, string fileName);
    CF public byte[] UploadFile(string address, string method,
                string fileName);
    CF public byte[] UploadValues(string address, NameValueCollection data);
    CF public byte[] UploadValues(string address, string method,
                NameValueCollection data);
    }
```

■ **KC** WebClient is an example of what we call "Aggregate Component". It's a façade on top of several different fine-grained—but at the same time more complex—APIs. It provides an easy single entry point to the most common functionality related

CONTINUED

383

to the `System.Net` namespace. With a library as extensive as the one in the framework, we observed that the most common and severe usability problems include problems with finding the type that the user needs to use and problems with initializing and hooking up several fine-grained objects just to do some very basic things. To address the problem, we added several Aggregate Components to some core namespaces.

▪ JM Component, which `WebClient` derives from here, does not exist in the ECMA standard. Instead, the ECMA standard has it derived from `System.Object`.

▪ LO Future versions of `WebClient` will include support for submitting requests asynchronously.

Description

[*Note:* The `WebClient` class provides common methods for sending data to or receiving data from any local, Intranet, or Internet resource identified by a URI. The `WebClient` class uses the `WebRequest` class to provide access to Internet resources. `WebClient` instances can access data with any class derived from `WebRequest` that is registered with the `WebRequest.RegisterPrefix` method. By default, the CLI supports URIs with the "http:", "https:", and "file:" schemes. The `WebClient` class provides the following methods for uploading data to a resource:

- `OpenWrite` returns a `System.IO.Stream` used to send data to the resource.
- `UploadData` sends a byte array to the resource and returns a byte array containing any response.
- `UploadFile` sends a local file to the resource and returns a byte array containing any response.
- `UploadValues` sends a `System.Collections.Specialized.NameValue-Collection` to the resource and returns a byte array containing any response.

The `WebClient` class also provides the following methods for downloading data from a resource:

- `DownloadData` downloads data from a resource and returns a byte array.
- `DownloadFile` downloads data from a resource to a local file.
- `OpenRead` returns the data from the resource as a `System.IO.Stream`.]

Example

```
using System;
using System.Net;
using System.IO;
```

```
using System.Collections.Specialized;

public class WebClientSample
{
    public static void Main()
    {
        try
        {
            WebClient wc = new WebClient();
            String target = "default.htm";
            wc.BaseAddress = "http://www.microsoft.com/";
            wc.Headers.Add("USER-AGENT", "My custom .NET code");
            wc.Headers.Add("WINDOW-TARGET", "my-window");
            NameValueCollection nvc = new NameValueCollection();
            nvc.Add("name", "value");
            wc.QueryString = nvc;
            Console.WriteLine("Reading '{0}{1}'...",
                wc.BaseAddress, target);
            Stream s = wc.OpenRead(target);
            StreamReader reader = new StreamReader(s);
            Console.WriteLine(reader.ReadToEnd());
            s.Close();
            Console.WriteLine("WebClient.ResponseHeaders are:");
            foreach (String key in wc.ResponseHeaders.AllKeys)
            {
                Console.WriteLine("- " + key + " = "
                    + wc.ResponseHeaders[key]);
            }
        }
        catch (Exception e)
        {
            Console.WriteLine("*ERROR: " + e.Message);
        }
        Console.WriteLine();
        Console.WriteLine();
        Console.WriteLine("Press Enter to continue");
        Console.ReadLine();
    }
}
```

The output is

```
Reading 'http://www.microsoft.com/default.htm'...
<!DOCTYPE HTML PUBLIC "-//W3C//DTD HTML 4.0 Transitional//EN" ><html><head><META
 http-equiv="Content-Type" content="text/html; charset=utf-8"><!--TOOLBAR_EXEMPT
--><meta http-equiv="PICS-Label" content="(PICS-1.1 &quot;http://www.rsac.org/ra
tingsv01.html&quot; l gen true r (n 0 s 0 v 0 l 0))"><meta name="KEYWORDS" conte
nt="products; headlines; downloads; news; Web site; what's new; solutions; servi
ces; software; contests; corporate news;"><meta name="DESCRIPTION" content="The
entry page to Microsoft's Web site. Find software, solutions, answers, support,
and Microsoft news."><meta name="MS.LOCALE" content="EN-US"><meta name="CATEGORY
" content="home page"><title>Microsoft Corporation</title><style type="text/css"
 media="all">@import "/h/en-us/r/hp.css";</style><script type="text/javascript"
    [output truncated]

WebClient.ResponseHeaders are:
```

WebClient Class

```
- Cache-Control = public
- Content-Length = 16843
- Content-Type = text/html
- Expires = Sun, 13 Feb 2005 21:54:05 GMT
- Last-Modified = Sun, 13 Feb 2005 19:07:25 GMT
- Server = Microsoft-IIS/6.0
- X-AspNet-Version = 1.1.4322
- P3P = CP="ALL IND DSP COR ADM CONo CUR CUSo IVAo IVDo PSA PSD TAI TELo OUR SAM
o CNT COM INT NAV ONL PHY PRE PUR UNI"
- X-Powered-By = ASP.NET
- Date = Sun, 13 Feb 2005 19:16:11 GMT


Press Enter to continue
```

A
B
C
D
E
F
G
H
I
J
K
L
M
N
O
P
Q
R
S
T
U
V
W
X
Y
Z

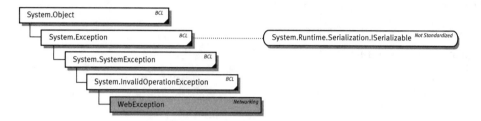

Summary

Represents an error that occurs while accessing the Internet through a pluggable protocol.

Type Summary

```
public class WebException : InvalidOperationException, ISerializable
    {
    // Constructors
        public WebException();
MS CF protected WebException(SerializationInfo serializationInfo,
                    StreamingContext streamingContext);
        public WebException(string message);
        public WebException(string message, Exception innerException);
        public WebException(string message, Exception innerException,
            WebExceptionStatus status, WebResponse response);
        public WebException(string message, WebExceptionStatus status);

    // Properties
        public WebResponse Response { get; }
        public WebExceptionStatus Status { get; }

    // Explicit Interface Members
MS CF void ISerializable.GetObjectData(SerializationInfo serializationInfo,
            StreamingContext streamingContext);
    }
```

Description

[*Note:* WebException is thrown by classes derived from WebRequest and Web-Response that implement pluggable protocols when an error occurs while accessing the Internet. When WebException is thrown by a method in a class derived from Web-Request, the WebException.Response property provides the Internet response to the application.]

Example

```
using System;
using System.Net;
using System.IO;

public class WebExceptionSample
{
    public static void Main()
    {
        try
        {
            CauseError();
        }
        catch (WebException wex)
        {
            Console.WriteLine("WebException occurred:");
            Console.WriteLine("- Message = '{0}'",
                wex.Message);
            Console.WriteLine("- Status = '{0}'",
                wex.Status);
        }
        catch (Exception e)
        {
            Console.WriteLine("*ERROR: " + e.Message);
        }
        Console.WriteLine();
        Console.WriteLine();
        Console.WriteLine("Press Enter to continue");
        Console.ReadLine();
    }
    private static void CauseError()
    {
        try
        {
            String target = "http://localhost/create500error.aspx";
            HttpWebRequest req = (HttpWebRequest)
                WebRequest.Create(target);
            HttpWebResponse result = (HttpWebResponse)req.GetResponse();
            result.Close();
        }
        catch (WebException wex)
        {
            throw(new WebException("Application Error !", wex));
        }
    }
}
```

The output is

```
WebException occurred:
- Message = 'Application Error !'
- Status = 'UnknownError'


Press Enter to continue
```

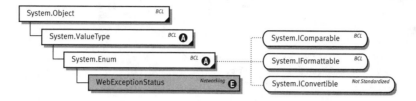

Summary

Defines status codes for the `WebException` class.

Type Summary

```
public enum WebExceptionStatus
    {
        ConnectFailure = 2,
        ConnectionClosed = 8,
        KeepAliveFailure = 12,
MS CF 1.1 MessageLengthLimitExceeded = 17,
        NameResolutionFailure = 1,
        Pending = 13,
        PipelineFailure = 5,
        ProtocolError = 7,
        ProxyNameResolutionFailure = 15,
        ReceiveFailure = 3,
        RequestCanceled = 6,
        SecureChannelFailure = 10,
        SendFailure = 4,
        ServerProtocolViolation = 11,
        Success = 0,
        Timeout = 14,
        TrustFailure = 9,
MS CF 1.1 UnknownError = 16,
    }
```

Description

This enumeration defines the status codes assigned to the `WebException.Status` property.

Example

```
using System;
using System.Net;
using System.IO;

public class WebExceptionStatusSample
{
    public static void Main()
    {
```

```
                    // create a custom WebException
                    WebException cex = new WebException("My Error Message",
                        WebExceptionStatus.ServerProtocolViolation);
                    ShowExceptionDetails(cex);

                    // handle a real WebException
                    try
                    {
                        HttpWebRequest req = (HttpWebRequest)
                            WebRequest.Create("http://doesnotexist.anywhere/");
                        HttpWebResponse result = (HttpWebResponse)req.GetResponse();
                    }
                    catch (WebException wex)
                    {
                        ShowExceptionDetails(wex);
                    }
                    catch (Exception ex)
                    {
                        Console.WriteLine("Exception: " + ex.Message);
                    }
                    Console.WriteLine();
                    Console.WriteLine();
                    Console.WriteLine("Press Enter to continue");
                    Console.ReadLine();
                }

                public static void ShowExceptionDetails(WebException ex)
                {
                    Console.WriteLine("WebException.Message = '{0}'",
                        ex.Message);
                    Console.WriteLine("WebException.Response = '{0}'",
                        ex.Response);
                    Console.WriteLine("WebException.Status = '{0}'",
                        ex.Status);
                    Console.WriteLine();
                }
            }
        }
```

The output is

```
WebException.Message = 'My Error Message'
WebException.Response = ''
WebException.Status = 'ServerProtocolViolation'

WebException.Message = 'The underlying connection was closed: The remote name co
uld not be resolved.'
WebException.Response = ''
WebException.Status = 'NameResolutionFailure'
```

A
B
C
D
E
F
G
H
I
J
K
L
M
N
O
P
Q
R
S
T
U
V
W
X
Y
Z

System.Net
WebHeaderCollection

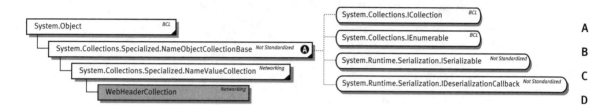

Summary

Contains protocol headers associated with a `WebRequest` or `WebResponse` instance.

Type Summary

```
public class WebHeaderCollection : NameValueCollection, ISerializable
    {
    // Constructors
        public WebHeaderCollection();
MS CF protected WebHeaderCollection(SerializationInfo serializationInfo,
                StreamingContext streamingContext);

    // Methods
        public void Add(string header);
        public override void Add(string name, string value);
        protected void AddWithoutValidate(string headerName,
                    string headerValue);
        public override string[] GetValues(string header);
        public static bool IsRestricted(string headerName);
MS CF public override void OnDeserialization(object sender);
        public override void Remove(string name);
        public override void Set(string name, string value);
MS public byte[] ToByteArray();
MS public override string ToString();

    // Explicit Interface Members
MS CF void ISerializable.GetObjectData(SerializationInfo serializationInfo,
            StreamingContext streamingContext);
    }
```

Description

This class is generally accessed through `WebRequest.Headers` or `Web-Response.Headers`.

Certain protocol headers are protected and cannot be set directly in a `WebHeader-Collection` instance. These headers can only be set through provided property accessors or by the system. The protected headers are:

Accept
Connection
Content-Length
Content-Type
Date
Expect
Host
If-Modified-Since
Range
Referer
Transfer-Encoding
UserAgent

Example

```
using System;
using System.Net;

public class WebHeaderCollectionSample
{

    public static void Main()
    {
        WebHeaderCollection whc = new WebHeaderCollection();
        whc.Add("MyCustomHeader1", "CustomValue1");
        whc.Add("MyCustomHeader2", "CustomValue2");
        whc.Add("MyMultiValueHeader", "MultiValue1");
        whc.Add("MyMultiValueHeader", "MultiValue2");
        Console.WriteLine();
        Console.WriteLine("Starting values:");
        ShowContents(whc);
        whc.Set("MyMultiValueHeader", "NewNonMultiValue");
        Console.WriteLine();
        Console.WriteLine("After Set(\"MyMultiValueHeader\", "
            + "\"NewNonMultiValue\"):");
        ShowContents(whc);
        whc.Set("MyMultiValueHeader", "NewMultiValue1,NewMultiValue2");
        Console.WriteLine();
        Console.WriteLine("After Set(\"MyMultiValueHeader\", "
            + "\"NewMultiValue1,NewMultiValue2\"):");
        ShowContents(whc);
        whc.Remove("MyCustomHeader1");
        Console.WriteLine();
        Console.WriteLine("After Remove(\"MyCustomHeader1\"):");
        ShowContents(whc);
        whc.Remove("MyMultiValueHeader");
        Console.WriteLine();
        Console.WriteLine("After Remove(\"MyMultiValueHeader\"):");
        ShowContents(whc);
```

```csharp
            // get headers from a request
            HttpWebRequest req = (HttpWebRequest)
                WebRequest.Create("http://www.microsoft.com/");
            HttpWebResponse result = (HttpWebResponse)req.GetResponse();
            WebHeaderCollection hdrs = result.Headers;
            Console.WriteLine();
            Console.WriteLine("Headers retrieved from a HttpWebResponse:");
            ShowContents(hdrs);

            Console.WriteLine();
            Console.WriteLine();
            Console.WriteLine("Press Enter to continue");
            Console.ReadLine();
        }

        private static void ShowContents(WebHeaderCollection whc)
        {
            foreach (String key in whc.AllKeys)
            {
                Console.Write("Key='{0}' ", key);
                Console.WriteLine("Value='{0}' ", whc[key]);
            }
        }
    }
}
```

The output is

```
Starting values:
Key='MyCustomHeader1' Value='CustomValue1'
Key='MyCustomHeader2' Value='CustomValue2'
Key='MyMultiValueHeader' Value='MultiValue1,MultiValue2'

After Set("MyMultiValueHeader", "NewNonMultiValue"):
Key='MyCustomHeader1' Value='CustomValue1'
Key='MyCustomHeader2' Value='CustomValue2'
Key='MyMultiValueHeader' Value='NewNonMultiValue'

After Set("MyMultiValueHeader", "NewMultiValue1,NewMultiValue2"):
Key='MyCustomHeader1' Value='CustomValue1'
Key='MyCustomHeader2' Value='CustomValue2'
Key='MyMultiValueHeader' Value='NewMultiValue1,NewMultiValue2'

After Remove("MyCustomHeader1"):
Key='MyCustomHeader2' Value='CustomValue2'
Key='MyMultiValueHeader' Value='NewMultiValue1,NewMultiValue2'

After Remove("MyMultiValueHeader"):
Key='MyCustomHeader2' Value='CustomValue2'

Headers retrieved from a HttpWebResponse:
Key='Cache-Control' Value='public'
Key='Content-Length' Value='16843'
Key='Content-Type' Value='text/html'
Key='Expires' Value='Sun, 13 Feb 2005 20:41:53 GMT'
```

A
B
C
D
E
F
G
H
I
J
K
L
M
N
O
P
Q
R
S
T
U
V
W
X
Y
Z

WebHeaderCollection Class

```
        Key='Last-Modified' Value='Sun, 13 Feb 2005 17:55:13 GMT'
        Key='Server' Value='Microsoft-IIS/6.0'
        Key='X-AspNet-Version' Value='1.1.4322'
        Key='P3P' Value='CP="ALL IND DSP COR ADM CONo CUR CUSo IVAo IVDo PSA PSD TAI TEL
        o OUR SAMo CNT COM INT NAV ONL PHY PRE PUR UNI"'
        Key='X-Powered-By' Value='ASP.NET'
        Key='Date' Value='Sun, 13 Feb 2005 19:33:34 GMT'


        Press Enter to continue
```

A
B
C
D
E
F
G
H
I
J
K
L
M
N
O
P
Q
R
S
T
U
V
W
X
Y
Z

System.Net
WebPermission

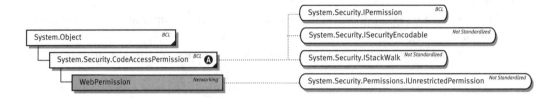

Summary

Controls access to Internet resources.

Type Summary

```
CF public sealed class WebPermission : CodeAccessPermission,
                                       IUnrestrictedPermission
     {
     // Constructors
MS CF public WebPermission();
MS CF public WebPermission(NetworkAccess access, Regex uriRegex);
   CF public WebPermission(NetworkAccess access, string uriString);
   CF public WebPermission(PermissionState state);

     // Properties
MS CF public IEnumerator AcceptList { get; }
MS CF public IEnumerator ConnectList { get; }

     // Methods
MS CF public void AddPermission(NetworkAccess access, Regex uriRegex);
MS CF public void AddPermission(NetworkAccess access, string uriString);
   CF public override IPermission Copy();
   CF public override void FromXml(SecurityElement securityElement);
   CF public override IPermission Intersect(IPermission target);
   CF public override bool IsSubsetOf(IPermission target);
MS CF public bool IsUnrestricted();
   CF public override SecurityElement ToXml();
   CF public override IPermission Union(IPermission target);
     }
```

Description

The XML encoding of a WebPermission instance is defined below in EBNF format. The following conventions are used:

- All non-literals in the grammar below are shown in normal type.
- All literals are in bold font.

The following meta-language symbols are used:

- "*" represents a meta-language symbol suffixing an expression that can appear zero or more times.
- "?" represents a meta-language symbol suffixing an expression that can appear zero or one time.
- "+" represents a meta-language symbol suffixing an expression that can appear one or more times.
- "('')" is used to group literals, non-literals, or a mixture of literals and non-literals.
- "|" denotes an exclusive disjunction between two expressions.
- ":= " denotes a production rule where a left-hand non-literal is replaced by a right-hand expression containing literals, non-literals, or both.

BuildVersion refers to the build version of the shipping CLI. This is a dotted build number such as "2412.0".

ECMAPubKeyToken::= `b77a5c561934e089`

HostName refers to a host name such as "www.contoso.com".

Portnumber denotes a `System.Int32` value indicating a port.

TransportProtocol::= `1 | 2 | 3 /*1= UDP, 2 = TCP, 3 = both */`

```
WebPermissionXML::=
<IPermission
class="
System.Net.WebPermission,
System,
Version=1.0.BuildVersion,
Culture=neutral,
PublicKeyToken=ECMAPubKeyToken"
version="1"
(
Unrestricted="true"/>
)
|
>
(<ConnectAccess>
(
<URI>HostName#PortNumber#TransportProtocol</URI>
)+
</ConnectAccess>
</IPermission>
)
|
>
(<AcceptAccess>
(
<URI>HostName#PortNumber#TransportProtocol</URI>
)+
</AcceptAccess>
</IPermission>
)
|
/>
```

Example

```csharp
using System;
using System.Net;
using System.Security;
using System.Security.Permissions;

public class WebPermissionSample
{
    public static void Main()
    {
        WebPermission perm = new
            WebPermission(PermissionState.Unrestricted);
        Console.WriteLine("XML encoding of WebPermission:");
        SecurityElement sec = perm.ToXml();
        Console.WriteLine(sec);

        WebPermission permCopy = (WebPermission)perm.Copy();
        Console.WriteLine("XML encoding of copy of WebPermission:");
        sec = permCopy.ToXml();
        Console.WriteLine(sec);

        Boolean result = perm.IsSubsetOf(permCopy);
        Console.WriteLine("Initial WebPermission instance "
            + "IsSubsetOf copied instance: {0}",
            result);
        Console.WriteLine();
        Console.WriteLine();
        Console.WriteLine("Press Enter to continue");
        Console.ReadLine();
    }
}
```

The output is

```
XML encoding of WebPermission:
<IPermission class="System.Net.WebPermission, System, Version=1.0.5000.0, Cultur
e=neutral, PublicKeyToken=b77a5c561934e089"
         version="1"
         Unrestricted="true"/>

XML encoding of copy of WebPermission:
<IPermission class="System.Net.WebPermission, System, Version=1.0.5000.0, Cultur
e=neutral, PublicKeyToken=b77a5c561934e089"
         version="1"
         Unrestricted="true"/>

Initial WebPermission instance IsSubsetOf copied instance: True


Press Enter to continue
```

A
B
C
D
E
F
G
H
I
J
K
L
M
N
O
P
Q
R
S
T
U
V
W
X
Y
Z

Summary

Used to declaratively specify permission to access Internet resources.

Type Summary

```
CF public sealed class WebPermissionAttribute : CodeAccessSecurityAttribute
     {
     // Constructors
     CF public WebPermissionAttribute(SecurityAction action);

     // Properties
     CF public string Accept { get; set; }
  MS CF public string AcceptPattern { get; set; }
     CF public string Connect { get; set; }
  MS CF public string ConnectPattern { get; set; }

     // Methods
     CF public override IPermission CreatePermission();
     }
```

Description

[*Note:* The security information declared by a security attribute is stored in the metadata of the attribute target, and is accessed by the system at runtime. Security attributes are used for declarative security only. For imperative security, use the corresponding permission class, `WebPermission`. The allowable `WebPermissionAttribute` targets are determined by the `System.Security.Permissions.SecurityAction` passed to the constructor.]

Example

```
using System;
using System.Net;
using System.Security;
using System.Security.Permissions;
```

```
public class WebPermissionAttributeSample
{
    public static void Main()
    {
        WebPermissionAttribute wpa = new
            WebPermissionAttribute(SecurityAction.Deny);
        wpa.Accept = "http://yoursite.com/page1.htm";
        wpa.Connect = "http://yoursite.com/page2.htm";
        Console.WriteLine("WebPermissionAttribute.Accept = '{0}'",
            wpa.Accept);
        Console.WriteLine("WebPermissionAttribute.Connect = '{0}'",
            wpa.Connect);
        Console.WriteLine();
        Console.WriteLine();
        Console.WriteLine("Press Enter to continue");
        Console.ReadLine();
    }
}
```

The output is

```
WebPermissionAttribute.Accept = 'http://yoursite.com/page1.htm'
WebPermissionAttribute.Connect = 'http://yoursite.com/page2.htm'


Press Enter to continue
```

A
B
C
D
E
F
G
H
I
J
K
L
M
N
O
P
Q
R
S
T
U
V
W
X
Y
Z

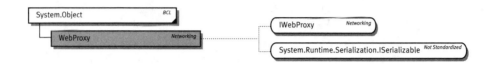

Summary

Contains HTTP proxy settings for the System.Net.WebRequest class.

Type Summary

```csharp
public class WebProxy : IWebProxy, ISerializable
{
    // Constructors
    public WebProxy();
MS CF protected WebProxy(SerializationInfo serializationInfo,
            StreamingContext streamingContext);
    public WebProxy(string Address);
    public WebProxy(string Address, bool BypassOnLocal);
CF  public WebProxy(string Address, bool BypassOnLocal,
            string[] BypassList);
CF  public WebProxy(string Address, bool BypassOnLocal,
            string[] BypassList, ICredentials Credentials);
    public WebProxy(string Host, int Port);
    public WebProxy(Uri Address);
    public WebProxy(Uri Address, bool BypassOnLocal);
CF  public WebProxy(Uri Address, bool BypassOnLocal, string[] BypassList);
CF  public WebProxy(Uri Address, bool BypassOnLocal, string[] BypassList,
            ICredentials Credentials);

    // Properties
    public Uri Address { get; set; }
CF  public ArrayList BypassArrayList { get; }
CF  public string[] BypassList { get; set; }
    public bool BypassProxyOnLocal { get; set; }
    public ICredentials Credentials { get; set; }

    // Methods
    public static WebProxy GetDefaultProxy();
    public Uri GetProxy(Uri destination);
    public bool IsBypassed(Uri host);

    // Explicit Interface Members
MS CF void ISerializable.GetObjectData(SerializationInfo serializationInfo,
            StreamingContext streamingContext);
}
```

> ■ **JM**   The design guidelines (Partition V in the public ECMA standard—will be Partition VI when edition 3 comes out) clearly state "Do parameter names with camelCasing." We missed the boat on some of these.
>
> ■ **DT**   `WebProxy` constructors would be easier to read and use if those `Bypass-OnLocal` parameters were an `enum` type instead of `Booleans`. Enums with descriptive element names are more explicit, easier to read, and easier to write at the call site. See the comments on `System.Net.Authorization` for an example.
>
> ■ **DT**   .NET Framework API Design Guidelines: Parameter names should be first letter lowercase, followed by word boundary camel-caps. The constructor parameters here should be `address`, `bypassOnLocal`, `bypassList`, `credentials`. Starting locals (including parameters) with lowercase helps the reader distinguish them from global type names. The issue is not ambiguity to the compiler, but to the human maintainers of the code.

Description

`WebRequest` instances use `WebProxy` instances to override the proxy settings in `GlobalProxySelection`.

[*Note:* Local requests are identified by the lack of a period (.) in the authority of the URI, as in "http://webserver/" versus "http://www.contoso.com/".]

Example

Example 1

The following example sets a `WebProxy` for a `WebRequest`. The `WebRequest` instance uses the proxy to connect to external Internet resources.

```
using System;
using System.Net;

public class WebProxyExample
{
    public static void Main()
    {

        WebProxy proxyObject =
            new WebProxy("http://proxyserver:80/",true);
        WebRequest req =
            WebRequest.Create("http://www.contoso.com");
        req.Proxy = proxyObject;
    }
}
```

Example 2

```
using System;
using System.Net;

public class WebProxySample
{
    public static void Main()
    {
        String[] bplist = new String[] {"mysite.com/*",
                                        "http://*.microsoft.com/*",
                                        "http://test.org/test.htm"};
        NetworkCredential nc = new NetworkCredential("test", "secret");
        Uri path = new Uri("http://mysite.com");
        CredentialCache cc = new CredentialCache();
        cc.Add(path, "BASIC", nc);
        WebProxy wp = new WebProxy(new Uri("http://myproxy/"),
            true, bplist, cc);

        Console.WriteLine("WebProxy property values:");
        Console.WriteLine("Address = '{0}'", wp.Address);
        Console.Write("BypassList = ");
        foreach (String item in wp.BypassList)
        {
            Console.Write(item + " ");
        }
        Console.WriteLine();
        Console.WriteLine("BypassProxyOnLocal = {0}",
            wp.BypassProxyOnLocal);
        NetworkCredential found =
            wp.Credentials.GetCredential(path, "BASIC");
        Console.WriteLine("Credentials.UserName = '{0}'",
            found.UserName);
        Console.WriteLine("Credentials.Password = '{0}'",
            found.Password);
        Console.WriteLine();
        Console.WriteLine();
        Console.WriteLine("Press Enter to continue");
        Console.ReadLine();
    }
}
```

The output is

```
WebProxy property values:
Address = 'http://myproxy/'
BypassList = mysite.com/* http://*.microsoft.com/* http://test.org/test.htm
BypassProxyOnLocal = True
Credentials.UserName = 'test'
Credentials.Password = 'secret'


Press Enter to continue
```

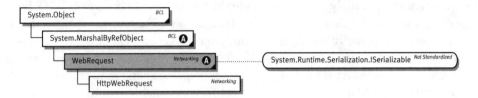

Summary

Makes a request to a Uniform Resource Identifier (URI).

Type Summary

```
public abstract class WebRequest : MarshalByRefObject, ISerializable
    {
    // Constructors
        protected WebRequest();
MS CF protected WebRequest(SerializationInfo serializationInfo,
                StreamingContext streamingContext);

    // Properties
        public virtual string ConnectionGroupName { get; set; }
        public virtual long ContentLength { get; set; }
        public virtual string ContentType { get; set; }
        public virtual ICredentials Credentials { get; set; }
        public virtual WebHeaderCollection Headers { get; set; }
        public virtual string Method { get; set; }
        public virtual bool PreAuthenticate { get; set; }
        public virtual IWebProxy Proxy { get; set; }
        public virtual Uri RequestUri { get; }
        public virtual int Timeout { get; set; }

    // Methods
        public virtual void Abort();
        public virtual IAsyncResult BeginGetRequestStream(
                            AsyncCallback callback, object state);
        public virtual IAsyncResult BeginGetResponse(AsyncCallback callback,
                            object state);
        public static WebRequest Create(string requestUriString);
        public static WebRequest Create(Uri requestUri);
        public static WebRequest CreateDefault(Uri requestUri);
        public virtual Stream EndGetRequestStream(IAsyncResult asyncResult);
        public virtual WebResponse EndGetResponse(IAsyncResult asyncResult);
        public virtual Stream GetRequestStream();
        public virtual WebResponse GetResponse();
        public static bool RegisterPrefix(string prefix,
                            IWebRequestCreate creator);

    // Explicit Interface Members
MS CF void ISerializable.GetObjectData(SerializationInfo serializationInfo,
            StreamingContext streamingContext);
    }
```

> **■ LO**   We argued for many days about whether to have a separate class for request
> and reply or to put them all together on one HTTP class. In the end we went with a
> separate request and reply class. This made the request/reply nature of HTTP more
> explicit. It was also consistent with the model used on the server side (ASP.NET). For
> a while there was actually an attempt to unify the server and client classes on the
> same common base classes but the overhead of unification proved to be greater than
> the potential benefits and the effort was abandoned. Today the request/reply model
> remains intact. Had the focus been less on HTTP we probably would have gone the
> other direction.

Description

WebRequest is an abstract class that models the request side of transactions used for
accessing data from the Internet.

Classes that derive from WebRequest are required to override the following members of the WebRequest class in a protocol-specific manner:

- Method—Gets or sets the protocol method to use in the current instance.
- RequestUri—Gets the System.Uri of the resource associated with the current
  instance.
- Headers—Gets or sets the collection of header name/value pairs associated with the
  request.
- ContentLength—Gets or sets the content length of the request data being sent.
- ContentType—Gets or sets the content type of the request data being sent.
- Credentials—Gets or sets the credentials used for authenticating the client using
  the current instance.
- PreAuthenticate—Gets or sets a value that indicates whether to send authentication information with a request for resources.
- GetRequestStream—Returns a System.IO.Stream for writing data to a resource.
- BeginGetRequestStream—Begins an asynchronous request for a stream in which
  to write data to be sent in the current request.
- EndGetRequestStream—Returns a System.IO.Stream for writing data to the
  resource accessed by the current instance.
- GetResponse—Returns a response to a request.
- BeginGetResponse—Begins an asynchronous request for a resource.
- EndGetResponse—Returns a WebResponse that contains a response to a specified
  pending request.

In addition, derived classes are required to support the IWebRequestCreate interface.

[*Note:* An application that uses the request/response model can request data be sent from the Internet in a protocol-agnostic manner, in which the application works with instances of the WebRequest class while classes that derive from WebRequest and implement specific protocols perform the details of the request. Requests are sent from an application to a particular Uniform Resource Identifier (URI), such as a Web page on a server. Using the URI, the Create method creates an instance of a type derived from WebRequest to handle the request. The type is selected from the set of registered types. Types may be registered to handle a specific protocol, such as HTTP or FTP, or to handle a request to a specific server or path on a server. [*Note:* For information on registering types, see RegisterPrefix.] The System.Net.WebRequest class throws a WebException exception when an error occurs while accessing a resource. Use the Create method to initialize a new instance of a class that derives from WebRequest. Do not use the WebRequest constructor.]

Example

Example 1
The following example demonstrates using Create to create an instance of HttpWebRequest.

```
using System;
using System.Net;

public class WebRequestExample
{

    public static void Main()
    {

        // Initialize the WebRequest.
        WebRequest myRequest =
            WebRequest.Create("http://www.contoso.com");

        // Print the type of the request.
        Console.WriteLine(myRequest);
    }
}
```

The output is

```
System.Net.HttpWebRequest
```

Example 2
```
using System;
using System.Net;
using System.IO;
using System.Text;
using System.Threading;
```

WebRequest Class

```
public class WebRequestSample
{
    private static Boolean bDone = false;
    private static byte[] data;

    public static void Main()
    {
        try
        {
            String target = "http://localhost/default.aspx";
            String value = "Some data to send as the request";
            HttpWebRequest req = (HttpWebRequest)
                WebRequest.Create(target);
            req.Method = "POST";
            req.ContentType = "multipart/formdata";
            data = new ASCIIEncoding().GetBytes(value);
            req.ContentLength = data.Length;
            req.Timeout = 2000;
            IAsyncResult ar = req.BeginGetRequestStream(new
                AsyncCallback(GetRequestHandler), req);
            while (!bDone)
            {
                Thread.Sleep(500);
            }
        }
        catch (Exception e)
        {
            Console.WriteLine("*ERROR: " + e.Message);
        }
        Console.WriteLine();
        Console.WriteLine();
        Console.WriteLine("Press Enter to continue");
        Console.ReadLine();
    }

    private static void GetRequestHandler(IAsyncResult ar)
    {
        try
        {
            HttpWebRequest req = (HttpWebRequest)ar.AsyncState;
            Stream s = req.GetRequestStream();
            s.Write(data, 0, data.Length);
            HttpWebResponse result = (HttpWebResponse)req.GetResponse();
            Console.WriteLine("Data has been sent");
            Console.WriteLine("HttpWebResponse.StatusCode = {0}",
                result.StatusCode.ToString());
            result.Close();
            Console.WriteLine("Page that was requested was: {0}",
                req.RequestUri.ToString());
        }
        catch (Exception e)
        {
            Console.WriteLine("*ERROR: " + e.Message);
        }
        finally
        {
```

```
            bDone = true;
        }
    }
}
```

The output is

```
Data has been sent
HttpWebResponse.StatusCode = OK
Page that was requested was: http://localhost/default.aspx


Press Enter to continue
```

A
B
C
D
E
F
G
H
I
J
K
L
M
N
O
P
Q
R
S
T
U
V
W
X
Y
Z

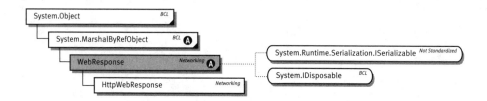

Summary

Represents a response received from a Uniform Resource Identifier (URI).

Type Summary

```
public abstract class WebResponse : MarshalByRefObject, ISerializable,
                                    IDisposable
   {
   // Constructors
      protected WebResponse();
MS CF protected WebResponse(SerializationInfo serializationInfo,
               StreamingContext streamingContext);

   // Properties
      public virtual long ContentLength { get; set; }
      public virtual string ContentType { get; set; }
      public virtual WebHeaderCollection Headers { get; }
      public virtual Uri ResponseUri { get; }

   // Methods
      public virtual void Close();
      public virtual Stream GetResponseStream();

   // Explicit Interface Members
MS CF void ISerializable.GetObjectData(SerializationInfo serializationInfo,
               StreamingContext streamingContext);
   CF void IDisposable.Dispose();
   }
```

Description

WebResponse is the base class from which protocol-specific response classes, such as HttpWebResponse, are derived.

Classes that derive from WebResponse are required to override the following members in the WebResponse class:

- ContentLength—Gets or sets the content length of the data being received.
- ContentType—Gets or sets the media type of the data being received.

- `GetResponseStream`—Returns a `System.IO.Stream` that contains data from the current host.
- `ResponseUri`—Gets a `System.Uri` containing the URI of the resource associated with the current instance.
- `Headers`—Gets or sets the collection of header name/value pairs associated with the current instance.

[*Note:* Applications can participate in request/response transactions in a protocol-agnostic manner using instances of the `WebResponse` class while protocol-specific classes derived from `WebResponse` carry out the details of the request. Applications do not create `WebResponse` objects directly; they are created by calling `WebRequest.GetResponse`.]

Example

Example 1
The following example creates a `System.Net.WebResponse` instance from a `System.Net.WebRequest`.

```
using System;
using System.Net;

public class WebResponseExample
{
    public static void Main()
    {

        // Initialize the WebRequest.
        WebRequest myRequest =
            WebRequest.Create("http://www.contoso.com");

        // Return the response.
        WebResponse myResponse = myRequest.GetResponse();

        // Code to use the WebResponse goes here.

        // Close the response to free resources.
        myResponse.Close();
    }
}
```

Example 2
```
using System;
using System.Net;
using System.IO;

public class WebResponseSample
{
    public static void Main()
```

A
B
C
D
E
F
G
H
I
J
K
L
M
N
O
P
Q
R
S
T
U
V
W
X
Y
Z

```
    {
        try
        {
            String target = "http://microsoft.com/";
            HttpWebRequest req = (HttpWebRequest)
                WebRequest.Create(target);
            HttpWebResponse result = (HttpWebResponse)req.GetResponse();
            Console.WriteLine("Page that was delivered was: {0}",
                result.ResponseUri);
            Console.WriteLine("HttpWebResponse.StatusCode = {0}",
                result.StatusCode);
            Console.WriteLine("HttpWebResponse.ContentLength = {0}",
                result.ContentLength);
            Console.WriteLine("HttpWebResponse.ContentType = '{0}'",
                result.ContentType);
            Console.WriteLine("HttpWebResponse.Headers are:");
            foreach (String key in result.Headers.AllKeys)
            {
                Console.WriteLine("- " + key + " = "
                    + result.Headers[key]);
            }
            StreamReader reader = new
                StreamReader(result.GetResponseStream());
            Console.WriteLine("Contents of the returned page:");
            Console.WriteLine(reader.ReadToEnd());
            reader.Close();
            result.Close();
        }
        catch (Exception e)
        {
            Console.WriteLine("*ERROR: " + e.Message);
        }
        Console.WriteLine();
        Console.WriteLine();
        Console.WriteLine("Press Enter to continue");
        Console.ReadLine();
    }
}
```

The output is

```
Page that was delivered was: http://www.microsoft.com/
HttpWebResponse.StatusCode = OK
HttpWebResponse.ContentLength = 16843
HttpWebResponse.ContentType = 'text/html'
HttpWebResponse.Headers are:
- Cache-Control = public
- Content-Length = 16843
- Content-Type = text/html
- Expires = Sun, 13 Feb 2005 23:19:15 GMT
- Last-Modified = Sun, 13 Feb 2005 20:32:35 GMT
- Server = Microsoft-IIS/6.0
- X-AspNet-Version = 1.1.4322
- P3P = CP="ALL IND DSP COR ADM CONo CUR CUSo IVAo IVDo PSA PSD TAI TELo OUR SAM
  o CNT COM INT NAV ONL PHY PRE PUR UNI"
- X-Powered-By = ASP.NET
```

```
- Date = Sun, 13 Feb 2005 20:59:26 GMT
Contents of the returned page:
<!DOCTYPE HTML PUBLIC "-//W3C//DTD HTML 4.0 Transitional//EN" ><html><head><META
 http-equiv="Content-Type" content="text/html; charset=utf-8"><!--TOOLBAR_EXEMPT
--><meta http-equiv="PICS-Label" content="(PICS-1.1 &quot;http://www.rsac.org/ra
tingsv01.html&quot; l gen true r (n 0 s 0 v 0 l 0))"><meta name="KEYWORDS" conte
nt="products; headlines; downloads; news; Web site; what's new; solutions; servi
ces; software; contests; corporate news;"><meta name="DESCRIPTION" content="The
entry page to Microsoft's Web site. Find software, solutions, answers, support,
and Microsoft news."><meta name="MS.LOCALE" content="EN-US"><meta name="CATEGORY
" content="home page"><title>Microsoft Corporation</title><style type="text/css"
 media="all">@import "/h/en-us/r/hp.css";</style><script type="text/javascript"
    [output truncated]
```

A
B
C
D
E
F
G
H
I
J
K
L
M
N
O
P
Q
R
S
T
U
V
W
X
Y
Z

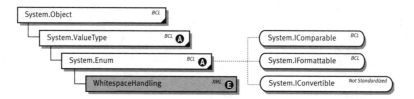

Summary

Specifies the type of white space returned by instances of the `XmlTextReader` class.

Type Summary

```
public enum WhitespaceHandling
    {
    All = 0,
    None = 2,
    Significant = 1,
    }
```

Description

Significant white space is white space between markup in a mixed content model, or white space within an element that has the `xml:space="preserve"` attribute. Insignificant white space is any other white space between markup.

Example

```
using System;
using System.Xml;

/// <summary>
/// Reads an input .xml file three times, each time handling the white space
/// in different ways by setting the WhitespaceHandling enum to one of
/// its three possible values
/// </summary>

public class WhitespaceHandlingSample
{
    public static void Main()
    {
        ReadXmlDocument(WhitespaceHandling.All);
        ReadXmlDocument(WhitespaceHandling.None);
        ReadXmlDocument(WhitespaceHandling.Significant);
        Console.WriteLine();
        Console.WriteLine();
```

```
        Console.WriteLine("Press Enter to continue");
        Console.ReadLine();
    }

    static void ReadXmlDocument(WhitespaceHandling wspace)
    {
        XmlTextReader r = new XmlTextReader("sample.xml");
        r.WhitespaceHandling = wspace;
        Console.WriteLine();
        Console.WriteLine("With Whitespacehandling {0}:", wspace);
        while (r.Read())
        {
            Console.WriteLine("Node ({0}) {1}", r.Name, r.NodeType);
        }
        r.Close();
    }
}
```

The output is

```
With Whitespacehandling All:
Node (xml) XmlDeclaration
Node () Whitespace
Node (root) Element
Node () Whitespace
Node (child) Element
Node () SignificantWhitespace
Node (grandchild) Element
Node () Text
Node (grandchild) EndElement
Node () SignificantWhitespace
Node (child) EndElement
Node () Whitespace
Node (root) EndElement
Node () Whitespace

With Whitespacehandling None:
Node (xml) XmlDeclaration
Node (root) Element
Node (child) Element
Node (grandchild) Element
Node () Text
Node (grandchild) EndElement
Node (child) EndElement
Node (root) EndElement

With Whitespacehandling Significant:
Node (xml) XmlDeclaration
Node (root) Element
Node (child) Element
Node () SignificantWhitespace
Node (grandchild) Element
Node () Text
Node (grandchild) EndElement
```

A
B
C
D
E
F
G
H
I
J
K
L
M
N
O
P
Q
R
S
T
U
V
W
X
Y
Z

WhitespaceHandling Enum

```
Node () SignificantWhitespace
Node (child) EndElement
Node (root) EndElement
```

```
Press Enter to continue
```

A
B
C
D
E
F
G
H
I
J
K
L
M
N
O
P
Q
R
S
T
U
V
W
X
Y
Z

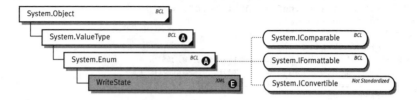

Summary

Specifies the write state of an instance of a class derived from the XmlWriter class.

Type Summary

```
public enum WriteState
    {
    Attribute = 3,
    Closed = 5,
    Content = 4,
    Element = 2,
    Prolog = 1,
    Start = 0,
    }
```

Description

When a writer is instantiated, the write state is set to Start. While content is written, the write state is set to reflect the type of content being written. When the XmlWriter.Close method is called, the write state is set to Closed. The XmlWriter.WriteEndDocument method resets the write state back to Start, allowing the writer to write a new XML document.

Example

```
using System;
using System.Xml;

/// <summary>
/// Writes the WriteState at each point in the writing of an .xml input file
/// </summary>

public class WriteStateSample
{
    public static void Main()
    {
        XmlTextWriter w = new XmlTextWriter("sample.xml", null);
        ShowWriteState("constructor", w);
        w.WriteStartDocument();
```

```
                ShowWriteState("WriteStartDocument", w);
                w.WriteStartElement("root");
                ShowWriteState("WriteStartElement", w);
                w.WriteStartAttribute("sample", "");
                ShowWriteState("WriteStartAttribute", w);
                w.WriteString("value");
                ShowWriteState("WriteString", w);
                w.WriteEndAttribute();
                ShowWriteState("WriteEndAttribute", w);
                w.WriteElementString("subelement", "sample");
                ShowWriteState("WriteElementString", w);
                w.WriteEndElement();
                ShowWriteState("WriteEndElement", w);
                w.WriteEndDocument();
                ShowWriteState("WriteEndDocument", w);
                w.Close();
                ShowWriteState("Close", w);
                Console.WriteLine();
                Console.WriteLine();
                Console.WriteLine("Press Enter to continue");
                Console.ReadLine();
        }

        static void ShowWriteState(string s, XmlTextWriter w)
        {
                Console.WriteLine("Called method {0}, "
                     + "WriteState is {1}",
                     s, w.WriteState);
        }

}
```

The output is

```
Called method constructor, WriteState is Start
Called method WriteStartDocument, WriteState is Prolog
Called method WriteStartElement, WriteState is Element
Called method WriteStartAttribute, WriteState is Attribute
Called method WriteString, WriteState is Attribute
Called method WriteEndAttribute, WriteState is Element
Called method WriteElementString, WriteState is Content
Called method WriteEndElement, WriteState is Content
Called method WriteEndDocument, WriteState is Start
Called method Close, WriteState is Closed


Press Enter to continue
```

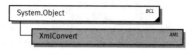

Summary

Encodes and decodes XML names and provides methods for converting between common language infrastructure (CLI) types and XML Schema Definition language (XSD) types. When converting data types, the values returned are locale independent.

Type Summary

```
public class XmlConvert
{
   // Constructors
      public XmlConvert();

   // Methods
      public static string DecodeName(string name);
      public static string EncodeLocalName(string name);
      public static string EncodeName(string name);
      public static string EncodeNmToken(string name);
      public static bool ToBoolean(string s);
      public static byte ToByte(string s);
      public static char ToChar(string s);
      public static DateTime ToDateTime(string s);
      public static DateTime ToDateTime(string s, string format);
      public static DateTime ToDateTime(string s, string[] formats);
      public static decimal ToDecimal(string s);
      public static double ToDouble(string s);
   MS public static Guid ToGuid(string s);
      public static short ToInt16(string s);
      public static int ToInt32(string s);
      public static long ToInt64(string s);
      public static sbyte ToSByte(string s);
      public static float ToSingle(string s);
      public static string ToString(bool value);
      public static string ToString(byte value);
      public static string ToString(char value);
      public static string ToString(DateTime value);
      public static string ToString(DateTime value, string format);
      public static string ToString(decimal value);
      public static string ToString(double value);
      public static string ToString(float value);
   MS public static string ToString(Guid value);
      public static string ToString(int value);
      public static string ToString(long value);
      public static string ToString(sbyte value);
      public static string ToString(short value);
      public static string ToString(TimeSpan value);
      public static string ToString(uint value);
```

A
B
C
D
E
F
G
H
I
J
K
L
M
N
O
P
Q
R
S
T
U
V
W
X
Y
Z

```
        public static string ToString(ulong value);
        public static string ToString(ushort value);
        public static TimeSpan ToTimeSpan(string s);
        public static ushort ToUInt16(string s);
        public static uint ToUInt32(string s);
        public static ulong ToUInt64(string s);
        public static string VerifyName(string name);
        public static string VerifyNCName(string name);
    }
```

> **■ MF**   The XmlConvert class encapsulates the CLR to XSD type conversions so that
> you can read XML strings and convert these into CLR types and vice versa. For
> example, the following XML element called date has a serialized XSD DateTime:
>
> `<date>1967-08-04T04:00:00</date>`
>
> which can be converted to a CLR type using the ToDateTime method. One of the
> main features in the v2.0 release of the .NET Framework is to integrate this type
> conversion support into the processing classes such as the XmlReader. That way you
> can work with XML simple types as CLR types.

Description

Element and attribute names or ID values are limited to a range of XML characters according to the Extensible Markup Language (XML) 1.0 (Second Edition) recommendation,
located at www.w3.org/TR/2000/REC-xml-20001006.html. When names contain invalid
characters, they need to be translated into valid XML names.

Many languages and applications allow Unicode characters in their names, which are
not valid in XML names. For example, if "Order Detail" were a column heading in a database, the database allows the space between the words Order and Detail. However, in
XML, the space between Order and Detail is considered an invalid XML character. Thus,
the space, the invalid character, needs to be converted into an escaped hexadecimal encoding and can be decoded later.

The EncodeName and DecodeName methods are used to translate invalid XML
names into valid XML names and vice versa.

XmlConvert provides methods that enable the conversion of a String to a CLI data
type and vice versa. Locale settings are not taken into account during data conversion.

XmlConvert also provides methods that convert between XML Schema Definition
(XSD) data types (see http://www.w3.org/TR/xmlschema-2/#built-in-datatypes) and
their corresponding common language infrastructure (CLI) data types. The following
table shows the XSD data types and their corresponding CLI data types.

XSD Data Type	CLI Data Type
hexBinary	A `System.Byte` array
base64Binary	A `System.Byte` array
Boolean	`System.Boolean`
Byte	`System.SByte`
normalizedString	`System.String`
Date	`System.DateTime`
duration	`System.TimeSpan`
dateTime	`System.DateTime`
decimal	`System.Decimal`
Double	`System.Double`
ENTITIES	A `System.String` array
ENTITY	`System.String`
Float	`System.Single`
gMonthDay	`System.DateTime`
gDay	`System.DateTime`
gYear	`System.DateTime`
gYearMonth	`System.DateTime`
ID	`System.String`
IDREF	`System.String`
IDREFS	A `System.String` array
int	`System.Int32`
integer	`System.Decimal`

A
B
C
D
E
F
G
H
I
J
K
L
M
N
O
P
Q
R
S
T
U
V
W
X
Y
Z

XSD Data Type	CLI Data Type
language	System.String
long	System.Int64
month	System.DateTime
Name	System.String
NCName	System.String
negativeInteger	System.Decimal
NMTOKEN	System.String
NMTOKENS	A System.String array
nonNegativeInteger	System.Decimal
nonPositiveInteger	System.Decimal
NOTATION	System.String
positiveInteger	System.Decimal
short	System.Int16
string	System.String
time	System.DateTime
timePeriod	System.DateTime
token	System.String
unsignedByte	System.Byte
unsignedInt	System.UInt32
unsignedLong	System.UInt64
unsignedShort	System.UInt16
anyURI	System.Uri

A
B
C
D
E
F
G
H
I
J
K
L
M
N
O
P
Q
R
S
T
U
V
W
X
Y
Z

Example

```
using System;
using System.Xml;

/// <summary>
/// Converts strings to other data types using XmlConvert methods
/// </summary>

public class XmlConvertSample
{
    public static void Main()
    {
        string s = "true";
        bool c = XmlConvert.ToBoolean(s);
        Console.WriteLine("String: '{0}', Boolean value: {1}",  s, c);

        s = "2004-10-03T14:04:34";
        string f = "yyyy-MM-ddTHH:mm:ss";
        DateTime t = XmlConvert.ToDateTime(s, f);
        Console.WriteLine();
        Console.WriteLine("String: '{0}'", s);
        Console.WriteLine("Format: '{0}'", f);
        Console.WriteLine("DateTime value: {0}", t);

        s = "57.4033";
        decimal d = XmlConvert.ToDecimal(s);
        Console.WriteLine();
        Console.WriteLine("String: '{0}', Decimal value: {1}", s, d);

        s = "39";
        int i = XmlConvert.ToInt32(s);
        Console.WriteLine();
        Console.WriteLine("String: '{0}', Int32 value: {1}", s, i);

        Console.WriteLine();
        Console.WriteLine();
        Console.WriteLine("Press Enter to continue");
        Console.ReadLine();
    }
}
```

The output is

```
String: 'true', Boolean value: True

String: '2004-10-03T14:04:34'
Format: 'yyyy-MM-ddTHH:mm:ss'
DateTime value: 10/3/2004 2:04:34 PM

String: '57.4033', Decimal value: 57.4033

String: '39', Int32 value: 39


Press Enter to continue
```

A
B
C
D
E
F
G
H
I
J
K
L
M
N
O
P
Q
R
S
T
U
V
W
X
Y
Z

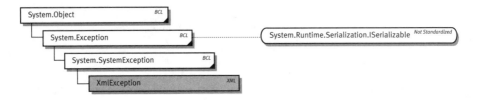

Summary

Represents the error that occurs when an XML document or fragment cannot be parsed.

Type Summary

```
      public class XmlException : SystemException
         {
         // Constructors
  MS CF 1.1 public XmlException();
      MS CF protected XmlException(SerializationInfo info,
                  StreamingContext context);
  MS CF 1.1 public XmlException(string message);
         public XmlException(string message, Exception innerException);
  MS CF 1.1 public XmlException(string message, Exception innerException,
                  int lineNumber, int linePosition);

         // Properties
            public int LineNumber { get; }
            public int LinePosition { get; }
            public override string Message { get; }

         // Methods
      MS CF public override void GetObjectData(SerializationInfo info,
                           StreamingContext context);
         }
```

■ **MF** LineNumber and LinePosition support is probably the most useful information to know when you get an error parsing XML documents. The line information is also usually included in the Message property.

■ **CL** This class is where it becomes painfully obvious that the entire System.Xml framework was designed for "runtime" processing of XML and not for XML tools. This was a deliberate design decision that we made up front. You cannot use XmlTextReader to build an XML editor, for example, because any time it runs into

CONTINUED

illegal XML it throws an exception and stops. You cannot force it to continue. The thinking was that in a mission-critical runtime environment you want predictability of guaranteed exceptions on bad input, and most customers are perfectly happy with this. But in the "tool" space you want a more forgiving XML processing model. Can one framework satisfy both needs? Well, probably not at the parser level. Higher up the stack when you're dealing with XSD validation, reporting more than one error is doable, but error recovery in an XML parser gets pretty tricky to deal with. You have to be building a pretty sophisticated tool (like an XML editor) to need error recovery, in which case the actual parsing step is probably the least of your concerns.

Example

```csharp
using System;
using System.Xml;
using System.Text;

/// <summary>
/// Reads in a badly formed Xml file and prints out detailed information on the
/// issue
/// </summary>

public class XmlExceptionSample
{
    public static void Main()
    {
        try
        {
            ReadXmlFile("sample.xml");
        }
        catch (XmlException xe)
        {
            Console.WriteLine("* XmlException: {0}", xe.Message);
            Console.WriteLine("* InnerException: {0}",
                              xe.InnerException.Message);
        }
        catch (Exception e)
        {
            Console.WriteLine("* Error: {0}", e.Message);
        }
        Console.WriteLine();
        Console.WriteLine();
        Console.WriteLine("Press Enter to continue");
        Console.ReadLine();
    }
    static void ReadXmlFile(string f)
    {
        XmlTextReader r = null;
        try
        {
            r = new XmlTextReader(f);
            Console.WriteLine("Reading file {0}...", f);
```

XmlException Class

```
            while (r.Read())
            {
                Console.WriteLine("Node: {0}", r.NodeType);
            }
        }
        catch (XmlException e)
        {
            StringBuilder sb = new StringBuilder("Error reading '");
            sb.Append(f);
            sb.Append("' at line: ");
            sb.Append(e.LineNumber);
            sb.Append(", position: ");
            sb.Append(e.LinePosition);
            XmlException xe = new XmlException(sb.ToString(), e);
            throw xe;
        }
        catch (Exception )
        {
            throw;
        }
        finally
        {
            r.Close();
        }
    }

}
```

The output is

```
Reading file sample.xml...
Node: XmlDeclaration
Node: Whitespace
Node: Element
Node: Whitespace
Node: Element
Node: Text
Node: EndElement
Node: Whitespace
Node: Element
Node: Whitespace
* XmlException: Error reading 'sample.xml' at line: 7, position: 3
* InnerException: The 'badtag' start tag on line '6' doesn't match the end tag
of 'root' in file 'file:///C:/System.Xml/XmlException/sample.xml'. Line 7, posi
tion 3.


Press Enter to continue
```

System.Xml
XmlNamespaceManager

Summary

Resolves, adds, and removes namespaces in a collection and provides scope management for these namespaces. This class is used by the `XmlReader` and `XmlTextReader` classes.

Type Summary

```
public class XmlNamespaceManager : IEnumerable
    {
    // Constructors
        public XmlNamespaceManager(XmlNameTable nameTable);

    // Properties
        public virtual string DefaultNamespace { get; }
        public XmlNameTable NameTable { get; }

    // Methods
        public virtual void AddNamespace(string prefix, string uri);
        public virtual IEnumerator GetEnumerator();
        public virtual bool HasNamespace(string prefix);
        public virtual string LookupNamespace(string prefix);
        public virtual string LookupPrefix(string uri);
        public virtual bool PopScope();
        public virtual void PushScope();
        public virtual void RemoveNamespace(string prefix, string uri);
    }
```

> ■ **CL**   You will notice that `System.Xml` exposes a lot more than MSXML in terms of classes like this, the `NameTable`, the `XmlNamespaceManager`, and so on. This is because the general philosophy was to design `System.Xml` to be as transparent as possible about how it was doing XML processing. This gives you many extensibility points, and makes the overall framework a lot more reusable.

Description

This class stores prefixes and namespaces as unique `String` objects.

 `XmlNamespaceManager` assumes all prefixes and namespaces are valid.

A
B
C
D
E
F
G
H
I
J
K
L
M
N
O
P
Q
R
S
T
U
V
W
X
Y
Z

425

XmlNamespaceManager Class

If the prefix and namespace already exist within the current scope, they will replace the existing prefix/namespace combination. The same prefix and namespace combination can exist across different scopes.

The following prefix/namespace pairs are added by default to the `XmlNamespace-Manager`. They can be determined at any scope.

Prefix	Namespace
xmlns	http://www.w3.org/2000/xmlns/ (the xmlns prefix namespace)
xml	http://www.w3.org/XML/1998/namespace (the XML namespace)
`System.String.Empty`	`System.String.Empty`. The empty namespace can be reassigned a different prefix. For example, `xmlns=""` defines the default namespace to be the empty namespace.

Example

```
using System;
using System.Xml;

/// <summary>
/// Creates a new XmlNamespaceManager based on an XmlTextReader
/// Demonstrates adding and removing namespaces, and displaying
/// namespace information
/// </summary>

public class XmlNamespaceManagerSample
{
    public static void Main()
    {
        XmlTextReader r = new XmlTextReader("sample.xml");
        XmlNamespaceManager nm = new XmlNamespaceManager(r.NameTable);
        nm.AddNamespace("", "http://www.default");
        string ns = nm.DefaultNamespace;
        Console.WriteLine("DefaultNamespace Prefix: '{0}', "
            + "Namespace: '{1}'",
            nm.LookupPrefix(ns), ns);
        nm.AddNamespace("test", "http://www.test");
        ShowNamespaces("Before:", nm);
        if (nm.HasNamespace("test"))
        {
            string tns = nm.LookupNamespace("test");
            nm.RemoveNamespace("test", tns);
        }
        ShowNamespaces("After RemoveNamespace:", nm);
        r.Close();
        Console.WriteLine();
        Console.WriteLine();
```

```
        Console.WriteLine("Press Enter to continue");
        Console.ReadLine();
    }

    private static void ShowNamespaces(string s,
        XmlNamespaceManager nm)
    {
        Console.WriteLine();
        Console.WriteLine(s);
        foreach (string p in nm)
        {
            Console.WriteLine("Prefix: '{0}', Namespace: '{1}'",
                p, nm.LookupNamespace(p));
        }
    }
}
```

The output is

```
DefaultNamespace Prefix: '', Namespace: 'http://www.default'

Before:
Prefix: 'test', Namespace: 'http://www.test'
Prefix: 'xmlns', Namespace: 'http://www.w3.org/2000/xmlns/'
Prefix: 'xml', Namespace: 'http://www.w3.org/XML/1998/namespace'
Prefix: '', Namespace: 'http://www.default'

After RemoveNamespace:
Prefix: 'xml', Namespace: 'http://www.w3.org/XML/1998/namespace'
Prefix: 'xmlns', Namespace: 'http://www.w3.org/2000/xmlns/'
Prefix: '', Namespace: 'http://www.default'


Press Enter to continue
```

A
B
C
D
E
F
G
H
I
J
K
L
M
N
O
P
Q
R
S
T
U
V
W
X
Y
Z

Summary

Creates a table that stores unique instances of `String` objects.

Type Summary

```
public abstract class XmlNameTable
    {
    // Constructors
        protected XmlNameTable();

    // Methods
        public abstract string Add(char[] array, int offset, int length);
        public abstract string Add(string array);
        public abstract string Get(char[] array, int offset, int length);
        public abstract string Get(string array);
    }
```

> **▪ CL** We made `XmlNameTable` abstract so you could plug in your own implementation, so if you have explicit knowledge about your domain you could potentially optimize even further, or you might want to implement a thread safe version if you need that.

Description

Only a single instance of any given string is stored even if the string is added multiple times to the table.

Using this class provides an efficient means for an XML parser to use the same `String` object for all repeated element and attribute names in an XML document. If the same object is used for all repeated names, the efficiency of name comparisons is increased by allowing the names to be compared using object comparisons rather than string comparisons.

[*Note:* This class is `abstract` and is implemented in the `NameTable` class.]

Example

```csharp
using System;
using System.Xml;

/// <summary>
/// Checks to see if a particular string is in the XmlNameTable
/// </summary>

public class XmlNameTableSample
{
    public static void Main()
    {
        NameTable n = new NameTable();
        n.Add("the value");
        if (n.Get("the value") == "the value")
        {
            Console.WriteLine("String 'the value' is in NameTable");
        }
        else
        {
            Console.WriteLine("String 'the value' is not in NameTable");
        }
        Console.WriteLine();
        Console.WriteLine();
        Console.WriteLine("Press Enter to continue");
        Console.ReadLine();
    }
}
```

The output is

```
String 'the value' is in NameTable


Press Enter to continue
```

A
B
C
D
E
F
G
H
I
J
K
L
M
N
O
P
Q
R
S
T
U
V
W
X
Y
Z

A
B
C
D
E
F
G
H
I
J
K
L
M
N
O
P
Q
R
S
T
U
V
W
X
Y
Z

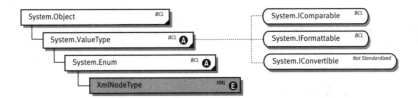

Summary

Specifies the type of node.

Type Summary

```
public enum XmlNodeType
    {
    Attribute = 2,
    CDATA = 4,
    Comment = 8,
    Document = 9,
    DocumentFragment = 11,
    DocumentType = 10,
    Element = 1,
    EndElement = 15,
    EndEntity = 16,
    Entity = 6,
    EntityReference = 5,
    None = 0,
    Notation = 12,
    ProcessingInstruction = 7,
    SignificantWhitespace = 14,
    Text = 3,
    Whitespace = 13,
    XmlDeclaration = 17,
    }
```

■ MF   The `XmlNodeType` enumeration epitomizes the very essence of XML. On the one hand XML is very simple, if all you care about are elements and attributes. On the other hand XML has numerous complex constructs like entity references and notations, which the majority of developers never encounter. XML is an easy-to-learn syntax with many arcane processing rules.

Description

A given set of XML data is modeled as a tree of nodes. This enumeration specifies the different node types.

Example

```
using System;
using System.Xml;

/// <summary>
/// Reads in an .xml file and writes out the NodeType for each node read.
/// </summary>

public class XmlNodeTypeSample
{
    public static void Main()
    {
        string s = "sample.xml";
        Console.WriteLine("Reading file '{0}'", s);
        XmlTextReader r = new XmlTextReader(s);
        while(r.Read())
        {
            Console.WriteLine("Node name: {0}, Node type: XmlNodeType.{1}",
                r.Name, r.NodeType);
        }
        r.Close();
        Console.WriteLine();
        Console.WriteLine();
        Console.WriteLine("Press Enter to continue");
        Console.ReadLine();
    }
}
```

The output is

```
Reading file 'sample.xml'
Node name: xml, Node type: XmlNodeType.XmlDeclaration
Node name: root, Node type: XmlNodeType.Element
Node name: subelement, Node type: XmlNodeType.Element
Node name: , Node type: XmlNodeType.Text
Node name: subelement, Node type: XmlNodeType.EndElement
Node name: root, Node type: XmlNodeType.EndElement


Press Enter to continue
```

A
B
C
D
E
F
G
H
I
J
K
L
M
N
O
P
Q
R
S
T
U
V
W
X
Y
Z

A
B
C
D
E
F
G
H
I
J
K
L
M
N
O
P
Q
R
S
T
U
V
W
X
Y
Z

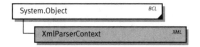

| System.Object | BCL |
| XmlParserContext | XML |

Summary

Provides all the context information required by instances of the `XmlTextReader` class to parse an XML fragment.

Type Summary

```
public class XmlParserContext
    {
    // Constructors
        public XmlParserContext(XmlNameTable nt, XmlNamespaceManager nsMgr,
                string docTypeName, string pubId, string sysId,
                string internalSubset, string baseURI, string xmlLang,
                XmlSpace xmlSpace);
        public XmlParserContext(XmlNameTable nt, XmlNamespaceManager nsMgr,
                string docTypeName, string pubId, string sysId,
                string internalSubset, string baseURI, string xmlLang,
                XmlSpace xmlSpace, Encoding enc);
        public XmlParserContext(XmlNameTable nt, XmlNamespaceManager nsMgr,
                string xmlLang, XmlSpace xmlSpace);
        public XmlParserContext(XmlNameTable nt, XmlNamespaceManager nsMgr,
                string xmlLang, XmlSpace xmlSpace, Encoding enc);

    // Properties
        public string BaseURI { get; set; }
        public string DocTypeName { get; set; }
        public Encoding Encoding { get; set; }
        public string InternalSubset { get; set; }
        public XmlNamespaceManager NamespaceManager { get; set; }
        public XmlNameTable NameTable { get; set; }
        public string PublicId { get; set; }
        public string SystemId { get; set; }
        public string XmlLang { get; set; }
        public XmlSpace XmlSpace { get; set; }
    }
```

> ▪ **MF**   This class should have been called `XmlReaderContext` rather than `XmlParserContext`, and is an example of not thinking about naming consistency enough.
>
> *CONTINUED*

> **■ CL**   This is a perfect example of making `System.Xml` as transparent as possible.
> The fact that you can cook up an `XmlParserContext` and tell the `XmlTextReader`
> to continue parsing some random fragment of XML based on the context that you
> give it is an awesome feature that I haven't seen in any other XML processing API.

Example

```csharp
using System;
using System.Xml;
using System.Text;


public class XmlParserContextSample
{
    public static void Main()
    {
        string xml = "<?xml version='1.0'?><sample><book publisher='"
            + "&pub;'>Microsoft .NET by &pub;</book></sample>";
        NameTable nt = new NameTable();
        XmlNamespaceManager nm = new XmlNamespaceManager(nt);
        string lang = "en-us";
        XmlSpace xs = XmlSpace.None;
        UTF8Encoding enc = new UTF8Encoding();
        XmlParserContext pc = new XmlParserContext(null, nm, lang,
            xs, enc);
        pc.BaseURI = "http://baseuri";
        pc.DocTypeName = "sample";
        pc.InternalSubset = "<!ENTITY pub 'Addison Wesley'>";
        pc.PublicId = "-//ADWES//Test Language 1.0//EN";
        ShowProperties(pc);
        ReadXml(xml, pc);
        Console.WriteLine();
        Console.WriteLine();
        Console.WriteLine("Press Enter to continue");
        Console.ReadLine();
    }

    private static void ShowProperties(XmlParserContext pc)
    {
        Console.WriteLine("BaseURI: '{0}'", pc.BaseURI);
        Console.WriteLine("DocTypeName: '{0}'", pc.DocTypeName);
        Console.WriteLine("Encoding.EncodingName: '{0}'",
            pc.Encoding.EncodingName);
        Console.WriteLine("InternalSubset: {0}", pc.InternalSubset);
        Console.WriteLine("PublicId: '{0}'", pc.PublicId);
        Console.WriteLine("SystemId: '{0}'", pc.SystemId);
        Console.WriteLine("XmlLang: '{0}'", pc.XmlLang);
        Console.WriteLine("XmlSpace: {0}", pc.XmlSpace);
        Console.WriteLine();
    }

    private static void ReadXml(string xml, XmlParserContext pc)
```

```
        {
            XmlTextReader r = new XmlTextReader(xml,
                XmlNodeType.Element, pc);
            Console.WriteLine();
            Console.WriteLine("Parsing XML document...");
            while (r.Read())
            {
                Console.Write("NodeType: {0} ({1})", r.NodeType, r.Name);
                if (r.HasValue)
                {
                    Console.Write(" Value: '{0}'", r.Value);
                }
                Console.WriteLine();
                if (r.HasAttributes)
                {
                    while (r.MoveToNextAttribute())
                    {
                        Console.WriteLine("- Attribute '{0}', Value: '{1}'",
                            r.Name, r.Value);
                    }
                }
            }
            r.Close();
        }

    }
```

The output is

```
BaseURI: 'http://baseuri'
DocTypeName: 'sample'
Encoding.EncodingName: 'Unicode (UTF-8)'
InternalSubset: <!ENTITY pub 'Addison Wesley'>
PublicId: '-//ADWES//Test Language 1.0//EN'
SystemId: ''
XmlLang: 'en-us'
XmlSpace: None


Parsing XML document...
NodeType: XmlDeclaration (xml) Value: 'version='1.0''
- Attribute 'version', Value: '1.0'
NodeType: Element (sample)
NodeType: Element (book)
- Attribute 'publisher', Value: '&pub;'
NodeType: Text () Value: 'Microsoft .NET by '
NodeType: EntityReference (pub)
NodeType: EndElement (book)
NodeType: EndElement (sample)


Press Enter to continue
```

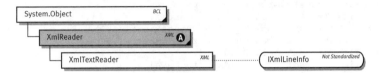

Summary

Represents a reader that provides non-cached, forward-only access to XML data.

Type Summary

```
public abstract class XmlReader
    {
    // Constructors
    protected XmlReader();

    // Properties
    public abstract int AttributeCount { get; }
    public abstract string BaseURI { get; }
    public virtual bool CanResolveEntity { get; }
    public abstract int Depth { get; }
    public abstract bool EOF { get; }
    public virtual bool HasAttributes { get; }
    public abstract bool HasValue { get; }
    public abstract bool IsDefault { get; }
    public abstract bool IsEmptyElement { get; }
    public abstract string LocalName { get; }
    public abstract string Name { get; }
    public abstract string NamespaceURI { get; }
    public abstract XmlNameTable NameTable { get; }
    public abstract XmlNodeType NodeType { get; }
    public abstract string Prefix { get; }
    public abstract char QuoteChar { get; }
    public abstract ReadState ReadState { get; }
    public abstract string Value { get; }
    public abstract string XmlLang { get; }
    public abstract XmlSpace XmlSpace { get; }
    public abstract string this[int i] { get; }
    public abstract string this[string name] { get; }
    public abstract string this[string name, string namespaceURI] { get; }

    // Methods
    public abstract void Close();
    public abstract string GetAttribute(int i);
    public abstract string GetAttribute(string name);
    public abstract string GetAttribute(string name, string namespaceURI);
    public static bool IsName(string str);
    public static bool IsNameToken(string str);
    public virtual bool IsStartElement();
    public virtual bool IsStartElement(string name);
    public virtual bool IsStartElement(string localname, string ns);
```

XmlReader Class

```
    public abstract string LookupNamespace(string prefix);
    public abstract void MoveToAttribute(int i);
    public abstract bool MoveToAttribute(string name);
    public abstract bool MoveToAttribute(string name, string ns);
    public virtual XmlNodeType MoveToContent();
    public abstract bool MoveToElement();
    public abstract bool MoveToFirstAttribute();
    public abstract bool MoveToNextAttribute();
    public abstract bool Read();
    public abstract bool ReadAttributeValue();
    public virtual string ReadElementString();
    public virtual string ReadElementString(string name);
    public virtual string ReadElementString(string localname, string ns);
    public virtual void ReadEndElement();
    public virtual string ReadInnerXml();
    public virtual string ReadOuterXml();
    public virtual void ReadStartElement();
    public virtual void ReadStartElement(string name);
    public virtual void ReadStartElement(string localname, string ns);
    public virtual string ReadString();
    public abstract void ResolveEntity();
    public virtual void Skip();
}
```

■ **MF**   The XmlReader was a significant innovation in XML parsing due to its pull model approach and caused a significant amount of acclaim in the industry. Until then developers had to endure the SAX push model, which although great for XML parser implementers (just push out an event when something happens), was painful for developers to use. The XmlReader reversed this position allowing you to do simple, procedural code where you could get the XmlReader to do the heavy lifting for you, like skipping elements that you did not care about or throwing away white space from the document. The XmlReader was inspired by seeing the use of other readers in the .NET Framework such as the StringReader class and applying the same principles to XML.

■ **MF**   There are aspects of the XmlReader design where we had to choose between usability and performance. For example, due to the attribute indexer methods all the attributes for an element have to be cached, which does not allow for a complete streaming API. On the whole the majority of XML documents have small numbers of attributes so improved usability was the best design.

■ **CL**   In addition to the reason Mark just noted, you have to cache all the attributes anyway in order to know the namespace of the element. SAX had the exact same problem—only worse. In SAX, an Array object is created with all of the attributes that is then passed to your handler. At least here we avoid that array creation.

CONTINUED

■ **JM**   The Read and Skip methods are, of course, different beasts. But they are more similar than you might think. If the reader is on any node besides a non-empty element node, Read and Skip behave the same. Otherwise, Skip positions the reader following the corresponding EndElement node, not exposing any properties along the way (while Read will expose the properties).

■ **CL**   In general the XmlReader makes recursive descent parsing of a given XML document a snap. In fact, it is so easy that the XmlSerializer generates IL code for you that calls the XmlReader to parse the XML while it builds your own custom objects from what it finds in the stream. Hence, XmlSerialization is probably the #1 customer of the XmlReader class in terms of overall volume of XML parsed.

Notice that XmlReader is abstract. If you want to just parse XML text, you need the concrete subclass XmlTextReader discussed later. Why did we bother with an abstract base class? Because we envisioned the creation of lots of different kinds of XML readers that took their data from other sources besides text. It also means you can plug in additional behavior into the XML processing pipeline. Suppose someone consumes an XML reader. Well, you can wrap the XmlTextReader with an XmlValidatingReader and pass that instead, and now you are causing your consumer to validate while they parse without them even knowing it.

■ **HK**   Although the XmlReader was designed as an abstract class, it has a few properties that are bound to the text representation of XML, such as QuoteChar or IsEmptyElement. As was pointed out quite a few times by our users, it is annoying that the XmlReader reports empty and non-empty elements differently. For non-empty element <a>...</a> the reader returns Element and EndElement events, but for empty element <a/> it only returns a single Element event. The user has to check the IsEmptyElement property to see whether he should expect a closing EndElement or not. In many cases this causes two similar code paths in the handling code, one for empty elements and one for non-empty ones.

Description

This class provides forward-only, read-only access to a stream of XML data. This class enforces the rules of well-formed XML but does not perform data validation.

This class conforms to the W3C Extensible Markup Language (XML) 1.0 and the Namespaces in XML recommendations.

A given set of XML data is modeled as a tree of nodes. The different types of nodes are specified in the XmlNodeType enumeration. The reader is advanced to the next node using the Read method. The current node refers to the node on which the reader is positioned. The following table lists the node properties exposed for the current node.

Property	Description
AttributeCount	The number of attributes on the node.
BaseUri	The base URI of the node.
Depth	The depth of the node in the tree.
HasAttributes	Whether the node has attributes.
HasValue	Whether the node can have a text value.
IsDefault	Whether an `Attribute` node was generated from the default value defined in the DTD or schema.
IsEmptyElement	Whether an `Element` node is empty.
LocalName	The local name of the node.
Name	The qualified name of the node, equal to `Prefix:LocalName`.
NamespaceUri	The URI defining the namespace associated with the node.
NodeType	The `System.Xml.XmlNodeType` of the node.
Prefix	A shorthand reference to the namespace associated with the node.
QuoteChar	The quotation mark character used to enclose the value of an attribute.
Value	The text value of the node.
XmlLang	The `xml:lang` scope within which the node resides.

This class does not expand default attributes or general entities. Any general entities encountered are returned as a single empty `EntityReference` node.

This class checks that a Document Type Definition (DTD) is well-formed, but does not validate using the DTD.

To read strongly typed data, use the `XmlConvert` class.

This class throws an `XmlException` on XML parse errors. After an exception is thrown, the state of the reader is not predictable. For example, the reported node type may be different than the actual node type of the current node.

[*Note:* This class is `abstract` and implemented in the `XmlTextReader` class.]

Example

```
using System;
using System.Xml;


public class XmlReaderSample
{
    public static void Main()
    {
        XmlTextReader r = new XmlTextReader("sample.xml");
        while (r.Read())
        {
            if (r.NodeType == XmlNodeType.XmlDeclaration
                || r.NodeType == XmlNodeType.Element)
            {
                Console.WriteLine("NodeType {0} ('{1}') is at Depth: '{2}'",
                    r.NodeType, r.Name, r.Depth);
                if (r.HasValue)
                {
                    Console.Write(" Value: '{0}'", r.Value);
                }


                Console.WriteLine("Element <{0}> has {1} attribute(s)",
                    r.Name, r.AttributeCount);
                if (r.AttributeCount > 0)
                {
                    string fn = String.Empty;
                    string ln = String.Empty;
                    string ns = String.Empty;
                    while (r.MoveToNextAttribute())
                    {
                        fn = r.Name;
                        ln = r.LocalName;
                        ns = r.NamespaceURI;
                        Console.WriteLine("- Attribute: '{0}', "
                            + "LocalName: '{1}', Value: '{2}'",
                            fn, ln, r.GetAttribute(ln, ns));
                    }

                }
            }
        }
        r.Close();
        Console.WriteLine();
        Console.WriteLine();
        Console.WriteLine("Press Enter to continue");
        Console.ReadLine();

    }
}
```

The output is

```
NodeType XmlDeclaration ('xml') is at Depth: '0'
 Value: 'version="1.0"'Element <xml> has 1 attribute(s)
- Attribute: 'version', LocalName: 'version', Value: '1.0'
NodeType Element ('root') is at Depth: '0'
Element <root> has 1 attribute(s)
- Attribute: 'xmlns:test', LocalName: 'test', Value: 'http://mysite/prefixes'
NodeType Element ('test:subelement') is at Depth: '1'
Element <test:subelement> has 2 attribute(s)
- Attribute: 'test:first', LocalName: 'first', Value: 'one'
- Attribute: 'test:second', LocalName: 'second', Value: 'two'


Press Enter to continue
```

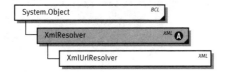

Summary

Resolves external XML resources named by a URI.

Type Summary

```
public abstract class XmlResolver
    {
    // Constructors
       protected XmlResolver();

    // Properties
       public abstract ICredentials Credentials { set; }

    // Methods
       public abstract object GetEntity(Uri absoluteUri, string role,
                            Type ofObjectToReturn);
       public virtual Uri ResolveUri(Uri baseUri, string relativeUri);
    }
```

▪ **JM**   You will notice that some methods within this class (e.g., `GetEntity`) take `Uri` parameters. `Uri` is part of the Networking library (see Partition IV of the ECMA specification for more details on the term "library"). Initially this was a problem because the XML library was not required to have the Networking library implemented for it to be implemented (e.g., a kernel profile implementation could have chosen to implement XML functionality without networking). Due in large part to this type, the ECMA CLI committee decided to mandate a networking library dependency on the XML library.

▪ **CL**   The `XmlResolver` is another example of transparency in the `System.Xml` framework. You can plug in at any level and customize the XML processing behavior. All kinds of `XmlResolvers` have been written to do different custom things. For example, if you are in ASP.NET, a simple URL resolution will not work; instead, you have to call `Server.MapPath`, so no problem, plug in a little `AspXmlResolver` and

CONTINUED

441

> you are back in business. Another classic application of this nifty little class is caching. Suppose you know that your application always downloads a DTD or schema from the same place off the Web, and you don't want to pay that price every time you want to validate your XML? No problem, plug in a `CachingXmlResolver` that saves the files to disk, then override `ResolveUri` to map the URI from http to the local file if you have it.

Description

This class is used to resolve external XML resources such as entities, document type definitions (DTDs), or schemas. It is also used to process include and import elements found in Extensible StyleSheet Language (XSL) stylesheets or XML Schema Definition language (XSD) schemas.

This class is `abstract` and implemented in the `XmlUrlResolver` class.

Example

```
using System;
using System.Xml;
using System.Net;

/// <summary>
/// Show how XmlResolver behaves differently in relative and nonrelative cases.
/// </summary>

public class XmlResolverSample
{
    public static void Main()
    {
        XmlResolver res = new XmlUrlResolver();
        Uri ubase = new Uri("http://mysite.com/myxmldoc.xml");
        string s1 = "sample.xsd";
        string s2 = "http://othersite.com/sample.xsd";
        Console.WriteLine(res.ResolveUri(ubase, s1));
        Console.WriteLine(res.ResolveUri(ubase, s2));
        Console.WriteLine();
        Console.WriteLine();
        Console.WriteLine("Press Enter to continue");
        Console.ReadLine();
    }
}
```

The output is

```
http://mysite.com/sample.xsd
http://othersite.com/sample.xsd


Press Enter to continue
```

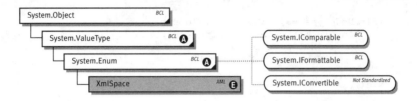

Summary

Specifies the white space attribute, xml:space, which indicates whether white space should be preserved in an element.

Type Summary

```
public enum XmlSpace
    {
    Default = 1,
    None = 0,
    Preserve = 2,
    }
```

Description

[*Note:* This enumeration is used by instances of the XmlParserContext, Xml-TextReader, and XmlTextWriter classes.]

Example

```
using System;
using System.Xml;

/// <summary>
/// Reads in xml documents and outputs the XmlSpace value for each.
/// </summary>

public class XmlSpaceSample
{
    public static void Main()
    {
        ReadXmlDocument("default.xml");
        ReadXmlDocument("none.xml");
        ReadXmlDocument("preserve.xml");
        Console.WriteLine();
        Console.WriteLine();
        Console.WriteLine("Press Enter to continue");
        Console.ReadLine();
    }
```

A
B
C
D
E
F
G
H
I
J
K
L
M
N
O
P
Q
R
S
T
U
V
W
X
Y
Z

```
static void ReadXmlDocument(string s)
{
    XmlTextReader r = new XmlTextReader(s);
    while(r.Read())
    {
        if(r.NodeType == XmlNodeType.Element)
            Console.WriteLine("Element <{0}> in '{1}',"
                + "XmlSpace is {2}",
                r.Name, s, r.XmlSpace);
    }
    r.Close();
}

}
```

The output is

```
Element <root> in 'default.xml',XmlSpace is Default
Element <subelement> in 'default.xml',XmlSpace is Default
Element <root> in 'none.xml',XmlSpace is None
Element <subelement> in 'none.xml',XmlSpace is None
Element <root> in 'preserve.xml',XmlSpace is Preserve
Element <subelement> in 'preserve.xml',XmlSpace is Preserve


Press Enter to continue
```

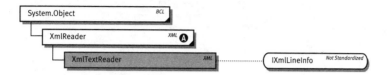

Summary

Represents a reader that provides fast, non-cached, forward-only access to XML data.

Type Summary

```
public class XmlTextReader: XmlReader, IXmlLineInfo
{
    // Constructors
    protected XmlTextReader();
    public XmlTextReader(Stream input);
    public XmlTextReader(Stream input, XmlNameTable nt);
    public XmlTextReader(Stream xmlFragment, XmlNodeType fragType,
            XmlParserContext context);
    public XmlTextReader(string url);
    public XmlTextReader(string url, Stream input);
    public XmlTextReader(string url, Stream input, XmlNameTable nt);
    public XmlTextReader(string url, TextReader input);
    public XmlTextReader(string url, TextReader input, XmlNameTable nt);
    public XmlTextReader(string url, XmlNameTable nt);
    public XmlTextReader(string xmlFragment, XmlNodeType fragType,
            XmlParserContext context);
    public XmlTextReader(TextReader input);
    public XmlTextReader(TextReader input, XmlNameTable nt);
    protected XmlTextReader(XmlNameTable nt);

    // Properties
    public override int AttributeCount { get; }
    public override string BaseURI { get; }
    public override int Depth { get; }
    public Encoding Encoding { get; }
    public override bool EOF { get; }
    public override bool HasValue { get; }
    public override bool IsDefault { get; }
    public override bool IsEmptyElement { get; }
    public override string this[int i] { get; }
    public override string this[string name] { get; }
    public override string this[string name, string namespaceURI] { get; }
    public int LineNumber { get; }
    public int LinePosition { get; }
    public override string LocalName { get; }
    public override string Name { get; }
    public bool Namespaces { get; set; }
    public override string NamespaceURI { get; }
    public override XmlNameTable NameTable { get; }
    public override XmlNodeType NodeType { get; }
```

A
B
C
D
E
F
G
H
I
J
K
L
M
N
O
P
Q
R
S
T
U
V
W
X
Y
Z

445

```
          public bool Normalization { get; set; }
          public override string Prefix { get; }
          public override char QuoteChar { get; }
          public override ReadState ReadState { get; }
          public override string Value { get; }
          public WhitespaceHandling WhitespaceHandling { get; set; }
          public override string XmlLang { get; }
          public XmlResolver XmlResolver { set; }
          public override XmlSpace XmlSpace { get; }

       // Methods
          public override void Close();
          public override string GetAttribute(int i);
          public override string GetAttribute(string name);
          public override string GetAttribute(string localName,
                             string namespaceURI);
          public TextReader GetRemainder();
          public override string LookupNamespace(string prefix);
          public override void MoveToAttribute(int i);
          public override bool MoveToAttribute(string name);
          public override bool MoveToAttribute(string localName,
                             string namespaceURI);
          public override bool MoveToElement();
          public override bool MoveToFirstAttribute();
          public override bool MoveToNextAttribute();
          public override bool Read();
          public override bool ReadAttributeValue();
          public int ReadBase64(byte[] array, int offset, int len);
          public int ReadBinHex(byte[] array, int offset, int len);
          public int ReadChars(char[] buffer, int index, int count);
          public override string ReadInnerXml();
          public override string ReadOuterXml();
          public override string ReadString();
          public void ResetState();
          public override void ResolveEntity();

       // Explicit Interface Members
          bool IXmlLineInfo.HasLineInfo();
       }
```

▪ MF The XmlTextReader class is the one everyone should reach for to read an XML document, especially when performance is a critical issue.

▪ CL Well, this class is the be all and end all of XML text parsing. You should never need to write another XML parser—this guy can do it all. Unless, that is, you're building an XML editor and you need to parse non–well-formed XML. This class is designed for efficient runtime parsing of XML in mission-critical environments where you only care about well-formed XML.

CONTINUED

■ **HK**   Unfortunately, XmlTextReader is not a fully conformant XML parser. It does not expand entity references or include default attributes. To get this functionality the user needs to create XmlValidatingReader over XmlTextReader and explicitly turn off its validation. This layering created various problems since entity resolution is designed to happen on a low-level parsing layer. One example is when an entity reference is surrounded by white space; for example, `<a> &ent; </a>`. When the XmlTextReader is set up to ignore white space nodes, the XmlValidatingReader will never see the spaces before and after &ent; and therefore cannot merge them with the expanded entity value. The correct value of the text node between `<a>` and `</a>` should include the spaces.

■ **HK**   XmlTextReader also does not normalize new lines and attribute values according to the XML spec by default. The user needs to turn it on explicitly with the Normalization property. In my opinion this was a big mistake as it deviates from the XML spec and many users became dependent on this. It is also a problem for XML digital signatures, as it needs to work on normalized XML. Since XML digital signatures can accept any XmlReader, it does not know whether the input is already normalized and hence has to re-normalize it. Unfortunately, in some cases the result of this is not the same as if the normalization was done by the XmlReader itself during parsing.

Turning off this normalization was supposed to improve the XmlTextReader performance, but in the v2.0 release of the .NET Framework we discovered other ways that the XmlTextReader can be optimized without compromising on conformance to the XML spec.

Description

This class provides forward-only, read-only access to a character stream of XML data. This class enforces the rules of well-formed XML but does not perform data validation.

This class implements the XmlReader class and conforms to the W3C Extensible Markup Language (XML) 1.0 and the Namespaces in XML recommendations.

A given set of XML data is modeled as a tree of nodes. The different types of nodes are specified in the XmlNodeType enumeration. The current node refers to the node on which the reader is positioned. The reader is advanced using any of the "read" or "moveto" methods. The following table lists the node properties exposed for the current node.

XmlTextReader Class

Property	Description
AttributeCount	The number of attributes on the node.
BaseUri	The base URI of the node.
Depth	The depth of the node in the tree.
HasAttributes	Whether the node has attributes (inherited from System.Xml.XmlReader).
HasValue	Whether the node can have a text value.
IsDefault	Whether an Attribute node was generated from the default value defined in the DTD or schema.
IsEmptyElement	Whether an Element node is empty.
LocalName	The local name of the node.
Name	The qualified name of the node, equal to Prefix:LocalName.
NamespaceUri	The URI defining the namespace associated with the node.
NodeType	The System.Xml.XmlNodeType of the node.
Prefix	A shorthand reference to the namespace associated with the node.
QuoteChar	The quotation mark character used to enclose the value of an attribute.
Value	The text value of the node.
XmlLang	The xml:lang scope within which the node resides.

This class does not expand default attributes or resolve general entities. Any general entities encountered are returned as a single empty EntityReference node.

This class checks that a Document Type Definition (DTD) is well-formed, but does not validate using the DTD.

To read strongly typed data, use the XmlConvert class.

This class throws an XmlException on XML parse errors. After an exception is thrown, the state of the reader is not predictable. For example, the reported node type may be different than the actual node type of the current node.

Example

```
using System;
using System.Xml;

/// <summary>
/// Reads in an xml file and writes out some information
/// about its contents
/// </summary>

public class XmlTextReaderSample
{
    public static void Main()
    {
        XmlTextReader r = new XmlTextReader("sample.xml");
        r.WhitespaceHandling = WhitespaceHandling.None;
        Console.WriteLine("ReadState is {0}", r.ReadState);
        while (r.Read())
        {
            Console.WriteLine("NodeType {0} ('{1}'), "
                + "IsStartElement: {2}",
                r.NodeType, r.Name,
                r.IsStartElement());
            if (r.NodeType == XmlNodeType.XmlDeclaration
                || r.NodeType == XmlNodeType.Element)
            {
                Console.WriteLine("Element <{0}> has {1} attribute(s)",
                    r.Name, r.AttributeCount);
            }
            Console.WriteLine("ReadState is {0}", r.ReadState);
            Console.WriteLine("Line Number {0}, Position {1}",
                r.LineNumber, r.LinePosition);
        }
        r.Close();
        Console.WriteLine();
        Console.WriteLine();
        Console.WriteLine("Press Enter to continue");
        Console.ReadLine();
    }
}
```

The output is

```
ReadState is Initial
NodeType XmlDeclaration ('xml'), IsStartElement: True
Element <root> has 0 attribute(s)
ReadState is Interactive
Line Number 2, Position 2
NodeType Element ('subelement'), IsStartElement: True
Element <subelement> has 2 attribute(s)
ReadState is Interactive
Line Number 3, Position 4
NodeType Text (''), IsStartElement: False
ReadState is Interactive
Line Number 3, Position 40
NodeType EndElement ('subelement'), IsStartElement: False
```

A
B
C
D
E
F
G
H
I
J
K
L
M
N
O
P
Q
R
S
T
U
V
W
X
Y
Z

XmlTextReader Class

```
ReadState is Interactive
Line Number 5, Position 5
NodeType EndElement ('root'), IsStartElement: False
ReadState is Interactive
Line Number 6, Position 3


Press Enter to continue
```

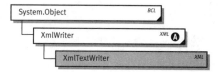

Summary

Represents a writer that provides a fast, non-cached, forward-only way of generating streams or files containing XML data that conforms to the W3C Extensible Markup Language (XML) 1.0 and the Namespaces in XML recommendations.

Type Summary

```csharp
public class XmlTextWriter : XmlWriter
{
    // Constructors
        public XmlTextWriter(Stream w, Encoding encoding);
        public XmlTextWriter(string filename, Encoding encoding);
        public XmlTextWriter(TextWriter w);

    // Properties
        public Stream BaseStream { get; }
        public Formatting Formatting { get; set; }
        public int Indentation { get; set; }
        public char IndentChar { get; set; }
        public bool Namespaces { get; set; }
        public char QuoteChar { get; set; }
        public override WriteState WriteState { get; }
        public override string XmlLang { get; }
        public override XmlSpace XmlSpace { get; }

    // Methods
        public override void Close();
        public override void Flush();
        public override string LookupPrefix(string ns);
        public override void WriteBase64(byte[] buffer, int index, int count);
        public override void WriteBinHex(byte[] buffer, int index, int count);
        public override void WriteCData(string text);
        public override void WriteCharEntity(char ch);
        public override void WriteChars(char[] buffer, int index, int count);
        public override void WriteComment(string text);
        public override void WriteDocType(string name, string pubid,
                          string sysid, string subset);
        public override void WriteEndAttribute();
        public override void WriteEndDocument();
        public override void WriteEndElement();
        public override void WriteEntityRef(string name);
        public override void WriteFullEndElement();
        public override void WriteName(string name);
        public override void WriteNmToken(string name);
```

XmlTextWriter Class

```
            public override void WriteProcessingInstruction(string name,
                                string text);
            public override void WriteQualifiedName(string localName, string ns);
            public override void WriteRaw(char[] buffer, int index, int count);
            public override void WriteRaw(string data);
            public override void WriteStartAttribute(string prefix,
                                string localName, string ns);
            public override void WriteStartDocument();
            public override void WriteStartDocument(bool standalone);
            public override void WriteStartElement(string prefix, string localName,
                                string ns);
            public override void WriteString(string text);
            public override void WriteSurrogateCharEntity(char lowChar,
                                char highChar);
            public override void WriteWhitespace(string ws);
        }
```

■ **MF**   A mistake that we made on the `XmlTextWriter` was to not make it a fully conformant XML 1.0 writer. That is, you can use it to write invalid XML which the `XmlTextReader` then cannot parse. This was partly because there is no standard for writing XML, unlike reading XML, and partly because that we felt that some aspects of writing, such as element name checking, provided a significant performance overhead, which later turned out to be false or at least not as significant as we thought. This is a classic case of sticking to your primary design requirements and not letting performance or implementation dictate functionality or API design. In the v2.0 release of the .NET Framework the `XmlReader` and `XmlWriter` have static `Create` methods to create `XmlReaders` and `XmlWriters` that are fully conformant to the XML 1.0 standard and twice as fast, which just goes to show that you can have your performance cake and eat it too!

■ **CL**   The thinking was that when you are in control of the elements you are writing, you can usually guarantee some other way that your output will be correct (by doing a code review, for example). So, why pay for expensive name validation when you can already prove the names will be correct? On the `XmlReader` side, however, you are probably consuming XML from some random third party, so it makes sense to be a bit more paranoid in that case.

Even though the performance of the `XmlWriter` has improved such that this issue is now irrelevant, I still wonder if I can turn off validation of names and then make it three times faster. I guess I hate to see resources wasted if a good API design can avoid

CONTINUED

A B C D E F G H I J K L M N O P Q R S T U V W X Y Z

it. But I do agree that we definitely should have made the default behavior do more XML 1.0 compliance checking, and only if you deliberately turn off that behavior do you see the performance benefits.

■ **HK**   As with XmlReader, even though we have an abstract XmlWriter class, it is still very much bound to the text representation of XML. For example, it is hard to write an XmlWriter that builds an XmlDocument when the XmlWriter needs to support lexical methods such as WriteCharEntity, WriteSurrogateCharEntity, or WriteRaw, since XmlDocument does not have a way to represent character entities or "unparsed blobs."

Description

This class maintains a namespace stack corresponding to all the namespaces defined in the current element stack. Namespaces can be declared manually to override the current namespace declaration. Prefixes can be specified to associate with a namespace. If there are multiple namespace declarations mapping different prefixes to the same namespace URI, this class walks the stack of namespace declarations backwards and picks the closest one.

If namespace conflicts occur inside an element, this class resolves the conflict by generating alternate prefixes. The generated prefixes are named ni, where n is the literal character 'n' and i is a number beginning at one. The number is reset to one for each element. See the example section for a demonstration of this behavior.

Attributes which are associated with a namespace URI must have a prefix (default namespaces do not apply to attributes). This conforms to section 5.2 of the W3C Namespaces in XML recommendation. If an attribute references a namespace URI, but does not specify a prefix, the writer generates a prefix for the attribute.

When writing an empty element, an additional space is added between tag name and the closing tag, for example <item />. This provides compatibility with older browsers.

When a String is used as method parameter, null and String.Empty are equivalent. String.Empty follows the W3C rules.

This class implements the XmlWriter class.

Example

Example 1
The following example demonstrates how this class resolves namespace conflicts inside an element. In the example, the writer writes an element that contains two attributes. The element and both attributes have the same prefix but different namespaces. The resulting XML fragment is written to the console.

A
B
C
D
E
F
G
H
I
J
K
L
M
N
O
P
Q
R
S
T
U
V
W
X
Y
Z

```
using System;
using System.Xml;

public class WriteFragment
{
    public static void Main()
    {
        XmlTextWriter xWriter = new XmlTextWriter(Console.Out);
        xWriter.WriteStartElement("prefix", "Element1", "namespace");
        xWriter.WriteStartAttribute("prefix", "Attr1", "namespace1");
        xWriter.WriteString("value1");
        xWriter.WriteStartAttribute("prefix", "Attr2", "namespace2");
        xWriter.WriteString("value2");
        xWriter.Close();
    }
}
```

The output is

```
<prefix:Element1 d1p1:Attr1="value1" d1p2:Attr2="value2" xmlns:d1p2="namespace2"
xmlns:d1p1="namespace1" xmlns:prefix="namespace" />
```

Example 2

```
using System;
using System.Xml;
using System.Text;
using System.IO;

/// <summary>
/// Creates a new xml document called output.xml and writes to it
/// </summary>

public class XmlTextWriterSample
{
    public static void Main()
    {
        string s = "output.xml";
        Encoding e = new UTF8Encoding();
        XmlTextWriter w = new XmlTextWriter(s, e);
        w.Formatting = Formatting.Indented;
        w.IndentChar = ' ';
        w.Indentation = 2;
        w.QuoteChar = '\'';
        w.WriteStartDocument();
        w.WriteComment("This is a test document");
        w.WriteStartElement("root");
        w.Flush();
        w.WriteStartAttribute("sample", "");
        w.WriteString("value");
        w.WriteEndAttribute();
        w.WriteElementString("subelement", "sample");
        w.WriteEndElement();
        w.WriteEndDocument();
        w.Close();
        DisplayDocument(s);
```

```
            Console.WriteLine();
            Console.WriteLine();
            Console.WriteLine("Press Enter to continue");
            Console.ReadLine();
        }

        private static void DisplayDocument(string s)
    {
        Console.WriteLine("Created document {0}:", s);
        StreamReader sr = new StreamReader(s);
        Console.WriteLine(sr.ReadToEnd());
        sr.Close();
    }

}
```

The output is

```
Created document output.xml:
<?xml version='1.0' encoding='utf-8'?>
<!--This is a test document-->
<root sample='value'>
  <subelement>sample</subelement>
</root>


Press Enter to continue
```

A
B
C
D
E
F
G
H
I
J
K
L
M
N
O
P
Q
R
S
T
U
V
W
X
Y
Z

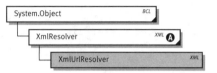

Summary

Resolves external XML resources named by a URI.

Type Summary

```
public class XmlUrlResolver : XmlResolver
    {
    // Constructors
        public XmlUrlResolver();

    // Properties
        public override ICredentials Credentials { set; }

    // Methods
        public override object GetEntity(Uri absoluteUri, string role,
                            Type ofObjectToReturn);
        public override Uri ResolveUri(Uri baseUri, string relativeUri);
    }
```

> **MF** This type is an XML abstraction over the `WebRequest` and file handling classes and enables you to resolve the location of the XML document and any references that it contains, such as DTDs. The `GetEntity` method is where the work is done by returning a stream from the resolved URI. The role parameter was included since this was expected to be used in the W3C Xlink standard, but to this date remains unused.

Description

This class is used to resolve external XML resources such as entities, document type definitions (DTDs), or schemas. It is also used to process include and import elements found in Extensible StyleSheet Language (XSL) stylesheets or XML Schema Definition language (XSD) schemas.

This class implements the `XmlResolver` class.

Example

```
using System;
using System.Xml;
using System.Net;

/// <summary>
/// Show how XmlUrlResolver behaves differently in relative and nonrelative cases.
/// </summary>

public class XmlUrlResolverSample
{
    public static void Main()
    {
        XmlUrlResolver res = new XmlUrlResolver();
        Uri ubase = new Uri("http://mysite.com/myxmldoc.xml");
        string s1 = "sample.xsd";
        string s2 = "http://othersite.com/sample.xsd";
        Console.WriteLine(res.ResolveUri(ubase, s1).ToString());
        Console.WriteLine(res.ResolveUri(ubase, s2).ToString());
        Console.WriteLine();
        Console.WriteLine();
        Console.WriteLine("Press Enter to continue");
        Console.ReadLine();
    }
}
```

The output is

```
http://mysite.com/sample.xsd
http://othersite.com/sample.xsd


Press Enter to continue
```

A
B
C
D
E
F
G
H
I
J
K
L
M
N
O
P
Q
R
S
T
U
V
W
X
Y
Z

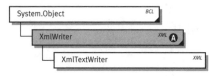

Summary

Represents a writer that provides a non-cached, forward-only means of generating streams or files containing XML data.

Type Summary

```
public abstract class XmlWriter
{
    // Constructors
    protected XmlWriter();

    // Properties
    public abstract WriteState WriteState { get; }
    public abstract string XmlLang { get; }
    public abstract XmlSpace XmlSpace { get; }

    // Methods
    public abstract void Close();
    public abstract void Flush();
    public abstract string LookupPrefix(string ns);
    public virtual void WriteAttributes(XmlReader reader, bool defattr);
    public void WriteAttributeString(string localName, string value);
    public void WriteAttributeString(string localName, string ns,
            string value);
    public void WriteAttributeString(string prefix, string localName,
            string ns, string value);
    public abstract void WriteBase64(byte[] buffer, int index, int count);
    public abstract void WriteBinHex(byte[] buffer, int index, int count);
    public abstract void WriteCData(string text);
    public abstract void WriteCharEntity(char ch);
    public abstract void WriteChars(char[] buffer, int index, int count);
    public abstract void WriteComment(string text);
    public abstract void WriteDocType(string name, string pubid,
            string sysid, string subset);
    public void WriteElementString(string localName, string value);
    public void WriteElementString(string localName, string ns,
            string value);
    public abstract void WriteEndAttribute();
    public abstract void WriteEndDocument();
    public abstract void WriteEndElement();
    public abstract void WriteEntityRef(string name);
    public abstract void WriteFullEndElement();
    public abstract void WriteName(string name);
    public abstract void WriteNmToken(string name);
```

```
    public virtual void WriteNode(XmlReader reader, bool defattr);
    public abstract void WriteProcessingInstruction(string name,
                      string text);
    public abstract void WriteQualifiedName(string localName, string ns);
    public abstract void WriteRaw(char[] buffer, int index, int count);
    public abstract void WriteRaw(string data);
    public void WriteStartAttribute(string localName, string ns);
    public abstract void WriteStartAttribute(string prefix,
                      string localName, string ns);
    public abstract void WriteStartDocument();
    public abstract void WriteStartDocument(bool standalone);
    public void WriteStartElement(string localName);
    public void WriteStartElement(string localName, string ns);
    public abstract void WriteStartElement(string prefix, string localName,
                      string ns);
    public abstract void WriteString(string text);
    public abstract void WriteSurrogateCharEntity(char lowChar,
                      char highChar);
    public abstract void WriteWhitespace(string ws);
}
```

■ **MF**   In the same way that the XmlReader made it very easy to parse XML documents, the XmlWriter made it very easy to generate them. The approach was simple. Rather than the XML DOM-based API that has a bottom-up approach of creating node trees and attaching them to a parent node, the XmlWriter provided a streaming push API that enabled you to just think about the top-down structure of your XML document. Another usability win for developers.

■ **MF**   Where are the methods to write namespaces? Namespaces are serialized as attributes, but of course are not attributes. However we decided to use the write attribute methods to minimize the methods on the API, which caused some obscurity when using the XmlWriter to write namespaces. Having explicit methods would have been clearer.

Description

The output of this class conforms to the W3C Extensible Markup Language (XML) 1.0 and the Namespaces in XML recommendations.

[*Note:* This class is abstract and is implemented in the XmlTextWriter class.]

Example

```
using System;
using System.Xml;
using System.Text;
using System.IO;
```

```
public class XmlTextWriterSample
{
    public static void Main()
    {
        string s = "sample.xml";
        Encoding e = new UTF8Encoding();
        XmlTextWriter w = new XmlTextWriter(s, e);
        w.WriteStartDocument();
        w.WriteComment("This is a test document");
        w.WriteStartElement("root");
        w.Flush();
        w.WriteStartAttribute("sample", "");
        w.WriteString("value");
        w.WriteEndAttribute();
        w.WriteElementString("subelement", "sample");
        w.WriteEndElement();
        w.WriteEndDocument();
        w.Close();
        DisplayDocument(s);
        Console.WriteLine();
        Console.WriteLine();
        Console.WriteLine("Press Enter to continue");
        Console.ReadLine();
    }

    private static void DisplayDocument(string s)
    {
        Console.WriteLine("Created document {0}:", s);
        StreamReader sr = new StreamReader(s);
        Console.WriteLine(sr.ReadToEnd());
        sr.Close();
    }
}
```

The output is

```
Created document sample.xml:
<?xml version="1.0" encoding="utf-8"?><!--This is a test document--><root
sample="value"><subelement>sample</subelement></root>


Press Enter to continue
```

Annotations Index

Index

Microsoft .NET Development Series

.NET Framework Standard Library Annotated Reference
Volume 1:

Microsoft .NET Framework Class Libraries Team
Brad Abrams, Editor

0321154894

.NET Web Services
Architecture and Implementation

Keith Ballinger

0321113594

A First Look at SQL Server 2005 for Developers

Bob Beauchemin
Niels Berglund
Dan Sullivan

0321180593

Essential .NET
Volume 1
The Common Language Runtime

Don Box
with Chris Sells

0201734117

Graphics Programming with GDI+

Mahesh Chand

0321160770

The C# Programming Language

Anders Hejlsberg
Scott Wiltamuth
Peter Golde

0321154916

A First Look at ADO.NET and System Xml v 2.0

Alex Homer
Dave Sussman
Mark Fussell

0321228391

Essential ASP.NET
with Examples in C#

Fritz Onion

0201760401

Essential ASP.NET
with Examples in Visual Basic .NET

Fritz Onion

0201760398

The Visual Basic .NET Programming Language

Paul Vick

0321169514

For more information go to
www.awprofessional.com/msdotnetseries/

0321228960

0321154932

0201734958

0321116208

0321125193

0201770180

0201745682

0321174038

0321174046

Register
Your Book
at www.awprofessional.com/register

You may be eligible to receive:
- Advance notice of forthcoming editions of the book
- Related book recommendations
- Chapter excerpts and supplements of forthcoming titles
- Information about special contests and promotions throughout the year
- Notices and reminders about author appearances, tradeshows, and online chats with special guests

Contact us

If you are interested in writing a book or reviewing manuscripts prior to publication, please write to us at:

Editorial Department
Addison-Wesley Professional
75 Arlington Street, Suite 300
Boston, MA 02116 USA
Email: AWPro@aw.com

Addison-Wesley

Visit us on the Web: http://www.awprofessional.com

CD-ROM Warranty

Addison-Wesley Professional warrants the enclosed CD-ROM to be free of defects in materials and faulty workmanship under normal use for a period of ninety days after purchase (when purchased new). If a defect is discovered in the CD-ROM during this warranty period, a replacement CD-ROM can be obtained at no charge by sending the defective CD-ROM, postage prepaid, with proof of purchase to:

Disc Exchange
Addison-Wesley Professional
Pearson Technology Group
75 Arlington Street, Suite 300
Boston, MA 02116
Email: AWPro@aw.com

Addison-Wesley Professional makes no warranty or representation, either expressed or implied, with respect to this software, its quality, performance, merchantability, or fitness for a particular purpose. In no event will Addison-Wesley Professional, its distributors, or dealers be liable for direct, indirect, special, incidental, or consequential damages arising out of the use or inability to use the software. The exclusion of implied warranties is not permitted in some states. Therefore, the above exclusion may not apply to you. This warranty provides you with specific legal rights. There may be other rights that you may have that vary from state to state. The contents of this CD-ROM are intended for personal use only.

More information and updates are available at:

http://www.awprofessional.com/

NOTE: To ensure optimal performance of the PDF file on this CD, you first need to configure your Web browser to open PDF files in a separate Adobe Acrobat window. For more information, see "Important Information About Viewing the eBook" in the eBook Instructions on the CD.